GENETIC STUDIES OF GENIUS

Edited by

Lewis M. Terman

VOLUME IV

THE GIFTED CHILD GROWS UP

Twenty-five Years' Follow-up of a Superior Group

GENETIC STUDIES OF GENIUS

EDITED BY LEWIS M. TERMAN

VOLUME I. MENTAL AND PHYSICAL TRAITS OF A THOUSAND GIFTED CHILDREN
By LEWIS M. TERMAN *and* OTHERS

VOLUME II. THE EARLY MENTAL TRAITS OF THREE HUNDRED GENIUSES
By CATHARINE M. COX

VOLUME III. THE PROMISE OF YOUTH: FOLLOW-UP STUDIES OF A THOUSAND GIFTED CHILDREN
By BARBARA S. BURKS, DORTHA W. JENSEN, *and* LEWIS M. TERMAN

VOLUME IV. THE GIFTED CHILD GROWS UP; TWENTY-FIVE YEARS' FOLLOW-UP OF A SUPERIOR GROUP
By LEWIS M. TERMAN *and* MELITA H. ODEN

THE GIFTED CHILD GROWS UP

TWENTY-FIVE YEARS' FOLLOW-UP OF A SUPERIOR GROUP

VOLUME IV

GENETIC STUDIES OF GENIUS

BY

LEWIS M. TERMAN AND MELITA H. ODEN

IN ASSOCIATION WITH

NANCY BAYLEY

HELEN MARSHALL

QUINN MC NEMAR

ELLEN B. SULLIVAN

STANFORD UNIVERSITY PRESS

STANFORD, CALIFORNIA

OXFORD UNIVERSITY PRESS :: LONDON: GEOFFREY CUMBERLEGE

STANFORD UNIVERSITY PRESS, STANFORD, CALIFORNIA
LONDON: GEOFFREY CUMBERLEGE, OXFORD UNIVERSITY PRESS

THE BAKER AND TAYLOR COMPANY, 55 FIFTH AVENUE, NEW YORK 3
HENRY M. SNYDER & COMPANY, 440 FOURTH AVENUE, NEW YORK 16
W. S. HALL & COMPANY, 457 MADISON AVENUE, NEW YORK 22

PRINTED AND BOUND IN THE UNITED STATES OF AMERICA BY
STANFORD UNIVERSITY PRESS

PUBLISHED, DECEMBER 1947

TO THE GIFTED "CHILDREN" AND
THEIR PARENTS, IN GRATEFUL
APPRECIATION OF THEIR LOYAL
AND PATIENT CO-OPERATION
OVER MANY YEARS

ACKNOWLEDGMENT OF FINANCIAL ASSISTANCE

The investigations summarized in this volume have been financed by grants-in-aid and anonymous gifts totaling in all close to $150,000.

Three separate grants from the Commonwealth Fund of New York City defrayed the greater part of the expenses incurred between 1921 and 1929. The Carnegie Corporation of New York provided two grants which made possible the extensive follow-up of 1939–41 and the statistical work on the resulting data between 1941 and 1943. The National Research Council, through its Committee for Research on Problems of Sex, financed the studies on marital adjustments reported in chapter xix, and the Columbia Foundation of San Francisco provided three annual grants which met approximately three-fourths of the expenses incurred between 1943 and 1946 in continued follow-up of the subjects and in the preparation of this volume for publication.

Stanford University, through the Thomas Welton Stanford Fund, financed the follow-up study of 1936–37 and contributed minor supplementary funds as needed between 1928 and 1936. Material assistance was provided from time to time, from the beginning of the study in 1921 to the end of 1946, by gifts from various individual donors including several parents of the subjects, a few of the subjects themselves, a member of the Stanford faculty, and the proprietor of a well-known magazine; the total of such gifts amounts to about one-sixth of the entire cost of the study to date. Follow-up of the subjects beyond 1946 is being financed in part by the Marsden Foundation of Palm Springs, California.

By special arrangement all net profits from publications in the series, *Genetic Studies of Genius,* have been added to the research funds without payment of royalty to any of the authors.

ACKNOWLEDGMENT OF FINANCIAL ASSISTANCE

The investigations summarized in this volume have been financed at the outset and in large part by [illegible] in all [illegible]. Three separate grants from the Commonwealth Fund of New York paid for a large part of the expense incurred between 1921 and 1928. The Carnegie Corporation of New York made three grants which made possible the extensive follow-up field and the statistical work on the resulting data between 1941 and 1945. The National Research Council, through its Committee for Research on Problems of Sex, made possible studies on marital adjustment in [illegible] and the Columbia Foundation of San Francisco provided three annual grants which met approximately the cost of the field work between 1945 and 1949 in continuing follow-up of the subjects and in the preparation of this volume for publication.

Stanford University, through the Thomas Welton Stanford Fund, financed the follow-up study of 1936–37 and contributed substantially toward other studies made between 1928 and 1947. Also financial assistance was provided from time to time, from the beginning of the study in 1921 to the end of 1946, by gifts from various individual donors, including several parents of the subjects, a few of the subjects themselves, a member of the Stanford family, and the [illegible] of a well-known magazine; the total of such gifts amounts to about [illegible] of the entire cost of the study to date. Follow-up of the subjects beyond 1946 is being financed in part by the [illegible] Foundation, [illegible] Springs, California.

By special arrangement all net profits from publications in the series Genetic Studies of Genius have been added to the research fund without payment of royalty to any of the authors.

PREFACE

This is the fourth volume resulting from the Stanford studies of gifted children. Those which preceded it have dealt successively with *The Mental and Physical Traits of a Thousand Gifted Children* (Terman *et al.,* 1925), *The Early Mental Traits of Three Hundred Geniuses* (Cox, 1926), and *The Promise of Youth: Follow-up Studies of a Thousand Gifted Children* (Burks, Jensen, and Terman, 1930). The present volume is an over-all report of the work done with the California group of gifted subjects from 1921 to 1946, the greater part of it being devoted to a summary of the follow-up data obtained in 1940 and 1945. At the latter date the average age of the group was approximately thirty-five years, a period of life when the adult careers of the subjects are rapidly taking form. The chief aim of the report is to give as complete a picture as possible, within a single volume, of what the group is like at the end of the first twenty-five years of testing and observation.*

It is unnecessary to discuss here the general plan of the investigation or the significance of what has been accomplished. The nature and purpose of the project have been set forth in the introductory chapter, and in the final chapter will be found a retrospective appraisal of methods used, a list of generalizations believed to be warranted by the results to date, and a preview of plans for the continuation of the study.

Although the investigation was a logical outgrowth of my earlier studies in the field of mental testing, it will be obvious that the launching and prosecution of a research program as ambitious as the present one would have been impossible without the co-operation of many persons. First of all, I wish to acknowledge my profound indebtedness to the late Professor Ellwood P. Cubberley, revered friend and counselor, for the research opportunities he opened to me when I was a member of his department faculty, and for his hearty support of my plans for a comprehensive study of gifted children. To President Ray Lyman Wilbur of Stanford University I owe a similar debt of

* Anything like a complete summary of the data at hand would have necessitated an additional volume, and several segments of the material least germane to the stated aim have therefore been reserved for separate publication.

gratitude for his unfailing encouragement in all our relationships, and for his active support in obtaining needed financial assistance.

Formal acknowledgment has been made elsewhere of the grants-in-aid from various foundations and of the anonymous contributions that have come from private individuals. To all the donors I am grateful not merely for the material aid they have provided but also for their repeated expressions of confidence in the value of this long-term project. I am particularly indebted to Dr. Max Farrand, formerly Director of Educational Research for the Commonwealth Fund, and to the other officers of that foundation, for the grants which made possible the initiation of the study and supported it through its early and most critical stages. It was their faith in my long-cherished dream that transformed the dream into reality.

But neither the merits of the project nor the financial support that has been so generously provided could alone have insured its success. No less crucial throughout the years have been the competence and devotion of those who have collaborated as assistants, consultants, or coauthors. The quality of the field work was especially important in the testing of subjects, in the compilation of case histories, and in enlisting the co-operation of parents, teachers, and school officials. In respect to these matters the study was given an auspicious start by Florence Goodenough and Helen Marshall, who, with the assistance of Florence Fuller and Dorothy Hazeltine Yates, conducted the field testing program in 1921–22 and made the initial contacts with parents and teachers. Dr. Goodenough and Dr. Marshall assisted me during two additional years in the treatment of results and in preparing the first published report. Another valuable member of the office staff at this period was Raymond R. Willoughby.

A number of significant contributions to the research in this early period were in the form of doctoral dissertations by Stanford graduate students in psychology. Among these were the character tests devised by A. S. Raubenheimer, the interest test devised by Jennie Benson Wyman, and the study by J. C. DeVoss on specialization of the abilities of gifted subjects. Another of my graduate students, Giles M. Ruch, and my faculty colleague, Truman L. Kelley, collaborated with me in preparing the first edition of the Stanford Achievement Tests in time for use with the gifted group. Margaret Lima assisted in a comparative study of the reading interests of gifted and unselected children.

Shortly after the research got under way, a second grant was made available by the Commonwealth Fund to finance a parallel study of the childhood traits of historical geniuses. This was brilliantly executed as a doctoral dissertation by Catharine M. Cox, who was assisted in various aspects of her study by Lela Gillan, Ruth Haines Livesay, Florence Goodenough, and Maud A. Merrill. The two lines of investigation, one dealing with living gifted children, the other with the early lives of men and women who achieved great eminence, have crosslighted each other in important ways and have demonstrated the value of the two-directional approach to the problem of genius.*

In the first follow-up of the California gifted group in 1927–28, my chief assistant was Barbara Stoddard Burks, who was also coauthor of the resulting volume issued in 1930. Assistants in the field work were Alice Leahy, Helen Marshall, and Melita Oden. An evalution of the literary juvenilia produced by members of the group was embodied in a doctoral dissertation by Dortha Williams Jensen and published in the 1930 report.

Mrs. Oden has served continuously as my research associate in the follow-up of the group since 1936. She helped to plan the large-scale field study of 1940 and assisted me in the office while the field work was in progress. She later supervised the preparation of both the old and the new data for Hollerith treatment, and as coauthor of the present volume has contributed importantly to both the content and form of all but three or four of the chapters.

The field work of 1940, on which so much depended, was carried out by Dr. Helen Marshall, Dr. Nancy Bayley, and Dr. Ellen B. Sullivan, all of whom devoted full time to the task for a year. The study was indeed fortunate to enlist the services of three clinical psychologists so experienced and competent. Dr. Marshall, my only associate who has participated in all the major field studies from the beginning, has done much to promote uniformity of procedures in the field work and to enlist the continued co-operation of the subjects and their parents.

* I wish to record here my conviction that the psychobiographical methods used by Cox are so promising that they ought to be refined and extended for use in evaluating the early mental development of living persons who have achieved outstanding fame for accomplishment in science, literature, art, music, statesmanship, or social philosophy. The method should be especially fruitful in the study of living geniuses because they are in better position to co-operate with the investigator than is the subject of a post-mortem analysis!

In connection with the chapters which deal with marital adjustments I wish to acknowledge my indebtedness to the following persons: to Dr. Robert M. Yerkes for his help in obtaining grants-in-aid from the National Research Council; to Dr. Winifred B. Johnson for assistance in formulating the test of marital happiness and the test of aptitude for marriage; to Marian Ballin who coded the blanks of both these tests for Hollerith treatment, and to Robert Morris who sorted the Hollerith cards for item analysis of the marriage data and performed much of the computational labor.

I am deeply grateful to my colleague and former student, Dr. Quinn McNemar, not only for the chapter he contributed on the adult intellectual status of the group but also for the constructive help he has given over many years on statistical problems growing out of the investigation. His wife, Olga W. McNemar, as part-time research associate, checked many of the statistical computations and has assisted in other phases of the work. Both Mrs. Oden and Mrs. McNemar have checked the typed chapters against manuscript copy and have read both sets of printer's proof. Their meticulous attention to detail resulted in the elimination of many errors, but in view of the amount and variety of factual data reported it would be too much to hope that no errors have been overlooked.

Mrs. Ella Bale, as secretarial assistant, has handled for several years a heavy load of correspondence with the subjects and typed both the preliminary and final drafts of the manuscript.

I am proud to record the fact that of twenty persons who have been most closely associated with my studies of gifted children—most of them as youthful assistants—the large majority have made important contributions of their own to American psychology.

Lewis M. Terman

Stanford University
January 12, 1947

TABLE OF CONTENTS

CHAPTER I

INCEPTION AND NATURE OF THE RESEARCH

Because the investigations reported in this volume are concerned so largely with the later stages of a longitudinal study which has been under way for a quarter of a century, it seems desirable to devote a few chapters to a restatement of the original problem and to a résumé of the more important findings reported in preceding publications of the series. Such an orientation is especially necessary for those who have not read the earlier reports, and may be helpful to those who have.

Historical Background

Attention may be called to a curious circumstance relating to the historical background of our problem, namely, that in western Europe and in America a definite change took place eighty or a hundred years ago in the attitude of people toward what we now call the gifted child. Prior to that time the youthful prodigy was generally regarded with a mixture of admiration, awe, and hopeful expectation. His parents were envied, and the child was likely to be made the protégé of a prince or king.

Then, after 1850 or thereabouts, one finds an increasing number of treatises, written chiefly by doctors and educational theorists, in which the "precocious" child was classed with the abnormals, depicted as a neurotic, and alleged, if he survived at all, to be headed for post-adolescent stupidity or insanity. Gradually the view came to prevail that a rich and well-balanced maturity demands the prolongation of infancy and the fullest living-out of each developmental stage. Not only should the bright child be protected from intellectual stimulation; any tendency toward early cleverness should be positively discouraged. "Early ripe, early rot" was the slogan of those who favored slow maturation. The myth became prevalent that many of the great geniuses were dunces in childhood.

This attitude is less common today than formerly, but is still encountered. One occasionally finds a teacher who exibits something of resentment and dislike toward the pupil of exceptionally high IQ. The latter, sensing the situation, sometimes finds it profitable to hide his intellectual enthusiasm and even to feign ignorance in his classroom recitations. Examples could be cited in the case histories of subjects in our gifted group.

When, in 1904, Terman surveyed the literature on mental precocity that had appeared in the preceding decades in America, England, Germany, and France, he found the sentiment against the intellectual prodigy so nearly unanimous that he was inclined to assume it must be well grounded.[61]* The following year, as it happened, his faith in the current theory was considerably weakened by the results of an experimental study of two contrasting groups of bright and dull children,[62] but it was not until some time later, when the task of revising the Binet scale led him to test and follow up many bright subjects, that his skepticism was complete. It had become evident that here was a problem of major social and educational importance.

The problem has many ramifications, but in its simplest form it may be stated as follows: What are the physical, mental, and personality traits that are characteristic of intellectually superior children, and what sort of adult does the typical gifted child become? The opportunity for a large-scale attack on this problem was made possible in 1921 by a generous grant to Stanford University from the Commonwealth Fund of New York City, a source from which later grants were to follow. By that time the senior author was already following the development of about a hundred children who had tested above 130 IQ on the Stanford-Binet scale. It was now proposed to sift a school population of a quarter-million in order to identify and study a thousand or more of highest IQ.

Plan of the Research

There were five essential features of the investigation as planned:

1. The subjects selected for study must be as nearly as possible an unbiased sampling of their kind, so that whatever might be found true of the group investigated would be true of any other representative group of the same degree of mental superiority, living in a comparable culture. In earlier studies of gifted children there had been

* Numerals refer to numbered and alphabetically arranged references on pages 383 ff.

several instances of questionable generalizations based upon observations of small and unrepresentative groups.

2. It was regarded as important that the procedures used should be as objective as possible and so clearly defined that the investigation could be repeated and its conclusions checked. It was necessary that this rule should be followed both in the selection of subjects and in the choice of techniques for physical, psychological, and educational measurements. Even the case-history methods, although inevitably more subjective than anthropometric and psychometric measures, were highly systematized to provide as much objectivity as could be secured.

3. From the beginning it was planned that the subjects should be followed as closely and as far into adult life as finances and other circumstances would permit. Retesting at intervals was an essential part of the follow-up program, but only a part of it. The problem was not only to investigate the degree of constancy of measurable childhood traits, but also to throw light on the factors responsible for such changes as might be found in educational achievement, personality, social adjustment, and tested abilities. Obviously the second of these problems is more difficult than the first. *How* a gifted child turns out can be objectively determined; *why* he turns out as he does is necessarily a matter of inference. In this connection the reader should bear in mind that the best evidence obtainable will not lead all observers to exactly the same conclusions, and that it is accordingly necessary to discriminate between verifiable facts and inferences from those facts.

4. Another feature of the original plan, though not realizable until the main investigation had been under way for more than a year, involved a companion study of the childhood of a representative group of historical geniuses.[18] The purpose was to discover the extent to which the early mental development of such persons parallels that of living children selected on the basis of superior IQ. Evidence especially was desired on childhood IQ, personality, special abilities, and the influence of educational and other environmental factors in shaping the life career.

5. One other thing should be made clear: the investigation as planned was not a direct attack upon the pedagogy of gifted children; it was instead a search for the basic facts that would provide a necessary prologomenon to further advances in this field of special training. Information must precede reform. It was lack of information that

had made this region the darkest Africa of education. Once the physical and mental characteristics and the developmental tendencies of intellectually superior children have been definitely established, then, and only then, is it possible to plan intelligently for their education.

Selection of Assistants and Their Preparation for the Survey

It was obvious that the success of an investigation so ambitious in scope would depend largely on the selection of gifted, well-trained, and objective-minded assistants. Several months before the field work was to begin, the senior author visited the leading universities of the country in a search for likely candidates, and was fortunate to secure as his chief assistants, Florence L. Goodenough of Columbia University, and Helen Marshall of Ohio State University. Both were highly skilled in psychometrics, interested in gifted children, and endowed with the qualities of personality necessary to insure the co-operation of the subjects, their parents, and their teachers.

Two months were spent with the assistants after they reached Stanford in preparing for the field work. Their Binet procedures were carefully checked for uniformity. Previous studies of gifted children were reviewed and discussed; the supplementary tests to be given the subjects were selected; information blanks to be filled out by parents and teachers were formulated; various rating schemes were devised; and the entire plan of search for subjects was agreed upon. In all of this preliminary work the assistants were active collaborators, not passive agents being coached on a cut-and-dried program. As a result of the careful planning, it was possible to carry out the field work with dispatch and with uniformity of procedure. The field work began in September 1921, and continued until July 1922.

The Selection of Subjects

The problem was to discover in the schools of California a thousand or more subjects with IQ's that would rate them well within the highest 1 percent of the child population. For financial reasons it was not possible to give mental tests to the entire school enrollment of the state, desirable as that would have been. Instead, the search was limited chiefly to the larger and medium-sized urban areas. The following procedures were used to identify the children of highest IQ in the areas surveyed.

In grades three to eight each classroom teacher filled out a blank which called for the name of the brightest child in the class, the second brightest, the third brightest, and the youngest. In addition, the teacher was asked to give the name of the brightest child she had in her class the previous year. The children thus nominated in a particular school building were called together and given a group intelligence test (National, Scale B). Those who scored promisingly high on the group test were given an individual examination on the abbreviated Stanford-Binet, and those scoring above a given point on this test were given a complete Stanford-Binet. The method of search in grades one and two involved merely the Binet testing of pupils nominated by the teacher, since group tests then available at this level were unsatisfactory.

The original standard set for inclusion in the experimental group was an IQ of 140 or above, but for various reasons sixty-two subjects were included in the IQ range of 135 to 139. Most of those below 140 IQ were either siblings of subjects already admitted to the group, or were older subjects whose scores were deemed to be spuriously low because of insufficient top in the 1916 Stanford-Binet. The standard set was purely arbitrary and was intended to insure that the subjects included for study should be in the highest 1 percent of the school population in general intelligence as measured by the test used. Its choice was not based on any assumption that children above this IQ level are potential geniuses.

As a check on the efficiency of the method of search, mental tests were given to the entire population of three schools after the teacher nominations had been made in the usual way. The results indicated that the method used was identifying close to 90 percent of all who could have qualified if every pupil had been given a Stanford-Binet test. The proportion is high enough to insure that the group selected for study constitutes a reasonably unbiased sampling. It is possible, however, that those missed may have been less outstanding in school achievement or less vocal in classroom recitations than those who were discovered.

All of the five kinds of nominations yielded subjects who were able to qualify. As was to be expected, the proportion qualifying dropped rapidly from those nominated as brightest to those nominated as second or third brightest. However, the most fruitful single kind of nomination was that of youngest in the class; it yielded a slightly larger proportion of qualifying subjects than nomination of brightest in the class. In other words, if you are allowed only one method of locating the highest IQ in a classroom, your chance of getting the right child is better if you merely look in the class register and take the youngest than if you trust the teacher's judgment! At least, this was true in the California schools of 1921–22. The tendency of teachers is to judge the intelligence of their pupils on the basis of absolute achievement, with little regard for age differences. The tendency is only partly corrected even when definite instructions are given—as they were in this case—to take account of age.

A large proportion of the subjects qualifying had received two or three kinds of nominations. A small number qualified who had not been nominated in any way but were tested because they were known to have rated high in an earlier test given by someone else. The number qualifying would undoubtedly have been greater if we had tested not only the youngest in every class but also the second youngest.

The search above described yielded 661 subjects—354 boys and 307 girls—from a school population of about 160,000. Because the methods used in this part of the survey were so systematic and uniform, these subjects were designated as the Main Experimental Group (Group I). They were especially suitable for comparison with a control group made up of a random sampling of comparable age.

There was a second Binet-tested group of 365 subjects—197 boys and 168 girls—located in grades below the high school by less systematic procedures. About a third of these had been tested and followed up prior to 1921. Most of the others in this group were discovered by the help of volunteer testers in smaller urban communities of California not covered in the main survey. These have been designated as the Outside Binet Cases (Group II).

A third group of 444 subjects—273 boys and 171 girls—were admitted to the study on the basis of group intelligence tests and are classified as the Outside Group Test Cases (Group III). All but 24 of the Group III subjects were in grades seven to twelve (junior and senior high school), and these were referred to as the High School Group. With the exception of 6 cases, the high-school subjects were selected on the basis of the Terman Group Test of Mental Ability—the TGT. The majority of those taking the TGT were located in a survey made of ninety-five California high schools, but a smaller number not attending high schools included in the survey were brought to our attention by their school principals as a result of the testing programs of their particular schools. In addition, a few older siblings of Group I were admitted on a Terman Group Test at the time of the original survey. Six of the students included in the high-school group had made outstanding scores on the Army Alpha test.

The 24 pre-high-school subjects of Group III (10 boys and 14 girls) had qualified for the gifted study on the National Intelligence Test given in a survey of a southern California community. These subjects ranged in age from seven to eleven years.

The standards for admission on all the group tests required the subject to score within the top 1 percent of the general school population on which the norms were established.

These three groups just described number 1,470 (824 boys and 646 girls) and were selected from a total school population of about a quarter-million. The addition of 58 siblings who qualified for the gifted group in tests administered during the 1927–28 follow-up, brought the total number of subjects in this investigation to 1,528 (857 male and 671 females).* Table 1 gives the classification of the subjects into the various subgroups.

TABLE 1

ORIGINAL CLASSIFICATION OF THE SUBJECTS

	Males	Females	Total
A. Subjects selected 1921–23			
I. Main Experimental Group	354	307	661
II. Outside Binet Cases	197	168	365
III. Outside Group Cases			
1. High-school group			
Terman Group Test	258	156	414
Army Alpha test	5	1	6
2. Pre–high-school group			
National Intelligence Test	10	14	24
B. Siblings added to study in 1927–28 follow-up			
Qualifying on the Stanford-Binet test	26	18	44
Qualifying on the Terman Group Test	7	7	14
Total number of subjects	857	671	1,528

* Attention is called to the fact that the N's given here for the three groups are not quite the same as those given in Volumes I and III of *Genetic Studies of Genius*. The discrepancies are partly accounted for by later additions of siblings who were too young to test in 1921–22, partly by the fact that some of the IQ's in the Outside Binet group had not originally been "corrected" to compensate for lack of top in the Stanford-Binet test, and to a minor degree by the elimination of a few subjects whose test scores for other reasons were deemed questionable.

Kinds of Information Secured

Besides the intelligence test scores on which the selection of subjects was based, information of eleven different kinds was obtained for a part or all of the subjects in connection with the original survey. Unless otherwise indicated, the data were secured in 1921–22. The sources were as follows:

1. A twelve-page Home Information Blank was filled out by parents for all three groups of subjects (Groups I, II, and III).* This called for information on developmental case history, circumstances of birth, early feeding, age of walking and talking, illnesses, nervous symptoms, home training, indications of intelligence, age of learning to read, reading habits, educational and occupational achievement of parents, genealogical records, and ratings on twenty-five traits.

2. An eight-page School Information Blank was filled out by the child's teacher. The blank called for information on school health records, quality of schoolwork in each separate subject, evidence of superior ability, amount and kinds of reading, nervous symptoms, social adjustment, and ratings on the same twenty-five traits that were rated by the parents. This information was obtained for all three groups of gifted subjects and also for a control group of 527 unselected subjects.

3. A one-hour medical examination was given to 783 subjects, 591 of whom were in the Main Experimental Group. The examination covered vision, hearing, nutrition, posture, teeth, heart, lungs, genitals, glandular disorders, blood pressure and hemoglobin tests, pulse and respiration rates, urine tests, and neurological conditions. Basal metabolism tests were also given to 93 of the subjects. The medical data were obtained in 1922–23, a year after the study began.

4. Thirty-seven anthropometrical measurements were made of 594 subjects in the Main Experimental Group. The physical measurements, like the medical, were carried out in 1922–23.

5. A three-hour battery of school achievement tests was given to about 550 subjects of the Main Experimental Group enrolled in grades two to eight. The battery covered reading, arithmetical computation, arithmetical reasoning, language usage, spelling, science information, language and literature information, history and civics in-

* All of the information blanks and record forms used in the original study are reproduced in Volume I of *Genetic Studies of Genius,* published by the Stanford University Press.[68]

formation, and art information. The same tests were given to a control group of unselected subjects.

6. A battery of seven character tests was administered to 532 gifted subjects of the Main Experimental Group and to 533 unselected subjects of a control group. These included two tests of overstatement; three tests of questionable interests, preferences, and attitudes; a test of trustworthiness under temptation to cheat; and a test of emotional stability.

7. A four-page Interest Blank was filled out by the subjects of all three groups who were able to read and write. The blank called for information on occupational preferences, reading interests, school-subject interests, relative difficulty of school subjects, number and size of collections, and various activities and accomplishments. This blank was also filled out by a control group of unselected subjects.

8. A record of all books read over a period of two months was obtained from the subjects of the Main Experimental Group and also from a control group of 808 unselected children. Each book read was rated by the child for degree of interest.

9. A test of play interest, play practice, and play information was given to the subjects of all three groups above grade two, and to a control group of nearly 500 subjects. This test yielded scores on masculinity, maturity, and sociability of interests, and a play information quotient.*

10. A test of interests was given, based upon the method of word association, which yielded separate measures of the strength of intellectual interests, social interests, and activity interests. It was administered to 689 gifted subjects, chiefly of the Main Experimental Group, and to 609 subjects of a control group.

11. Home ratings, based on the Whittier Scale for Home Rating, were made by field workers of 574 gifted homes selected at random;† ratings were also made of the neighborhoods in which the homes were located.

It would have been desirable, of course, to have all the foregoing kinds of information for all the gifted subjects and also for a matched control group, but funds were not available to permit the

* These scores have not been statisticized for members of the High School Group because of lack of age norms for unselected subjects at this level.

† The 288 home ratings mentioned on page 73 of Vol. I in this series[68] include only those for the Main Experimental Group.

attainment of this ideal. It is believed, however, that in nearly all cases the data were adequate to provide a safe basis for generalization regarding the characteristic traits of the gifted child as compared with the average child in the school population.

The nature and results of the investigation from 1921 to 1924 have been fully described in an earlier publication,[68] of which the four chapters that follow are a highly condensed summary.

CHAPTER II

COMPOSITION AND SOCIAL ORIGIN OF THE GIFTED GROUP

Of the total 1,528 subjects, 1,070 (70 percent) were selected for the study by the Stanford-Binet, 428 by the Terman Group Test, 24 by the National Intelligence Test, and 6 by the Army Alpha. The distributions of IQ's for the two largest groups (Stanford-Binet and TGT) are given in Table 2 and Table 3. The IQ's of the older subjects in both of these tables have undergone a "correction" to allow for lack of adequate top in the tests, but in a good many cases the correction is insufficient to express the true intellectual status of the subjects.

TABLE 2

DISTRIBUTION OF STANFORD-BINET IQ'S
PRE-HIGH-SCHOOL SUBJECTS

IQ	Boys	Girls	Boys and Girls
200–	..	1	1
195–199	..	..	..
190–194	4	2	6
185–189	1	2	3
180–184	13	3	16
175–179	8	11	19
170–174	19	13	32
165–169	22	18	40
160–164	43	27	70
155–159	57	52	109
150–154	119	76	195
145–149	114	125	239
140–144	143	132	275
135–139	34	31	65
N	577	493	1,070
Mean	151.5	150.4	151.0
S.D.	10.8	10.4	10.6

The 24 subjects, seven to eleven years of age, who were admitted to the study on the National Intelligence Test ranged in IQ from 135 to 194 with a mean of 147. The Army Alpha scores of the 6 subjects admitted on that test were all equivalent to an IQ of at least 140.

TABLE 3

DISTRIBUTION OF TERMAN GROUP TEST IQ'S
HIGH-SCHOOL SUBJECTS

IQ	Boys	Girls	Boys and Girls
165–169	1	..	1
160–164	..	1	1
155–159	5	2	7
150–154	16	12	28
145–149	48	29	77
140–144	136	70	206
135–139	59	49	108
N	265	163	428
Mean	142.8	142.4	142.6
S.D.	4.7	4.9	4.8

The age range of subjects in Table 2 when first tested was from 3 to 13 years, with an average of 9.7 years. The high-school subjects in Table 3 ranged from 11 to 19 years, with an average of 15.2 years.

As shown in the tables, the IQ's of the Binet subjects ranged from 135 to 200, with a mean of 151; while the range of the Terman Group Test IQ's was from 135 to 169, with a mean of 142.6. Although the mean IQ of the subjects tested on the Terman Group Test is 8.4 points below the mean of the Binet-tested group, our follow-up data to 1945 indicate that the High School Group is at least as highly selected as the Binet group. The difference is due to inadequate top in the TGT.

THE SEX RATIO

The relative incidence of superior ability in the sexes has long been a matter of controversy. Our most crucial data on the subject are furnished by the Main Experimental Group because of the systematic procedures used in locating the subjects in this group. The sex ratio here is 115.3 boys to 100 girls. In the Outside Binet group the ratio is 117.3 to 100. For all the Binet-tested subjects of Table 2 (577 boys and 493 girls) the ratio is 116.4 to 100. The much higher ratio in the High School Group (Table 3) could possibly be due to the less systematic procedures used in locating these subjects.

How shall we account for the excess of boys among the Binet-tested subjects? Conceivably it could be due to (1) bias in the selection of subjects to be tested; (2) a real average superiority of boys in the intellectual functions tested; (3) greater biological variability of boys; or (4) a combination of these factors.

A statistical analysis of the nominations made by the teachers failed to support the hypothesis of biased selection, for, among children who were nominated but failed to qualify on the tests, the sex ratio was only 103.7 boys to 100 girls. This was almost exactly the same as the ratio for the entire population in grades one to eight of the cities canvassed. With regard to the second hypothesis, the evidence on sex differences in the functions tested fails to reveal any consistent superiority of either sex. For the 905 subjects on whom the 1916 Stanford-Binet was standardized, the mean IQ was slightly but not reliably higher for girls. From two carefully drawn samplings of Scottish children tested by the Stanford-Binet at or near the age of ten years, there was no reliable sex difference in mean IQ.

There remains the hypothesis of a sex difference in variational tendency. A summary was made by McNemar and Terman[45] of the literature available to 1935 on anthropometric, psychological, and educational measurements. The data on physical traits indicated reliably greater variability of boys above ten years, and particularly for the ages fifteen years and up. On educational and special ability tests the data were highly inconsistent, but on tests such as the Stanford-Binet, the National Intelligence Test, the Pressey Group Test, and Thorndike's CAVD, 29 of 33 sex comparisons based on age groupings showed greater variability of boys.

Probably the most valid data that have been reported on sex differences in variability are those from two Scottish investigations. The first involved group tests of 87,000 children, comprising almost the entire child population of Scotland born in 1921. The age at testing was close to ten years. Stanford-Binet tests administered to a random sampling of 500 boys and 500 girls of this group gave an S.D. of distribution of approximately 17 for the boys and 16 for the girls.[53] The second Scottish group was composed of 444 boys and 430 girls who were born on four particular days of the calendar year 1926 and were tested near the age of ten. This sample is the most nearly perfect that has ever been given a phychological examination, for of the 875 children born in Scotland on the four given days and still living, all but one were located and tested! The mean IQ was 100.5

for boys and 99.7 for girls. The S.D. of IQ distribution was 15.9 for boys and 15.2 for girls.[43] If we take account of the sex differences both in mean and S.D. of distribution, the figures for this group give a ratio of 158 boys to 100 girls of IQ 140 or higher. If we disregard the small difference of 0.8 in mean, and base our calculation only on the obtained difference in S.D. of the distribution, the ratio becomes 134 to 100. The vastly greater ratio of males to females among historical geniuses (about 20 to 1) may also involve biological as well as cultural factors, for if males are in fact more variable than females in intellectual endowment, the sex ratio as figured above should increase rapidly in the higher levels of achievement. Against this theoretical probability, however, is the fact that the three highest IQ's we have found were those of girls. In view of the contradictory nature of the evidence now available, any positive conclusion will have to await further investigation.

Racial and Social Origin

The information on racial and social origin was obtained chiefly through the Home Information Blank filled out by a parent, usually the mother. Although the data are much the same for all three groups of subjects, they are most complete for the Main Experimental Group, and our summary is accordingly based on this group except where otherwise specified. It should be noted that the information was obtained in 1922 when the average age of the fathers was only forty-five years and that of the mothers only forty-one. In regard to such things as occupational status of father, family income, home library, home ratings, and neighborhood ratings, the situation could be expected to improve for another decade or more.

The reports on racial origin indicate that, in comparison with the general populations of the cities concerned, there is about a 100 percent excess of Jewish blood, a 25 percent excess of native-born parentage, a probable excess of Scottish parentage, and a deficiency of Italian, Portuguese, Mexican, and Negro ancestry. However, nearly all of the racial and nationality groups with any considerable representation in the cities canvassed have contributed one or more subjects for our research. The ancestral strains stem back to all the European countries, and to China, Japan, the Philippines, Mexico, black Africa, and pre-Columbian America. No race or nationality has any monopoly on brains. The non-Caucasian representation in our gifted group would certainly have been larger than it was but for handicaps of language, environment, and educational opportunities. It is especially to be regetted that schools attended only by Chinese and Japanese children were not canvassed in the search for subjects.

Three-fourths of the parents of our subjects were born in urban or semiurban communities and only a quarter in rural areas or in towns of less than a thousand population. Surprisingly, the grandparents were almost as predominantly urban or semiurban as the parents. The figures are, of course, greatly influenced by the fact that the search for subjects was conducted chiefly in urban areas. States most frequently given as the birthplace of native-born grandparents were, in order of frequency, those of New England, the Middle Atlantic, and the Middle West.

Classification of the occupations of fathers into the five grades of Taussig's scale gave 31.4 percent for Class I (professional); 50 percent for Class II (semiprofessional and business); 11.8 percent for Class III (skilled work); and a total of 6.8 percent for Classes IV and V (semiskilled and unskilled labor).* Earlier investigations had shown that the occupational status of parents is reliably correlated with the achievement of the offspring; this study shows that it is correlated with the childhood intelligence of offspring. Cattell and Brimhall report as belonging to the professional class 43.1 percent of the fathers of 885 leading American men of science,[13] and Clarke so reports 49.2 percent of the fathers of 666 American men of letters.[16] In all of these figures, including those for our gifted group, the proportion of fathers in the professions is several times that for the generality, and the proportion in the lower occupational classes is correspondingly less. The relative influence of heredity and environment in producing this result cannot at present be accurately assessed; both are certainly involved.

The tendency toward superiority in the social and cultural background of our subjects was evidenced in many ways. For example, the mean amount of schooling for both fathers and mothers was approximately 12 grades; that for grandfathers was 10.8 grades, and for grandmothers 9.7 grades. The average parent of these subjects had received 4 or 5 grades more schooling than the average person of his generation in the United States. A third of the fathers and 15.5 percent of the mothers had graduated from college. Parents who

* See page 183 for a classification as of 1940 on the Minnesota Occupational Scale. This scale has seven occupational groups instead of Taussig's five.

had taken a Ph.D. degree included twenty-eight fathers and six mothers.

The number of books in the home library, as estimated by parents, ranged from none to 6,000, with a mean of 328. Only 6.4 percent of the homes had 25 books or fewer, as against 16.5 percent reporting 500 or more. Comparative figures for the general population of California are not available, but the mean for the generality would certainly be far less than 328.

Information on family income (as of 1921) was requested from only one hundred seventy families representing a fairly random sampling of all families. These reported a median of $3,333 and an average of $4,705. Only 4.4 percent of the families reported $1,500 or less, and only 35.3 percent reported $2,500 or less. At the other extreme were 14.1 percent reporting $8,500 or more, and 4.1 percent reporting $12,500 or more. Although the median for the one hundred seventy families was more than twice as high as for the generality of families in California, only one family in twelve had an income above $10,000.

Field assistants rated 574 homes (a random selection) on the Whittier Scale for Grading Home Conditions. This scale called for separate ratings from 0 to 6 on necessities, neatness, size, parental conditions, and parental supervision. The mean rating was above 4.5 on each of the five conditions rated, and the total score was distinctly poor for only 10 percent of the homes. Field assistants also rated the neighborhoods in which 305 of the gifted homes were situated. The ratings were on a scale of five steps ranging from very inferior to very superior. On this rather subjective scale the ratings were distributed as follows:

Superior or very superior	60.3 percent
Average	30.2 percent
Inferior or very inferior	9.5 percent

It was the impression of the field assistants that as a rule the homes themselves tended to be distinctly superior to the neighborhoods in which they were situated.

Characterizations of home background by teachers were obtained both for the gifted group and for a control group of randomly selected children attending the same schools. Unfavorable circumstances were mentioned for 8.6 percent of the gifted homes and 24.1 percent of the unselected homes; favorable circumstances were mentioned for 85.1 percent of the former and 61.8 percent of the latter.

The incidence of parental divorce or separation is of interest in this connection. Up to 1922, the percentage of parents who had been divorced was 5.2, and of those separated 1.9, making a total of 7.1 percent either divorced or separated. The incidence of broken families was definitely below that for the general population of comparable age in California in 1922, and has remained below since that date.*

Additional Information Regarding Relatives

Much additional information on the family background was provided by four pages of questions on family history in the 1922 Home Information Blank. The data called for included facts regarding the child's sibs, the child's parents and their sibs, and the child's grandparents. Information was also sought on the abilities and outstanding achievements of more remote relatives. The information thus provided by the Home Blank was considerably amplified in the field assistants' conferences with parents.

So far as possible the information on relatives has been brought down to date with each follow-up, both by questionnaire and by personal interviews. As of 1945 we have a fairly complete picture of the family background, including for both the parents and the siblings, age, education, occupation, marital status, number of offspring, honors, accomplishments, misfortunes, and mortality. For several hundred siblings we have intelligence test scores.

We note first the number of families in which more than one child qualified for inclusion in the research. Among the families of all gifted subjects, 151 contributed two subjects, 20 contributed three, 9 contributed four, and 2 contributed five. There are also 28 pairs of first cousins in the group. By the laws of chance, unaided by influences of common heredity and common environment, the likelihood of even two highly gifted children appearing in one sibship is very small. For example, if only one child in a hundred of the generality tests as high as 135 IQ, the chance probability that both children in a family of two will reach this standard is $1/100 \times 1/100$, or 1 in 10,000. That so many families contributed two or more means that something besides

* By 1940 the incidence of divorce among parents had increased to 13.9 percent. This is still below that of the generality in California of comparable age range.

chance was operating, such as common ancestry, common environment, or, more probably, both of these influences.

Among relatives of the entire group, those known to be listed in *Who's Who*[73] up to 1923 were 4 fathers, 2 mothers, 4 grandfathers, and 35 more remote relatives. By 1940 the number of parents known to have achieved this distinction had increased to 44 fathers and 3 mothers.

Posts of important responsibility that had been held by parents or grandparents to 1923 included 20 cases of major national office, 26 of major state office, 67 of major religious or fraternal office, 4 college presidencies, 23 professorships in colleges, 74 positions as superintendent or manager of a large factory or corporation, and 18 bank presidencies. Many additional parents had become distinguished by 1945. These include a major general, a famous playwright, several outstanding novelists, a top-ranking motion-picture director and producer, a dozen prominent scientists (of whom 3 are members of the National Academy), and numerous others who have achieved notably. On the other hand, we also find fathers in such occupations as watchman, gardener, postman, and carpenter.

Among 58 remote relatives who had achieved eminence were 6 signers of the Declaration of Independence, 2 Presidents and 2 Vice-Presidents of the United States, 4 generals, 6 writers, 4 statesmen, 2 inventors, 3 artists, and 2 Supreme Court judges. Nearly a quarter of the members of the Hall of Fame are known to be related to one or more of our subjects.

That superior achievement tends to run in families has been noted by all students of genius, especially by Galton,[26] Ellis,[24] and Woods.[75] Perhaps the study of most direct interest for comparison with our data is that by Brimhall[5] on the families of Cattell's *American Men of Science*.

By 1940, when all the families had been completed, our data showed that the parents of the gifted subjects had produced slightly over 4,000 children or an average of 3.09 per family.* This rate, if continued, would more than maintain the stock, but, as will be shown in chapter xviii, it appears likely that the subjects themselves will not equal the fertility rate of their parents.

* It should be noted that although there are 1,528 subjects in the gifted group, there are not 1,528 families, since 182 families are represented more than once. Allowing each of these one representative in the group, the number of families is 1,302.

By 1940 approximately 31 percent of the fathers and 15 percent of the mothers were deceased. At that time the mean age of parents (living and deceased) would have been approximately sixty-three years for fathers and fifty-nine years for mothers.

There are 22 parents and 15 siblings who are known to have been insane, and there are 13 parents and 2 siblings who have suffered other forms of mental breakdown. There are 17 parents and 6 siblings who committed suicide. In one family both parents, and in two families both a parent and a sibling committed suicide. Among siblings there are 7 known cases of feeble-mindedness.

CHAPTER III

CHARACTERISTIC TRAITS OF THE GIFTED CHILD: PHYSIQUE, HEALTH, AND EDUCATIONAL ACHIEVEMENT

The information summarized in this chapter includes anthropometric measurements, health histories, medical examinations, educational histories, and tests of school achievement.

Anthropometric Measurements

In the spring of 1923, thirty-seven anthropometric measurements were made of 594 subjects (312 boys and 282 girls). Nearly all the subjects were members of the Main Experimental Group, and all but a few were in the age range seven to fourteen, inclusive. The measurements were made by Dr. Beth Wellman under the direction of Dr. Bird T. Baldwin of the University of Iowa.

It is unnecessary to summarize here the extensive statistical data yielded by these numerous measurements. The most important findings were as follows:

The gifted children as a group were above the best standards for American-born children in growth status as indicated by both height and weight; they were also above the established norms for unselected children of California. In lung capacity, considered in relation to height, weight, and age, the means for the gifted subjects were above the Baldwin norms. The gifted subjects, on the average, exceeded the norm groups in breadth of shoulders and hips, and in muscular strength. In all respects the results of the measurements showed that the gifted group was slightly superior physically to the various groups used for comparison.

Physical History

The information on physical history was supplied by parents, teachers, and two physicians who gave medical examinations to 591 subjects in the Main Experimental Group. The information from parents and teachers was obtained for all three groups of subjects. In addition, teachers supplied similar information for a control group of 527 children enrolled in the classes attended by members of the gifted group.

The Home Blank called for information on twenty-nine items, including gestation, birth conditions, infancy, breast feeding, age of walking and talking, childhood diseases, minor ailments, accidents, and surgical operations. The School Blank called for information from school medical records. Health-history data obtained from the parents by our physicians at the time the child was medically examined served as a valuable check on the reports made by parents in the Home Blank. The conclusions which follow are based entirely upon data secured for the Main Experimental Group, since medical examinations were not given to all the subjects in the other two groups.

The mother's health during pregnancy was in the great majority of cases good; in only 7.8 percent of cases was it rated distinctly poor. The proportion of premature births (at eight months or less) was 2.7 percent. The mean birth weight as reported was approximately three-fourths of a pound above the norm according to accepted standards at the time.

About 19 percent of male births and 12 percent of female births involved instrumental delivery. These figures are probably higher than for run-of-the-mill births in California at the period in question, and may reflect chiefly the quality of obstetrical service obtained by parents of superior intelligence and above-average income. This high proportion of instrumental deliveries among gifted children suggests that the role of birth injury in the causation of mental deficiency may be less than is commonly supposed.

The proportion of breast feeding was considerably in excess of the figures reported by Woodbury[74] for the general population; it was slightly though not reliably higher for those above 160 IQ than for the entire gifted group. The child's health during the first year was rated by the mothers as "excellent" or "good" for 74 percent of cases, and as "very poor" for only 3.3 percent.

The reported age of learning to walk averaged about a month less, and of learning to talk about three and a half months less, than the mean ages that have been reported for normal children. However, attention should be called to the fact that memory reports of this kind have a low reliability.

The contagious-disease histories showed no important deviations of this group from normal children except, perhaps, for the rather high incidence of scarlet fever (9.1 percent) and diphtheria (5.9 percent). About a third of the group had suffered one or more accidents, 8 percent having had bone fractures. The number of surgical operations averaged slightly more than one per child, over half of which were for adenoids or tonsils.

The gifted children showed a significant excess of daily hours of sleep as compared with 2,692 unselected children studied by Terman and Hocking.[64] The excess was slight with the younger children, but amounted to about 50 minutes by age twelve. The average amount of time spent out-of-doors per day was about 3 hours for the boys and 2½ hours for the girls.

The health histories obtained by the physicians indicated that the dietary regime of the gifted subjects was above the average for the general child population, and that constipation was relatively rare. The physicians reported the gifted boys of twelve years and older to be slightly accelerated in pubescence as indicated by amount and kinkiness of pubic hair. Parents' reports regarding age when voice changed confirm this, and their reports on first menstruation of girls show the mean age of reaching this stage of maturity to be 13.02. Data summarized by Dennis[20] indicated that the mean age for American girls in general is somewhat higher than the mean we have found.

The School Blank filled out by teachers for the gifted subjects, and also for a control group attending the same classes, furnished interesting comparative data. As compared with control subjects, "general weakness" was nearly a third less common in the gifted group, "frequent headaches" half as common, "poor nutrition" a third as common, "marked" or "extreme" mouth-breathing two-thirds as common, and the incidence of defective hearing less than half as great. In frequency of colds the two groups did not differ significantly. The same was true for "excessive timidity" and "tendency to worry," but indications of "nervousness" were reported for about 20 percent fewer gifted than control subjects. On the other hand, teachers reported defective vision about 25 percent more common among the gifted, and the proportion who had undergone tonsillectomy twice as great. Tests of vision by our physicians revealed about the same incidence of visual defect as tests reported by others have shown for general school populations. In the gifted group, defective vision had nearly always been corrected by glasses, a circumstance which doubtless caused defects to be reported by teachers that otherwise would have gone unnoticed. The higher incidence of tonsillectomy among the gifted probably reflects the superior medical care which the gifted group had enjoyed.

Results of Medical Examinations

Although the data just reviewed gave valuable indications of the health conditions among the gifted subjects, there was obvious need for the more crucial evidence that could come only from thorough medical examinations. The physicians secured for this purpose were Dr. Albert H. Moore of the Hollywood Medical Group in Los Angeles, and Dr. Edith Bronson, assistant professor of pediatrics in the University of California Medical School. They were selected as among the ablest and most highly trained child specialists belonging to the younger generation of pediatricians in their respective areas. Both had completed two years of postgraduate work in the same department of pediatrics—namely at the University of California Medical School—a circumstance which helped to assure comparability of their procedures and findings.

Dr. Moore examined the subjects who lived in and around Los Angeles, and Dr. Bronson those in San Francisco and the Bay area. All examinations were made in the physician's office, the child usually being brought in by the mother. The examinations averaged an hour or more in length, including the time needed for securing case-history data from the mother. The examination schedule to be followed was worked out by the physicians in a series of conferences in which the exact procedures to be used in connection with each item of data were agreed upon.

The medical examinations were given to 783 subjects, of whom 591 were members of the Main Experimental Group. All but 24 were in the age range six to fourteen when examined. It is possible to include here only a brief outline of the physical conditions found in this special group of 591 subjects.

The incidence of physical defects and abnormal conditions of almost every kind was below that usually reported by school doctors in the best medical surveys of school populations in the United States. This is certainly true for defects of hearing and vision, obstructed breathing, dental caries, malnutrition, postural defects, abnormal conditions of the heart or kidneys, enlargement of the bronchial glands, and tuberculosis. The sleep and dietary regimes of the group as a whole were found to be definitely superior. The incidence of nervous habits, tics, and stuttering was about the same as for the generality of children of corresponding age. Because thyroid deficiency is often associated with mental defect, it would not have been unreasonable to expect a high incidence of hyperthyroidism in a mentally superior group. This condition was found in only 6 percent of cases, most of which were of moderate degree. The examining physicians, notwithstanding occasional disagreements in their results, were in complete accord in the belief that on the whole the children of this group were physically superior to unselected children.

The results of the physical measurements and the medical examinations provide a striking contrast to the popular stereotype of the child prodigy so commonly depicted as a pathetic creature, overserious and undersized, sickly, hollow-chested, stoop-shouldered, clumsy, nervously tense, and bespectacled. There are gifted children who bear some resemblance to this stereotype, but the truth is that almost every element in the picture, except the last, is less characteristic of the gifted child than of the mentally average. However, we shall not pride ourselves prematurely on having destroyed a myth by means of a few facts. Stereotypes have almost nothing to do with facts; this one has probably been shaped by a Freudian mechanism to cloak the common man's sense of inferiority and make him feel superior at least in physique to his envied intellectual betters.

Educational History

The information on educational history to 1922 was obtained for the subjects of all three gifted groups by the inclusion of twenty-seven questions in the Home Blank and twenty in the School Blank. The school information was also obtained for the control group of unselected children. The summary that follows is limited to the salient facts for the Main Experimental Group of gifted subjects, supplemented by comparative data for the control group:

The average age on entering school (above kindergarten) was six and a quarter years. Three-fifths had previously attended a kindergarten, the average length of such attendance being a little more than half a school year. Low first grade was skipped by 21 percent of the children, and the entire first grade by 10 percent.

According to the usual standards, about 85 percent of the gifted children were accelerated and none retarded. The average progress quotient was 114, which means that the average gifted child was accelerated to the extent of 14 percent of his age. Approximately 85 percent had skipped one or more half-grades, as compared with 4 percent who had repeated. The mean net gain from skipping was one full grade. According to the testimony of the teachers, the average gifted child merited additional promotion to the extent of 1.3 half-grades, or about two-thirds of a grade. In all, 82 percent were said to merit some additional promotion. However, from the scores on achievement tests summarized in the section which follows, it appears that teachers greatly underestimated the amount of additional promotion merited.

The average gifted child had attended 2 different schools by the age of eight years, and 3 by the age of eleven. For this group, no amount of shifting about from one school to another appeared to have had appreciable effect on achievement as measured by the test scores. The mean number of days of absence from school during the school year was 12.

Only one gifted child in a hundred was reported by parents as having a positive dislike for school, but with 4 percent more the liking was "slight." It was "very strong" with 54 percent of boys and 70 percent of girls. According to the school reports, less than half as many gifted as control children displayed an undesirable attitude toward school.

Nearly half of the gifted children learned to read before starting to school; at least 20 percent before the age of 5 years, 6 percent before 4, and 1.6 percent before 3. Most of these learned to read with little or no formal instruction. One of our gifted girls demonstrated by test that she could read almost as well at the age of 25 months as the average child at the end of the first school grade.*

Early indications of superior intelligence most often noted by parents were quick understanding, insatiable curiosity, extensive information, retentive memory, large vocabulary, and unusual interest in such things as number relations, atlases, and encyclopedias. There is no evidence that these abilities and preoccupations were to any considerable degree the result of artificial stimulation or forced cul-

* This subject has since taken a Ph.D. degree, and is now teaching in a state university.

ture. Although a majority of the parents had encouraged the child by answering his questions and by showing an interest in the things which concerned him, less than a dozen had carried out any systematic scheme of child training. In regard to the rate of school progress, 70 percent of the parents said they had allowed the child to go his own pace, 20 percent that they had encouraged rapid progress, and 10 percent that they had tried to hold the child back. In line with this, the amount of time reported by parents as spent in home study of school lessons averaged only two hours a week in the grades below the ninth. It was reported as none at all for 42 percent. A majority of these children did a great deal of reading, but it was nearly all free reading.

Objective Tests of School Achievement

Subjective estimates of school achievement, whether expressed in school marks or in steps on a rating scale, are notoriously inaccurate. That this should be true of ratings made by parents is understandable, for most parents have not had opportunity to compare their child's day-by-day performance in school with that of unselected children of the same age or grade. Since teachers do have such opportunity, one might expect their estimates of achievement to be rather accurate. Actually they are often astonishingly inaccurate, for when school marks in the various subjects are compared with scores on reliable and valid achievement tests, large discrepancies are found. During the course of this investigation we have found gifted children in almost every school grade whose achievement in one or more subjects had been rated by the teacher as average or below for the grade, but whose achievement test scores showed them to be as much as two years *above* their grade norms in those same subjects.

The errors in teachers' ratings have many sources. For one thing, not all children in the classroom situation manifest their knowledge to the same degree. Some are shy and recite as little as possible; others speak up boldly and often. Some who have learned much get low marks because written work is done carelessly, lacks neatness, or is turned in tardily. Often the assigned tasks are so far below their capacity as not to command their attention. Others are penalized in marks for all sorts of things that have nothing to do with their actual knowledge of the school subjects. Among these are the troublemakers, the saucy, and the conceited.

In order to secure more precise information about the educational achievement of our gifted subjects than either the home or school could provide, it was necessary to make use of objective measurements. In the spring of 1922, immediately after the search for subjects was completed, 565 children of the Main Experimental Group were given the Stanford Achievement Tests of reading, computation, arithmetical reasoning, language usage, and spelling. In addition, they were given information tests in general science, language and literature, history and civics, and the arts. The total working time for all the achievement tests was about three hours and was divided into two sittings.

These achievement tests were so standardized as to permit the expression of scores in terms of educational ages and achievement quotients. For example, if a child of 10 years earns a total achievement score as high as the average child of 13, his educational age is 13 and his achievement quotient is 130. The educational age and achievement quotient were computed not only for total score but also for the score in each of the nine subtests: reading, computation, arithmetical reasoning, language usage, spelling, science information, literature information, history and civics information, and art information. The large, unselected populations on which the tests were standardized, served as a control group with which the gifted were compared.

Two comparisons have been made, both of extraordinary interest. One is between educational age and mental age, the other between IQ and AQ (achievement quotient). Together, they show in a dramatic way how well each child was living up to his intellectual potentialities. The necessary data for such comparisons had never before been available for a large and representative group of gifted children. Let us see what the comparisons reveal.

The average achievement quotient for the children of this group was approximately 144. This means that, on an average, the gifted child's educational age was 44 percent above his chronological age. Or, to state it somewhat differently, the average gifted child's school knowledge was on a par with that of a strictly average child whose age was 44 percent greater. Only one achievement quotient in six was as low as 130. How does this compare with the child's grade placement? In the preceding section it was shown that the average grade progress quotient for the children in this group was 114; that is, the typical gifted child was accelerated by 14 percent of his age. By subtracting the mean progress quotient (114) from the mean achievement quotient (144) we get a measure of the amount the typical gifted child was retarded in grade placement below the level of achievement he had already reached. The amount was 30 percent of his chronological age (144 — 114 = 30). For the ten-year-old this is equal to three years, or three full school grades. This is the central tendency; some had been held back more, others not so much. *It is a conservative estimate that more than half of the children with IQ's of 135 or above had already mastered the school curriculum to a point two full grades beyond the one in which they were enrolled, and some of them as much as three or four grades beyond.*

The achievement quotients of the gifted were not equally high in all the school subjects. For the fields of subject matter covered in our tests, the superiority of gifted over unselected children was greatest in reading, language usage, arithmetical reasoning, and information in science, literature, and the arts. In arithmetical computation, spelling, and factual information about history and civics, the superiority of the gifted was less marked. Computation and spelling do not make very great demands on the higher thought processes—even borderline morons have been known to excel in them. History and civics ought to call for thinking, but as taught they often do not. It has been found that in such subjects as penmanship, manual training, sewing, and cooking, children of high IQ do not do much better than average children.

There were minor differences between gifted boys and gifted girls on the various school subjects, but these were trifling as compared with the enormous distance that separated the average achievement scores of the gifted from those of unselected children.

Is the gifted child's high achievement quotient chiefly a result of his formal education, or is it primarily a reflection of his superior intelligence? This is the age-old question of nature versus nurture, still so controversial. Some of our data provide interesting, even though not crucial, evidence on the problem. Among gifted children of a given age there was a wide range in the months of formal schooling they had had; in our ten-year gifted group of 109 children, the length of school attendance ranged from less than 24 months to more than 72 months. The IQ's of these children ranged from 139 to 190, and their achievement quotients in the various subjects ranged from 110 to 180. A correlation was run to determine how closely their achievement quotients were related to months of school attendance. The answer for this group of subjects is unequivocal: *the correlations for the various school subjects range from —.10 to +.13, not one being reliably different from zero.*

It is true that the majority of these children came from good or superior homes where the intellectual environment was stimulating rather than depressing. But given this environment, the number of months spent in school had almost no effect in raising the achievement quotient. Once started in the three R's, the gifted child increased his knowledge in most fields of the curriculum without much help from the teacher. Given reasonable encouragement in the home, he can pretty well educate himself, at least as far as the seventh or eighth grade. One of our subjects attended school a total of only two years before entering Stanford University at the age of fourteen.

Another question answered by the objective achievement tests was whether the gifted child tends to be more uneven or one-sided in his abilities than the average child. There is a widespread tradition that such is the case. The majority of people cling tenaciously to this belief in the law of compensation in respect to human endowment, for it helps our ego to believe that the fellow who is so much our superior in certain abilities is probably our inferior in others. This consoling doctrine was not supported by the evidence from achievement test scores of gifted and average children. Dr. J. C. DeVoss made a searching statistical analysis of the amount of unevenness in the subject quotients (for reading, arithmetic, *et cetera*) of our gifted children as compared with the unevenness found in unselected children.[68] * The outcome of the analysis can be expressed in a single statement: *The amount of unevenness in the subject-matter profiles of gifted children does not differ significantly from that shown in the profiles of unselected children.* A considerable proportion of children in both groups scored higher in some subject or subjects than in others; the only difference between the gifted and the normal was that the unevenness of the gifted child occurred on a high level of achievement, that of the normal child on a much lower level.

* Chapter xii of Volume I.

CHAPTER IV

CHARACTERISTIC TRAITS OF THE GIFTED CHILD: INTERESTS AND PREOCCUPATIONS

A four-page Interest Blank was filled out by the subjects of all three gifted groups who were able to read. This called for information on scholastic interests, occupational preferences, and interests in miscellaneous activities.

Scholastic Interests

The first page of the blank contained a list of practically all the school subjects taught in California public schools, and the children were asked to rate for both interest and difficulty all they had ever studied. Because of difficulties experienced by the younger children in reading and understanding the instructions, especially by children in the control group, the following summary of results is limited to the responses of children of ages eleven to thirteen inclusive. These included 209 gifted subjects and 262 of the control group.

The ratings were on a five-step scale: (1) "like very much"; (2) "like fairly well"; (3) "neither like nor dislike"; (4) "rather dislike"; (5) "dislike very much." The rating for difficulty called for placing one cross (x) "before each subject that is very easy for you," and two crosses (xx) "before the one subject that is easiest of all."

The preference ratings showed that, in general, the gifted children were more interested than were unselected children in school subjects which are most abstract, and somewhat less interested in the more "practical" subjects. However, the two groups expressed about the same degree of interest in games and sports. Literature, debating, dramatics, and ancient history were rated as much more interesting by the gifted, while penmanship, manual training, drawing, and painting were rated somewhat higher by the control group.

The school subjects were ranked by us according to order of preference, separately for gifted boys, control boys, gifted girls, and control girls. This revealed that the scholastic interests of gifted boys and control boys were much more alike than were the interests of gifted and control girls. The two rankings for boys gave a rank-order correlation of .72; the two rankings for girls only .16. In fact, the scholastic interests of gifted girls resemble those of gifted boys much more than they resemble those of control girls. In other words, the scholastic interests of girls appear to be more influenced by superior intelligence than are those of boys.

Ratings were obtained from teachers on the quality of work the children were doing in the school subjects they were taking, and it is interesting to note the relationship between these ratings and the preference ratings given by the children. The correlation of .41 which was found would have been considerably higher but for the low reliability of teachers' ratings.

When rank orders of school subjects were made for the four groups on the basis of how "easy" they were said to be, it was found that these rankings were much like those for preference. The correlations for the two sets of rank orders (for ease and for preference) were all between .56 and .64. When cross-sex comparisons were made on ratings for ease, it was again found that gifted girls resembled gifted boys far more closely than they resembled control girls, the respective correlations being .70 and .09. A correlation of .37 was found between gifted and control boys. Ratings for ease were more affected by high intelligence than were ratings for preference, but on both ease and preference gifted boys resembled unselected boys more than gifted girls resembled unselected girls.

Occupational Preferences

Occupational preferences expressed by children in the pre-high-school grades have little prognostic value. In making such preference judgments the young child is doubly handicapped; he has little understanding of himself, and his knowledge of many occupations is also vague and inaccurate. Even so, it seemed desirable to secure occupational interest ratings by gifted and control subjects for whatever they might be worth. A list of 125 occupations was presented in the Interest Blank, and the child was instructed to place one cross before each occupation he might possibly wish to follow and two crosses before his one first choice. The data were treated for ages eight to thirteen for both gifted and control groups.

Analysis of the data revealed that gifted subjects showed greater preference for professional and semiprofessional occupations, for various kinds of public service, and for the arts. The control group expressed greater preference for mechanical and clerical occupations, transportation, and athletics. When the choices made by each group were rated on the Barr Scale of Occupational Intelligence, it was found that the mean Barr rating of preferences expressed by the gifted was significantly higher than the corresponding mean for the control group. Both groups displayed a good deal of ambition, but when the Barr rating of the child's preference was compared with the Barr rating of the father's occupation, the ambitions of the control group were, intelligence considered, much more extravagant than those of the gifted.

Interest in Miscellaneous Activities

The Interest Blank contained a list of twelve miscellaneous activities which subjects were asked to rate on a scale of 1 to 5 to indicate their liking for each. The activities were: (1) studying lessons; (2) general reading; (3) music, drawing, or dancing; (4) games requiring little exercise; (5) games requiring much exercise; (6) playing with several other persons; (7) playing with one other person; (8) playing alone; (9) parties, picnics, or club meetings; (10) tools or machinery; (11) sewing or cooking; (12) being leader in a team or club.

The activities were selected to test the accuracy of some of the traditional beliefs about gifted children: whether they are solitary, averse to active games, dislike tools, *et cetera.* The conclusions that follow are based on the mean ratings given the individual activities by the gifted and control children of each sex.

A majority of the activities showed a higher mean rating by the gifted than by the control group. Gifted children of both sexes seem to have a little more enthusiasm about things in general than do unselected children. The three largest differences between means were all in the direction of greater liking by the gifted; these were for general reading, games requiring much exercise, and playing with one other person. A fourth reliable but smaller difference was for playing alone. Both groups rated this activity far lower than any other, but it appeared to be a little better tolerated by the gifted than by the control subjects. This does not necessarily mean that gifted children are more inclined to be solitary; it may only mean that they are more resourceful in amusing themselves. The latter interpretation is supported by the fact that "playing with several other persons" was rated a trifle higher by the gifted than by the control group. The evidence on the whole suggests that the interests of gifted children in these twelve activities follow rather closely the normal patterns. Although there are exceptions to the rule, the typical gifted child likes active games, plays with tools and machinery, likes the companionship of others, and shows no abnormal fondness for study or for solitude.

Information on another activity—the making of collections—was obtained for the same groups. For the gifted it was obtained from the children themselves and also from their parents; for the control group, only from the children. Three main facts emerged: (1) nearly twice as many gifted as control subjects had made collections, (2) the collections of the gifted tended to be larger, and (3) they were more often of a scientific nature.

Interest in Plays, Games, and Related Activities

Data on play interests and play activities were obtained for about 1,200 children of the three gifted groups and for a control group of about 500 unselected children in grades three to nine. The data were of two kinds: (1) results of a questionnaire-test of play interests and play information, and (2) replies by parents and teachers to numerous questions in the Home Blank and School Blank. The results of the test proved to be particularly significant, as it was so devised as to yield for each child numerical scores on several aspects of play interests, and in addition a score on play information.

The test made use of a list of 90 plays and games which previous investigations had shown to be widely popular among school children in various parts of the United States. The test was designed to yield a preference score on each of the 90 items for each age and sex group of gifted and control subjects. The preference score for a particular play or game was a composite of two ratings given it by the children: (1) a rating for the degree of liking, and (2) another on the frequency with which it was played.

The following summary of test results is based on comparison of the preference scores of 554 gifted children of the Main Experimental Group and 474 unselected children of the control group:

As compared with the control boys, gifted boys showed much

greater preference for jackstraws, coasting, hiking, dancing, swimming, rowing, croquet, wrestling, racing or jumping, handball, soccer, tennis, dominoes, crokinole, parchesi, authors, guessing games, cards, checkers, and chess; they showed much less preference for rolling hoops, walking on stilts, flying kites, riding bicycle, garden work, shooting, riding horseback, hunting, ring-around-a-rosy, farmer-in-the-dell, drop the handkerchief, cat-and-mouse, ante-over, jump the rope, fox and geese, volleyball, basketball, and playing house.

As compared with the control girls, gifted girls showed much greater preference for jackstones, skating, hiking, dancing, fishing, swimming, sewing, using tools, shinny, cards, puzzles, and chess; and they showed much less preference for walking on stilts, riding bicycle, hunting, cooking, ring-around-a-rosy, hopscotch, cat-and-mouse, ante-over, dare base, fox and geese, baseball, racing or jumping, handball, volleyball, basketball, and charades.

The gifted and control children of both sexes differed from the opposite sex on much the same activities and usually in the same direction. Some of the differences between the gifted and control groups may have been due to the influence of social-economic factors, since the gifted more often came from homes of superior education and culture. Other differences are probably dependent upon intelligence; for example, the greater preference among the gifted for such games as cards, authors, puzzles, checkers, and chess.

The above differences are interesting, but their interpretation is not always easy; indeed, it is hardly likely that any two readers would draw exactly the same conclusions from them. One needs to know more precisely the psychological meaning of a high or low preference score for a given activity, what it signifies in regard to such things as mental masculinity, interest maturity, sociability, and enjoyment of strenuous physical activity. Fortunately, it is possible to obtain information of this kind directly from the preference indices, and we have in fact derived scores for the four variables just mentioned.

Masculinity-Femininity of Play Interests

First, a masculinity index was computed for each of the 90 plays and games on the basis of the amount and direction of sex difference in the preference scores of the control group. If a given activity had a high preference score for boys and a low one for girls, the activity in question was considered masculine; if the difference was in the opposite direction, the activity was considered feminine. On a masculinity-femininity scale ranging from 24 (most masculine) to 2 (most feminine), with 13 as the line of neutrality, the 90 activities received scores as follows:

24. Tools
23. . . . .
22. . . . .
21. Shooting
20. Kites, bicycle, marbles, wrestling, boxing, football
19. Tops, machinery, baseball
18. Fishing
17. Bow and arrow, skiing, tug of war, soccer
16. Stilts, garden work, basketball, pool
15. Hoops, swimming, rowing, hunting, snap-the-whip, shinny, racing and jumping
14. Coasting, hiking, riding, duck-on-a-rock, leapfrog, bowling, handball, backgammon, checkers, chess, billiards
13. *(Line of neutrality)* Red Rover, pom-pom-pullaway, follow-the-leader, ante-over, roly-poly, fox and geese, croquet, volleyball, dominoes, crokinole, parchesi, tiddlywinks, snap, cards, history cards, geography cards, word building
12. Jackstraws, post office, blackman, fox and hounds, tennis, authors
11. Tag, hide-and-seek, puss-in-the-corner, dare-base, Simon-says, playing church, solving puzzles
10. Jackstones, skating, drop the handkerchief, blindfold
9. Ring-around-a-rosy, London Bridge, farmer-in-the-dell, in-and-out-the-window, cat-and-mouse, jumping rope, guessing games, charades
8. Dancing, sewing, playing store
7. Knitting or crocheting
6. Playing school
5. Cooking, playing house
4. Hopscotch
3. Dressing up
2. Dolls

The next step was to compute a masculinity score *for each child* according to the masculinity of the activities for which preference was expressed. These indices showed that in play interests gifted boys tended to be rather more masculine than unselected boys at all ages from eight to twelve years, after which there was little difference. The means for gifted and unselected girls did not differ significantly at ages eight, nine, and ten, but at ages eleven, twelve, and thirteen gifted girls tended to be more masculine.

In both gifted and control groups the means for the sexes were far apart, as would be expected, although the sex distributions overlapped considerably. One gifted boy received a masculinity rating lower than that of any girl in either group. On the other hand, there were three girls (two gifted, one control) who rated more masculine than the mean of boys.

Measure of Interest Maturity

A majority of plays and games wax or wane in interest as the child gets older. The curve of mean preference score for successive ages may rise or fall rapidly or slowly. For a child of age 10 to express great liking for a type of play that is most popular at age 6 and then rapidly declines, is evidence of interest immaturity. For a child of 10 years to like a type of play that is sharply increasing in popularity at this age level would be evidence of interest maturity. By using the angle at which the curve of mean preference scores rose or fell, each of the ninety activities was given a numerical weight as an index of interest maturity. As in the case of masculinity, these weights were based on responses made by children in the control group. The next step was to compute an interest maturity score *for each child*, according to the maturity indices of the various activities for which the child had expressed preference. When gifted subjects were compared with control subjects on the maturity of their play interests, it was found that the gifted of both sexes showed greater average maturity at all ages. The differences were all statistically significant except at ages 8 and 9 for girls, and age 13 for boys. The typical gifted child is accelerated in the maturity of his play interests.

Play Interests as a Basis for Sociability and Activity Ratings

The ninety play activities were rated by several judges for the amount of social participation and social organization they involve, and were classified into three groups; the nonsocial, the mildly social, and the markedly social. By noting the distribution of a child's preferences it was possible to assign him a sociability score. In a similar manner it was possible to compute for each child an activity score on the basis of his preferences between the relatively quiet and the relatively active games. On both of these variables the control group scored higher than the gifted group at all ages. On sociability nearly

45 percent of the gifted of each sex fell within the lowest quartile of the respective sex norm for the control group. The superiority of the control on activity scores is hardly less marked.

These data do not entirely agree with other information we have secured on the social and activity interests of gifted and control subjects. The discrepancies are in part accounted for by the fact that several of the very mildly social games which appeal to gifted children are unpopular with average children because of the demands they make on intelligence (e.g., authors, anagrams, puzzles, checkers, chess). Another explanation is the fact that the gifted child is usually a year or two younger than his classmates and is therefore handicapped in the more strenuous competitive sports like football, baseball, basketball, and soccer.

A Measure of Play Information

A test of play information was used which consisted of one hundred twenty-three questions of the following types:

You pick up jackstraws with a magnet, hook, fingers.
A drop kick scores 1, 2, 3.
The score in tennis is tied at deuce, love-thirty, vantage in.
Roly-poly is played with a mallet, net, rubber ball.
The number of strikes needed to "fan" a player is 3, 4, 5.

Age norms available for unselected children made it possible to compute, for the gifted group, play information quotients analogous to intelligence quotients. These ranged from 75 to 195, with a mean of 137. Only 7.5 percent of the quotients were below 110 and only 3 percent were below 100. The average gifted child of 9 years had acquired more information of this kind than the average unselected child of 12 years.

Reported Experiences

Another section of the questionnaire-test on plays and games contained forty-five questions about a great variety of experiences. They were in form as follows:

Did you ever make a trap? Yes No
Did you ever swim 100 feet? Yes No
Have you ever been captain of an athletic team? Yes No
Do you belong to a hiking club? Yes No

The mean scores of the gifted in this test were almost identical, age by age, with those of the control group. The validity of the scores depends, of course, on the relative frequency of exaggeration in the two groups. The test of overstatement, described in chapter v, showed the gifted less prone to this fault than were the unselected children.

Home and School Data on Play Life

Both the Home Blank and School Blank contained several questions relating to the child's play life. As the School Blank was filled out for both gifted and control subjects, and the Home Blank only for the gifted, the comparisons that follow are based upon the school reports:

A third of the control subjects but only a quarter of the gifted were described by teachers as playing with other children "very much." Of the gifted, 25 percent preferred playmates who were older than themselves, as compared with only 9 percent of the control group. Teachers reported the gifted as showing less preference than control subjects with regard to sex of playmates; this difference is slight for boys but more marked for girls.

There was no difference between gifted and control in the frequency with which a child's companionship was sought or avoided, and no reliable difference on the child's tendency to cry or get angry when he could not have his way. However, 12 percent of the gifted but only 5 percent of control subjects were said to be regarded by others as "queer" or "different." This is hardly surprising in view of the fact that our typical gifted child of eight, with physique close to that of the average eight-year-old, was on a par with the average twelve-year-old in intelligence, general information, and command of language. The gifted children *were* different, and it speaks well for their social cleverness that in seven cases out of eight their classmates either did not notice the difference or chose to ignore it.

Reading Interests

Parents of the gifted subjects were asked in the Home Blank to estimate the average number of hours per week of home reading, not including schoolwork. In the School Blank, teachers were asked to rate the amount of home reading on a five-step scale from "much more than average" to "much less than average." Teachers' ratings were obtained for both the gifted and control groups. Information of greater value was obtained by having the children keep a record of the books they read over a period of two months. Such records were kept by 511 members of the Main Experimental Group and by 808 unselected children in a special control group. The record of each child was kept in a thirty-two-page booklet, size three by five inches, providing space for recording one book on each page, and for rating on a five-point scale how well it was liked.

The data showed that the majority of gifted children were inveterate readers. The amount of home reading per week, as estimated by parents, averaged about 6 hours at age 7 and increased to an average of 12 hours at age 13. At every age from 6 to 13 there were gifted children who were reported as reading 20 hours a week or more. The teachers reported 88 percent of the gifted as reading more than the average child and none as reading less than the average; they reported 34 percent of the control group as reading more than average and 22 percent as reading less.

The two months' record kept by the children showed the average gifted child reading about 10 books by age 7 and 15 by age 11, with little increase after 11. Few of the control group reported reading any books below 8 years; and after 8 years the average reported for the two months ranged between 40 percent and 50 percent of the average for the gifted. In both groups the means were a trifle higher for girls than for boys.

Classification of the books read by the two groups brought out the fact that the gifted children read over a considerably wider range than the control children, and that they read more science, history, biography, travel, folk tales, informational fiction, poetry, and drama. On the other hand, in proportion to the total number of books read, the gifted read fewer books of adventure or mystery, and far less emotional fiction.

Sex differences in kinds of books read during the two months followed much the same pattern for the gifted as for the control group. In both groups the reading of boys showed greater variety and a marked preference for books of adventure, while the girls read about five times as many books classed as emotional fiction. Rereading of the same book in the two months' period was reported only by girls.

Measures of Intellectual, Social, and Activity Interests

Some of the evidence we have presented regarding the interests of gifted children has been indirect or inferential. Much of it is inadequate in the same way that class marks and teachers' ratings are inadequate to establish the exact status of a child with respect to his educational accomplishment. The estimates supplied by parents and teachers are always open to the suspicion of having been influenced by suggestion, "halo" effects, or other forms of bias. Even the testimony of the children themselves in regard to their interests cannot be accepted at face value. Children lack standards by which to judge the absolute strength of their interests, and they are likely to be misled as to the relative amount of interest they have in various things by the influence of associations and other extraneous factors. What is needed is a measure of interest as objective, as consistent, and as valid as the best measure of intelligence or educational achievement.

However, the quantitative study of interests is inherently difficult. Interest seems very intangible in comparison, for example, with intelligence. Intelligence is abiding; it does not take wings or completely alter its form and substance, as interest is so likely to do, the moment one approaches it with a test. For this reason a test of interest needs to be disguised so that its purpose will not be known to the subject.

Dr. J. B. Wyman[68] devised for use with our gifted group an interest test which for the first time meets the standard requirements with respect to objectivity, reliability, and validity, and in addition the requirement of disguise. This was a word-association test of the Kent-Rosanoff type. The test was adapted for use with small groups by presenting each stimulus word visually, in large print on a card, and having the children write down the first word which it made them think of. As the stimulus word was presented it was also pronounced by the examiner.

It has long been recognized by investigators who have worked with association tests that responses to a stimulus word are greatly influenced by the subject's habitual mental preoccupations. Dr. Wyman's problem was, first of all, to select important aspects of interest that would be amenable to such a technique and, secondly, to make up a list of stimulus words the responses to which would be influenced by those particular aspects of interest which the test was designed to measure.

It was decided to try to measure simultaneously, and by the use of a single list of stimulus words, the strength of three kinds of interest: intellectual, social, and activity interests. It was assumed that these are the aspects of interest that help to determine whether one will be primarily a thinker, a mixer, or a doer. Their importance for the total personality picture is sufficiently obvious.

The next task was to make up a list of words that would afford measures of these three aspects of interest. All the words in Thorndike's word lists were examined and 800 of the words that seemed most promising were scrutinized for probable merit by several judges. A stimulus word like *ball,* for example, could be expected to bring, among others, such responses as *sphere* or *earth* (indicative of intellectual interest), *gay* or *partner* (social interest), *bat* or *soccer* (activity interest). The response *dance* might deserve a weight for both social and activity interest. Similarly, the stimulus word *ring* might bring such responses as *circle, engagement,* or *target.*

On the basis of such considerations, a trial list of 80 stimulus words was made up and administered to 175 children. Analysis of the responses resulted in the elimination of 37 of the 80 words, and afforded clues as to the kinds of words that would be fruitful. A new list was then made up containing 160 words, later reduced to 120 after trial with several groups of subjects. This was the final form of the test which was given to gifted and unselected subjects.

The validation of the test and the method of assigning score weights to responses were based on the results of the test with 265 seventh-grade children who had been specially selected by their teachers as representing either high or low intellectual interests, high or low social interests, high or low activity interests. A particular response to any given stimulus word was given a score weight according as it discriminated between children of high or low interest in any of the three fields. The sums of weights for all of a child's responses yielded three total scores, one for each of the three types of interest. The reliabilities of the three total scores were all between .80 and .90, which is not far below the reliabilities of group intelligence tests. Finally, 128 children who had been given the test were also rated individually by two teachers on each of the three aspects of interest. The correlations between Wyman scores and the teachers' ratings were, respectively, .65, .50, and .31 for intellectual interest, social interest, and activity interest. The first two of these coefficients are about as high as are usually found between intelligence test scores and teachers' ratings on intelligence; that for activity interest is so low as to be useful only in the comparison of rather large groups.

The test was given to 689 gifted subjects of ages eight to fifteen, belonging chiefly to the Main Experimental Group, and to a control group of ages ten to fifteen. The subjects of both groups were in grades four to nine.

On strength of intellectual interests, the mean of the gifted children at most ages exceeded that of the control group by about 1.4 times the S.D. of the control distribution. For the ages combined, about 90 percent of the gifted were above the mean of the control group in intellectual interest. In social interests the superiority of the gifted was somewhat less marked but still very decisive, the mean of the gifted exceeding that of unselected children by about 1 S.D. of the distribution of the latter. Approximately 84 percent of the gifted were above the mean of the control group in social interest. In activity interests there was no reliable difference between the gifted and control groups except for a moderate superiority of the gifted boys at age ten.

The data yielded by the Wyman test are believed to be the most reliable and valid evidence we have regarding the differences between the interests of gifted and of unselected children. As measured by this test, the difference is very great for intellectual interests, a third less for social interests, and practically zero for activity interests. The *relative* magnitudes of differences for the three kinds of interest are pretty certainly correct; the *absolute* magnitudes are more in doubt. The order of relative differences is supported by other evidence. For example, we know that the gifted average about 3 S.D. higher in IQ than unselected children, that they are only slightly above unselected children in physique (on which activity interests must in considerable measure depend), and that on the social traits which favor election to school offices their degree of superiority is intermediate between IQ difference and the difference in physique.

Consider next the superiority of the gifted in intellectual interest (as measured by the Wyman test) with their superiority in intelligence. The former, we have seen, is represented by a mean interest score 1.4 S.D. above the mean for unselected subjects, the latter by a mean 3 S.D. above that of unselected subjects. In other words, the gifted average only about 50 percent as superior in intellectual interest as in IQ. Although it is a matter of common observation that some children of high IQ display little intellectual interest, it is unlikely that the true average discrepancy is as great as this. The Wyman test, valuable as it is, is not offered as a completely adequate measure of all the intellectual interests a child may have.

Another estimate of the intellectuality of a child's interest could be based on the relative magnitude of his IQ and his achievement quotient. We have previously shown that our gifted group was about 80 percent as superior in achievement quotient as in IQ. Which of the two estimates (80 percent or 50 percent) is more nearly correct it is impossible to say. In all probability the truth lies somewhere between. The fact that not all of intellectual interest is measured by the Wyman test suggests that 50 percent must be too low. That the 80 percent may be too high is suggested by the observation that a child's school achievement is likely to be influenced by a number of things that have nothing to do with the strength of his intellectual interests, including, for example, his personal liking for the teacher.

Whatever the exact magnitude of the average discrepancy may be, it is a matter of common knowledge that some persons of high IQ have little intellectual interest. The extent to which school achievement is influenced by the kind of intellectual interest measured by this test was estimated by applying the method of partial correlation to the scores of 81 children who had been given the National Intelligence Test, the Stanford Achievement Test, and the Wyman Test of Intellectual Interests. The correlation between intelligence and achievement when intellectual interest was held constant was .76. The correlation between intellectual interest and achievement when intelligence was held constant was .49. These correlations give a comparative measure of the effect of the two variables on school achievement. The effect of intellectual interest on achievement was significant for all the school subjects except spelling. Similar treatment of the data for social and activity interests indicated that these two variables as here measured have practically no effect upon school achievement.

CHAPTER V

CHARACTERISTIC TRAITS OF THE GIFTED CHILD: CHARACTER TESTS AND TRAIT RATINGS

Are superior traits of character evenly distributed among all intellectual levels, or do they appear with unequal frequency among the gifted, the average, and the mentally inferior? One's answer to this question may profoundly influence one's attitudes toward various social and occupational classes. Because the issue is one which people cannot face with mental objectivity, any unbiased evidence that psychometrics can offer should be doubly welcome.

Such evidence we have obtained, but only for children of school age. There is no certainty that the relationship between intelligence and character during childhood persists throughout life, though a majority of psychologists believe that it does. The evidence brought together by Chassell[14] strongly suggests that such is the case. However this may be, it seemed desirable to establish as accurately as possible the relative standing of gifted and unselected children in a number of character traits for which tests of demonstrated validity had been devised. The scores made by the gifted subjects in such tests acquire additional interest in connection with the follow-up studies of their later careers.

A battery of tests was given to 532 gifted subjects aged seven to fourteen (chiefly of the Main Experimental Group), and to 533 unselected subjects aged ten to fourteen used as a control group. The battery included two tests of the tendency to overstate in reporting experience and knowledge; three tests of the wholesomeness of preferences and attitudes (reading preferences, character preferences, and social attitudes, respectively); a test of cheating under circumstances that offered considerable temptation; and a test of emotional instability. The subjects were tested in groups.

The tests of cheating and of emotional instability were selected as among the best of a battery of character tests used by Cady;[8] the others were all from a battery devised by Raubenheimer.[49] Both of these batteries had been found to yield satisfactory reliability coefficients and to discriminate rather effectively between boys of known delinquent tendencies and boys of superior social and behavioral adjustment. Total scores of the seven character tests have a reliability of .80 to .85 and a validity (based on discrimination between delinquent and well-adjusted boys of ages twelve to fourteen) in the neighborhood of .60. Whether the validity is equally high for girls is not known. The seven tests will be briefly described.

1. *Overstatement A.* Each child was given a printed list of 50 book titles and was told to put a cross before each book he had read. Twenty of the titles in the list were fictitious, and the overstatement score was the ratio of fictitious to genuine titles checked. Temptation to overstate was provided by informing the children that, when they were through, each would be asked to stand up and tell the number of books he had read.

2. *Overstatement B.* First the child was given a list of 80 questions, each to be answered by underlining "Yes" or "No." Examples:

Do you know who discovered America?	Yes	No
Do you know who wrote *Huckleberry Finn*?	Yes	No

Each child counted the number of his "yes" responses and announced it to the group.

The second part of this test was a check on the child's honesty of response in the first part, and for this reason was not given until all the other tests in the series had been completed. It was an information test of 80 items, each item corresponding to one in the first part of the test. Examples:

America was discovered by Drake Columbus Balboa Cook

Huckleberry Finn was written by Alger Dickens Henty Mark Twain

The score is the percentage of overstatement or understatement.

3. *Test of questionable reading preferences.* The child was given a list of 10 alleged book titles (all fictitious), and was told to number each book from 1 to 10 to indicate how well he thought he would like it. The items were:

A Daring Rescue
Roy Black, the Master Thief
Captains of Great Teams
Hobo Stories
Running Away with the Circus
The Adventures of Boys Who Became Great Men
Summer Camp Adventures
With the Gang in the Back Streets
The Boy Inventor
The Escape Through the Woods

The score was the sum of the squares of the individual deviations of responses from a hypothetical "best" order. The "best" order was based on the judgments of several psychologists regarding the probable wholesomeness of interest represented by the individual titles.

4. *Test of questionable character preferences.* This consisted of 16 character sketches made up in two lists of 8 each. The persons described in each list were to be numbered from 1 to 8 to indicate their relative appeal as a possible chum. The score was derived as in the test of reading preferences. Two of the items were as follows:

DICK joined the Boy Scouts as soon as he was old enough. He did not like it at first; the drill and the rules were hard. Now he is a troop leader and is planning a camp in the mountains next summer.

BILL EVANS is fourteen and is the leader of his gang. He always manages to get his men home safely after they have had a good time around the pool room. Just last week they saw Tom Mix at the movies without paying.

5. *Test of questionable social attitudes.* Twenty-four things, persons, or ideas were named, each followed by four statements indicating possible attitudes toward it. The subject was asked to check the *one* statement that most nearly told how he felt about it. Score was the number of questionable attitudes checked. Two of the items were as follows:

BOY SCOUTS: They have too many rules.
They have to drill too hard; it is no fun.
They are regular fellows and have lots of fun.
They are like sissies.

POLICEMEN: They have it in for the kids.
They are glad to help you out.
It is fun to fool them.
They are just big bluffs.

6. *Test of cheating.* This was disguised as a test of skill and was in two parts. In the first part, the child was given a sheet with irregularly placed circles printed on it. The task was to note carefully the position of each circle, then shut the eyes tight and try to place a cross in every circle. The second part was similar except that four square maze paths were to be traced with the eyes shut. As only a very small amount of success in either part of this test is possible without "peeping," the cheating score was the number of correct responses above the average success norm experimentally established under conditions which excluded cheating.

7. *Test of emotional instability.* This was Cady's modification of the Woodworth questionnaire, and consisted of 85 questions to be answered by "Yes" or "No." Score was the number of "Yes" or "No" responses given of those that had previously been found to discriminate between normal and delinquent boys. Examples of test items:

Are you afraid in the dark?	Yes	No
Do you ever dream of robbers?	Yes	No
Do people find fault with you much?	Yes	No

The results of the character tests were decisive; the gifted group scored "better" than the control group on every subtest at every age from ten to fourteen. Below the age of ten no comparison was possible because the control subjects below this age were not sufficiently literate to take the tests. Table 4 shows, for the sexes separately, the proportion of gifted subjects who equaled or surpassed the mean of the control group on each subtest and on the total score for ages ten to fourteen combined.

It can be seen from Table 4 that the overlap on most of the subtests, and even on the total score, was rather large. For ages ten to fourteen the superiority of the gifted on the total score amounted to about 1 S.D. of the distribution of the control group, which is only about a third as great as their superiority over unselected children in IQ.

The question may be raised whether a part of this superiority is spurious because of the possibility that bright subjects would be more likely to divine the purpose of the tests and so respond in the socially approved way. This factor would be most likely to be present in the tests of reading preferences, character preferences, social attitudes, and emotional instability. It is believed hardly to have entered at all in the case of the cheating test and the two overstatement tests, all three of which gave highly reliable differences between the gifted and control groups. It has previously been noted that the second part of Overstatement B, which is most likely to arouse suspicion, was not given until all the other tests had been completed. In his study of delinquent and well-adjusted boys, Raubenheimer questioned his subjects after they had completed the tests, to find out whether they had guessed their purpose. Less than 5 percent of his subjects (all thirteen years old) guessed correctly.

TABLE 4

PROPORTION OF GIFTED SUBJECTS WHO EQUALED OR SURPASSED THE MEAN OF CONTROL SUBJECTS IN EACH OF SEVEN CHARACTER TESTS AND IN TOTAL SCORE

Tests	Percentage Boys	Percentage Girls
1. Overstatement A	57	59
2. Overstatement B	63	73
3. Book preferences	74	76
4. Character preferences	77	81
5. Social attitudes	86	83
6. Cheating tests	68	61
7. Emotional stability	67	75
Total score	86	84

TRAIT RATINGS

The subjective rating of abilities and personality traits is a technique widely used in individual psychology. Notwithstanding its many limitations, it is often capable of yielding valuable data where more exact psychometric procedures are not available, or where a check is needed on the results obtained by other methods. Among the limitations are: (1) low reliability, as indicated by disagreements between judges who rate the same individuals; (2) the rather low correlations with objective measures of the trait in question, where accurate objective measures are possible; (3) the difficulty of avoiding "halo" effects resulting from the tendency of a judge to rate a subject high or low in all traits according to his good or bad opinion of the one being rated.

There are various ways of reducing the error from these sources.

For example, reliability and validity can be improved by carefully defining the trait to be noted, by choosing raters who have had ample opportunity to observe the person to be rated, by forewarning them against specific types of error, and by selecting for rating only such traits as are likely to manifest themselves in everyday behavior. The setup of the rating scale is also important.

The plan of trait rating used with the gifted subjects was the result of several years' experience in trying out various rating schemes with children of average and superior ability. The traits finally selected for rating numbered 25 and can be classified in the following categories: intellectual (4), volitional (4), moral (4), emotional (3), aesthetic (2), physical (2), social (5), and the single trait, mechanical ability. The individual traits are listed by category in Table 5. However, in the blanks in which the ratings were made, the traits were presented in a mixed order.

The rating scheme with instructions filled five pages in the Home Blank and School Blank. The first page, including instructions and illustrative ratings, is here reproduced.

Effort was made to have each child in all three gifted groups rated on all the 25 traits by a teacher and by one of the parents. Both parent ratings and teacher ratings were obtained for almost 95 percent of the Main Experimental Group. In addition, teacher ratings were obtained for 523 children of ages eight to fourteen in a control group composed of children enrolled in the same classes as the gifted.

When ratings of the gifted subjects by parents and teachers were compared it was found that on a majority of the traits the parent ratings averaged higher for both boys and girls. They were much higher for Appreciation of beauty, Leadership, Sympathy and tenderness, and Desire to know. On the other hand, teacher ratings averaged higher for Prudence and forethought, Permanency of moods, and Common sense. On Self-confidence, boys averaged higher on teacher ratings, girls higher on parent ratings. On Freedom from vanity, boys averaged higher on parent ratings, girls higher on teacher ratings. On General intelligence the mean of parent ratings was almost identical with the mean of teacher ratings for boys and girls.

Parents and teachers agreed fairly well regarding the traits on which the gifted children were most or least superior to average children. The rank order of the traits from highest to lowest mean rating by parents correlated .70 with the corresponding rank order

RATINGS ON PHYSICAL, MENTAL, SOCIAL, AND MORAL TRAITS

Directions: (1) In each trait or characteristic named below, compare this child with the *average child of the same age.* Then make a small cross somewhere on the line for each trait, to show how much of that trait the child possesses. Note that in each case, one end of the line represents one extreme for the trait in question, and the other end of the line the other extreme. The middle of the line represents an average amount of the trait. The meanings of other points are stated in fine print above the line. Before making the cross, read very carefully everything that is printed in small type above the line.

(2) Try to make real distinctions. Do not rate a child high on all traits simply because he is exceptional in some. Children are often very high in some traits and very low in others.

(3) Locate your cross *any place on the line* where you think it belongs. It is *not* necessary to locate it at any of the little vertical marks.

(4) Do not study too long over any one trait. Give for each the best judgment you can, and go on to the next. Please omit none. The ratings will be held absolutely confidential.

(5) Below each line, underline the word that tells how certain you feel about your judgment.

Examples: In *Example 1* the cross shows how one child was rated for beauty, and the line underneath the words "very certain" shows that the one who made the rating felt "very certain" of his judgment. In *Example 2* the cross shows how the same child was rated for obstinacy, and the line under "fairly certain" shows that the one who made the rating felt "fairly certain" of his judgment. Do not rate this child on the "examples."

Example 1. Beauty.

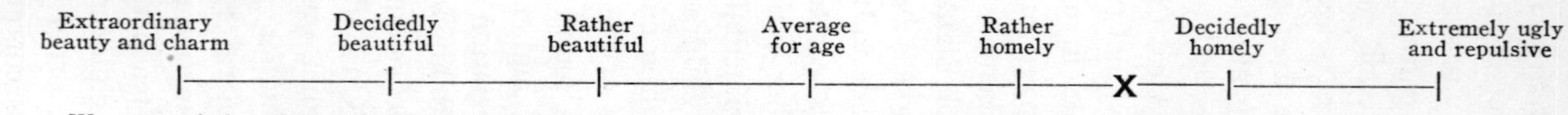

Was your judgment on the above trait very certain, fairly certain, rather uncertain, very uncertain?

Example 2. Obstinacy.

Extraordinarily obstinate and stubborn — Decidedly obstinate and stubborn — Rather obstinate — Average for age — Less than average — Decidedly less than average — Extreme lack of obstinacy

Was your judgment on the above trait very certain, fairly certain, rather uncertain, very uncertain?

based on teachers' ratings. However, the agreement was much less in their ratings on individual children; for most of the traits it was represented by a Pearsonian correlation of only about .30. This figure should not be regarded as a reliability coefficient in the true sense, for the reason that a child's personality behavior in the school is often very different from that which he exhibits in the home.

More important is the comparison of gifted and control subjects on ratings given to both groups by teachers. Table 5 gives the comparative data both for the 25 individual traits and for groups of traits as classified in various categories. The comparison is in terms of the percentage of gifted subjects who equaled or exceeded the control subjects in mean rating. The figures in Table 5 are for the sexes combined and for all ages combined, since the mean ratings varied only slightly either with age or sex. The instructions specifically requested that the child should be rated in comparison with the average child of the same age. The instructions made no reference to sex, but it is probable that boys were rated in comparison with boys and girls in comparison with girls. Combining ages and sexes greatly enhanced the reliability of the comparisons in Table 5.

For the most part, the results of the trait ratings by teachers present a picture of the gifted child that agrees fairly well with the data from other sources. This is especially true in regard to the kinds of traits in which the superiority of the gifted group is most or least marked. At the top of the list is General intelligence, in which 97 percent of the gifted were rated at or above the mean of the control group. A little below are the other intellectual traits including Desire to know (90 percent), Originality (85 percent), Common sense (84 percent). The average of the percentages for the 4 intellectual traits is 89 percent. As noted in the preceding chapter, 90 percent of the gifted equaled or exceeded the mean of unselected children in intellectual interest as measured by the Wyman test. The agreement of the two lines of evidence is here almost perfect.

Next highest in the order of superiority of the gifted subjects are the volitional traits: Will power and perseverance (84 percent), Desire to excel (84 percent), Self-confidence (81 percent), Prudence and forethought (81 percent). The average of these is 82.5 percent.

The figures for emotional traits are: Sense of humor (74 percent), Cheerfulness and optimism (64 percent), Permanence of moods (63 percent). The average of these is 67 percent, which is exactly the same as the proportion of gifted who equaled or exceeded the control group in the Woodworth-Cady Test of Emotional Stability.

TABLE 5

PERCENTAGES OF GIFTED SUBJECTS RATED BY TEACHERS ABOVE THE MEAN OF THE CONTROL GROUP

	Percent	
1. *Intellectual traits*		
General intelligence	97	
Desire to know	90	
Originality	85	
Common sense	84	
Average of intellectual traits		89
2. *Volitional traits*		
Will power and perseverance	84	
Desire to excel	84	
Self-confidence	81	
Prudence and forethought	81	
Average of volitional traits		82.5
3. *Emotional traits*		
Sense of humor	74	
Cheerfulness and optimism	64	
Permanence of moods	63	
Average of emotional traits		67
4. *Aesthetic traits*		
Musical appreciation	66	
Appreciation of beauty	64	
Average of aesthetic traits		65
5. *Moral traits*		
Conscientiousness	72	
Truthfulness	71	
Sympathy and tenderness	58	
Generosity and unselfishness	55	
Average of moral traits		64
6. *Physical traits*		
Health	60	
Physical energy	62	
Average of physical traits		61
7. *Social traits*		
Leadership	70	
Sensitivity to approval	57	
Popularity	56	
Freedom from vanity	52	
Fondness for large groups	52	
Average for social traits		57.4
8. *Mechanical ingenuity*	47	

The figures for moral traits are: Conscientiousness (72 percent), Truthfulness (71 percent), Sympathy and tenderness (58 percent), Generosity and unselfishness (55 percent). The average of these is 64 percent.

Two of the moral traits, Conscientiousness and Truthfulness, are more or less comparable with three of the character tests; namely, the two tests of overstatement and the test of cheating. On the two tests of overstatement combined, 63 percent of the gifted were at or above the mean of the control group; on the test of cheating 64 percent were at or above the mean. These figures are to be compared with 72 percent on the ratings for Conscientiousness and 71 percent on the ratings for Truthfulness. The disagreement here between the two lines of evidence is not very great, but it is enough to indicate that in objective tests of truthfulness and honesty the gifted did not quite live up to their reputation. In ratings of the other two moral traits, Sympathy and Generosity, the superiority of the gifted was less marked. These traits are perhaps as much social as moral; at any rate, their means are closely in line with the means of the social traits.

In respect to physical traits, both the anthropometric measurements and the medical examinations showed the gifted definitely though not greatly superior to unselected children. The ratings on physical traits were in harmony with this finding; 60 percent of the gifted were rated at or above the average of the control group on Health, and 62 percent on Physical energy. The Wyman scores on activity interests showed no reliable difference between the gifted and the control groups, but activity interests are perhaps only in part dependent upon physique.

On ratings of social traits the proportions of gifted at or above the mean of the control group were 70 percent for Leadership, 57 percent for Sensitivity to approval or disapproval, 56 percent for Popularity, 52 percent for Freedom from vanity, and 52 percent for Fondness for large groups. The average of the figures for the social traits was 57 percent. However, on the Wyman test of social interests, about 84 percent of the gifted equaled or exceeded the mean of the control group. The large discrepancy between these two figures (57 percent and 84 percent) indicates that social interest and social effectiveness are not the same thing.

The singular position of Leadership among the social traits deserves comment. On this trait 70 percent of the gifted equaled or exceeded the mean of the control group, while for the other four social traits the proportions ranged between 52 percent and 57 percent. Obviously Leadership depends largely upon other factors than Fondness for large groups, Sensitiveness to approval or disapproval, Freedom from vanity, and Popularity. One surmises that these other necessary factors are largely intellectual and volitional, in both of which the gifted notably excel. The ratings on Leadership are consistent with the facts reported in chapter xiii on the frequency with which our gifted subjects are elected to class offices and honors despite their usual age disadvantage.

On the two aesthetic traits—Musical appreciation and Appreciation of beauty—approximately 65 percent of the gifted equaled or exceeded the mean of the control group. We have no comparable test data for these traits, but other investigators have reported low yet reliable positive correlations between intelligence scores and scores in tests of musical and artistic talent. We do have preference ratings of the different school subjects by the gifted and control groups, but these are not very enlightening; they tell us primarily how well a subject is liked in comparison with other subjects, not the absolute degree of liking or appreciation. The ratings in question showed modeling to be the only art subject relatively more liked by the gifted than by the control group. Painting and drawing were relatively more liked by the control group (both sexes). Instrumental music and singing were both relatively more liked by control girls than by gifted girls, while boys of the two groups showed about equal preference for these subjects. Perhaps all this means nothing more than that average children are more likely than the gifted to appreciate relief from school subjects that require thinking, and the opportunity to shift to subjects which involve less thinking and more motor activity.

Mechanical ingenuity was the one trait in which teachers rated the gifted below unselected children. It is certain that the teachers were here in error, for test scores in mechanical ability have been consistently found to yield positive, not negative, correlations with intelligence scores. This is a trait which the average classroom teacher has little opportunity to observe; moreover, she is prone to overlook the fact that the gifted child in her class is usually a year or two younger than the others.

Degree of Certainty in Trait Ratings

In the rating instructions, raters were asked to indicate the certainty of each judgment by underlining one of the phrases "very certain," "fairly certain," "rather uncertain," "very uncertain." The average degree of certainty was about the same for girls and boys and changed little with the age of the subject. As would be expected, parents rated the gifted with more certainty than the teachers rated them. This was true for every trait. The teachers rated the gifted with more certainty than they rated the control subjects, which suggests that the gifted child, on the average, has a more positive and striking personality than the average child.

Some traits were rated with a much greater feeling of certainty than others. The mean degree of indicated certainty was high for such traits as General intelligence, Desire to know, and Desire to excel. It was very low for Musical appreciation, Appreciation of beauty, Permanence of moods, Sympathy and tenderness, Generosity and unselfishness, Prudence and forethought, Mechanical ingenuity, and Leadership.

Composite Portrait of the Gifted Child

The material presented in this and the two preceding chapters constitutes what might be called a composite portrait of the gifted child. The outstanding features of this delineation will now be briefly summarized in terms of deviations from the central tendencies of the general child population.

First of all, we have seen that despite many exceptions to the rule the typical gifted child is the product of superior parentage—superior not only in cultural and educational background but apparently also in heredity. As a result of the combined influence of inheritance and environment, the typical member of our group is a slightly better physical specimen than the average child of the generality: the evidence obtained from anthropometric measurements, health histories, and medical examinations is unanimous and conclusive on this point.

Educationally, the average gifted child is accelerated in grade placement about 14 percent of his age, but in mastery of the subject matter taught he is accelerated about 44 percent of his age. The net result is that a majority of the members of our group, during the elementary-school period, were kept at school tasks two or three full grades below the level of achievement they had already reached. In the earlier years, at least, the school appears to play only a minor role in the education of the gifted child, for among those of a given age there is almost no correlation between achievement test scores and length of school attendance. Notwithstanding this gross neglect of their educational needs, the vast majority of gifted children like school and prefer the hard subjects to the easy ones.

The interests of gifted children are many-sided and spontaneous. They learn to read easily, read more and better books than the average child, and largely educate themselves. At the same time, they make numerous collections, engage in all kinds of childhood activities, and acquire far more knowledge of plays and games than the average child of their years. Their preferences among plays, games, and amusements follow fairly closely the normal sex trends with regard to masculinity and femininity of interest, although gifted girls tend to be a little more masculine in their play life than average girls. Perhaps the most significant thing about the play preferences of gifted children is that they reveal a degree of interest maturity two or three years beyond the age norm. On the Wyman Interest Test, 90 percent of the gifted subjects score above the average of unselected children in intellectual interests and 84 percent of them score above the average in social interests. In activity interests the gifted differ little from unselected children of the same age.

A battery of seven character tests showed gifted children above average on every one. As compared with unselected children they are less inclined to boast or to overstate their knowledge; they are more trustworthy when under temptation to cheat; their reading preferences, character preferences, and social attitudes are more wholesome; and they score higher in emotional stability. On total score of the character tests, the typical gifted child of nine years tests as high as the average child of twelve.

Ratings on 25 traits by parents and teachers confirm the evidence from tests and case histories. The proportion of gifted subjects rated superior to unselected children of corresponding age was 89 percent for 4 intellectual traits, 82 percent for 4 volitional traits, 67 percent for 3 emotional traits, 65 percent for 2 aesthetic traits, 64 percent for 4 moral traits, 61 percent for 2 physical traits, and 57 percent for 5 social traits. Only on one trait—mechanical ingenuity—were they rated as low as unselected children, and this verdict is contradicted by the results of mechanical aptitude tests.

There are two facts which stand out clearly in the composite portrait: (1) The deviation of the gifted subjects from the generality is in the upward direction for nearly all traits. This is another way of saying that desirable traits tend to be postively rather than negatively correlated. There is no law of compensation whereby the intellectual superiority of the gifted is sure to be offset by inferiorities along nonintellectual lines. (2) The amount of upward deviation is not the same in all traits. It is greatest in those aspects of behavior most closely related to intelligence, such as originality, intellectual interests, and ability to score high in achievement tests. In school achievement the superiority is greatest in the abstract subjects and least in penmanship, spelling, and routine arithmetical computations. This unevenness is no greater in amount for gifted than for average children, but it is different in direction; whereas the gifted are at their best in the "thought" subjects, average children are at their best in subjects that make least demands upon concept manipulation.

The reader is cautioned, however, to bear in mind the limitations of composite portraiture. The method is useful in calling attention to central tendencies and in providing a basis for generalization as a guide to educational practice, but it would be unfortunate if this emphasis should lead one to overlook the wide range of variability within the gifted group on every trait we have studied. Gifted children do not fall into a single pattern but into an infinite variety of patterns. One can find within the group individual examples of almost every type of personality defect, social maladjustment, behavior problem, and physical frailty; the only difference is that among gifted children the incidence of these deviations is, in varying degrees, lower than in the general population. There will be ample opportunity in later chapters of this volume to call attention to the individual differences among our subjects.

CHAPTER VI

SIX YEARS LATER: THE PROMISE OF YOUTH

After the survey of 1921–22, effort was made to keep in touch with the subjects by sending annual report blanks to parents and teachers requesting certain physical, educational, and social data. Such blanks were mailed in 1923–24, 1924–25, and 1925–26. Each year about 90 percent of the Home Blanks were filled out and returned, but only about 75 percent of the School Blanks. Although the information received in this way was of considerable value, it was so limited in scope that it offered a rather insecure basis for generalizations in other matters than educational progress.

In 1927 a grant from the Commonwealth Fund of New York City made it possible to undertake a more thorough follow-up by field assistants. Plans for the work were formulated during the spring and summer of 1927 and, in September of the same year, the field assistants began their work of testing children and interviewing parents and teachers. The work required the full time of three assistants for a year, and the tabulation and interpretation of the material required an additional year.

The six-year interval between the original research and the follow-up investigation was in a number of respects favorable as to length; it was great enough to make a comparison between earlier and later findings significant and interesting, but not so long as to make it impossible to use any of the kinds of tests employed in the original study. Data were secured as follows:

Intelligence tests. The Stanford-Binet was given to subjects under thirteen years of age, and one form of the Terman Group Test to all others. Scores on the Thorndike Intelligence Examination for High School Graduates were available for a considerable number of the older subjects.

Achievement tests. The Stanford Achievement Test was used with subjects who were in grades four to eight. Other achievement tests used were the Hotz Algebra Test, the Stanford Comprehension in Literature Test for subjects in grades nine, ten, and eleven, and the Iowa High School Content Examination for high-school seniors and college freshmen. Scholastic marks of subjects in high school were also secured.

Personality tests. The Woodworth-Cady Test of Emotional Stability, used in 1922, was given to subjects aged eleven to eighteen who lived in the San Francisco Bay area. The Wyman Test of Intellectual Interests was repeated for some of those who took this test in 1922–23. The Stanford Masculinity-Femininity Test, devised by Terman and Miles, was given to subjects in grade nine or above, including those who had discontinued school at high-school graduation. The George Washington Social Intelligence Test was given to high-school seniors and college freshmen, and to subjects under twenty who were not in school. The Goodwin Watson Test of Social Attitudes was given to high-school seniors and college freshmen.

Vocational interest tests. The Strong Vocational Interest Test was given to boys of the Main Experimental Group who were over fourteen, and the Zyve Test of Scientific Aptitude to gifted subjects attending Stanford University.

The age range of the subjects was so great that no test, either of intelligence, achievement, or personality was suitable for all. Furthermore, because of limitations of time and expense it was not possible in the case of most of the tests to give them to all the subjects for whom they were applicable. A majority of them were given to random samplings of 100 to 200 subjects—samplings large enough to afford a basis for generalizations regarding the entire group of subjects. The testing schedule was planned primarily for subjects who had originally been given the Stanford-Binet test.

Other types of data were secured as follows: a Home Information Blank of four pages was filled out by parents of subjects up to and including age nineteen. An Interest Blank of two pages was filled out by the subjects under twenty, and a two-page Information Blank by those age twenty or over. A School Information Blank of two pages was filled out by the teachers of the children who were still in elementary or high school. A Trait Rating Blank provided ratings by parents and teachers on 12 traits selected from the 25 on which ratings were secured in 1921–22. Finally, blanks were provided for the field workers' reports on home visits and on conferences with the children themselves and their teachers. It was not possible, unfortunately, to repeat the medical examinations and physical measurements of the original study, but considerable information on physical development and health history was secured from parents and teachers.

The follow-up staff included Barbara Stoddard Burks, Alice Leahy, Helen Marshall, and Melita Oden. Miss Marshall had assisted in the investigation of 1921–22, and in the present follow-up was concerned primarily with the collection of field data in the San Francisco area. Miss Leahy and Mrs. Oden also gave their time to field work, while Dr. Burks' duties were divided between field work and office administration. In the published report it was possible to include a valuable study by Dr. Dortha Jensen of the literary juvenilia of certain members of the group.

The remainder of this chapter will be devoted to a brief summary of the most important results of the follow-up as published in Volume III of *Genetic Studies of Genius*.[7] It will be understood, of course, that the results here reported are incapable of answering the question, how gifted children finally turn out. It is believed, however, that they do give a fairly good picture of the typical gifted child in early youth. At the time of the follow-up, the average age of the Main Experimental Group was in the neighborhood of sixteen years, and the average age of the high-school group not far from twenty-one years.

Retesting of Intelligence

The Stanford-Binet was given to members of the group below the age of thirteen years. These included 38 boys and 35 girls. The boys showed an average drop of 3 points in IQ after the six-year interval, the girls an average drop of 13 points. On the Terman Group Test there was a gain in point score but a slight drop in IQ as estimated by this test. The mean score on the Thorndike Intelligence Examination for students entering Stanford was about 1 S.D. above the average of Stanford University students.

Twenty-seven subjects whose IQ's had changed by 15 points or more on the Stanford-Binet test were given the Herring-Binet, and 26 whose estimated IQ's on the Terman Group Test had decreased markedly were given a second form of the same test. In the majority of cases the additional data confirmed the results of the first retest. Moreover, the school achievement test scores of subjects whose IQ's had dropped averaged below those of the other members of the gifted group. On the whole, the data pointed to the conclusion that, although a majority of gifted subjects were in 1927–28 about as superior to the generality as they were in 1921–22, there were some cases which showed a reliable drop in IQ. There were also some reliable gains, but these were less numerous than the losses. The reader is referred to chapters xi and xii, in which the intellectual status of the group as of 1940 has been evaluated.

Achievement Tests

The mean educational quotients of the subjects young enough to be given the Stanford Achievement Test in 1928 were slightly lower than those of gifted subjects of similar age who took the test in 1922. The average difference amounted to 6 points in educational quotient for boys and 10 points for girls.

The Hotz Algebra Test showed the gifted subjects somewhat above the high-school norms published by the author. The Iowa High School Content Examination, covering the fields of English, mathematics, science, and history, showed the gifted group on an average nearly 2 S.D. above the Iowa norms for high-school seniors. The Zyve Test of Scientific Aptitude was given to 53 of the gifted subjects attending Stanford University; the resulting mean score was nearly 1 S.D. above that of Stanford students in general, and only a little below the average of Stanford *graduate students majoring in science.*

Scholastic and Other Interests

Both questionnaire and test data on interests were in line with the results secured in 1921–22, though naturally there were changes resulting from increase in age. The average number of hours per week devoted to general reading was approximately seven and one-half, but this decreased after age fourteen as a result of home-study requirements. The sex differences in reading preferences almost exactly paralleled those found six years earlier. Both boys and girls tended to prefer reading to all other occupations, and to prefer "games that require lots of exercise" to "games that require little exercise." The gifted subjects had taken part in a wide variety of extracurricular activities both in the grades and in high school.

It was possible to give the Wyman Interest Test to 91 subjects who had taken the test in 1922–23. The resulting distributions of scores for intellectual interest, social interest, and activity interest, were almost identical with those in the original test, but the correlations between the individual scores on the original test and the retest were low; namely, .38 for intellectual interests, .50 for social interests, and .15 for activity interests. Obviously, this test given in childhood is not very predictive of interests in the middle and late teens.

Social and Personality Traits

Repetition of the Woodworth-Cady Test of Emotional Stability with 150 subjects showed a correlation of .42 between the original results and those of 1928.

The Goodwin Watson Test of Social Attitudes, intended primarily as a test of fair-mindedness, gave results with the gifted group closely resembling the scores of other well-educated groups tested by Watson.

On the Terman-Miles test of masculinity-femininity* the gifted boys rated almost exactly on a par with unselected boys of corresponding age, but gifted girls averaged reliably more masculine than unselected girls.

The George Washington Social Intelligence Test was administered to 184 of the gifted subjects, and gave average scores considerably above the norms furnished by the author of the test. The scores on this test are perhaps as much influenced by general intelligence as by social intelligence.

Case-history data on social and personality traits gave a picture which differed little from that of 1921–22. The proportion of gifted subjects whose companionship was sought by others, and the proportion who were teased or regarded as "queer" had changed little. However, the gifted subjects by mid-youth showed an even greater tendency to prefer companions older than themselves than they did during their childhood years. About 5 percent of the boys and 2 percent of the girls were, in 1928, regarded either by parents or by teachers as presenting personality problems. There was some indication that difficulties in making social adjustments were more often encountered among subjects who as children had tested above 170 IQ.

* Described in reference number 66. This M-F test is not to be confused with that used in 1921–22, or with the one used in 1940.

Trait Ratings

The traits selected for ratings in 1927–28 were the following: Perseverance, Fondness for groups, Leadership, Popularity, Desire to excel, Freedom from vanity, Sympathy, Conscientiousness, Desire to know, Originality, Common sense, and General intelligence. These were the traits of the original 25 previously used which had yielded the most reliable and objective data. In 1927–28, teachers' ratings of the gifted group on these traits were lower by a very small fraction than they were in 1921–22, but they were still above the mean ratings of the control group of 1921–22 in all but the social traits. Actually, the changes between 1922 and 1928 in the mean ratings, both by teachers and parents, were slight. There was still rather close agreement between parents and teachers in the rank order of the 12 traits based upon mean ratings, and this rank order agreed closely with that found six years earlier.

Health History

The incidence of physical defects and of diseases reported by parents and teachers yielded a picture which differed from the norm about the same as did the results of the original study. In the home and school reports, approximately 85 percent of the subjects were described as having "good" general health, and less than 5 percent as having "poor" health. It is unnecessary to present the physical data in more detail, especially as medical examinations were not given.

Literary Juvenilia

The literary juvenilia, both of a number of our gifted subjects and of several eminent authors, were evaluated by Dr. Jensen in terms of a scale specially devised for the purpose. The results indicated that at least seven of the gifted subjects had by the age of twelve years or earlier produced juvenilia which were on a par with those produced by eminent English or American authors of corresponding age. It is rather surprising that almost all of the gifted subjects who showed outstanding literary ability in childhood were girls. This suggests that literary composition, especially the writing of poetry, is looked upon by children as something more suitable for girls than for boys. As we shall see later, only a few of those who produced very superior juvenilia adopted a literary career. This is one of the many indications that exceptional ability in a particular line during childhood does not necessarily bear fruit in later years. With the development from childhood to youth and to adulthood, interests and motivation may so change as to lend the appearance of increased or decreased ability.

Summary

Perhaps the most important outcome of the 1927–28 follow-up was the fact that the composite portrait of the group had changed only in minor respects in six years. As a whole, the group was still highly superior intellectually, for the most part within the top 1 or 2 percent of the generality. There was some evidence that the boys had dropped slightly in IQ and that the girls had dropped somewhat more. This conclusion, however, needs to be qualified in two respects. For one thing, the intelligence tests used in the follow-up lacked sufficient top to yield IQ's strictly comparable with those of 1921–22. Secondly, it should be pointed out that some regression toward the mean is to be expected from purely statistical considerations. When any group is selected on the basis of *either* a very high or a very low IQ, a later test, even the following week, will ordinarily show some regression toward the mean of the generality. This tendency is accentuated if the second test does not measure precisely the same functions as the test originally used. With allowance made for these considerations, one can say that the group as a whole had pretty well maintained its intellectual status. There were, however, exceptions to this rule. Individuals were found who had almost certainly dropped 20 or more points in IQ. The data strongly indicate that a few of the subjects had undergone a definite change in rate of intellectual growth during the six-year period. This matter will be discussed more fully in connection with the intelligence test scores earned by the group in the 1940 follow-up.

The showing in school achievement was in line with that for intelligence. There was less skipping of school grades after the age of eleven or twelve years, but the quality of work for the group in general remained at an exceedingly high level. For example, nearly two-thirds of the high-school grades of the girls and more than one-half of the high-school grades of the boys were A's. The significance of this is accentuated by the fact that the gifted group in the high-school period averaged considerably younger than the generality of high-school students. In evaluating school achievement at the high-school or college period, it is also necessary to bear in mind that the higher we go in the grades the more highly selected is the school population with whom the gifted subjects are compared.

The composite-portrait method is useful, just as concepts and generalizations are useful in the shorthand of thinking. Nevertheless, the composite portrait, like any other kind of average, fails to convey any sense of the uniqueness of the individual subjects who compose the group. Although deviations below average intelligence were not found in the 1927–28 follow-up, extreme deviations both from the group average and from the generality were found in almost every physical, mental, and personality trait, including size, athletic ability, health, scientific ability, literary ability, masculinity, social and activity interests, vocational aptitude, social intelligence, leadership, ambition, and moral dependability. It is true that on all of these traits the mean for the gifted group tends to be higher than for unselected children of corresponding age, but the range of variability in these and other traits was if anything greater in mid-youth than it had been in mid-childhood. The characteristic features of a personality are formed gradually. The traits of childhood often foreshadow to some extent the adult personality, but the traits of youth approximate it more closely.

CHAPTER VII

LATER FOLLOW-UP: 1936, 1940, 1945

For eight years after the follow-up described in the preceding chapter there was no systematic attempt to contact all the members of the gifted group. During that period, however, a half-time assistant was employed to help with the correspondence that was carried on with individual subjects of the group. Many wrote about their activities, or came to Stanford for personal interviews. Many who had no special occasion to write kept us informed of changes in their mailing address. Between 1928 and 1936 contact of one sort or another was had with a considerable proportion of the entire group, with the result that for many subjects a great deal of information was obtained. Regarding others of the group little information was secured during this period. Since the beginning of the study numerous parents have written us from time to time or have come to Stanford for conferences.

In 1936 plans were laid for an extensive field study to be made as soon as funds should become available. First, however, it seemed desirable to get in touch with as many as possible of the original group by mail, and to secure certain information that would aid in planning for the projected field study. It was first of all necessary to locate the subjects, many of whom had moved from their earlier addresses. In the second place, it was important to do everything possible to put the members of the group in a co-operative mood. Accordingly, a letter was sent out detailing the study and its purposes, and asking for the address of the subject, of his parents, and of a relative or friend through whom the subject might be located in later years. The letter was usually sent to the parents, though occasionally to the subject himself, at the most recent address in our files. When the addresses had been received, a four-page Information Blank was sent to each subject, and a four-page Home Information Blank to the parents or, if both parents were deceased, to a near relative. The blank was accompanied by a letter emphasizing our continued interest in the subject, and the value both to science and to education of exact knowledge regarding the adult careers of persons who had tested high in intelligence during childhood.

The subject's Information Blank called for detailed information regarding educational history, occupations since leaving school, avocational interests and activities, general health, marital status, and deaths among relatives since 1928. The Home Information Blank called for information on the subject's physical and mental health, indications of special abilities, personality and character traits, education and occupations of siblings, and the accomplishments and activities of the subject's parents. Both blanks gave ample space for "additional information" not called for by specific questions and this brought, in many cases, extremely valuable and detailed replies. The blanks were sent out in the spring of 1936 and, though the great majority of the reports had been received by midsummer, there was considerable difficulty in locating some of the subjects, and it was nearly a year before blanks could be placed in the hands of all those who finally were located.

This mail follow-up was more successful than had been expected, for approximately 90 percent of the subjects were located, and from nearly all of them considerable information was obtained. It is unnecessary to summarize this information since, for the most part, it is rendered obsolete by the follow-up of 1940. The important thing is that this preliminary roundup showed that it was possible to contact a great majority of the subjects, and to secure their wholehearted co-operation. The stage was accordingly set for the more searching investigation that was to follow.

Scope of 1940 Follow-up

Early in 1939 a generous grant for follow-up purposes was obtained from the Carnegie Corporation of New York City. This was supplemented by grants from the National Research Council Committee for Research on Problems of Sex, by a second grant from the Carnegie Corporation, by three grants from the Columbia Foundation of San Francisco, by a sizable gift from an anonymous donor, and by other personal contributions. All told, more than $40,000 was available for the collection of new material and for correlating it with the extensive information secured between 1921 and 1928. This was sufficient to make possible the administration of numerous tests to the subjects by field assistants and the collection of a large amount of case-history data. The blanks, tests, and reports by means of which the information was secured, may be listed as follows:

1. A General Information Blank of eight pages filled out by the gifted subjects.

2. A four-page Supplementary Information Blank filled out by a parent or other close relative of subject.

3. The Strong Vocational Interest Test for all the men, and for those women who were interested in taking it.

4. The Concept Mastery test, which is a brief but reliable test of "abstract" intelligence, given both to gifted subjects and to their spouses.

5. The Marriage Blank of seven pages, which yielded a numerical index of marital happiness, filled out by married gifted subjects and by their spouses.

6. The Personality and Temperament test, devised as a measure of aptitude for marital adjustment, given to both married and unmarried gifted subjects, and to the spouses of the married.

7. A Stanford-Binet test of the gifted subjects' offspring above the age of two and a half years, together with birth and developmental data on each child tested.

8. Detailed reports by field workers on conferences with the subjects, their parents, spouses, or other relative. These reports called for supplementary information on education, occupation, interests, special abilities, attitude toward the gifted study, health, nervous tendencies and general adjustment, marital status, family constellation, and socioeconomic status. The field workers also rated the subjects and their spouses on twelve traits.

The General Information Blank and the Strong Vocational Interest Blank could be and usually were filled out by the subjects at their convenience and without supervision. The Concept Mastery test, the test of marital happiness, and (in most cases) the test of aptitude for marriage, were filled out under supervision by the subjects and their spouses at small group meetings held by the field assistants at intervals during the course of the follow-up. The resulting information will be summarized in the chapters which follow.

Selection of Research Associates

Because of the age and professional status of the subjects, it was deemed necessary to utilize only mature psychologists as assistants.

It was fortunate for the investigation that the following could be secured for ten months of field work: Dr. Helen Marshall, who had assisted both in the original investigation of 1921–22 and in the follow-up of 1927–28; Dr. Nancy Bayley, Research Associate in the Child Research Institute of the University of California; and Dr. Ellen Sullivan, Associate Professor of Psychology in the University of California at Los Angeles. Dr. Sullivan's field work was confined chiefly to the Los Angeles area and San Diego; Dr. Bayley worked entirely in the San Francisco Bay region, while Dr. Marshall covered outlying sections of California from the northern to the extreme southern end of the state and co-operated with Dr. Sullivan and Dr. Bayley in the Los Angeles and San Francisco areas. It was impossible to send field workers outside of California, but in nearly all cases extensive information was secured by mail from the subjects residing in other parts of the country. These included about one-fourth of the total group.

Co-operation of Subjects

It was feared that after so long a lapse of time many of the subjects would fail to co-operate either because of waning interest in the investigation or because of the difficulty of finding the time (averaging perhaps five or six hours) to be interviewed, to fill out our blanks, and take our schedule of mental tests. As it turned out, however, the group was almost incredibly co-operative, although not every one was able to do everything that was asked by our field assistants. The vast majority were willing to go to almost any amount of trouble to further the aims of the investigation. During childhood the subjects had taken the tests with little knowledge of or interest in their purpose, and even in the follow-up of 1927–28 a good many had not shown any marked personal interest in the investigation. By 1940 the situation had so changed that almost every member of the group had a definite scientific curiosity about the outcome of the study. They were quite willing to serve as "guinea pigs" if thereby they could help to answer the question, how children of high IQ turn out. This curiosity, surprisingly, was about as evident among the less successful as among the more successful members of the group.

In some cases co-operation may have been stimulated by the fact that certain services were offered by us, including the testing and educational guidance of offspring, the vocational testing of the men and also of such women as wished to have the test, and finally the permission to give the senior author as reference in connection with applications for positions or special appointments. Far more influential, however, was the professional skill of the field assistants. In many years devoted to clinical psychology and other forms of individual counseling, they had acquired the ability to win confidence quickly and to secure personal information of the most intimate kind.

Conditions under which the field work had to be carried out were in a number of respects difficult. It is easy to command the time of school children, provided only the teacher is willing to co-operate, but in the case of busy adults time for conferences could often be found only on evenings or week ends. The result was that the field assistants spent their forenoons chiefly in writing up reports and making appointments by telephone for afternoons, evenings, or Sundays. It is impossible to overpraise either the quality or the quantity of field work accomplished.

It was with some misgivings that plans were made to include in the greater part of the testing schedule the spouses who had married into the group. It was feared that some of them would be found more or less reluctant to enter into competition with the highly intellectual group into which they had married. Ordinarily the spouses wanted to know what we had learned about gifted children, and were quite willing to enter into the investigation as in-laws. Humorous comments were not infrequently encountered, but beneath these and other evidenced attitudes, a wholesome respect for a high IQ could usually be observed.

The hearty co-operation of the subjects and their spouses is all the more remarkable in view of the fact that many of the questions in the marital happiness test called for extremely intimate information about personal attitudes toward the marriage and toward the spouse, and still more intimate information about sexual relationships. Even on these tests there were few refusals to co-operate.

Hollerith Coding of Results

Neither in the original survey nor in the earlier follow-up work had use been made of Hollerith techniques. In the present investigation, however, it was deemed necessary to prepare for Hollerith treatment not only the new data of 1940, but also the most important test scores, measurements, and case-history data collected during the preceding twenty years. This was a truly enormous task, one made more difficult by the fact that much of the information to be coded was of the semiqualitative sort imbedded in case-history material. The task was carried out by Mrs. Oden with the help of trained assistants over a period of nearly two years. It may be mentioned here that the most essential parts of the original data and of the present follow-up were coded on seven Hollerith cards. In view of the fact that it is not easy to correlate data on one Hollerith card with data on another, certain items of information, requiring in all 30 of the 80 columns on a Hollerith card, were repeated on all the cards. The seven cards just mentioned did not include the item data on the test of marital happiness or the test of marital aptitude. These alone required the use of nine Hollerith cards to make possible an item analysis of everything included in the two tests.

The use of the punched card and of machine tabulation made possible a more thorough analysis of the material at hand than would otherwise have been possible. It will be recalled that in the earlier reports, except for a general description of the composition of the gifted group as a whole and a short summary of the material on the High School Group, the discussion of findings and the statistical analyses were confined largely to data for the subjects in the Main Experimental Group. The Hollerith technique now made it possible to handle with ease the data for all the subjects whose development had been followed.

The Group as of 1940

In the follow-up undertaken in the autumn of 1939, every attempt was made to reach all subjects regardless of the original subgroup classification (I. Main Experimental Group, II. Outside Binet Cases, III. Outside Group Test Cases.)* No distinction in membership was made either in follow-up procedures or in treatment of the data gathered. All the evidence indicated that the heretofore less extensively reported groups were at least the equal of the Main Experimental Group; in fact, most of the small differences actually favored the High School Group.

Not only those of high-school age who had qualified on the Terman Group Test, but also the older subjects from the elementary grades

* Table 1, p. 7.

who qualified on the Binet test, made a somewhat better showing in 1940 than those who were tested at earlier ages. Two factors are undoubtedly involved. In the first place, both of these tests lacked sufficient top to measure adequately the older subjects in the original survey. As a result, the subjects qualifying at the upper ages were more highly selected than those qualifying at lower ages. A second factor is the well-established fact that the older a subject is when measured by *any* given test, the better the score on that test will predict adult intellectual status.[2]

As complete case data as possible had been collected for all the subgroups, both at the time of the original survey and in the subsequent follow-up studies, even though the published reports were concerned chiefly with the Main Experimental Group. Most of the differences were in the number and type of tests given. Some differences in testing were unavoidable, since several of the achievement, personality, and interest tests were inapplicable to intellectually superior subjects of high-school age. The large majority of the Outside Binet group, however, were given the complete battery of tests at the time of the original survey. Only a few of the group-test subjects were given the physical examination of 1922–23, but a good many of the Outside Binet cases had the same physical examinations as the Main Experimental Group. There are few subjects for whom we do not have, in addition to the intelligence-test data, fairly complete information on family background; on developmental, educational, vocational, and marital history; and on interests, character, and personality. The information was provided by the subjects themselves, their parents, their teachers, and the field assistants.

As stated in chapter i, the total number of subjects selected for study in this investigation was 1,528. However, in the period elapsing between the original selection of subjects and the 1940 follow-up, 35 males and 26 females had died, leaving a total of 1,467 subjects (822 men and 645 women) on our active list when the 1940 work was undertaken. Although as much information as possible has been secured for the deceased up to the time of death, they are not included in the report of the 1940 and 1945 findings except where specifically noted.* The 1,467 subjects who were alive in 1940 were distributed

* Chapter viii, "Mortality" and chapter x, "Mental Health, Nervous Disorders, and General Adjustment."

as follows, according to the type of the test on which they were selected, and their age at the time of selection:

	Male	Female	Total
1. *Pre-high-school subjects* (*age 3 to 13 years*)			
Stanford-Binet	554	476	1,030
National Intelligence Test	10	14	24
2. *High-school subjects* (*age 12 to 19 years*)			
Terman Group Test	253	154	407
Army Alpha	5	1	6
Total N of surviving subjects (1940)	822	645	1,467

The success of the follow-up is shown by the figures in Table 6, from which it will be seen that of the 1,467 living subjects, data were secured for 97.7 percent. Of the total group, almost 1,100 were interviewed by field workers, including nearly all who resided in California and some from out of the state who visited California and called at Stanford. The great majority of those contacted only by mail were living outside of California. The second part of Table 6 shows that 1,348 of the 1,467 subjects (91.89 percent) filled out the General Information Blank, 1,235 (84.18 percent) the test of personality and temperament (marital aptitude), and that 697 (47.58 percent of all subjects, or 69.49 percent of the married) took the test of marital happiness. The latter test was limited to married subjects, and chiefly to those who could be tested under the supervision of a field assistant.

In addition to the data listed in Table 6, we were able to secure Stanford-Binet tests of 364 offspring of the gifted subjects, including 182 boys and 182 girls; also the following data from spouses who had married into the gifted group: Concept Mastery test, 527; test of marital happiness, 636; and the test of marital aptitude, 636.

Two things stand out clearly in the following table. First, the almost incredible amount of co-operation that was secured. No other comparably large group of any kind—superior, average, or inferior—has been tested and followed up over so long a period. The resulting data provide, if not a final answer, at least a better answer than has hitherto been available to the age-old question regarding the later careers of superior children.

The second fact to be noted is the enormous amount of data which had to be statisticized in connection with the present follow-up.

Information included not only the numerous test scores and case-history material secured in 1940, but also the most important data secured in 1921–22, 1927–28, and 1936. Moreover, the recent data included extensive information regarding spouses and offspring of of the subjects.

TABLE 6

OUTCOME OF THE STUDY (1940)

	Male	Female	Total	Percent
I. *Follow-up contacts and co-operation*				
Subjects interviewed by field workers..	593	493	1,086	
Subjects contacted by mail...........	198	125	323	
Total actively co-operating			1,409	96.04
Information only from interview with parent or sibling	10	6	16	
No direct contact with subject or family but information secured from other sources	6	3	9	
Total in touch with directly or indirectly			1,434	97.7
Unable to trace. No information since 1928 or earlier*	15	18	33	
Total group			1,467	
II. *Blanks filled out*				
General Information (from subjects)..	758	590	1,348	
Personality and Temperament (test of aptitude for marriage)	697	538	1,235	
Your Present Marriage (test of marital happiness)	391	306	697	
Strong Vocational Interest Blank.....	627	199	826	
Concept Mastery test	527	427	954	
Supplementary Information (from parents or close relative)	432	337	769	

* Between 1940 and 1945 there were 5 (4 men and 1 woman) of the 33 subjects in this category who were located and with whom co-operation was re-established.

In the chapters that follow, the number of subjects varies somewhat for different items because of differences in the data secured originally for the various subgroups, or because of the failure of subject or parents to supply some of the information called for. There are, however, a few subjects with whom we have not been in contact for a number of years. In 1940 this group of "lost subjects" numbered 33 (15 men and 18 women), but since that time 5 of these have been located, so that the number lost now stands at 28 (11 men and 17 women).

There is no reason to think that any considerable part of the loss has been due either to the death of subjects or their unwillingness to co-operate. In nearly all cases the entire family had moved to parts unknown before the children had grown up, and our best efforts to locate them have been unsuccessful. Only in one case had there been outright and sustained refusal to co-operate. This subject was a member of the High School Group whose parents had only partially co-operated in 1922 and had failed to reply to any of the follow-up letters until 1936 when our questionnaire was returned with the notation "this subject does not wish to be studied." We still hope eventually to locate more of the lost members of the group. On several occasions in the past, subjects who were thought to be lost have spontaneously written us saying that they had taken certain tests and filled out questionnaires some years ago, had then moved away and heard nothing more of the study, and were anxious to know whether the research was still in progress. Sometimes it is a newspaper or magazine article that gives us a clue as to the whereabouts of a lost member, and once it was a "Letter to the Editor" published in a widely read magazine.

Following are some of the pertinent available facts regarding the 28 with whom we were still out of touch in 1945. Among these there were 10 from the Main Experimental Group, 9 from the Outside Binet cases, and 9 who had qualified on a Terman Group Test. The Binet-tested subjects ranged in IQ from 143 to 182 with a mean of 153. The IQ equivalent of the TGT scores ranged from 139 to 151, with a mean of 143. In 18 cases contact had been maintained until 1928, but in the interval between that follow-up and the one of 1936 we lost track of them. We kept in touch by mail with 7 subjects until 1926, but were unable to locate them in 1927–28 or subsequently, and in 5 other cases we were never in touch with the subject or his family after the data for the original survey (1922) had been gathered.

In addition to the individuals who have been lost there is a small number whose co-operation has been limited, but regarding whom we have some information. Our knowledge usually includes such items as place of residence, occupation, extent of schooling, marital status, *et cetera,* but the information has been secured indirectly from a parent, sibling, friend, or more remote source. It has been our experience that, once personal contact has been made with these subjects, co-operation is no longer a problem; but a majority of them live so far away that personal contact is impossible.

At the time of the 1940 follow-up, the mean age of the living subjects was 29.8 years (S.D. 3.9) for males and 29.1 years (S.D. 3.5) for females. The mean age for the sexes combined was 29.5 years. The range of ages for males was from 14 to 39 years, and for females from 16 to 37 years. The distribution of ages as of the last birthday was as follows:

Age in Years	Males (N = 822)	Females (N = 645)
Under 20	4	6
20–24	75	68
25–29	377	320
30–34	275	220
35–39	91	31

The Group as of 1945

Between 1940 and 1945 letters and visits from members of the group had kept us in touch with many subjects, but, since for the majority no information had been secured during the war years, it was decided to make another survey of the group. Accordingly, in April of 1945 a two-page information blank* was sent to each subject at the most recent address in our files. As had been expected, a good many letters were returned undelivered from the first mailing because of changes of address during the war years. In such cases letters of inquiry were then sent to relatives or friends, and eventually close to 98 percent of the group were located. All but a small proportion of those for whom addresses were secured supplied the information requested.

The information blanks were filled out and returned by 1,320 subjects, and an additional 31 who did not fill out the form either called in person or wrote letters supplying information comparable to that asked for in the questionnaire. Thus, the number of subjects for whom information on 1945–46 status was received is 1,351, or 93.0 percent of all subjects.† For another 67 we either received the 1945 address directly from the subject or his family, or were able to verify it through the telephone directory or university alumni records. In 14

* Appendix, pages 437 ff.

† The number of living subjects was 1,454, there having been 13 who died in the interval between 1940 and 1945.

of these cases, information regarding the subject had been received from a sibling who was also a member of the gifted group. The returns according to sex were as follows: Information was obtained for 760 men (93.6 percent) and 591 women (92.1 percent), and addresses were verified and prospects for later co-operation good for an additional 38 men and 29 women.

In all, 1,418 subjects or 97.5 percent of the total had been located by mid-1946, and 95.3 percent of these supplied the information called for.

The information asked for included a record of military service and nonmilitary war work; schooling since 1940; occupation and earned income for the years 1941, 1942, 1943, and 1944; publications; general health (physical and mental); marital history; and offspring. In addition, there was a question asking for "any other significant information regarding yourself or your family which has not been covered in this questionnaire . . . ."

Considering the confusion incident to war activities, and the numerous occupational changes following the cessation of hostilities, the response of the subjects has been extraordinary. Replies have come to us from all over the world, including Britain, France, Germany, Italy, North Africa, China, India, Japan, and various islands of the Pacific. Blanks were filled out on naval ships, in Army camps and hospitals, and even in fox holes of combat areas.

The time chosen for the survey of 1945–46 turned out to be most fortunate, since we were able to get very nearly complete war records from our subjects. In a large number of cases, those whose blanks were returned before the end of the war have written subsequent letters to tell us of their postwar activities.

The inquiry of 1945–46 was not a detailed one, but was designed rather to maintain contact with the subjects and to bring our records up to date on the main events in their lives. Not all of the data received in this follow-up have been thoroughly analyzed, but results on the more important items have been tabulated and are reported as supplementary material in the chapters which they concern. The war records, of course, are wholly new material and have been reported in a separate chapter.

CHAPTER VIII

MORTALITY

There had been 61 deaths among the gifted subjects by 1940 (35 males and 26 females). The incidence for males was 4.14 percent and for females 3.98 percent. For the sexes combined the mortality rate was 4.07 percent. These proportions are based on the 1,500 subjects for whom information was available; that is, the 28 subjects (11 men and 17 women) with whom we have lost contact are excluded from the calculations of mortality rate. As pointed out in the preceding chapter, there is no reason to believe that our loss of contact with these subjects has been due to greater mortality among them.

The mortality rate for the generality in a particular age span can be determined from a life table by finding the number out of an arbitrarily large number of live births who are living at a given age, and the proportion of those who survive to a specified older age. We used the life tables from Dublin and Lotka,[23] based on the mortality rate in 1929–31. Age 11 was chosen as the initial age on the table and 30 as the upper limit, since these ages closely approximated the mean age of the gifted group at the time of the original survey and at the 1940 follow-up, respectively. The mortality rate for the generality of white population in this age period was 5.37 percent for males, 4.68 percent for females, and 5.02 percent for the sexes combined. As noted above, of the 1,500 gifted subjects for whom we had information, 4.07 percent died between 1922 and 1940. It appears, therefore, that the death rate among the gifted subjects was definitely below that of the general population.

Causes of Death

The causes of death to 1940 are summarized in Table 7, which gives both the N and percentage incidence for each category. It will be noted that the death rate from accident was much higher for males than for females. This is true also in the general white population, for whom the accidental death rate among males in recent years has been nearly twice as great as that among females. According to

Dublin and Lotka, at age 10 the chances per 1,000 general population of eventually dying from accidental causes are 80.8 for males and 44.9 for females.

TABLE 7

CAUSES OF DEATH TO 1940, WITH PERCENTAGE INCIDENCE

	MALES (N = 846)		FEMALES (N = 654)		TOTAL (N = 1,500)	
	N	%	N	%	N	%
Natural causes	18	2.13	21	3.21	39	2.60
Accidents	12	1.42	3	0.46	15	1.00
Suicides	5	0.59	1	0.15	6	0.40
No information as to cause	..	....	1	0.15	1	0.07
Deaths from all causes	35	4.14	26	3.98	61	4.07

Suicide in the gifted group follows the pattern of the general population in its greater frequency among males, the ratio of men to women in both cases being more than 3 to 1. Dublin and Lotka's calculations of the probability of dying from specified causes offer the most nearly comparable data we have found on the incidence of suicide in the general population. Their estimate of the probability of eventual suicide is based on the mortality conditions of 1930. According to these authors, 2.13 percent of the generality of males alive at age 10 will eventually die by suicide. The corresponding figure for females is 0.59 percent. In the gifted group 0.59 percent of males and 0.15 percent (one case) of females had committed suicide by 1940 when the average age of the group was about 30 years. If our group is ever to equal the rate for the generality as estimated by Dublin and Lotka, 3.61 as many men and 3.93 as many women as had committed suicide by 1940 will have to take their own lives in the years to come. The incidence of suicide in our group may be expected to increase since, in the general population, the median age of those committing suicide is 49, with about two-thirds of the deaths from this cause occurring between the ages of 33 and 65. If the gifted group should follow this pattern of increase with age, the ultimate number of suicides would be only a little over three times the number in 1940. As stated above, to reach the ultimate rate for the generality, the 1940 incidence would have to be multiplied by 3.61 for males and 3.93 for females, which on the basis of present evidence appears unlikely. In this connection, attention should be called to the probability that estimates for the general population are too low; not only does the individual committing suicide often take pains to make his death appear accidental, but also relatives and friends sometimes prefer to conceal the fact of suicide. So far, except for one case, we have had full information regarding the circumstances and causes of death of all deceased gifted subjects.

Additional Deaths to End of 1945

With 1945 reports in from more than 90 percent of the subjects, the following deaths are known to have occurred between 1940 and the end of 1945:

	Men	Women
Natural causes	2	2
Accidents	3	..
Suicides	..	1
War deaths	5	..
All causes	10	3

In addition to the five men who lost their lives in military service, two of the accidental deaths are indirectly attributable to the war. One man, a chemical engineer, was engaged in work in an atomic bomb laboratory when he came in contact with materials which proved fatal. The other was overcome by fumes while working as a welder in a war plant.

We estimate that the total number of deaths reported here would not be increased by more than one or two if all returns were in. At the end of 1945 the mean age of the group was close to 35 years. It would appear that the incidence of mortality in the group, as compared with that of the generality, was no less favorable at the later date than in 1940.

Subjects Who Have Died

The mean age at death of gifted subjects deceased by 1940 was 21.9 years for males (S.D. 5.5 years) and 21.8 years for females (S.D. 6.5 years), and the age range was from 8 to 35 years. Of the 35 deceased men, 20 were still in school at the time of death—16 in college and 4 in high school or below. The 15 who had completed their schooling included 13 college graduates and 2 who had completed a year or more of college but had not graduated. Nine of the 26 women had died before completing their education. Among the

17 who had finished their schooling were 6 college graduates, 1 who had finished high school and taken nurse's training, and 10 who had not gone beyond high school.

The average IQ of deceased subjects who had been given the Binet test was 149, and the IQ range was from 135 to 184. Space does not permit case notes on all who have died, but the following paragraphs give brief descriptions of several who are fairly representative of those deceased after the age of seventeen years.

Deaths from natural causes. Of the 39 deaths from natural causes to 1940, tuberculosis accounted for 8. Appendicitis, nephritis, and infantile paralysis each claimed 3, and the other 22 were distributed among 12 diseases, with no more than 2 deaths resulting from any one of them.

F 142 died of infantile paralysis at the age of eighteen. She was then in her second year at college and was exceptionally well adjusted socially. In high school she had entered into several activities and won various honors. She had not been in college long enough to become prominent in extracurricular activities, but was participating in several and was making an excellent scholastic record.

F 784 was one of four very gifted children in an unusually happy and congenial home. She was in the last term of her senior year at college when it was discovered that she had a brain tumor. An immediate operation resulted in a temporary recovery of health, but after a few months the symptoms returned and her death followed about a year later at the age of twenty-three. In the brief period of apparent recovery she completed *in absentia* the work she had been compelled to drop at the time of her operation, and she was awarded the A.B. degree shortly before her death.

M 846 was making rapid strides in the field in which he had worked so hard to become established when he died suddenly of a heart attack at the age of twenty-six. This subject had had fewer advantages than the majority of our group. Finishing high school at the time of the depression, he was able to take only one year at college before having to go to work. He held a variety of jobs, but was constantly on the alert for some way of getting into newspaper work. He finally succeeded and had made good as a sports writer on a large metropolitan daily when death ended his career.

F 1503 succumbed to nephritis at the age of thirty. At the time of her death she was employed as psychologist in a social-service agency, and was engaged in compiling the results of her research for the doctorate. She was to have received her Ph.D. degree within a few months.

M 908 finished the eighth grade at ten years eleven months, high school at fourteen years eleven months, graduated *cum laude* from college at nineteen, and was awarded his Ph.D. in physics at the exceptionally early age of twenty-two. He was elected to both Phi Beta Kappa and Sigma Xi. Embarking at once on his professional career, he soon became a university instructor and later assistant professor. He published a number of research articles, and at twenty-nine was listed in *American Men of Science*. At the age of thirty he contracted tuberculosis and was thereafter incapacitated. He died at the age of thirty-five. During his illness he wrote a popular book on physics which, published posthumously, received high praise both for its scholarly nature and for its superior literary quality.

F 575 became interested in astronomy when only nine years old, and this later became her major in college and was the professional field she planned to enter. She was elected to both the scholastic and activity honor societies on graduation from high school, and was chosen graduation speaker. She was doing graduate work in astronomy at the time of her death at the age of twenty-four. Her interests were unusually broad and included, besides astronomy: politics, international relations, history, and literature. She had been awarded a fellowship and was within a few months of her Ph.D. degree when stricken with leukemia.

F 1128 gave promise of being one of our most outstanding women. She finished high school at fifteen with scholarship honors, and was commencement speaker. As a result of her A record throughout her university career, she was awarded the University Medal, given each year to the senior having the highest scholarship standing. She took her Ph.D. in Latin and was Sterling Research Fellow in linguistics at Yale. At the time of her death from pneumonia at the age of twenty-nine she was a college instructor. Her publications include several scholarly articles on philology.

M 282. In this case death from infantile paralysis at twenty-four cut short a career of unusual accomplishment and promise. After graduating from college he took an executive position in New York with a world-wide service organization. He demonstrated such marked qualities of leadership and executive ability that he had many offers of fine positions, and had just accepted one when stricken. His school record presaged the extraordinary talents that were later to be so widely recognized. In high school he was business manager of the school paper, assistant editor of the yearbook, a member of the press club and of the fish and game club, president of a service club, and president of a national federation of service clubs. He was the winner in a state oratorical contest, and had the leading part in several operettas and plays. In college he became editor-in-chief of an off-campus magazine of national scope dedicated to interesting youth in the problems of democracy and to developing methods of training for government service. Gifted in speaking, writing, and leadership, he devoted himself unsparingly to the work of service organizations. At the time of his death, leaders in youth organizations all over the country wrote of the high esteem in which he had been held.

Deaths from accidents. Of the 15 fatal accidents, 10 were caused by automobiles and 3 by airplanes. One was an industrial accident, and one an accidental shooting while hunting. Following are brief case histories of 6 of the 15 subjects who died from accidents.

M 771, one of the most gifted young scientists in our group, lost his life in an automobile accident at the age of twenty-two years. He had graduated from Stanford University at twenty, with a major in geology and a minor in zoology. His interests in science were evidenced very early; he was only fifteen when he wrote a paper on molluscan fauna which was published by the United States National Museum. While still in high school he wrote a manual of the mollusks of Lower California, which, though never offered for publication, contained considerable original material. At twenty, under the auspices of Cornell University, he made a large collection of fishes from Hawaii. Later, under the direction of the California Academy of Sciences, he took part in a number of geological and biological surveys. Several of his scientific papers have been published. At the time of his death he was a graduate student in paleontology and assistant curator in the California Academy of Sciences. A half-page obituary published in *Science* shortly after his death characterized him as "a clear-headed and persistent worker, also a born executive and a master of English," and added that "his love for biological studies approached genius."

M 1529 met his death in an airplane accident at the age of twenty-five. An adopted child, he had been something of a behavior problem in his adolescent years; repeated truancy and various pranks got him into frequent trouble. On graduating from high school before the age of sixteen, he joined the Marines (overstating his age) and spent the following two years in China. He then took the examination for admission to the Naval Academy and passed with high honors, entering Annapolis a little before the age of eighteen, although officially listed as two years older. At Annapolis he made an excellent scholastic record, but was disqualified at the end of his second year for a breach of military discipline. Married at twenty, he continued his education at a state university. After graduating, he entered law school and had been in attendance less than a year when the accident occurred that took his life.

M 1088 was well established in his professional career when his hobby of mountain climbing resulted in death from a fall. This subject first came to our attention at the age of ten years when he was already in the eighth grade. He completed high school at fourteen, and was awarded his M.D. degree when barely twenty-three. He became associated with a prominent medical group and was achieving promising success when death occurred at the age of thirty-one.

M 1092, a boy of Jewish ancestry, was tested at seven years ten months, earning an IQ of 173. He had the advantage of unusually good home training and fine heredity. He showed exceptional scholastic attainment in both the original and follow-up investigations, and was a member of the honor society during his entire high-school course. He also manifested qualities of leadership and executive ability, holding various responsible positions in the Boy Scout organization and student-body groups. In university he was soon among the first ten in his class, a part of the time holding second or third place. He nevertheless found time for several activities in athletics and journalism. He lost his life in an automobile accident shortly before the age of twenty.

F 495 was killed in an automobile accident at the age of eighteen. When she was tested at the age of twelve, her mother was dead and she lived with her father and stepmother. Discipline at home was capricious, and the atmosphere not one to foster cultural or educational ambitions. The father and stepmother later separated, and our subject was placed in a boarding school. She was a brilliant pupil but somewhat moody and temperamental. In spite of these traits she was elected secretary and later president of the student body. She left high school at the end of her third year to take a position as a stenographer, and at the time of her death was planning to take extension courses in literature and journalism.

Deaths by suicide. Our case notes on the subjects who committed suicide have been made purposely brief and in some instances have been disguised in order to prevent identification. The five men in this category ranged at the time of their deaths from eighteen to thirty-five years of age. All had been in the study from the beginning, three having been admitted on the basis of a Binet test, and two on a Terman Group Test. None of the five had been married.

M 1314 was the youngest of our suicides. His hereditary background, especially on the maternal side, was streaked with insanity and constitutional inferiority. The parents were divorced following the father's desertion of the family when our subject was only three, and the father died a few years later. The subject was reared in an orphanage and attended public schools. His Binet IQ at the age of eleven was 165, and his achievement test scores were all several grades above his school placement. In high school his marks ranged from A in the subjects he liked to D in those he disliked. Although rather unsocial in his interests, he was rated by both the school and the orphanage as being above average in popularity and leadership, and in his junior year at high school he was elected class treasurer. Soon thereafter he got into trouble and was sent by the juvenile court to a detention home. He escaped, was found in another city, and escaped from the detention home there. After a year or so of wandering, he settled in an Eastern city and took up sculpturing. Shortly afterward he became despondent over a disappointment in love and committed suicide at the age of eighteen.

M 913 was admitted to the gifted group on a Terman Group Test at the age of fourteen. His IQ was 141. The parents were divorced when he was ten years old, and thereafter he lived with his mother and two siblings on a very restricted family income. The only case of mental difficulty reported in the family background was a paternal uncle who was described as "decidedly queer." When he was located, it was noted that the subject was rather undeveloped socially, and was in danger of becoming overly introverted. In high school he grew somewhat more sociable, but was shy with girls and disliked parties.

He graduated at sixteen with a very superior record despite the fact that he had to work for self-support most of his free time. He then worked full time for two years to earn money for college, but after entering college he had to drop out several times to help support the family. Although an honor student in science, he was constantly afraid of failing. However, he got his Bachelor's degree at age twenty-three, and continued for graduate study while working part time. Worry over his responsibilities and the outlook for his future was accentuated by several weeks of illness from pneumonia. It was while convalescing from this illness that his depression led him to commit suicide. He was twenty-four years old at the time.

M 131 earned an IQ above 180 when tested by us at the age of seven. Subsequent tests substantiated this early superiority. At eleven years his score on the Army Alpha exceeded by a wide margin the median for university graduate students, and at twelve years his score on the Thorndike test for high-school graduates equaled that of superior Ph.D. candidates. His family background included a number of relatives who had won distinction in such fields as law, finance, the ministry, music, and literature. Five cousins who were tested had IQ's of 157, 156, 150, 130, and 122. At the age of five he could read fluently and perform complicated arithmetic problems. He never attended the elementary school, but entered a junior high school at the age of nine, and the following year was advanced to the tenth grade. He graduated from high school at thirteen and from college at sixteen. After getting his Master's degree in science, he took a position in industry that allowed him to use both his scientific and business talents. He advanced rapidly and was soon earning $500 per month. This was in a depression period when a large proportion of men, including many college graduates, were unable to find jobs at all. Quite unexpectedly and without his friends being aware of his personal difficulties, he committed suicide before the age of thirty.

M 249 qualified for the group at the age of seventeen with a very high score on the Terman Group Test. He finished high school at eighteen, and was considered by his teachers a very superior student as well as a fine all-round boy who enjoyed both fun and work. He got his B.S. *cum laude,* took both a Master's degree and a Ph.D. degree in the biological sciences, was awarded a postdoctorate fellowship, and was soon appointed an assistant professor in a large university. He was well liked by his students, and was considered an exceptional teacher and able research man. He published a number of scientific articles and was listed in *American Men of Science*. His heredity was apparently clear of mental disease or defect, and the subject himself had shown no signs of instability in his earlier years. At the age of twelve years he developed an organic disorder, but the condition was later arrested and he was able to live a normally active life. The cause of his suicide, which occurred when he was in the middle thirties, is unknown.

M 57 was twenty when he committed suicide. A review of his case history up to 1930 revealed little of significance in his background or development except that he was somewhat overprotected and dependent. At the time of our 1927–28 follow-up he was eleven years old and in the eighth grade. He was described by the field assistant as a fine-looking boy with great personal charm. His IQ on the Stanford-Binet was 162 as compared with an IQ of 140 when he was originally tested at the age of five. Both home and school reports rated him above average in all traits, and particularly in the intellectual and social traits. He finished high school at sixteen and attended college for two years. Because of ill health and financial handicaps he left school and worked at various jobs for the next two years. At this time he developed marked traits of egocentricity and dissatisfaction which were evidenced both at home and at work. His self-centeredness and lack of consideration for others alienated both family and friends and cost him several jobs, but his desire for friends and social approval was strong, and the consequent conflict resulted eventually in suicide.

Only two women are known to have committed suicide; one of these committed suicide after 1940 and so is not included in Table 7.

F 502 earned an IQ of 143 when she was first tested in childhood. There was a history of insanity and suicide on both sides of the family. She graduated from high school at an early age with a fine record both in scholarship and extracurricular activities. After entering college she suffered a nervous breakdown that kept her out of school for a time. Apparently recovered, she returned to college, but had another breakdown and later committed suicide.

F 878, deceased after 1940 and therefore not included in Table 7, had given no indications of mental instability or maladjustment prior to the act that caused her death. There was no history of mental disease of any kind in her family background. She was one of several children in a well-to-do, cultured, and very congenial home with close family ties. Her IQ at the age of seven was 153. Her score on the Terman Group Test six years later was equally superior. She attended college for two years, but financial difficulties in the family caused her to drop out. She was married in her early twenties to a college man well started on a professional career. She herself was a strikingly beautiful and talented girl with many cultural and intellectual interests. The only known cause for unhappiness was her inability to bear children. In a period of depression, following a series of miscarriages, she committed suicide at the age of thirty.

The mean IQ (Binet) of the suicide cases was 157.0, as compared with 147.2 for those who died of natural causes and 150.1 for those who died of accidents, but these differences are not statistically reliable. Of the 7, only one (*F 502*) had a history of mental breakdown serious enough to require hospitalization before suicide occurred, although in the case of 2 of the 5 men there had been recognized difficulties in social or mental adjustment dating from early adolescence. Three of the 7 cases had a record of insanity or suicide, or both, in the immediate family. The amount of school acceleration was extreme in only one of the suicide cases (*M 131*).

War deaths. Following are case notes on each of the 5 men who lost their lives while in military service:

M 759 was one of our cases of lesser accomplishment. Although his school record was mediocre and his vocational achievement negligible, his score on the 1940 Concept Mastery test was far above the average for Stanford seniors. Soon after he entered high school, his father died, and it was necessary for him to work outside of school hours to supplement his mother's earnings. He was five years finishing high school. He entered college, but left before the end of the first year for financial reasons. After that he continued to work at relatively menial jobs—bus boy, fry cook, and day laborer. He began to drink, and a few years later alcohol had become such a problem that he voluntarily entered a state hospital for treatment. He was discharged after a few months, and so far as is known did not revert to drinking. He worked for about two more years as bus boy and cook in restaurants, then entered the Army Air Corps. He rose to staff sergeant, and was tail gunner on a bomber when he was killed in action after a year of service. In addition to the Purple Heart he held two Presidential Citations. He was thirty years old and unmarried at the time of his death.

M 265 had been followed by us from the age of eleven until his death at thirty-two. His childhood IQ was 162 and, although no follow-up tests were given because of his leaving California soon after the original survey, his achievements indicated a high level of intellectual ability. He attended the Royal Military College in Canada and, later, the University of London. He spent several years as a journalist in both South Africa and England and, at the outbreak of the war in Europe, was an executive with the International Broadcasting Company in London. With the coming of the war he joined the R.A.F., and after two years of service in England was sent to India with the rank of squadron leader. A year later he was killed in the crash of a transport plane in which he was traveling on a tour of duty.

M 389 lost his life in 1943 while piloting a paratroop plane in North Africa. He was thirty-seven years old, a university graduate, and had been a successful business man, active in civic affairs. Long interested in flying, he had held a civilian pilot's license before joining the American Air Forces. At the time of his death he held the rank of lieutenant colonel and had shortly before been awarded the Distinguished Flying Cross.

M 95 had gone through a stormy period in childhood and youth but later overcame his maladjustment and at the outbreak of the war was making a splendid record as an instructor in a leading university. As soon as war was declared, he resigned his position and entered the Navy as a noncommissioned officer. Given a highly important assignment, he made a record that was described by his commander as one of the finest he had ever known. He lost his life on active sea duty when his ship was destroyed in the southwest Pacific. Outstanding characteristics of this subject were high moral principles, fidelity to duty, and mental originality.

M 687 was first tested at seven when he earned an IQ of 152. He did commendable work in elementary and high school, and entered college in 1930. Adverse economic circumstances made it impossible for him to stay in college beyond the first two years. The following three years were spent at any sort of employment he could find because of the necessity of helping to support his parents. In 1935, discouraged by the employment situation, he joined the medical department of the United States Army and had attained the rank of sergeant by 1940. He was stationed in the Philippines at the outbreak of the war, taking part in action both at Bataan and Corregidor. He was taken prisoner by the Japanese, and lost his life two years later when the Japanese prison ship on which he was being transferred from the Philippines to China was sunk.

Summary

Of 1,500 gifted subjects, 61 or 4.07 percent died between 1922 and 1940. The proportion of deaths in this period among male subjects was 4.14 percent and among females 3.98 percent, as compared with 5.02 percent and 4.68 percent, respectively, for comparable groups of males and females in the general population. One-third of the male deaths were due to accidents, as compared with 11.6 percent from this cause among females. Death by suicide also has a higher incidence among men than among women, just as it is more a masculine than feminine type of reaction in the general population. Tuberculosis led for both sexes in deaths from natural causes.

The findings from studies of the death rate and causes of death in the general population by Dublin and his collaborators indicate a lower mortality rate among the gifted to 1940 than among the generality of comparable age. Deaths from accident and suicide have approximately the same sex ratio among the gifted as among the total population; that is, both occur with markedly greater frequency among males. It is difficult to estimate accurately the relative frequency of suicide in the gifted group as compared with the generality, but the data suggest that the ultimate suicide rate of the group is not likely to exceed that of the generality.

On the basis of somewhat incomplete data between 1940 and the end of 1945, it appears that the incidence of mortality in the group compared as favorably with incidence in the generality at the latter date as at the former. Of the 13 known deaths since 1940, war casualties accounted for 5.

Comparisons of childhood IQ showed that those who committed suicide averaged a little higher than those who died from natural causes or from accidents. However, the cases are too few to establish the reliability of this difference.

The deceased subjects include several who were among the most promising members of our group. The nation's resources of superior talent are appreciably reduced by such premature deaths.

CHAPTER IX

GENERAL HEALTH AND PHYSIQUE

Although it was not possible to have the subjects medically examined in the 1940 follow-up, considerable information on health conditions was secured from the subjects themselves and from their parents or other relatives. Much of this was obtained by the field assistants and some by questions in the General Information Blank. Table 8 gives the results of self-ratings on health which were made by 700 men and 563 women in 1940. Ratings by this scale are not available for a comparable adult population, but the distributions of ratings presented in the table indicate that ill health is relatively rare in this group of subjects.

TABLE 8

SELF-RATINGS ON HEALTH

	MEN (N = 700)		WOMEN (N = 563)		
Self-rating	N	%	N	%	CR
Very good	366	52.3	251	44.7	2.54
Good	270	38.6	219	39.0	....
Fair	51	7.3	72	12.8	....
Poor	7	1.0	18	3.2	....
Very poor	6	0.9	3	0.5	....
Fair or lower	64	9.2	93	16.5	3.82

The proportion in the "very good" category is higher for men than for women (CR = 2.54). The proportion in the combined categories "fair" to "very poor" is reliably higher for women (CR = 3.82). Whether these differences are real or due only to the vagaries of self-rating, we cannot say. At any rate, it is a sex difference that appears in all subgroups, such as Jewish, non-Jewish, accelerates, and non-accelerates. Similar sex differences have been reported by Ciocco[15] for the general population.

Physical Defects

Our records for practically all subjects include information on the presence or absence of physical defects.

Loss of hearing has been reported by 8 subjects, 5 men and 3 women. In the case of 3 men and 1 woman the deafness is severe enough to require the use of a hearing aid. For 2 of these men deafness followed childhood illnesses (scarlet fever and severe tonsillitis). In the case of the third man and the woman seriously afflicted, the onset was in early adulthood as a result of chronic sinusitis. Another man is deaf in one ear as a result of a childhood illness; the fifth man, whose hearing was affected by typhoid fever in childhood, improved later so that he is only slightly hard of hearing. Of the remaining 2 women, 1 became partially deaf during her high-school years as a result of infection, but there has been no further deterioration; in the other case, no mention is made of deafness until adulthood when the subject reported it without giving the cause or extent of impairment. It is quite likely that there are other cases of partial deafness, but it is believed that all of those with seriously impaired hearing are known.

We do not have figures on the incidence of minor visual defects. Only one subject has reported serious visual impairment, and in this case the defect is sufficiently correctable to permit of any occupation except one requiring an unusual amount of close eye work.

There are 6 men and 5 women with orthopedic handicaps of more or less serious nature. Five of these had a congenital hip dislocation which resulted in only slight lameness for 4, but in the fifth case arthritis developed at an early age and resulted in extreme physical disability. Infantile paralysis was the cause of severe crippling in one case and less serious in 2 additional cases. Perthe-Legge disease in one subject and a minor bone infection in another resulted in slight lameness. One subject has a congenital deformity of one hand.

In no case has the physical disability prevented achievement. The 2 subjects who are badly enough crippled to be physically dependent upon others have both been outstanding in accomplishment. One holds a Ph.D. degree, teaches in a university, and is a distinguished writer; the other had an excellent scholastic record and at last report was planning to be a chemist. Both are well adjusted socially and personally. Six of the remaining 9 who are crippled graduated from college and took graduate professional work; the other 3 had two years of college. Two of the slightly lame have had mental breakdowns, but in both cases the physical impairment was scarcely noticeable and seems not to have been related to the mental condition. In one of these the mental problems had become apparent before the onset of the disease that caused lameness.

Reported Height and Weight

Information on height (without shoes) was requested in the General Information Blank of 1940 and was supplied by 708 men and 568 women. The distributions are given in Table 9. The range for

TABLE 9

Height as Reported by Subjects

Height in Inches*	Men (N = 708)	Women (N = 568)
81	1	..
80	..	..
79	1	..
78	1	..
77	7	..
76	12	..
75	27	..
74	47	..
73	48	..
72	124	1
71	115	5
70	92	6
69	82	13
68	73	38
67	41	69
66	24	80
65	9	88
64	3	94
63	1	67
62	..	61
61	..	26
60	..	15
59	..	2
58	..	1
57	..	..
56	..	1
55	..	..
54	..	1
Median	71.26 inches	65.19 inches
Mean	70.65	64.69
S.D.	2.58	2.39

* Height was calculated to the nearest inch.

men is from 5 feet 3 inches to 6 feet 9 inches, with a mean of 5 feet 10.65 inches and S.D. of 2.58 inches. The range for women is from 4 feet 6 inches to 6 feet, with a mean of 5 feet 4.69 inches and S.D. 2.39 inches. The coefficient of variability is slightly but unreliably lower for men than for women: 3.65 as against 3.69.

The subjects filling out the General Information Blank were also asked to state their weight, specifying whether with or without clothing. If the weight given was with clothing, four pounds were deducted for men and two pounds for women; thus, the height-weight comparison of Table 10 is based on weight without clothing and height without shoes. The mean weight for this group of men, 5 feet 10.65 inches tall on the average, was 162.81 pounds (S.D. 21.39); for the women, with an average height of 5 feet 4.69 inches, the mean weight was 126.62 pounds (S.D. 17.66).

TABLE 10
HEIGHT-WEIGHT COMPARISON

Height	N	Mean Weight in Pounds	S.D.
	MEN		
6′ 3″ and above	49	186.74	18.66
6′ 0″ to 6′ 2″	218	172.34	18.01
5′ 9″ to 5′ 11″	287	160.14	18.84
5′ 6″ to 5′ 8″	138	147.54	16.53
5′ 2″ to 5′ 5″	13	133.73	.....
Total	705	162.81	21.39
	WOMEN		
5′ 9″ and above	25	149.70	27.88
5′ 6″ to 5′ 8″	185	132.77	15.40
5′ 3″ to 5′ 5″	246	123.48	14.06
5′ 0″ to 5′ 2″	101	118.56	17.98
4′ 6″ to 4′ 11″	5	100.50	.....
Total	562	126.62	17.66

As we have stated in chapter iii, the anthropometric measurements made at the time of the original investigation showed the gifted children as a group to rank above the generality of American-born children in physical development, and also to excel unselected California children in average height and weight. Now we find them as adults exceeding in stature not only the generality of Americans, but also selected groups such as college students and the offspring of old American stock studied by Hrdlička.[32]

The average full-stature male in the United States is approximately 67.5 inches tall and weighs 150 pounds according to both medico-actuarial tables and the selective-service measurements of 1940.[51]

Jackson[33] reports the average height of entering male students at the University of Minnesota as 68.7 inches. At Stanford University,* 3,000 entering male students measured during the period 1937–43 had a mean height of 69.57 inches and a mean weight of 158.46 pounds. When the Stanford students are broken into age groups the heights in inches are 69.88 for eighteen-year-olds, 70.03 for nineteen-year-olds, and 68.88 for twenty- to twenty-four-year-olds. The drop in height for the oldest group may be due to a preponderance in this category of men rejected for military service.

In the case of women, Hrdlička's analysis of the medico-actuarial figures yields a mean height of 63.5 inches and a mean weight of 130 pounds for American women in general; his women of old American stock averaged 63.7 inches tall and 125.5 pounds in weight. Jackson,[34] at the University of Minnesota, and Steggerda,[57] at Smith College, have summarized information on anthropometric measurements of women students at these and other colleges. There is close agreement among the various investigators, and when the figures are pooled one can conclude that the average height for college women in the late 1920's was just under 5 feet 4 inches (63.9 inches). Their weight averaged approximately 122 pounds. Three thousand women at Stanford University (1937–43) of seventeen to twenty averaged 64.69 inches in height and had an average weight of 122.8 pounds. The seventeen-year-old group averaged tallest (64.75 inches). Means of the eighteen-, nineteen-, and twenty-year-old groups were as follows: 64.71, 64.63, and 64.68 inches*

The preceding comparative data have been based on objective measurements, whereas the data for our gifted group were based on self-report. It is not possible to estimate either the amount or the direction of error in the self-reports. The tendency in the case of men might be in the direction of overstatement of height, but there is no certainty that the direction of error would be the same for women. An examination of the corresponding figures for spouses offers some basis for evaluation of the self-reports. Our data include the figures on self-reported height for 249 husbands and 316 wives of gifted subjects supplied in response to a question included in the marriage blank.

* Personal communication to the authors. Unpublished data.

The mean reported height of husbands of gifted women was 70.07 inches, and of the wives of gifted men 64.31 inches.

The spouse group closely resembles in intelligence, educational record, and social-economic background the college population in general and can therefore be expected also to resemble such a population in physique. On this basis it would appear that husbands of gifted women may have overstated their height about one inch, if no allowance is made for selective mating; their mean was a half-inch greater than the mean of Stanford men and 1.4 inches greater than the mean of University of Minnesota men. Women, on the other hand, appear to overstate their height very little if at all. The wives of the gifted men, according to their own statements, are 0.4 inches shorter than Stanford women and 0.4 inches taller than the composite average of college women from the group of colleges reported by Jackson and by Steggerda.

Since there is no reason to think that the gifted subjects would be any more prone to inaccuracy in stating their height than are their spouses, any constant error in self-reports by the gifted subjects should also occur in the spouse reports on themselves. If we can assume this to be the case, then the differences between the gifted and the spouse group of like sex are approximately correct. That the differences of 0.58 inches for men and 0.38 for women are probably not due to chance is indicated by the critical ratios (2.98 for men and 2.27 for women). Because of the assumptions involved it will be understood that any conclusions regarding height must be quite tentative.

From the foregoing it appears that the gifted men *probably* average about a half-inch taller than college men in general, and about one and a half inches taller than the generality of men in the United States. Likewise, gifted women average close to a half-inch taller than college women in general, and approximately an inch taller than women of the general population. Age differences do not affect the relative heights in our comparisons since all measurements are for approximately full-stature men and women.

We have not attempted to estimate the amount of error in the self-reports of weight, nor are we able to evaluate very satisfactorily weight differences between the gifted and the norm groups. In the age range of our group, weight has usually been found to increase with age; however, there are no striking changes in the relation of weight to height in the gifted group up to the average age of thirty years.

Summary

It has not been possible to give medical examinations to our gifted adults, but self-ratings on general health in 1940 indicated that the incidence of ill health was low. Ratings of "poor" or "very poor" were made by only 1.9 percent of men and 3.7 percent of women. Ratings of "good" to "very good" were made by 90.9 percent of men and 83.7 percent of women. To what extent these sex differences are real or spurious is not known, but they are in line with sex differences found by Ciocco on morbidity in the generality.

Data are fairly complete on the presence of certain physical defects in the gifted group. Only 4 subjects were seriously deaf in 1940, and in no case had this affliction been a marked deterrent to accomplishment. No figures are available on the incidence of minor defects of vision. In 1940 only one subject reported extremely poor vision, and even in this case glasses gave sufficient correction to permit entrance into almost any occupation except one making unusual demands upon the eyes. Six men and 5 women are crippled, the cause in 5 cases being a congenital hip dislocation. Infantile paralysis was responsible for 3 cases, bone infection for 2, and a congenital deformity of the hand for one. In no case has the physical disability prevented at least average or better-than-average achievement according to standards of accomplishment in the gifted group as a whole.

Height as reported by the subjects themselves is considerably above the average. Gifted men, according to self-reports, are 5 feet 10.65 inches tall on the average, and have a mean weight of 162.8 pounds. Figures on mean height for the general population range from 5 feet 7.5 inches for the selectees of the United States Army draft in 1940, to 5 feet 8.5 inches for unselected college men. Gifted women, according to their own report, average 5 feet 4.69 inches in height and 126.6 pounds in weight. The mean height for unselected college women is close to 5 feet 4 inches, and for American women in general, 5 feet, 3.5 inches.

The self-reports on height by husbands and wives of gifted subjects, as compared with measured height of comparable groups in the generality, suggest that husbands of the gifted may have overstated their height by an average of about one inch, wives of the gifted little if any. If gifted men overstated height as much as husbands of gifted women appear to have done, their mean height would be 69.6

inches instead of 70.6. On the basis of this correction, mean height of gifted men is about a half-inch greater than the mean of college men, and about 1.5 inches above the generality of men. The mean height of gifted women is estimated to be almost a half-inch above that of college women, and about an inch above the mean of women in general.

In conclusion, it may be said that the gifted group is probably at least equal or superior to the generality in respect to general health, height, weight, and freedom from serious defects. This is not surprising in view of the fact that medical examinations and anthropometrical measurements had demonstrated their clear superiority in childhood.

CHAPTER X

MENTAL HEALTH, NERVOUS DISORDERS, AND GENERAL ADJUSTMENT

The material to be summarized in this chapter includes ratings on mental health and general adjustment, and data on insanity, nervous disorders, alcoholism, delinquency, and homosexuality. Suicides have been treated in chapter viii.

Ratings on Mental Health and General Adjustment—1940

These ratings were limited to subjects living in 1940 and were based on all data available to that date. They were made by the authors on the basis of information obtained from various sources over a period of many years. The most important of these sources were personal conferences with the subjects and their parents by us and by our field workers of 1928 and 1940, letters from the subjects or their parents, and responses to questionnaires filled out by the subjects, the parents, and other informants. Both the 1936 and 1940 information schedules asked the question: "Has there been any tendency toward nervousness, worry, special anxieties, or nervous breakdown in recent years? . . . . nature of such difficulties . . . ." Each specific kind of information obtained was considered in the light of the total case history.

Subjects were classified into three categories representing, respectively, "satisfactory adjustment," "some maladjustment," and "serious maladjustment." The three degrees of adjustment were keyed as 1, 2, and 3. The third category is broken into two parts as follows: *3a,* those seriously maladjusted but not psychotic; *3b,* those with a history of psychosis or definite mental breakdown requiring hospitalization. The definitions of our three categories follow:

1. *Satisfactory.* Subjects classified in this category were essentially normal; i.e., their "desires, emotions, and interests were compatible with the social standards and pressures" of their group.[37] Everyone, of course, has adjustment problems of one kind or another. Satisfactory adjustment as here defined does not mean perfect contentment

and complete absence of problems, but rather the ability to cope adequately with difficulties in the personal make-up or in the subject's environment. Worry and anxiety when warranted by the circumstances, or a tendency to be somewhat high strung or nervous—provided such a tendency did not constitute a definite personality problem—were allowed in this category.*

2. *Some maladjustment.* Classified here were subjects with excessive feelings of inadequacy or inferiority, nervous fatigue, mild anxiety neurosis, and the like. The emotional conflicts, nervous tendencies, and social maladjustments of these individuals, while they presented definite problems, were not beyond the ability of the individual to handle, and there was no marked interference with social or personal life or with achievement. Subjects whose behavior was noticeably odd or freakish, but without evidence of serious neurotic tendencies, were also classified in this category.

3. *Serious maladjustment.*

a) Classified as 3*a* were subjects who had shown marked symptoms of anxiety, mental depression, personality maladjustment, or psychopathic personality. This classification also includes subjects who had suffered a "nervous breakdown," provided the condition was not severe enough to constitute a psychosis. Subjects with a previous history of serious maladjustment or nervous breakdown (without

* Few items are as relative and vague as "maladjustment." Surveys of problem children by Olson[46] and others show a widely varying proportion of children classified in this category by teachers and psychiatrists, the incidence ranging from about 5 percent to 20 percent of the total school population. The range is due almost entirely to lack of objective methods of diagnosis and to lack of uniform standards of classification. Every child has adjustment problems, and there is no general agreement on how numerous and serious these must be to warrant the designation "problem child." That the difficulty is no less great in rating the adjustment of adults is well illustrated by the study of 257 Harvard sophomores carried out under the Grant Foundation.[71] The subjects used in this study were not only a highly selected group from the mere fact that they had satisfied the difficult entrance requirements of Harvard, but were further selected as among the better adjusted and more scholastically successful of their class. Nevertheless, investigation of each subject by physicians, psychiatrists, psychologists, sociologists, and anthropologists brought to light one or more personality problems in the case of nearly every member of the group. A majority of the subjects mentioned one or more problems on their own initiative, and other problems in vast number were mentioned by parents or discovered by the team of experts. What one expert did not find, another did (or thought he did). For example, the following proportions were classified as possessing in "outstanding" degree these traits: unstable autonomic functions, 14.0 percent; the "just-so" (overmeticulous) personality, 13.6 percent; inhibited personality, 19.1 percent; shyness, 18.3 percent; asocial tendencies, 9.3 percent; lack of purpose and values, 21.8 percent. It is obvious that designations so freely applied to just noticeable defects of personality (if defects they be) have pretty much lost their common meanings. We have no idea what so microscopic a technique would have uncovered in our gifted group.

psychosis) were included here even though their adjustment at the time of rating may have been entirely satisfactory.

b) Classified as *3b* were those subjects who had at any time suffered a complete mental breakdown requiring hospitalization, whatever their condition at the time of rating. In the majority of cases the subjects were restored to reasonably good mental health after a brief period of hospital care.

The following examples of ratings assigned will give the reader an idea of the boundary lines separating the four groups. The first is selected as one of the least well adjusted in the "satisfactory" group. The next two cases represent, respectively, the upper and lower borders of the group classified as having "some maladjustment." Examples are also given of the least serious and most serious in category *3a*, i.e., those with marked maladjustment but not psychotic. The *3b* ratings were based on objective evidence—complete mental breakdown with hospitalization. Discussion of the psychotic subjects (*3b*) is reserved until later in this chapter where case notes will be presented for each.

M 1138 was considered to fall within the limits of the satisfactorily adjusted, but he represents the minimum degree of acceptability for this category. He was the older of two children in a home of modest financial status and atmosphere of strict decorum and propriety. The mother was the dominant parent, and our subject was very closely attached to her. During childhood and early youth he had no marked social difficulties, but he was not a good mixer and was inclined to be solitary in his interests. His scholastic record was excellent, including graduation from college *cum laude* and election to Phi Beta Kappa. On completing college, he accepted a position with a large business firm and in eight years advanced from a junior clerkship to the position of chief accountant. His leisure is devoted to the study of music and to church activities, and his reading is confined largely to material of a religious nature. He is inclined to pride himself on his independence and self-sufficiency. Although there are factors in this picture (mother attachment, nonsocial traits, and detachment from environment) that frequently lead to marked difficulties in personality functioning, they do not appear to constitute a serious problem in his case. He is well adjusted vocationally and finds reasonably satisfactory emotional outlet in his music and church work. He served three years in the Navy during the war, with promotions from ensign to lieutenant. Since the death of his mother he has married.

M 234, who is at the upper level of category 2, has had considerable success in his chosen field. His college record was excellent, and he has held fairly good positions. However, his personal adjustment has always been unsatisfactory. He grew up avoiding sports and the usual recreational pursuits of boys, and devoted much time to reading, with the result that he developed an introverted, withdrawn personality which made social contacts difficult. In his relationships with others he is on the defensive and sometimes gives the impression of being hostile or unfriendly. Endowed with a certain cleverness and wit, he has used it to the point of rudeness in compensating for his sense of inferiority. These feelings of inadequacy extended to matters of sex. He sought psychiatric help for this problem and a few years later was married. Professional success and a happy marriage have done much to help, but there appears to be sufficient basic weakness in his personality adjustment to make his rating 2. He was not called for military service because of his important scientific work in a war industry.

M 481 illustrates the lower limit of category 2. He was the eldest child in a home of somewhat better-than-average social-economic status. Not very robust, he was interested more in intellectual activities than in boys' games and sports. His mother tended to be overprotective and oversolicitous, whereas the father was reticent and undemonstrative. As a small child the subject was considered nervous, and until ten or twelve years of age he was troubled with enuresis. As he grew older the outward symptoms of nervousness were less evident. In adolescence his interest in artistic and literary pursuits developed, but he was still socially immature and had difficulty in making friends. The mother's ambition for her children resulted in considerable prodding, and our subject in particular had impressed on him the responsibility of his superior endowment. His score on the test measuring masculinity-femininity of play interests, taken when he was nine years old, showed him to be markedly feminine in his interests. Because he was slow to mix with other children he was looked upon as "different" by his fellow students in grade school. However, his social adjustment improved as he grew older, and in high school he won approval by his extensive participation in dramatic and literary activities. Both in high school and college he enjoyed portraying women's roles in dramatic productions. His score on the M-F scale of the Strong Vocational Interest Blank at the age of twenty-five was significantly below the mean for men. In early adulthood he had some difficulty in sex adjustments because of a strong homosexual tendency. After some years, during which he had both homosexual and heterosexual experiences, he married and has made a fairly satisfactory sexual adjustment. He has shown determination in sticking with the field of work he chose, although progress has been slow and financial returns small. Recently he has received gratifying recognition which promises well for the future. When called up for military service he was rejected on the basis of a psychiatric diagnosis, but he has not taken this too seriously or allowed it to worry him.

F 1375 was rated in category *3a* because of her general nervousness and emotional instability, although her adjustment difficulties have not been so great as to make her a serious problem to her family or to interfere, except for a short period of time, with earning a livelihood. Worry over the separation of her parents and over her own uncongenial relations with her mother resulted in a nervous breakdown at twenty-five. After a few months' rest she was sufficiently recovered to return to work, but it was some years before she was reasonably free from the extreme nervous tension that characterized her illness. She later attained a certain amount of stability after moving away from the highly emotional environment of her mother's home to an apartment by herself. Living alone has contributed to her self-reliance and peace of mind, but she is still emotional, self-centered, and immature in her personal adjustments.

M 374, also classified as *3a,* is an example of very poor adjustment, not sufficiently deep-rooted and serious, however, to be considered a psychosis. He is under par physically, extremely nervous, and a misfit socially. Worry over finances, unhappy family relationships, and his failure in college have accentuated his difficulties. He entered college with an A record from high school, but after three years of very uneven work was disqualified. His ability was evident to his instructors, but he was so inhibited, sensitive, and out of harmony with his environment that he was unable to function at his intellectual level. His occupational history since leaving college shows the effects of his instability and maladjustment. The only employment he had to 1940 was occasional clerical work. He has strong scientific interests, which he pursues as an avocation, and so intensive are his labors along this line that it is possible he may yet make a worth-while contribution. He has done considerable writing in the field of applied science, but without noteworthy success. In addition, he is artistic and quite clever as an illustrator and cartoonist. Although his dislike of sports and games, his preoccupation with intellectual and cultural interests, and his extreme sensitiveness have set him apart from his fellows, he is so objective about his shortcomings that a complete break or mental alienation seems unlikely. Information received in 1945 indicated that for the last four years he has held an important position in a war industry where his marked ability in scientific research proved valuable.

Results of Ratings

Our data were sufficiently adequate to permit ratings of 760 men and 603 women; for 62 men and 42 women the information was not complete enough to justify a rating. Among those not rated were 15 men and 18 women who were not located in 1940 and for whom no information had been secured for at least 12 years (see Table 6, page 74). For the remaining 71 (47 men and 24 women) who were not rated because of incomplete information, enough data were available to establish the fact that up to 1940 none had been hospitalized for mental disorder, and to indicate that few, if any, would fall as low as *3a* in classification. The results of the ratings are summarized in Part I of Table 11, and the figures for the unrated cases are given in Part II of this table.

No attempt was made to evaluate the mental adjustment of the 61 subjects (35 male and 26 female) who had died prior to 1940. Two of these had had mental breakdowns requiring hospitalization, and 3 of the suicide cases gave evidence of maladjustment before their deaths. There was no indication of serious personality difficulty among the others of the deceased group.

Sex differences in these ratings are small and not reliable; approximately four out of five of each sex were rated as having satisfactory adjustment, and about one out of twenty-five as having a record of serious maladjustment. Less than 1 percent of either sex had suffered a mental breakdown.

It is necessary to emphasize that ratings 2 and 3 were based on the existence of nervous tendencies, personal maladjustment, nervous breakdown, or psychosis *at any time* in the case-history record. Al-

TABLE 11

MENTAL HEALTH AND GENERAL ADJUSTMENT CLASSIFICATION (1940)

	Men		Women	
	N	%	N	%
Part I. Rating				
1. Satisfactory	605	79.60	493	81.76
2. Some maladjustment	124	16.32	84	13.93
3. Serious maladjustment				
a) Without psychosis	25	3.29	21	3.48
b) With psychosis	6	0.79	5	0.83
N for percentages	760		603	
Part II. Unrated Cases				
A. 1940 contacts effected. Information not complete enough for rating, but no case of mental breakdown	47		24	
B. Subjects deceased prior to 1940*	35		26	
C. No contact since 1928 or earlier, and no information regarding mental health	15		18	
Total N of subjects (living and deceased)	857		671	

* Two women in this category had had mental breakdowns requiring hospitalization before their deaths. No men in the deceased group had been hospitalized for mental disorder. If the deceased cases are added, the percentages in 3*b* become 0.75 for men and 1.11 for women.

though this method of rating makes for some distortion in the cross-section picture, it was felt to be desirable in order to avoid obscuring instances of earlier neurotic or psychotic tendencies.

In the 1940 Information Blank, subjects were asked to report on "present condition" with respect to nervous and mental difficulties by underlining one of the following responses: Free from difficulty, Improved, No change, Worse. These self-estimates were obtained from all of the 155 men and 110 women who had been classified in categories 2 and 3 on general adjustment. The replies were distributed as follows:

	Men (N = 155) %	Women (N = 110) %
Free from difficulty	7.89	9.43
Improved	43.42	51.88
No change	44.74	37.74
Worse	3.95	.94

Although self-ratings of this kind are obviously subject to error, their substantial accuracy in the great majority of cases was confirmed by the field data. Taken at their face value the figures indicate that of those who had been maladjusted, about half of the men and three-fifths of the women were improved or free from trouble in 1940, and that less than 4 percent of the men and less than 1 percent of the women were worse. As we shall see in the following section, all but 4 subjects—2 men (both epileptics) and 2 women—of the 11 with a history of psychosis had markedly improved by 1940.

Subjects with a History of Mental Disorder

A brief account of the cases classified as *3b* will be of interest here. Of the 6 men who had suffered a psychosis, 2 were epileptic, one was diagnosed as schizophrenic, 2 as manic depressive, and one was reported somewhat vaguely as a case of "complete mental and physical breakdown." By 1940 only one of the psychotic men had been married* and his marital history includes three marriages and two divorces. He had completed a year of graduate work in college and had made good progress professionally before his breakdown. Two of the men were working for advanced degrees (Ph.D. and LL.B.) when they became ill. Another had graduated from college and was trying to decide on his future work when his maladjustment became so aggravated as to require hospital treatment. Except for the two cases of epilepsy, these men had all recovered from the acute disorder from which they suffered and were able to live at home and carry on a limited amount of work. The 1945 reports showed no recurrence of their illness. One of the epileptics died in 1943 after several years of hospitalization; he had completed two years of college before his illness became so severe as to prevent further study. The other epileptic had had two periods of hospitalization, each resulting in marked improvement for a time but with subsequent relapses. He held a Bachelor's and a graduate professional degree, but because of his health was working at a part-time job as clerk.

Two of the 5 women were still hospitalized in 1940; one of these was suffering from dementia praecox, the other from a depression psychosis. The latter had recovered by 1945. Of the remaining 3, only one (a manic depressive) was still under the care of a psychiatrist, and she was able to live at home and work at a secretarial job. The other 2, also former manic-depressive patients, were fully recovered and making satisfactory adjustments to difficult life situations. In one of these cases the mental breakdown occurred in late adolescence and

* Another man in this group was married in 1944.

the subject is now considered normal; the other, always high strung, had a general nervous and mental breakdown following an unhappy marriage, but has made steady progress toward recovery. The former of these 2 women has taken a graduate degree at a university since her illness; both are competently filling positions of responsibility. Four of the 5 women in this category have been married and 3 of the 4 have been divorced.

We have been concerned so far only with the subjects living at the time of the 1940 follow-up. Among the 61 subjects who had died prior to 1940 and were therefore not included in Table 11, there had been 2 cases of mental breakdown requiring hospitalization. Both of these were women. The only others among the deceased whose sanity could be questioned were the subjects who had committed suicide.* Authorities differ as to whether suicide in itself necessarily implies mental disorder. Among our 6 cases of suicide only one had been considered psychotic prior to her death. This was *F 502,* who was one of the 2 cases of breakdown just mentioned. Two of the men who committed suicide, *M 57* and *M 913,* had shown psychoneurotic tendencies, but neither had reached the point where hospitalization was deemed necessary. Nothing in the behavior of the others prior to suicide indicated the presence of a psychosis.

The ages at hospitalization, including the 2 deceased and the 2 epileptic cases, were as follows:

Age	Men	Women
–19	..	1
20–24	3*	2†
25–29	2*	3†
30–34	1	1

* Includes one epileptic.

† Includes one deceased prior to 1940 and therefore not in Table 11.

The IQ's of these 13 subjects ranged from 140 to 165, and the schooling from one year of college to three years of graduate study. One had taken an M.D. degree, and 2 had M.A. degrees.

Except for the 2 epileptics and the 2 women still hospitalized in 1940, all the hospitalizations were for short periods of time, ranging from a few weeks to five or six months. All but 3 had been hospitalized in private sanitariums.

Not included among the insane were the 3 subjects (2 men and 1

* For a discussion of suicides in the gifted group see chapter viii.

woman) who had been voluntarily hospitalized for alcoholism. There was no evidence in 1940 that a psychosis was present in any of these cases, although one case later had a mental breakdown.

In considering the subject of mental disorder in the gifted group one is impressed by the high proportion of recovery. Except for the two epileptics, all the men had recovered sufficiently to live at home and to carry on a limited amount of activity. Two of the 5 women in category *3b* were so well recovered by 1940 as to carry on full-time work without the need of any particular safeguards against stress and strain. One, whose breakdown occurred in 1938, was just recovering and, though able to work, had to avoid carefully the tensions and complexities of life. Another who had been hospitalized for two years had improved greatly and was soon to be dismissed from the sanitarium. Only one case seemed hopeless. Thus, all of the 4 men, and 3 out of the 5 women afflicted with functional mental disorders had recovered, and a fourth woman gave promise of recovery. The 1945 reports showed continued progress by 8 of these 9 cases.

Superior intelligence does not appear to be a causal factor in mental disorder as found in this group but seems, rather, to have helped those affected to overcome their difficulties. The insight and intelligent cooperation shown by those who become mental patients has almost certainly contributed to the improvement noted in several of the cases.

Changes in Mental-Adjustment Status Since 1940

On the basis of reports received in 1945 it appears that 7 men and 3 women who were rated in category 2 in 1940 have since shown symptoms of more marked maladjustment that would now place them in category *3a*.

Four subjects (2 men and 2 women) have dropped to category *3b* from a higher rating as a result of mental breakdown requiring hospitalization. Of these, one man and one woman had been rated in category 1 (satisfactorily adjusted) in 1940, and one man and one woman had been rated *3a*. The 2 who dropped from category 1 to *3b* have recovered fully; the 2 who dropped from *3a* to *3b* have improved, but the prognosis for each is still uncertain.

Information was obtained in 1945 for 19 of the 25 men rated *3a* in 1940. Of these, 12 appeared to have improved greatly, and 4 did not show any change. One of the *3a*'s lost his life while on active military duty; he had been maladjusted in childhood and youth, but had completely recovered and made a splendid record in the Navy. Another was given a medical discharge shortly after being drafted; he had previously shown neurotic tendencies, but we do not know whether it was on this basis that he was discharged. Still another suffered a mental breakdown while in military service, was hospitalized for several months, but has since improved sufficiently to return to his civilian occupation.

Of 21 women rated *3a* in 1940, information to 1945 has been obtained for 19. The condition of 2 had not changed, 2 were somewhat better, and 13 were materially improved. One became worse after 1940, as a result of alcoholism, but later recovered and at present is doing well vocationally. One has had a complete mental breakdown since 1940, requiring hospitalization, but has greatly improved and is attending college.

The later condition of the 6 men and 5 women who were rated *3b* in 1940 has already been reported.

By the end of 1945 sufficient information was at hand to permit the ratings of 25 men and 12 women among the subjects who could not be rated in 1940 because of lack of adequate information (see Part II of Table 11). All of these 37 rated as satisfactorily adjusted with the exception of two men in category 2, two men in category *3a*, and one woman rated *3b* because of a mental breakdown (from which she has since recovered).

Mental-Adjustment Classification as of 1945

As shown in Table 11, the subjects rated for mental adjustment in 1940 included 760 men and 603 women, or a total of 1,363. We have been able to rerate about 93 percent of these on the basis of data secured in 1945. The recent reports, as we have seen, have also made it possible to rate 25 men and 12 women who could not be rated in 1940. These 37 ratings, added to those secured in 1940, give us a total of 1,400 subjects (785 men and 615 women) who have been classified for mental adjustment either in 1940 or 1945, or at both of these dates. The percentage classification of the 1,400 subjects, counting shifts from higher to lower categories between 1940 and 1945, now stands as shown in Table 12.

Comparing these percentages with those based upon 1940 ratings (Table 11), we find that the proportion in category 1 has decreased from 79.6 percent to 78.0 percent for men, and from 81.8 percent to

80.0 percent for women. During the same period, the proportion in category 2 has increased from 16.3 percent to 16.8 percent for men, and from 13.9 percent to 14.6 percent for women. In category *3a* the proportion has increased from 3.3 percent to 3.9 percent for men, and from 3.5 percent to 4.1 percent for women. In category *3b* (with psychosis) the figures are the same for men and women; the increase for each sex is from 0.8 percent to 1.3 percent. The 1945 percentages below category 1 are minimum figures; if the 1945 data had been obtained for all the subjects, instead of for 93 percent of them, the percentages falling in categories 2 and 3 might have been higher, though the error from this source is probably quite small. There is no reason to believe that the subjects we were not able to contact in 1945 represent a selected group, for recent difficulties in making contact have been due almost entirely to multiple changes of address caused by the war and postwar conditions.

Attention is called to the fact that the method of rating used permits a subject to drop to a lower category but not to rise to a higher category, however much the adjustment has improved.

TABLE 12

MENTAL HEALTH AND GENERAL ADJUSTMENT CLASSIFICATION (1945)

	Men		Women	
	N	%	N	%
Part I. Rating				
1. Satisfactory	612	77.96	492	80.00
2. Some maladjustment	132	16.82	90	14.63
3. Serious maladjustment				
a) Without psychosis	31	3.95	25	4.07
b) With psychosis*	10	1.27	8	1.30
N for percentages	785		615	
Part II. Unrated cases				
A. Information not complete enough for rating, but without history of mental breakdown	26		13	
B. Subjects deceased prior to 1940†	35		26	
C. No contact since 1928 or earlier, and no information regarding mental health	11		17	
Total N	857		671	

* If the cases in Part II, B, of this total are included, the percentages in *3b* become 1.22 for men and 1.56 for women.

† Those deceased between 1940 and 1945 have all been rated and are included in Part I of this table.

Insanity Rate in the Gifted Group Compared with That for the Generality

We have defined insanity as mental disorder requiring hospitalization. The reader will want to know how the incidence of insanity thus defined for the gifted group compares with that in the general population. In making such a comparison a number of difficulties are encountered. One is in the age range of the gifted group, which was 20 to 39 in 1940,* and 25 to 44 in 1945. At the former date the mean age was just below 30, and at the latter date just below 35. A second difficulty comes from the fact that our figures on insanity in the gifted group are based on summative data collected over a period of many years, and therefore represent the percentage of the group who have at any time in the course of the investigation undergone hospitalization for mental disorder. This is the kind of information needed, but it is not a kind that can be easily compared with statistics available for the generality. Perhaps the best approach to the problem is to compare the insanity rate in our group, as thus computed, with the expectancy for the general population in an age range having at its lower limit the average age of our subjects when located (about 11 years), and as its upper limit the average age when the follow-up data were secured (approximately 30 in 1940 and 35 in 1945).

Pollock,[47] using standard combined life and mental-disease tables, has computed the expectancy of insanity based on first admissions to all hospitals for mental disease in the state of New York during the years 1919, 1920, and 1921. Since New York State is considered fairly typical of the United States as a whole, and since there has been very little change in the rate of commitment of individuals under age 40 in recent years,[37] a comparison with Pollock's figures appears to be warranted. Pollock's data indicate that among males in New York State, 1.17 percent of those living at age 11 become mental patients by age 30, and 1.63 percent by age 35. The corresponding proportion for females is 0.83 percent by age 30, and 1.23 percent by age 35. For the sexes combined the proportion is approximately 1 percent by age 30, and 1.43 percent by age 35. The percentages of Pollock are to be compared with the percentages of gifted subjects in category 3*b* in 1940 and 1945.

Table 13 brings together the comparative data for Pollock's general

* Included here were 10 cases below the age of 20 in 1940, all of whom were younger siblings added to the group after the original survey.

population and for our total gifted group, living and deceased. Part I of the table compares the incidence of insanity in the gifted group based on the adjustment ratings of 1940 with Pollock's expectancy figures based on the percentage of persons living at age 11 who will become insane by age 30. Part II is the same kind of comparison between our 1945 figures for the gifted subjects and Pollock's expectancy figures to age 35.

TABLE 13

COMPARISON OF TOTAL INSANITY RATE (LIVING AND DECEASED SUBJECTS) IN THE GIFTED GROUP WITH POLLOCK'S EXPECTANCY FOR THE GENERALITY

	Males %	Females %	Total %
Part I			
Proportion of gifted rated 3*b* in 1940	0.75	1.11	0.91
Pollock's expectancy rate to age 30	1.17	0.83	1.00
Part II			
Proportion of gifted rated 3*b* in 1945	1.22	1.56	1.37
Pollock's expectancy rate to age 35	1.63	1.23	1.43

The figures indicate that the insanity rate in the gifted group in 1940 did not differ significantly from the expectancy for the generality; for gifted males it was below the expectancy rate, for females slightly above. The 1945 rate for the gifted males is still below the expectancy for the generality, and for gifted females it is still slightly higher than the expectancy.

In evaluating the comparative data, one must bear in mind the wide range of ages in our group. Although the mean of the group when located was about 11 years, the range was from 3 years to 19 years. Nearly half the subjects were in the age range from 30 to 39 in 1940, and in the range from 35 to 44 in 1945. Because the insanity rate increases with age, our younger subjects have an advantage in the comparison with Pollock's expectancy rates, and our older subjects are at a disadvantage. If the normal insanity rate increases more rapidly after age 30 or 35 than earlier, it follows that the comparative figures in Table 13 are less favorable to the gifted group than they should be.

Difficulties are again encountered when we attempt to forecast the future outlook for the gifted subjects on the basis of data for the generality. Lifetime expectancy calculations by Landis and Page[37] for the total population indicate that of those who survive to ten years, one out of 16 males and one out of 19 females will become mental patients; in other words, between 5 and 6 percent in the generality living at the age of ten become hospitalized at some time in their lives for mental disease. The rate of hospitalization is known to increase with age right up to the end of life.

Although the number of cases of insanity in our group can be expected to increase very considerably, it is doubtful whether the incidence will continue to parallel that for the general population. There are certain facts which suggest that the outlook for the gifted subjects, as compared with the generality, may become relatively more favorable. For one thing, our group in 1945 had passed, in terms of average age, the peak age for the onset of dementia praecox, which alone accounts for about 20 percent of all insanity in the generality. Secondly, evidence presented by Landis and Page on the relationship of education and social-economic status to the various mental-disease categories suggests that the future incidence of general paresis, cerebral arteriosclerosis, and senile dementia among the gifted should be less than in the general population. These three disorders are responsible for about 28 percent of the admissions to mental hospitals. Thus, with the peak of onset for 20 percent of all insanity behind us, and with the inverse relationship between certain mental diseases and superior educational-social-economic circumstances reducing the expected incidence among another 28 percent, it seems doubtful whether the final insanity rate in our group will ever rise from the 1.37 percent of 1945 to the 5 or 6 percent that is ultimately reached by the general population.

Other Nervous Disorders

Chorea. There are 13 subjects—10 men and 3 women—who had chorea in childhood. Of these, one man still has occasional symptoms, but these are limited to nervous mannerisms; he attended college, has a good position, and is married. All the others have fully recovered.

Stuttering. In childhood or adolescence there were 25 boys and 4 girls reported as stutterers, or approximately 1.8 percent of the total group. This is about the same proportion as in the general population according to the White House Conference on Child Health and Protection[72] which estimates the proportion in the child population as approximately 2 percent. In 1940 there were 4 men and 2 women still afflicted in some degree, but in none of these had the speech impediment seriously interfered with achievement. One man became a physician, another was studying medicine, another studied law but later entered teaching, and the fourth became a chemical engineer. Both of the women graduated from college and were married shortly thereafter. One has been occupied with the duties of housewife and mother; the other, who has no children, has taught school for several years.

Relation of Mental Health and General Adjustment to Education and Intelligence

The adjustment categories into which the subjects were classified in 1940 were compared for differences in education and intelligence. Table 14 gives the percentages of college graduates and nongraduates at the various levels of adjustment. From the table it will be seen that college graduates make a slightly better showing than nongraduates, although the difference is not very reliable for either sex. Such difference as exists has been largely due to leaving college before graduation because of social or general maladjustment.

TABLE 14

Mental Health and General Adjustment as Related to Education

	Men		Women	
Ratings	College Graduates (N=518) %	Nongraduates (N=220) %	College Graduates (N=388) %	Nongraduates (N=197) %
1. Satisfactory	80.1	76.8	84.0	75.6
2. Some maladjustment	16.2	17.7	12.6	17.8
3a, b. Serious maladjustment	3.7	5.5	3.3	6.6

The relationship between adjustment ratings and intelligence scores is given in Table 15. The figures show only a slight relationship between ratings and childhood IQ. The mean for the seriously maladjusted group is a little more than 2 points higher than the mean for the satisfactory group in the case of males but for females the difference runs to more than 4 points in IQ. Neither difference is reliable.

The ratings on general adjustment are much more clearly related to intelligence as measured in 1940 than to childhood IQ. It will be noted that the point score on the Concept Mastery test for the three groups, "satisfactory," "some maladjustment," and "serious maladjustment" increases in the case of males from 95 to 108 to 119, and that the corresponding increases for females are from 92 to 99 to 109. The critical ratio of the difference in mean score between men rated satisfactory and men in the other two categories combined is 4.48, but the corresponding critical ratio for women is 2.45.

TABLE 15

MENTAL HEALTH AND GENERAL ADJUSTMENT AS RELATED TO INTELLIGENCE

	ADJUSTMENT RATINGS OF MEN			ADJUSTMENT RATINGS OF WOMEN		
	1. Satisfactory	2. Some Maladjustment	3. Serious Maladjustment	1. Satisfactory	2. Some Maladjustment	3. Serious Maladjustment
Childhood IQ (Stanford-Binet)	(N=460)	(N=79)	(N=23)	(N=368)	(N=59)	(N=20)
Mean	150.1	151.6	152.3	149.8	153.5	154.0
S.D.	11.1	10.2	12.8	9.5	14.9	11.2
				CR: 1 vs. 3 = 1.7		
Concept Mastery Score (1940)	(N=407)	(N=91)	(N=18)*	(N=344)	(N=59)	(N=17)*
Mean	95.2	108.0	119.5	92.4	98.6	108.6
S.D.	30.9	31.2	23.6	28.7	25.4	27.1
	CR: 1 vs. 2+3 = 4.48			CR: 1 vs. 2+3 = 2.45		

* Two men and three women with a history of psychosis (rating 3*b*) were among those who took the Concept Mastery test in 1940. The men's scores were 60 and 107; the women's, 83, 108, and 127.

The reader will want to compare these findings with the data summarized in chapter xx for accelerated and nonaccelerated subjects, and with the data in chapter xxiii on the most and least successful men in the group. In the case of school acceleration there was no reliable difference between the accelerates and nonaccelerates in the proportion rated satisfactory in mental adjustment, although the accelerated averaged somewhat higher on the Concept Mastery test. Although severe mental maladjustment is in general somewhat more common among subjects who score high on the Concept Mastery test, many of the most successful men of the entire group also scored high on this test. Moreover, a larger proportion of the vocationally most successful than of the least successful rated satisfactory in mental adjustment.

Alcoholism

The General Information Blank contained a five-category scale* for self-rating on the use of alcohol. The subjects were asked to check the category appropriate to themselves. The reports of the 690 men and 546 women who responded are summarized in Table 16.

TABLE 16

Reported Use of Alcoholic Drinks

	Men (N=690) %	Women (N=546) %
1. I have never used liquor	8.55	11.54
2. I take a drink occasionally for social reasons	30.29	58.79
3. I am an occasional drinker; have not been drunk more than a few times	34.78	19.78
4. I am a moderate drinker; have been drunk occasionally but have never felt it necessary to stop	24.93	8.97
5. Alcohol is a problem; I drink periodically or steadily, am drunk fairly often, and attempts to stop have been unsuccessful	1.45	0.92

Ten men and 5 women rated themselves in the fifth category. Of these, 2 men and one woman had voluntarily sought treatment in a hospital. All 3 hospitalizations for alcoholism took place about the time of the 1940 follow-up; one had just been discharged, one was in the hospital for several months during 1940, and the other entered a hospital late in 1940. Of the 2 men, one enlisted in the Air Corps in 1942 and was killed while on a bombing mission a year later; the other made a fine record in the Merchant Marine during the war years and was still in that service when last heard from in 1945. The woman has had some relapses, but by 1945 appeared to have got command of herself and was making high grades in a premedical course.

In the 1940–45 interval, four of the remaining cases in category 5 of Table 16 had sought hospital care for alcoholism. Hospitalization had given only temporary relief in all of these cases. One was a woman who has since made a complete recovery through Alcoholics Anonymous. This organization was also responsible for the rehabilitation of one of the three men. Another has greatly improved under the care of a psychiatrist and the third was accidentally killed not long after his release from the hospital.

The total of 7 cases hospitalized for alcoholism to the end of 1945,

* This scale was formulated by Dr. Helen Marshall.

when the average age of the group was about thirty-five years, constitute a little more than a half of 1 percent of the subjects. We have not found authoritative data for a comparable age group of the general population, but there is reason to believe the incidence for our group is probably somewhat below that for the generality.

Delinquency

Four men in our group have been confined in reformatories, 3 as juvenile delinquents and one as an adult offender. Their infractions ranged from minor thefts to forgery. To prevent identification of these subjects, the case notes that follow are somewhat general in nature and have been disguised with respect to unimportant details.

M 287 came from one of the poorest home backgrounds in our group. His Binet IQ at ten years was 148, and the retest on the Terman Group Test when he was fifteen showed the same degree of superiority. The parents were divorced when our subject, the eldest of three children, was eight years old. The children were reared by the mother who did day work as a domestic to support them. By the time our subject reached high school he had become very cocksure about his ability, having been superior not only to his schoolmates but also to his siblings. In high school he neglected his studies, failed several courses, and finally left at the age of seventeen just short of graduating. He worked in a service station until he acquired money to buy an automobile, after which he worked only enough to supply himself with the requisites for having a good time—clothes, gasoline, and pocket money. Soon he began a series of small thefts, then followed with burglaries which eventuated in his arrest, six months in jail, and a three-year period of probation. The shock of this experience served to restore his good sense (his own expression), and so far as we know there has been no further delinquency. He is now married and is holding a responsible position.

M 364 (Binet IQ 152) was sent to reform school for a brief period in his late teens after a number of petty thefts climaxed by a burglary. A notable factor in this case was the lack of proper supervision in the home. Following his release from the reformatory he completed high school and attended college for a time. He has been fairly successful vocationally, and so far as we can learn there has been no further conduct problem. His 1940 score on the Concept Mastery was well above the mean for gifted men.

M 408 (Binet IQ 143) spent an unhappy childhood in an extremely unsatisfactory home. After one year in high school he ran away and spent the next two years in and out of the juvenile detention home and the foster home in which he was placed. Later he was sent to a reform school. Upon his release he roved as a vagabond, bumming his way all over the country. His career in this period reads like a story out of the autobiography of Jim Tully. At the time of the depression, when these wanderings occurred, there were thousands of boys and many teen-age girls who were riding the brake rods of trains and finding their keep in the same manner. As he grew older he tired of this mode of life and began to be interested in improving himself. Although he had attended high school only a short time, by reading and independent study he was able to qualify for admission to college. He attended somewhat more than a year and made a good scholastic record, but left to take a job and to get married. He has become quite a leader in the industrial plant where he is employed, and is prominent in employee activities. His Concept Mastery score, despite limited schooling and early environmental disadvantages, was equaled by only 10 percent of the entire gifted group. He has collected a sizable private library, described by our field worker as indicating aristocratic literary tastes. He has done considerable writing, but so far as we know has not sold any of his output.

M 122, our only adult with a criminal record, had a childhood IQ of 154. In his middle twenties he was given the revised Stanford-Binet, Form M, and passed all the tests; this gave him an IQ of at least 152. His Concept Mastery score in 1940 was considerably above the average of the gifted men. He was an excellent student in grade school and high school, although he began to be a conduct problem in the early teens. His family background was one of superior culture, but he was overindulged and spoiled, with the result that he became headstrong and difficult to manage. He did good work at college for a time, then took to gambling, neglected his studies, and was disqualified. For the next few years he was employed only occasionally, gambled frequently, and began forging checks to cover gambling debts. After being placed on probation several times he was sentenced to prison for forgery. He became an exemplary prisoner and was soon the editor of the institutional publication.

In addition to the cases just described there were among the men of our group two- or three-dozen minor brushes with the authorities, in which the charges were dropped or the offender was fined or given probation. Five were juvenile-court cases, of whom three were charged with larceny and were placed on probation. Zeal for scientific investigation led one boy to steal equipment needed in his experiments, but after his arrest the police department was so impressed by his ability that it gave him a job. His inventions later enabled him to earn $7,000 while in his undergraduate years at college, and today he ranks among the most successful of the gifted men. Another of the juvenile offenders stole candy and other small articles from stores during childhood, but was not brought to the attention of the police until several years later when he was caught stealing money at school. Placed on probation under the guidance of a Boy Scout leader, he soon developed wholesome interests and ceased to be a conduct problem.

Offenses resulting in arrests among adult men of the gifted group included college pranks, disturbing the peace, disorderly conduct, drunken or reckless driving, *et cetera.* Without opprobrium were the arrests of two adventurous subjects. One, a musician, was arrested on several occasions in 1939 in Japan, Greece, and Germany on suspicion of espionage. Another, who was a reporter-photographer for a popular magazine, was arrested for violating the maritime laws of a foreign country by going aboard an interned German ship to get interviews and pictures.

Among the deceased men were two additional subjects with records of juvenile delinquency. One was *M 1314,* who later committed suicide and whose case is briefly described in chapter viii. The other was brought before the juvenile authorities on several occasions for truancy during his high-school years.

Among the women, only two subjects are known to have had a history of encounters with the police. One was arrested once for vagrancy and was given a jail sentence; the other, a professional prostitute for several years, was arrested a number of times but never served a jail sentence. These two cases, with almost identical IQ's (152 and 153), present a striking contrast in background. The former was brought up in an atmosphere of wealth and luxury, the latter was orphaned in her early teens and lived with relatives under difficult economic circumstances. To avoid the possibility of identification, the case histories of these subjects must be withheld, but we are able to report that by 1940 both had apparently made normal behavioral adjustments.

There are other women in our group whose sex histories have been unconventional, but the two just noted are the only ones known to us whose conduct has brought them to the attention of the police. One was raped in her adolescent years and had an illegitimate child. Three or four others are reported to have given birth to illegitimate children.

One would like to be able to give comparative data on delinquency for the general population, but the task is made difficult by the lack of satisfactory statistics. Reckless and Smith,[50] writing in 1932, offer the most nearly comparable material. Their estimate of the total incidence of delinquency is based on 1927 and 1928 reports of the Children's Bureau of the United States Department of Labor. These data are more applicable to our group than material of recent date would be, since the average age of our subjects in 1928 was close to eighteen years. The upper-age limit of cases handled by juvenile courts varies from sixteen to twenty-one in the different states, but usually individuals are classified as juveniles up to the age of eighteen years.

From the data reported by Reckless and Smith, it appears that the incidence of juvenile-court arraignments in the generality was nearly twice that in the gifted group, namely, 1.2 percent as against 0.7 percent. No statistical comparison of adult criminality in the gifted group with that in the generality is warranted, since only one of our subjects has a prison record. The majority of our group are now well beyond the peak age for prison inmates in the general population. In 1940 the median age of felony prisoners in the state prisons of the United States was 26.7 years.

Homosexuality

Eleven men and 6 women of our group are known, or believed on good evidence, to have a history of homosexuality. The information has come from the subjects themselves in the case of all the men. Three of the women have reported homosexual episodes in their lives; in the case of the other 3 women the information was received from other sources. We believe that there are very few cases of marked homosexuality among the men about which we have not learned; among the women the number of unknown cases may be greater.

The data we have show an incidence of about 1 percent for

each sex. The precise incidence of homosexuality in the general population is unknown. It doubtless varies more or less in different countries and among the social and vocational classes in a given country, although few cultures have been found in which it was altogether absent. There have been historical periods when it was so prevalent as to be considered normal; ancient Greece, and Italy during the Renaissance, are outstanding examples. Studies of recent decades in western Europe and the United States have usually estimated the incidence among men at between 2 and 5 percent. The data of Davis[19] indicate that homosexual practices are very common among women. About half her subjects admitted having experienced homosexual feelings, and about a quarter admitted overt homosexual practices for at least a brief period. A searching investigation of the sexual histories of boys and young men has recently been reported by Kinsey[36] on the basis of standardized interviews of more than 1,600 subjects. Roughly half of these subjects admitted one or more overt homosexual experiences, and so many degrees of homosexuality and bisexuality were found that it was impossible to draw any rigid line between the normal and the abnormal. An overwhelming majority of persons who have had homosexual experiences make fairly easy transition to heterosexuality, but for a considerable number the transition is less easy. Our present concern is with gifted subjects for whom heterosexual adjustment has been difficult or impossible, or who have developed a pronounced tendency to bisexuality. It is this degree of homosexuality which is or has been present in about 1 percent of our group.

Four of the 11 men in this category have married, 3 of them in their late twenties. Marriage took place after some years of more or less frequent homosexual practices, dating from late high-school or early college days, and was the final step in a definite program to attain sexual normality. All but one of these 4 men appear to have made reasonably normal adjustment.

Of the 11 male homosexuals, 6 are college graduates, 1 had two years of college, 2 had several years of study in special schools beyond high school, and 2 had only a high-school education. Three are working in the field of fine arts, 2 are musicians, 3 are writers, 1 is a scientist, 1 is a mechanic, and 1 has been employed chiefly in office work. Their childhood IQ's range from 141 to 160. Four of the 11 have been so outstanding in their achievement as to be rated among the 150 most successful men of the gifted group.

Among the 6 women who have shown marked homosexual tendencies, 4 are college graduates and the other 2 attended college for one and two years respectively. Their IQ's ranged from 143 to 161. All but one of the 6 have married. Two of the marriages took place after homosexual episodes, and in both cases there is reason to believe that heterosexual adjustment has been achieved. Another had a brief homosexual experience after her marriage, but the affair was terminated without apparent injury to the marriage. The other 2 were married and divorced before becoming overt in their homosexuality. One of these was a patient in a mental hospital for some years, and it was after hospitalization that her homosexual traits became most evident, although her case history reveals premonitions of this tendency during adolescence. The other of these 2 subjects, a brilliant and highly successful professional woman, was married for a year and did not assume her homosexual relationship until sometime after her divorce.

The highly confidential nature of the information on homosexuality prevents the inclusion of case histories of the subjects involved. Most of the histories, particularly those of the men, follow the classical patterns in respect to masculinity or femininity of interests, strong attachment to the opposite-sex parent, and (in several cases) hatred of the same-sex parent. The histories of the women in this group follow a less definite pattern than those of the men.

Summary

On the basis of their case histories the gifted subjects were rated in 1940 and again in 1945 for general mental adjustment. They were classified into three categories: 1, satisfactory adjustment; 2, some maladjustment; and 3, serious maladjustment. Subjects in category 3 were further divided into two subgroups: *3a,* without psychosis, and *3b,* with psychosis. The criterion for classification in *3b* was a history of mental breakdown serious enough to require hospitalization. The border zones of these categories have been indicated by illustrative case descriptions.

These ratings were based upon the entire life histories of the subjects to the time the ratings were assigned. Each subject was placed in the lowest category warranted by the greatest degree of maladjustment that had been present at any considerable period, whatever the adjustment may have been at the time the classification was made. This means that between 1940 and 1945 it was possible for a subject to drop to a lower category but not possible to rise to a higher category. The percentages are therefore cumulative.

The ratings made in 1940 were based upon more adequate documentary evidence than were those of 1945. Sex differences in both ratings were small. For the sexes combined the percentages classified in the various categories in 1940 were as follows: satisfactory, 80.55 percent; some maladjustment, 15.26 percent; serious maladjustment, 3.38 percent without psychosis and 0.81 percent with psychosis. By 1945 the proportion in category 3 without psychosis was 4.00 percent, with psychosis 1.29 percent.

Except for the subjects classified as *3b,* there are no data available to permit a satisfactory comparison of our percentages with those that would be found for the general population. The percentage in *3b,* however, can be compared with insanity rates based on hospitalization for mental disorder in the generality. More specifically, the proportion of our subjects classified as *3b* in 1940, when their average age was approximately 30 years, was compared with Pollock's insanity expectancy rate to age 30 for persons in the generality who were alive at age 11 (the average age of our gifted subjects when they were first tested). Similarly, the proportion of gifted subjects rated *3b* in 1945, when the average age of the group was approximately 35, has been compared with Pollock's expectancy rate for the generality to age 35. The comparisons indicate that for the sexes combined the incidence of insanity for gifted subjects was very slightly below the expectancy for the generality both in 1940 and 1945.

No estimate of the probable ultimate rate for the gifted group has been attempted. However, because of certain inverse relationships that have been found between educational-social-economic status and insanity rate in later maturity, it seems doubtful whether the insanity rate for the group will ever equal the 5 or 6 percent reached by the general population.

The proportion of gifted subjects with a history of chorea or stuttering was about the same as that for the general child population, and recovery from these two disorders has been the rule.

For all grades of mental maladjustment, including category *3b,* there is a surprisingly large proportion of gifted subjects who have markedly improved or entirely recovered. It is suggested that superior intelligence may have been a factor in such improvement.

There was no correlation between the mental-adjustment ratings and childhood IQ, but a positive relationship was found between Concept Mastery scores of 1940 and the incidence of maladjustment. This relationship was more marked for men than for women. There was a slightly inverse relationship between the incidence of maladjustment and the amount of education.

A little less than 1.5 percent of the men and 1 percent of the women report a history of excessive drinking over periods of varying length. Five men and two women have voluntarily sought hospitalization for this reason.

The incidence of juvenile delinquency in the group was below that for the generality. However, four subjects (all males) have served terms in reformatories, three as juveniles and one as an adult. The three juveniles have since made a satisfactory adjustment. Two of the women have been arrested for "vagrancy."

Eleven men and six women, or slightly more than 1 percent of the group, are known to have had a history of homosexuality. Four of the men and five of the women have been married. Reasonably normal heterosexual adjustment seems to have been made by three of the men and by all but one or two of the women.

CHAPTER XI

INTELLIGENCE TESTS OF 1940

Some kind of measures of adult intelligence was regarded as an essential part of the follow-up program. We wanted to know, if possible, not only how well the intellectual superiority of childhood had been maintained, but also how adult achievement is related to adult intelligence regardless of early mental status. A test was needed which could be administered to a group of subjects in a brief period, which had sufficient top to differentiate at a very high level, and which would yield a statistically reliable measure of intellectual functions similar to those brought into play by the Stanford-Binet scale and other tests highly saturated with Spearman's "g" (general intelligence).

There was no existing test that satisfied all of these requirements. Only Thorndike's CAVD,[69] and a few tests devised for measuring the scholastic aptitude of college students, have sufficient top for our purpose, and all of these require more time for their administration than we could afford without omitting other tests that we were anxious to include in the testing schedule. Except for the limitation of testing time, the CAVD would have been almost ideal. It is a group test with ample top, it yields a reliable score, and it calls into play the kind of intellect we desired to measure.* It was ruled out, however, by the excessive time (three or four hours) required for its administration. There are several tests of college aptitude which satisfy most of our criteria fairly well, but these, too, required more time than we were willing to give. An attempt was therefore made to devise a test which would accomplish much the same result in only a fraction of the usual time, preferably not more than a half-hour.

The Concept Mastery Test

Before deciding upon the content of the proposed test we made a survey of the results yielded by the leading types of intelligence tests

* Composed of four subtests: completion, arithmetic, vocabulary, and directions.

that had been used: their reliabilities, their validities as measures of "intellect," and their relative efficiency per unit of time. As a result of this survey two tests were chosen: the synonym-antonym test devised by Otis in 1916, and the analogies test which also dates back to the early period of mental testing. Both, in one form or another, have been widely used and have an extensive literature. In the search for test items of these two kinds suitable for use with our highly selected group, we ransacked many collections of items, published and unpublished. A good many items of suitable difficulty could be borrowed from various sources with little or no change, but a large proportion of those needed had to be devised.* More items were prepared for tryout than were needed, so that those found to be nondiscriminative could be eliminated.

The tryout form of the test was given to a class of 136 second-year students at Stanford University, and a total score of the two subtests was computed for each. On the basis of total score the class was then divided into upper and lower halves, and percentages were computed showing the proportion in each half who answered each individual item correctly. Items which failed to give a reliably higher percentage of correct answers for the upper group than for the lower were eliminated. The number of items which satisfied this criterion was 120 for the synonym-antonym test and 70 for the analogies test. That is, the selection of items for retention was based on the principle of internal consistency. The resulting test is thus made up of items which hang together, or correlate with each other, instead of working at cross-purposes.

Directions and Sample Items

The test was printed in a four-page booklet measuring eight and one-half by eleven inches. The directions printed on the blank are reproduced below, together with several items from each test selected to illustrate the kinds of conceptual material used.

Directions for Test I, Synonyms and Antonyms. If two words mean the same, write S between them. If they mean the opposite, write O between them. Omit those that you could answer only by pure guess, but answer all you *think* you know, even if you are not quite certain. Do not study long over any pair.

* The new items were devised by the senior author with the assistance of Dr. Bayley, Dr. Marshall, Dr. Sullivan, Mrs. Oden, and Samuel Morford.

Examples

hot ....O.............. cold
big ....S.............. large

Selected items

2. decadence .... decline
7. if .... although
11. abjure .... renounce
24. peculation .... embezzlement
33. insouciant .... nonchalant
50. choleric .... apathetic
58. truculent .... violent
65. cenobite .... anchorite
71. ambiguous .... equivocal
80. devisor .... assignor
86. diatribe .... invective
89. viscosity .... viscidity
98. encomium .... eulogy
103. sophistry .... casuistry
116. abstruse .... recondite

Directions for Test II, Analogies. Each line below can be made a true sentence by using one of the three numbered responses in parentheses. In each line decide which numbered response is the correct one, then write its number on the dotted line.

Example 1. Shoe : Foot :: Glove : (1. Arm 2. Elbow 3. Hand) ..3..
This is read: Shoe is to Foot as Glove is to (1. Arm 2. Elbow 3. Hand). Here the third response is correct, so 3 is placed on the dotted line.

Example 2. Kitten : Cat :: Calf : (1. Horse 2. Cow 3. Lion) ..2..
Write answers in the answer column. Omit those that you have to answer by pure guess.

Selected items: Answer column

7. A : C :: X : (1. Y 2. V 3. Z)...................... ......
9. Darwin : Evolution :: Einstein : (1. Relativity 2. Mathematics 3. Magnetism) ....
14. Square : Cube :: Circle : (1. Sphere 2. Line 3. Round) ......
22. July 4 : United States :: July 14 : (1. England 2. Spain 3. France) ....
38. Mercury : Venus :: Earth : (1. Mars 2. Jupiter 3. Saturn) ....
44. Socrates : Plato :: Samuel Johnson : (1. Swift 2. Pope 3. Boswell) ....

47. Analysis : Synthesis :: Differentiation : (1. Integration 2. Frustration 3. Abomination) ....
58. Astrology : Astronomy :: Alchemy : (1. Physics 2. Chemistry 3. Phrenology) ....
63. Gascon : France :: Walloon : (1. Netherlands 2. Transvaal 3. Belgium) ....
70. Eight : Two :: Thousand : (1. Twenty-five 2. Twenty 3. Ten) ....

The total score on the synonym-antonym test is the number of right minus the number of wrong responses (R-W), and the total on the analogies test is the number of right minus half the number of wrong responses $\left(R - \frac{W}{2}\right)$. The purpose of this, of course, is to counteract the effects of guessing. Since there are 120 synonym-antonym items and 70 analogy items, the highest score that can be earned on the entire test is 190.

Characteristics of the C.M. Test

Both the synonym-antonym test and the analogies test are of the type commonly designated as "verbal." They are not as exclusively linguistic, however, as they appear to be. It is possible to devise verbal tests which measure not only vocabulary but a wide variety of information. In the selection of items, an effort was made to tap as many fields as possible by the use of concepts related to physical and biological science, medicine, mathematics, geography, history, logic, literature, psychology, art, religion, music, sports, *et cetera.* It was relatively easy to secure variety of this kind in the analogy items, but more difficult in the synonym-antonym items. The test has been named the Concept Mastery test because it deals chiefly with abstract ideas. Abstractions are the shorthand of the higher thought process, and a subject's ability to function at the upper intellectual levels is determined largely by the number and variety of concepts at his command and on his ability to see relationships between them.

This is not to say that the Concept Mastery test taps all the kinds of intellect one would like to measure. A huge battery of tests and many hours of testing time would be necessary to approach this goal even remotely. Some aspects of intelligence are so elusive that no tests man has been able to devise have so far enabled us to map them or quantify them. Creative intelligence, for example, or the ability to make new mental constructs out of one's repertoire of informational and conceptual raw material, has been faintly glimpsed but never adequately measured. The most that can be claimed for the Concept Mastery test is that, in terms of what it accomplishes per unit of time, it is a rather efficient measure of ability to deal with abstractions of the kind involved in scholastic aptitude. As we shall see later, it gives in a half-hour about as good a prediction of college grades as one can get from currently used tests that require two or three hours of working time.

It should go without saying that neither this nor any other test of intelligence measures native ability uninfluenced by schooling and other environmental factors. Like other group intelligence tests of the verbal type, its scores are probably more influenced by such factors than are scores on the Stanford-Binet. Although no amount of educational effort can furnish the naturally dull mind with a rich store of abstract ideas, it is obvious that one's wealth of concepts must inevitably reflect in some degree the extent of his formal education, the breadth of his reading, and the cultural level of his environment. The surprising thing is that despite such influences there are subjects in our gifted group with only a high-school education who score as high on the Concept Mastery test as others who have taken graduate degrees in superior universities and are successful lawyers, doctors, and college teachers. *Recency* of schooling does not, apparently, greatly affect the score.

Another merit of the Concept Mastery test is that it measures power rather than speed. Several studies have shown that the speed of mental processes declines more in middle and later maturity than does the level of power. Chess champions, for example, may retain most of their superb playing ability to an advanced age—a type of ability which demands a high degree of constructive imagination and abstract reasoning. Verbal abilities, even more notably, tend to survive the hazards of age. Sward's professors emeriti in the sixties and seventies scored as high in a difficult vocabulary test as his matched group of young university teachers ages twenty-five to thirty-five.[60] Specialized skills often atrophy from disuse, but one's thinking all life long involves the manipulation of concepts. The ability to deal with concepts is therefore one of the *fairest* measures of intellectual power from middle age onward, provided cultural opportunities have not been unduly limited.

Range, Reliability, and Validity of the C.M. Test

Range. The test was found to have ample top to differentiate at very superior levels. The highest score in our gifted group was 172, or 18 points below a perfect score, and the mean of the group was only 11 points above the middle of the scale. The analogies test, however, has less top than the synonym-antonym test. A few subjects made a perfect or near-perfect score on the former, but no one approached very closely the upper limit on the latter. The analogies test has enough easy items to discriminate among the lowest of our gifted subjects, but the synonym-antonym test would have been better for our purpose if it had been given a lower floor. Neither test has enough bottom to discriminate effectively among the less intelligent 50 or 60 percent of the general adult population.

Reliability. The true reliability of a test can only be found by testing a strictly random sample of the general population. This is impossible in the case of the Concept Mastery test in its present form because it does not measure ability at all in the lower half of the adult range. However, the reliability coefficients found for curtailed distributions enable us to estimate fairly closely what the reliability of the test would be if enough easier items of a similar type were added to extend the effective range of the test as low, say, as the borderline of mental deficiency. The reliability of the test (figured by the split-half method) was .81 for a group of 136 Stanford undergraduate students, and .87 for a group of 198 undergraduate students at Columbia tested by Dr. Robert Thorndike.* From these and other reliabilities found for similar tests, one can safely estimate that, if the C.M. test were given a lower floor, its true reliability for an unselected population would be in the neighborhood of .95.

Validity. There is no one-and-only criterion of validity for any psychological test. Instead, there are usually many criteria. An intelligence test may be validated in terms of the correlations it yields with scholarship marks, with subjective ratings of intelligence, with vocational success, or even with intelligence scores on a previously validated test. Our data for the C.M. test are limited chiefly to its correlations with scholastic grades and with other tests widely used as measures of general intelligence.

For 136 Stanford students the correlation of C.M. scores with

* Reported to the authors in a personal communication.

grade-point average was .49. These same students had been given a three-hour test of scholastic aptitude on entering the university, and their scores on this test correlated .50 with their grade-point rating—almost exactly the correlation yielded by the thirty-minute C.M. test. Not many correlations of this kind have been reported that were much above .50 or .55, however long the test used.

At Wilson College, 112 freshman students were given the American Council on Education test (used by many colleges as a measure of scholastic aptitude), the Wechsler-Bellevue Individual Test, and the 1937 revision of the Stanford-Binet. Eighty-one of this group were later given our Concept Mastery test. Correlations with grade-point rating for the year were as follows:

American Council on Education	.55
Stanford-Binet (1937 revision)	.55
Wechsler-Bellevue (full scale)	.45
Wechsler-Bellevue (verbal scale)	.52
Wechsler-Bellevue (performance scale)	.23
Concept Mastery	.66

The correlation of .66 for the Wilson College group is one of the highest of its kind ever reported.

Indirect evidence on the validity of the C.M. test is revealed by the high average score of our gifted subjects and by the fact that college teachers and accepted candidates for the Ph.D. degree in superior universities score much higher on the test than run-of-the-mill undergraduate students. Additional information on the C.M. scores of special groups will be found in later chapters, especially chapter xiv (vocational classification), chapter xxiii (vocational success), chapter xiii (education), and chapter xx (school acceleration).

Other indirect evidence is available from correlations of the test with other intelligence tests. For 136 undergraduate students at Stanford the correlation of C.M. scores with scores on the Thorndike college aptitude test for high-school graduates was .70. For 81 Wilson College freshmen its scores correlated .64 with the American Council on Education test and .58 with IQ's on the 1937 Stanford-Binet. Correlations with certain other tests will be found in Table 20 of chapter xii.

All of the correlations we have between scores on the C.M. test and other tests were obtained from relatively homogeneous groups as compared with a random sample of the generality. If both the C. M. test and a good test of scholastic aptitude (such as Thorndike's) were given sufficient bottom to measure a random sample of the adult population, the two tests would probably correlate in the neighborhood of .85 or .90.

There was also a positive relationship between C.M. scores of 1940 and the achievement quotients earned in 1922 on the three-hour battery of Stanford Achievement Tests. The subjects with achievement quotients below 131 had a mean C.M. point score of 70; the subjects whose achievement quotients were over 160 had a mean C.M. score of 116. The scholastic aptitude shown in childhood is clearly reflected in the C.M. scores eighteen years later.

Scores Yielded by the Concept Mastery Test

Table 17 gives the score distributions for 954 gifted subjects and 527 spouses of gifted who were tested in the 1940 follow-up. Table 18 gives distributions for specified groups of college students.

TABLE 17

C.M. Scores of Gifted Subjects and Spouses of Gifted

	Gifted Subjects			Spouses of Gifted		
Score Interval	Men	Women	Total	Husbands	Wives	Total
170–179	2	..	2	..	..	..
160–169	5	..	5	1	..	1
150–159	14	5	19	2	3	5
140–149	24	10	34	2	1	3
130–139	52	29	81	6	6	12
120–129	46	42	88	9	12	21
110–119	60	48	108	7	13	20
100–109	64	56	120	10	14	24
90– 99	51	60	111	15	15	30
80– 89	60	50	110	18	16	34
70– 79	49	34	83	22	18	40
60– 69	30	39	69	26	29	55
50– 59	35	24	59	15	37	52
40– 49	13	16	29	25	37	62
30– 39	19	9	28	25	35	60
20– 29	2	4	6	20	38	58
10– 19	1	1	2	14	20	34
0– 9	..	..	..	3	10	13
—10 to —1	..	..	..	2	1	3
N	527	427	954	222	305	527
Mean	98.10	93.94	96.24	64.32	58.93	61.20
S.D.	31.42	28.31	30.14	35.44	34.92	35.20

TABLE 18

C.M. SCORES OF COLLEGE GROUPS

Score Interval	Wilson Freshmen	Stanford Sophomores	Stanford Seniors	Gifted Subjects Elected To Phi Beta Kappa	Gifted Subjects Elected To Sigma Xi
170–179	..	..	..	1	..
160–169	..	..	..	2	..
150–159	..	..	1	1	1
140–149	..	..	1	11	6
130–139	..	..	..	16	8
120–129	1	..	2	11	6
110–119	1	3	2	19	7
100–109	2	4	1	15	8
90– 99	2	5	11	5	4
80– 89	6	11	4	11	3
70– 79	9	14	8	3	2
60– 69	7	22	18	3	2
50– 59	16	22	13	2	..
40– 49	14	21	16	1	1
30– 39	16	23	13	..	..
20– 29	7	8	5	..	..
10– 19	..	1	1	..	..
0– 9	..	1	..	..	..
N	81	135	96	101	48
Mean	55.3	58.0	63.2	113.7	113.3
S.D.	22.2	22.4	27.1	25.3	24.6

Table 17 shows that the C.M. scores of gifted subjects range all the way from the interval 10–19 to the interval 170–179. The scores of spouses range from slightly below zero* to the score interval 160–169. The means (to nearest whole number) were as follows:

Gifted Subjects			Spouses of Gifted		
Men	Women	Total	Husbands	Wives	Total
98	94	96	64	59	61

The mean of the total gifted group is about 96 points, or 1 S.D. of the spouse distribution, above the mean of spouses. It is 41 points higher than the mean of Wilson College freshman women, and 38 points above the mean of Stanford sophomores. The spouses of gifted subjects test slightly higher than undergraduate college students.

* Below-zero scores are the result of too many wrong guesses and may be regarded as zero scores.

The proportion of gifted subjects scoring as high as 98 is 50 percent. Ten percent score as high as 136, and 5 percent as high as 144. On the other hand, there were 65 (or 6.8 percent) of the 954 gifted subjects who scored below 50, which is probably close to the average for United States college students in general. Gifted subjects who were elected to Phi Beta Kappa or Sigma Xi had a C.M. mean 50 points above a miscellaneous group of Stanford seniors. Clearly, the test is quite discriminative in the higher ranges of intelligence.

The subjects who qualified for the group on the Stanford-Binet test had a mean C.M. score of 95, as compared with a mean of 102 for those who qualified on the Terman Group Test. This difference is probably due not so much to the original test used as to the age of the subject when tested. Those who qualified on the Stanford-Binet were of ages three to thirteen, those who qualified on the Terman Group Test were high-school students nearly all between the ages of twelve and eighteen. As J. Anderson[2] and others have shown, the older a child is when tested the better the test will predict later intelligence. Young children fluctuate more in their test scores than do older children, partly because their co-operation in the mental examination is less dependable, and partly because they are more likely to undergo changes in mental-growth rate. Of these two factors, the latter is probably the more important.

In view of the above facts it is not surprising to find that for those qualifying on the Stanford-Binet there is a positive correlation between 1940 C.M. scores and age when first tested. The C.M. mean was 78 for those who qualified below age seven; 93 for those who qualified at ages seven to ten, and 99 for those who qualified at ages eleven to thirteen.

Despite the attenuating effects of age when first tested, and despite the additional attenuation due to the highly curtailed distribution of the childhood IQ's (arbitrarily cut off at IQ 135), there is nevertheless for the group as a whole a positive correlation between Binet scores in childhood and C.M. scores eighteen to nineteen years later. Table 19 shows for both sexes a steady increase in mean C.M. score with increase in childhood IQ. As the IQ's of men increased from the interval 135–139 to the interval 170 and above, their mean C.M. increased from 84 to 118 points. In the case of women, the increase in mean C.M. score as we go from low to high childhood IQ is from 68 to 115.

TABLE 19

Concept Mastery Scores versus Stanford-Binet IQ's

Binet IQ	Concept Mastery (Men)			Concept Mastery (Women)		
	N	Mean	S.D.	N	Mean	S.D.
135–139	22	84.50	29.23	15	68.50	29.17
140–149	167	89.17	31.98	173	87.79	27.08
150–159	108	101.07	29.97	79	93.74	30.05
160–169	37	105.31	33.88	29	104.16	23.12
170 and above	22	118.14	29.93	17	115.09	19.24
Total............	356	95.96	32.51	313	91.37	28.70

Problems Involved in the Estimation of Intellectual Change

In order to estimate the amount of change that has taken place in the intelligence of the gifted subjects we need to have: (1) a statistically satisfactory measure of their superiority when selected, and (2) a comparable measure of their adult status *in the same intellectual functions*. The first of these requirements can be met with a fair degree of accuracy, but, for reasons that will presently be explained, the 1940 status of the group in the intellectual functions that were originally measured can be estimated only very roughly.

Consider first the superiority of the group at the time it was selected. As shown in Table 2, chapter ii, the 1,070 subjects who were selected by Stanford-Binet tests had a mean IQ of 151. The mean IQ of the 428 subjects who were selected on the Terman Group Test was 142.6, but because of the low ceiling of this test we estimate that the mean was spuriously reduced by at least 8 or 10 points. If so, the mean IQ of the total gifted group when selected was not far from 151 in terms of 1916 Stanford-Binet scores.

But this figure itself is not a satisfactory statistical expression of the original superiority of the group. We need to know the mean Stanford-Binet IQ for unselected child populations and the standard deviation of scores for such groups. Fortunately, both of these constants are fairly accurately known. The mean IQ yielded by this test for unselected subjects of ages four or five to twelve or thirteen is close to 100. The earlier figures on S.D. of IQ scores for the generality of children were underestimates, but the approximate true value has been reliably established by two large random samplings of Scottish children tested at the age of ten years. Both samples gave an S.D. of 16 IQ points.[43,53] This value is confirmed by data yielded by the 2,904 subjects tested in this country as a basis for the 1937 Stanford-Binet revision.[65] All of the 2,904 subjects were given both Form L and Form M of this test, and the S.D. of the distribution was computed separately for the two scales at each age from two to eighteen years. The average of these S.D.'s was 16.5 IQ points, which agrees fairly closely with the Scottish data. If we use 16.5 as the S.D., then the IQ of 151 found for our gifted subjects was 3.1 sigma above the generality; it figures at 3.2 sigma above if we use 16 as the S.D. value. The best estimate we can make of the average superiority of the Binet-tested subjects when they were selected at the age of three to thirteen years is that they were in the neighborhood of 3.15 sigma above the generality. The superiority of the high-school subjects who qualified on the Terman Group Test cannot be evaluated in terms of IQ, but this group appears to have been about as highly selected as the subjects who qualified on the Binet.

To obtain a satisfactory estimate of the amount of change in intellectual status by 1940, three conditions would have to be met: (1) the second test would have to measure the same functions as the original test; (2) it would have to be given to a large and truly representative sample of the adult population to determine the mean and S.D. of scores for the generality; and (3) the reliability of both the measuring instruments used would have to be known.

The first of these conditions is impossible to satisfy completely. One can never be sure that test items suitable for use at the higher mental levels measure precisely the same functions as items suitable at a lower level. Not even the same instrument can be guaranteed to bring exactly the same intellectual functions into play at all levels. Perhaps the Stanford-Binet comes as near to meeting this requirement as any test, but it was not used in the retest for two reasons: it lacks sufficient top to discriminate adequately at the higher adult levels, and it would have been too expensive to administer to so large a group. The Concept Mastery test was used instead because it could be given adequate top and because it is known to measure much the same (even though not exactly the same) functions as are measured by the Stanford-Binet.

The second condition, that the later test should be given to a random sample of adults, and that the S.D. of its score distribution for such a group be reliably established, has not been met at all. To secure such a sample of adults is a difficult and costly procedure.

Samplings like those used by Gallup and others in polling public opinions are not only expensive but are notoriously likely to be inadequate at the lower intellectual and cultural levels. There is reason to believe that persons in the dullest 10 percent of the generality are rarely caught in the Gallup net. Besides, the Concept Mastery test which was devised for our purpose lacks sufficient bottom to discriminate among the lower 50 or 60 percent of the adult population.

The third condition, high reliability of measuring instruments, is fairly well satisfied by both the Stanford-Binet and the C.M. test. Neither is perfectly reliable, of course, but their errors of measurement can be estimated within reasonable limits and the resultant effects upon obtained scores can be allowed for. *The reader should understand that when a group of subjects is selected on the basis of very high scores on any test with less than perfect reliability (which includes all psychological tests), and these subjects are later retested by the same test or by any other, the retest scores will show some regression toward the mean of the general population.* This will occur even if the second test follows the first by only a month or a week, provided there has been no carry-over of practice effect from the first test to the second. McNemar estimates that in the case of tests as reliable as the Stanford-Binet, the regression of retest scores would be equivalent to about 4 or 5 IQ points for subjects of 140 IQ or above on the first test. *That is, this amount of regression would be due to errors of measurement and would have no bearing on the question of change in mental status.* If the second test, in addition to being imperfectly reliable, should not measure exactly the same mental functions as the first test, this would result in further regression having nothing to do with mental change. It is doubtful if there is any intelligence test so reliable and so nearly equivalent to the Stanford-Binet in the functions it measures that it would not show a regression of something like 8 IQ points for subjects selected as the gifted group was selected. This means that the gifted subjects could be expected to show an apparent drop of about 0.5 S.D. on the C.M. test without having regressed at all in the mental functions originally tested.

Stanford-Binet IQ Equivalents of Concept Mastery Scores

The 81 Wilson College students mentioned earlier in this chapter are the only adult subjects who have been given the Stanford-Binet and have been retested within a few months with the Concept Mastery. This group, accordingly, affords the most *direct* evidence we have regarding Binet IQ equivalents of Concept Mastery scores.* Following are the medians, means, and standard deviations of the two sets of scores:

	Stanford-Binet (IQ's)	Concept Mastery (Point Scores)
Median	129.0	52.5
Mean	128.5	55.3
S.D. of distribution	9.6	22.2

The above figures provide a basis for estimating the metric sigma of the Concept Mastery scores in terms of the metric sigma of Stanford-Binet IQ's (metric sigma being defined as the S.D. of scores for an unselected population). We have already stated that the metric sigma of Stanford-Binet scores, as figured both from the Scottish data and from the United States 1937 revision data, is about 16 IQ points. The S.D. for the Wilson College group was 9.6 IQ points on the Stanford-Binet and 22 raw-score points on the Concept Mastery. Since the Stanford-Binet S.D. of 9.6 for this group is .6 of the Stanford-Binet metric sigma, the S.D. of 22.2 points for the C.M. scores can be assumed to be .6 of the C.M. metric sigma. On this basis the C.M. metric sigma would be 37 points.

The C.M. mean of the 954 subjects who took this test was 96, and the question now is how many metric sigma 96 is above the metric C.M. mean. We do not have the true metric C.M. mean, but on the basis of indirect evidence it has been estimated by McNemar (see p. 144) as 2 score points. If we can accept this estimate, the mean of 96 for the gifted subjects is about 2.5 metric S.D. above the adult generality $\left(\frac{96-2}{37} = 2.54\right)$. In terms of Stanford-Binet IQ this would be the equivalent of 2.5 x 16 above 100 IQ or approximately 140 IQ. That is, on the basis of the most nearly comparable data we have for C.M. and Stanford-Binet scores, there had been an *apparent* drop of 10.4 IQ points in the intellectual status of the group by 1940, a large part

* The tests referred to were made under the direction of Dr. E. E. Anderson. The 81 subjects were part of a larger group of first-year students who had been given the 1937 Stanford-Binet, the Wechsler-Bellevue scale, and the American Council on Education test. A few months later the Concept Mastery test was given to 81 members of the original group of 112. For a summary of results secured by the first three tests see E. E. Anderson, *et al* in References Cited. The results of the Concept Mastery test given later to 81 members of the same group of subjects were communicated to us privately by Dr. Anderson.

of which could be accounted for by imperfect reliability of the two tests and their failure to measure exactly the same kind of intellect.

This is the conclusion to which we are led by a consideration of the Wilson College data alone. However, there are other lines of evidence, somewhat less direct, which have to be taken into account. That evidence will be presented by Dr. McNemar in the chapter which follows. By giving equal weight to all the various lines of evidence (in proportion to the number of subjects involved), Dr. McNemar arrives at the conclusion that the 1940 status of the group is probably not more than 2.1 metric sigma above the metric mean, instead of the 2.5 metric sigma suggested by the Wilson College data. A metric sigma of 2.1 would correspond to an IQ of about 133 or 134 (depending on whether we take 16 or 16.5 as the metric sigma of the Stanford-Binet). This apparent drop of 17 or 18 points in IQ would be due to (1) errors of measurement, (2) failure of the Stanford-Binet and the Concept Mastery to measure exactly the same functions, and (3) maturational changes, environment, and education. The first two of these factors probably account for about half of the apparent drop, leaving perhaps 9 or 10 points to be accounted for in terms of maturational changes or environment. On the basis of the Wilson College data alone the drop due to the third factor would be only 3 or 4 IQ points, which is probably an underestimate in view of what is known about changes that take place in growth rate during the period of maturation. Probably the true net drop, beyond that due to errors of measurement and failure to test the same functions, is somewhere between 5 and 10 IQ points.

Gifted Subjects With Low C.M. Scores

That some of the gifted subjects have undergone considerable regression in mental ability is indicated by the fact that 65 (or 6.8 percent) of the 954 given the C.M. test in 1940 earned scores below 50—that is, below the estimated average of college students in general. However, one should not ignore the possibility that some of these low scores may be invalid because of failure to do their best. Especially suspicious are the low C.M. scores of subjects who have nevertheless graduated with honors from leading universities or who have attained outstanding success as lawyers, physicians, or engineers. One would like to know how such subjects would have scored if they could have been retested individually as they were tested in childhood.

CHAPTER XII

INTELLECTUAL STATUS OF THE GIFTED SUBJECTS AS ADULTS

(BY QUINN MCNEMAR)

The average IQ of the Binet-tested subjects (for whom C.M. scores are available) was 152* at the time they were selected. This figure is somewhat difficult to evaluate because of faulty standardization and various inadequacies of the 1916 Stanford Revision of the Binet Scale. If one accepts a standard deviation of 16[43,53,65] for the generality of children, this average was about 3.2 sigma above the mean of the population of school children of ages similar to those of the gifted at the time of the original testing. To what extent have the subjects, as a group, maintained this superiority?

In the 1927–28 follow-up study it was found, for 73 subjects who could be tested on the Binet, that an average loss of about 8 IQ points had taken place. This should not be surprising when one considers the likely causes for, or factors involved in, such regression. One factor which certainly contributed to the regression is the error of measurement. Had the group been retested only a month after their original testing, they would have averaged 4 or 5 points lower, and this "decline" would be attributable to unreliability of the test. When this amount of regression is considered along with regression due to possible, and likely, difference in the function measured by the 1916 revision at different age levels, plus regression due to the maturational, environmental, and educational factors which affect IQ constancy, one need not look further for an explanation of the drop which occurred during this six-year interval.

It is obvious that these same factors would also operate, and some with increased potency, to affect the IQ standing of the gifted as adults.

* The mean childhood IQ and the mean Concept Mastery score as given in this chapter differ by one point from the corresponding means used in the preceding chapter. This is due to the fact that the figures in this chapter are based upon only those subjects who took *both* tests.

In order to determine accurately their present superiority one would have to have a measuring stick meeting certain psychometric conditions necessary for the constancy of test scores over a long period; namely, a test with adequate norms for successive ages from three or four to thirty-five years, one yielding the same numerical mean and S.D. for the several age groups, and measuring the same intellectual functions at all age levels. No existing test adequately meets these standards. Sufficient top would also be necessary, a requirement which is not satisfied by either the 1916 or the 1937 Stanford-Binet. In an attempt to secure dependable test scores which would differentiate the gifted adults, the Concept Mastery test was devised. This has been described in the preceding chapter. It is on the basis of the scores made by the gifted on this test that we shall attempt to determine the present (adult) superiority of a group originally chosen on the basis of IQ's above 135 and who averaged 152. This average we interpret as being about 3.2 sigma above the mean for the entire population of school children.

The extent to which the Concept Mastery test is a measure of the kind of intellect measured by other tests of intelligence can be indicated by reference to some available correlations. These are given in the right-hand column of Table 20, wherein will also be found statistical measures for various groups which have been tested on C.M. and other scales.

Before concluding that the correlations in this table are too low to indicate that the Concept Mastery test has much in common with other tests of intelligence, one must consider the groups upon which they are based. All of the groups are so selected as to fall in the upper ranges of the distribution of intelligence and represent such a drastic curtailment in variation as inevitably to lead to a marked lowering of correlations. Since the curtailment for a given group has not been based solely on one of the variables being correlated, it is not possible to make any exact adjustments of these correlations for the effect of homogeneity. We estimate that adequate corrections would lead to a median r of about .85, and in particular we are inclined to believe that if the Concept Mastery test were adapted (made easier) for use with the general population it would yield a correlation between .85 and .90 with the 1937 Stanford-Binet IQ's for unselected cases.

Even if this were established as fact, we would not have the

TABLE 20

CONCEPT MASTERY VERSUS OTHER TESTS

Test	Group	N	M	S.D.	Metric M	Metric S.D.	Concept Mastery M	Concept Mastery S.D.	Concept Mastery r
a) 1916 Stanford-Binet	Gifted: childhood Binet; adult C.M.	632	152 IQ	9.8	100	16 ?	95	31	.30
b) 1937 Stanford-Binet	Wilson College students*	81	128 IQ	9.6	100	16.5	55	22	.58
c) Wechsler-Bellevue	Wilson College students	81	119 IQ	7.0	100	14.5	55	22	.32
d) American Council on Education	Wilson College students	81	120 pts.	22	?	?	55	22	.64
e) American Council on Education	Stanford AST†	66	134 pts.	17	?	?	71	27	.44
f) Army's General Classification test	Stanford AST	70	136 pts.	9.1	100	20	71	27	.30
g) Terman-McNemar Group	Stanford AST	58	130 IQ	7.5	100	16	71	27	.56
h) Terman-McNemar Group	Navy trainees‡ (air corps)	178	116 IQ	10.0	100	16	45	20	.62
i) Terman-McNemar Group	Stanford students†	37	125 IQ	8.3	100	16	70	30	.76
j) Otis Self-Administering	S.F. Junior Counseling Service§	100	115 IQ	8.4	100	14	54	30	.58
k) Thorndike college aptitude test	Stanford sophomores¶	136	80 pts.	14	?	?	58	22	.70
l) Thorndike college aptitude test	Gifted	170	90 pts.	11	?	?	102	28	.37

* Data supplied by Dr. E. E. Anderson. † Data collected in Stanford Psychology Department.
‡ Data supplied by Richard C. Miller. § Data collected by Barbara A. Mayer. ¶ From unpublished data of Dr. Robert T. Ross.

necessary information for stating the extent of regression which would be expected for a group selected in childhood on the basis of 1916 Stanford-Binet IQ's and tested as adults on the Concept Mastery test. To secure an estimate of such regression, one would obviously need to know the correlation for the generality between C.M. scores at adulthood and IQ's during childhood (or at ages three–thirteen). It would not be inconsistent with known facts concerning test-retest and inter-test correlations to expect that this correlation would be much lower than the correlation from an early retest by the same scale.

An approximate answer to the question of the present status of the gifted in regard to intelligence as tested can be obtained from a consideration of their average C.M. score as compared with the average score made by certain reference groups for which we have scores on other tests. The average C.M. score for 632 gifted subjects, all but a few of whom had Binet IQ's above 140, is 95 and the S.D. is 31. Our problem is that of determining how far a C.M. score of 95 is above the mean for the generality. We do not know the mean or the sigma for C.M. scores for the generality of individuals of any age, hence the problem becomes one of trying to specify the distance which 95 is above an unknown average, the distance to be expressed in terms of an unknown sigma. In the discussion to follow we shall refer to the S.D. (on any given test) for the general population as the "metric" sigma, and the general mean as the "metric" mean.

In Table 20 the metric M's and S.D.'s given for the several tests have been taken from the published norms. As a basis for estimating the unknown metric sigma for the Concept Mastery test, we shall assume that for two tests which measure much the same function, the ratio of the sigma obtained for a given group to the norm sigma for one test will tend to be the same as the ratio for the second test. Thus, from line *b* of Table 20, we would have 9.6 is to 16.5 as 22 is to an unknown metric sigma, from which we get 38 as one estimate for the C.M. metric sigma. Test groups *c, f, g, h, i,* and *j* provide other estimates for the unknown metric sigma. In order to strike an average of the several estimates, the two estimated variances (sigmas squared) for groups having two tests were averaged, then a weighted (for the respective N's) average of the five variances estimated from the five groups was computed. The square root of this average was 45, which we accept as our best approximation to the metric sigma for the Concept Mastery test.

Next we turn to the other unknown, the metric mean for the C.M. test. The same five reference groups provide a basis for estimating this unknown mean. We reason that, for instance, since the Wechsler mean for Wilson College students is 1.34 sigma above the Wechsler norm, their C.M. mean of 55 is approximately 1.34 sigma above the unknown C.M. metric mean. When the two estimates based on a group are averaged, and then a weighted average of the five estimates is taken it is found that the weighted mean C.M. of 58.4 corresponds to 1.25 sigma, whence the metric mean for C.M. would be about 2 score points.

If for the Concept Mastery test we accept 2 as the metric mean and 45 as the metric sigma, we find that the gifted average of 95 is 93 score points or about 2.1 metric sigma above the generality. Obviously, this is a crude approximation.

The critical reader may have noted that estimates from which the above was derived have been based on lines of equivalents rather than regression lines. In effect, the situation is this: a group selected as superior on the basis of one variable or a complex of variables, which selective variable or complex we will designate as Z, have been tested on other variables, say X and Y. Since the metric sigma, σ_x, is known, their standing on X can be expressed as $k\sigma_x$ above the generality. Can we, without having the numerical value for the metric sigma of Y, specify that the group's Y average is also $k\sigma_y$ above the generality? The answer is "yes" providing we are dealing with a group not selected on the basis of X, and providing it is reasonable to assume that the correlation between the complex Z and Y will tend to equal the correlation between Z and X for such X and Y variables as are involved in the discussion of this chapter. The regression of Y on X, and vice versa, need not be considered. If $r_{xz} = r_{yz}$ and individuals are selected as high on Z, it would be predicted that their superiority on X and Y will be the same; knowing their superiority on X, we can infer their standing on Y even though we don't know either r_{xz} or r_{yz}. It will be noted that the AST group's mean G.C.T. score of 136, which is 1.78 metric sigma above the norm, would need to be regressed before it is used in estimating their C.M. standing since G.C.T. is for this group a Z, not an X, type of variable. This was allowed for when making the estimates given in the foregoing paragraphs.

The meaning of a C.M. score of 95 can be evaluated by a second method which does not require estimates of the numerical values of the

C.M. metric mean and S.D. By drawing the line of equivalents on each of the correlation scatter plots for C.M. versus other tests for which norms for the generality are available, it is possible to read off the score on each of the other tests which is the equivalent of a C.M. score of 95. Each score thus found can be converted into its corresponding sigma value. The average of seven such estimates is 2.1 sigma, which agrees with the previous estimate. The use of regression lines instead of lines of equivalents leads to an average of 1.9 sigma as another estimate of the meaning of the average C.M. score for the gifted group.

Additional, though less precise, meaning can be attached to the performance of the gifted on the Concept Mastery test by considering the Wilson College data in Table 20. The Wilson College students, with a mean C.M. score of 55, average 120 on the A.C.E., which average falls at the 75th percentile for A.C.E. college norms. The mean A.C.E. score for the AST group is near the 87th percentile, yet their C.M. average is 24 points below the mean for the gifted group. The 136 Stanford sophomores with a mean score of 80 on the Thorndike college aptitude test average 58 on C.M. If we accept Thorndike's[70] own estimate that the metric mean and sigma for his test are 50 and 20 respectively, it is seen that the mean for the Stanford group is 1.5 sigma, a value which is accented by the fact that this test was one of the bases for selecting these students. The mean C.M. for this group is 37 points below that of the gifted.

Further evidence concerning the tested superiority of the gifted as adults can be found in the last line of Table 20. These 170 gifted, who took the Thorndike test as applicants for entrance to Stanford at about ages sixteen and seventeen, had the same average for their original IQ's as the total gifted group, but averaged somewhat higher (about .15 metric sigma) on the Concept Mastery test. On the basis of the aforementioned estimates by Thorndike, these gifted are 2.0 sigma above the generality.

The conclusion which we draw from the several rather crude approximations presented here is that the tested intellectual superiority of the gifted as adults (i.e., ages mostly twenty-five to thirty-five) is on the average at least 1.9 sigma and probably not more than 2.1 sigma above the mean for unselected cases. A regression from 3.2 sigma to 2.1 sigma would imply a correlation for the generality of .66 between 1916 Stanford-Binet IQ's earned at ages three to thirteen, and adult intellectual standing as measured by the Concept Mastery test. Since this degree of correlation is reasonable, we are inclined to believe that our estimate of the present standing of the gifted is tenable. For those who prefer IQ rather than sigma units, the 2.1 sigma position of the gifted would be the equivalent of about 134 IQ on a scale having the same mean and standard deviation as the 1937 Stanford-Binet revision.*

* *Note by L.M.T.:* As indicated on page 137, close to half of this apparent decrease in IQ can be accounted for by errors of measurement and by failure of the C.M. test to measure the same functions as are measured by the Stanford-Binet. On the basis of Dr. McNemar's estimates of the C.M. metric mean and metric sigma, this leaves a net decrease of 9 or 10 IQ points to be accounted for by maturational changes, environment, and school training. It will be recalled that data from the Wilson College group (the only adult group which has been given both the Stanford-Binet and the Concept Mastery test) indicate that the net decrease not accounted for by errors of measurement and difference in mental functions measured may be less than 5 IQ points. It is to be hoped that a random sampling of gifted subjects who were given the C.M. test in 1940 can be tested in the near future by the 1937 Stanford-Binet in order to secure a more direct basis for a comparison of childhood and adult mental status. The difficulties I have experienced in obtaining a random sample of adult subjects for use in the standardization of tests make me very suspicious of the metric means and metric sigmas furnished by the authors of several of the tests used by Dr. McNemar in Table 20.

CHAPTER XIII

EDUCATIONAL HISTORIES

This chapter will summarize the data on amount of schooling, major fields of study, scholastic records, awards of scholarships, fellowships, and assistantships, stipends from such awards, proportion of college expenses earned, extracurricular activities engaged in, and correlates of academic histories.

Amount of Schooling

Although the present chapter is primarily concerned with college and university histories, a brief account of the high-school record is necessary to complete the picture. Of the total group, approximately 84 percent of the men and 93 percent of the women earned the 15 or more high-school recommending (A or B grades) units required for admission to the top-ranking colleges and universities. Honor-society membership was held by 38 percent of the men and 55 percent of the women. About 6 percent of the men and 9 percent of the women were chosen as graduation speakers. Extracurricular activities in high school were participated in to some extent by more than 80 percent of the men and 87 percent of the women. Some 20 percent of the men and 27 percent of the women were outstanding in this regard, engaging in several activities and holding important elective offices or managerial positions in the student body. The foregoing achievements are impressive in view of the fact that the mean age at high-school graduation was at least a year below the average for California high schools.

There were 12 subjects (3 men and 9 women) who did not complete their high-school course, but nearly all of these had attended at least three years. The reason for leaving school was in some cases financial, the subject's help being needed to support the home; in some it was an impatience with school routine and a desire to be independent; and in three cases formal schooling was replaced by special training in theater arts.

The amount of undergraduate schooling completed by the gifted subjects to 1940 and to 1945 is shown in Table 21. Only in the case of a few members of the group was information lacking or incomplete. Of those whose schooling ended by 1940, the table shows that 87.3 percent of the men and 84.0 percent of the women entered college. Counting those who were still in attendance, the proportion entering college was around 90 percent of the men and 86 percent of the women. The proportion of the total group who graduated was about 70 percent of the men and 66.5 percent of the women. One man out of 14 and one woman out of 9 have had no education at all beyond high school.

The educational records of the gifted subjects were unfavorably influenced in many cases by the fact that a majority completed high school during the severe economic depression following 1929. We have positive knowledge that this circumstance rendered college attendance impossible in several cases, particularly for subjects who had to take over the support of other members of the family as soon as high school had been completed. However, the showing made by the group is very superior in comparison with the general population, of whom only about 5 percent graduate from college and only 30 or 40 percent graduate from high school. In California these figures (for the native white population) are somewhat higher, being approximately 8 percent for college and 43 percent for high school. The fact remains that practically all of the gifted subjects were potentially superior college material, and that probably a third left school with less—often much less—training than they should have had.

On the other hand, of the total group for whom 1940 data were complete, 47.6 percent of the men and 39.8 percent of the women had continued for graduate study beyond the Bachelor's degree, and 33.6 percent of the men and 17.7 percent of the women had taken one or more graduate degrees. Of those graduating from college, more than two-thirds of the men and 60 percent of the women returned for graduate study. The proportion of college graduates who continued to an advanced degree was 51.2 percent of the men and 29.3 percent of the women.

The highest degree taken by men beyond the Bachelor's was most frequently a law degree; following in order were the Doctor of Philosophy, the Master's degree, and Doctor of Medicine. The highest degree taken by women was most often the Master's. A few of the subjects have taken as many as three graduate degrees. For example, one woman has taken the M.A., the Ph.D., and the M.D.; and both a man and a woman have taken, besides an A.B., a Bachelor of Divinity, a Master of Sacred Theology, and a Ph.D. degree. Another man holds an M.A., and Ph.D. from American universities, and a D.Phil. from Cambridge.

TABLE 21

AMOUNT OF UNDERGRADUATE SCHOOLING TO 1940 AND 1945

	MEN				WOMEN			
	1940		1945		1940		1945	
	N	Percent	N	Percent	N	Percent	N	Percent
1. College graduation (includes graduate students)	545	69.8	555	69.5	402	66.5	417	66.8
2. From 1 to 4 years of college (no degree)*	100	12.8	108	13.5	83	13.7	89	14.3
3. One year or less of college	37	4.7	37	4.6	23	3.8	21	3.4
4. High school plus special training (technical, art, music, nursing, etc.)†	37	4.7	37	4.6	27	4.5	26	4.2
5. High-school graduation	59	7.6	59	7.4	61	10.1	62	9.9
6. High school not completed	3	0.4	3	0.4	9	1.5	9	1.4
N for percentages	781		799		605		624	
Undergraduate students	22		6		17		1	
Insufficient information	19		17		23		20	
Total N	822		822		645		645	

* May or may not include additional special training; e.g., technical, music, art, nursing, *et cetera.*

† In general, such courses were taken for at least one year. Brief business-school courses of 3 to 6 months, or other short courses, are classified in the next category (5).

It will be noted in Table 21 that data were complete for 18 more men and 19 more women in 1945 than in 1940. Except for 2 men and 3 women for whom there was insufficient information in 1940, these had all been undergraduate students at the earlier date. Nine of the men who were undergraduates in 1940 completed their work for a degree before entering military service. Of 13 men whose undergraduate schooling was interrupted by the war, 6 had resumed college work after the war, 6 had apparently decided to discontinue college, and one still in the service was undecided at last report. Of the 17 women who, in 1940, were undergraduates, 12 graduated from college and 3 of these continued for graduate study. Four who were married left school without a degree, and one died. Of the 5 subjects located subsequent to the 1940 follow-up, the 2 men had both completed about two years of college work; one woman was a college graduate and working for a Master's degree in 1945; one had had two years of college work; and one had not gone beyond high school except for a business training course.

Table 22 shows the amount of graduate training completed to 1940 and 1945, together with graduate degrees taken. Each individual appears only once in the listing of graduate degrees, hence only the highest degree obtained is given. For example, although 103 men and 92 women hold a Master's degree (1945), the figures in Table 22 are 58 and 76 respectively, the remainder having also taken a higher degree.

The order of frequency for all graduate degrees taken, including those reported in 1945, is given below. The total number does not correspond to the number of individuals who have taken advanced degrees, since a subject may hold more than one graduate degree.

NUMBER OF GRADUATE DEGREES

	Men	Women
Master's degree (arts or science)	103	92
Law degree (LL.B. or J.D.)	80	2*
Doctor of Philosophy (or other comparable doctorate)	60	13
Doctor of Medicine	48	6
Master of Business Administration	20	1
Graduate engineering degree	15	1
Graduate degree in theology	5	1
Graduate certificate in librarianship	2	17
Graduate diploma in social service	1	11
Other graduate professional degrees	3	2

* Two additional women attended law school only (without taking full college course), hold certificates in law, and have been admitted to the bar.

The 1945 reports do not change appreciably the percentages for either college graduation or graduate study, but the number of graduate degrees is increased somewhat. This increase is accounted for partly by the graduate students of 1940 who have since completed the work then in progress, and partly by the fact that some 25 of the college graduates, who supposedly had discontinued their schooling prior to 1940, later returned for further study and a graduate degree. By the end of 1945 all but one or two of these had completed at least one year of graduate study, and several had taken a Master's or a professional degree.

The number of both Bachelor's and graduate degrees may be expected to increase somewhat in the next few years, as those who have been in military service or war work take advantage of new educational opportunities.

TABLE 22

GRADUATE TRAINING AND GRADUATE DEGREES TO 1940 AND 1945
(Percentages based on N of college graduates)

	MEN				WOMEN			
	1940		1945		1940		1945	
	N	Percent	N	Percent	N	Percent	N	Percent
I. *Amount of graduate training*								
College graduation only	173	31.7	180	32.4	161	40.0	171	41.0
College graduates who proceed to graduate work	372	68.3	375	67.6	241	59.9	246	59.0
One or more graduate degrees	262	48.1	284	51.2	107	26.6	122	29.3
Graduate work 1 or more years without degree	59	10.8	57	10.3	92	22.9	96	23.0
Graduate work less than 1 year	14	2.6	15	2.7	21	5.2	20	4.8
Graduate student	37	6.8	19	3.4	21	5.2	8	1.9
II. *Highest graduate degree received**								
Ph.D. (or other comparable doctorate)	46	8.4	60	10.8	10	2.5	13	3.1
M.D.	44	8.1	47	8.5	5	1.2	5	1.2
LL.B.	78	14.3	79	14.2	2	.5	3	.7
M.B.A.	18	3.3	19	3.4	1	.3	1	.2
Master's degree in arts or science	58	10.6	58	10.5	66	16.4	76	18.2
Graduate engineering degree	14	2.6	14	2.5	..	..	..	..
Graduate degree in theology	3	.6	3	.5	..	..	..	..
Graduate certificate in librarianship	1	.2	2	.4	13	3.3	13	3.1
Graduate diploma in social work	..	..	..	..	7	1.7	8	1.9
Other graduate professional degrees	..	..	2	.4	3	.8	3	.7

* Among the subjects deceased before 1940 (not included in the data of this chapter) were: 1 man and 1 woman, each with a Ph.D.; 2 women lacking a few months of completing Ph.D. requirements; 2 men with LL.B. degrees; and 2 men with M.A. degrees.

TABLE 22 *(Continued)*

	MEN				WOMEN			
	1940		1945		1940		1945	
	N	Percent	N	Percent	N	Percent	N	Percent
III. *Graduate work for degree in progress*								
Ph.D.	23	4.2	16†	2.9	6	1.5	1	.2
M.D.	4	.7	..	..	..	..	1	.2
LL.B.	2	.4	1	.2	..	..	1	.2
M.B.A.	..	..	1	.2	N	..	..	..
M.A. or M.S.	7	1.3	1	.2	5	1.2	3	.7
Graduate certificate in librarianship	1	.2	..	..	2	.5	..	..
Graduate diploma in social work	..	..	..	..	..	..	2	.5
Graduate study for other professional certificates or degrees	..	..	..	..	8	2.0	..	..
N of college graduates	545		555		402		417	

† Three of these were still in military service at the time of the 1945 report but were planning to resume their work for a degree as soon as released.

Comparison with a study made by Greenleaf[28] of a representative sampling of college graduates* of the United States who had graduated between the years 1928 and 1935 inclusive is of interest here.† It was found that approximately half the graduates in this period continued later with graduate study for varying periods of time. About 25 percent of the men graduates and 12 percent of the women graduates took an advanced degree. In comparison, by 1940 approximately 48 percent of gifted men graduates and 27 percent of gifted women graduates had taken one or more advanced degrees. Of particular interest is the fact that 8.4 percent of gifted men graduating and 2.5 percent of gifted women graduating took the Ph.D. degree, as compared with 1.5 percent of the men and 0.3 percent of the women in the Greenleaf study.

* This study reports the findings of an investigation undertaken during 1936–37 by the United States Office of Education. Thirty-one universities considered representative of the United States as a whole and of the sections in which they were located were asked to co-operate. The colleges were located in twenty states in the North, East, South, and West. The graduates studied were from the classes of 1928–35 inclusive, nearly 50,000 participating. The questionnaire method was used, and the study done on a uniform basis, although each university handled the investigation among its own alumni. The information secured covered educational record, occupation, income, marital history, and offspring.

† Over 86 percent of our gifted college graduates completed their undergraduate work prior to 1936. Only 12 percent graduated from college before 1928.

Major Fields of Study

Table 23 shows the major fields of undergraduate study for 523 men and 388 women who in 1940 had completed a college course and supplied this information. The Social Sciences headed the list with both sexes, accounting for nearly 40 percent of all. For women, the field of Letters was a close second with better than 35 percent of the total. For men, Engineering and the Physical Sciences combined rated second with better than 32 percent for the two. Hardly more than one-fourth as many men as women majored in Letters; in Engineering and Physical Sciences combined, the sex ratio was about six men to one woman. The sex ratio for Education showed a marked preponderance of women; that for Law a still greater preponderance of men. Sex differences in the other fields were relatively small.

TABLE 23

Major Fields of Undergraduate Study

	Men		Women	
	N	Percent	N	Percent
Art or Architecture	15	2.9	16	4.1
Biological Sciences	52	9.9	24	6.2
Education	6	1.2	35	9.0
Engineering	79	15.1	1	0.3
Forestry	4	0.8	0	0.0
Law	13	2.5	1	0.3
Letters	49	9.4	138	35.6
Music	5	1.0	8	2.1
Physical Sciences	91	17.4	21	5.4
Religion	2	0.4	1	0.3
Social Sciences	207	39.6	143	36.9
N for percentages	523		388	

Table 24 shows the major fields of study at the graduate level. In its main features this table resembles the preceding one, although the proportion in the Social Sciences is here somewhat less for both sexes. The three fields attracting the most graduate men were, in order, Law, Social Sciences, and Biological Sciences (including Medicine). The three which attracted the most graduate women were Social Sciences, Letters, and Education.

Greenleaf's study offers comparative data on the preferences of college students in general in the matter of major fields of study. In the case of men the 5 top-ranking undergraduate fields are the same for our gifted as for the generality. However, these 5 (Social Sciences, Biological Sciences, Physical Sciences, Engineering, and Letters) account for 91.4 percent of gifted men as compared with 73.4 percent of all college men. Education as an undergraduate major attracted only 1.2 percent of our gifted men as compared with 6.6 percent of male college graduates in general.

TABLE 24

MAJOR FIELDS OF GRADUATE STUDY

	MEN		WOMEN	
	N	Percent	N	Percent
Art or Architecture	10	2.8	6	2.7
Biological Sciences	60	16.8	20	9.2
Education	23	6.5	42	19.3
Engineering	29	8.1	1	0.5
Forestry	2	0.6	0	0.0
Law	89	25.0	6	2.7
Letters	21	5.9	60	27.5
Music	4	1.1	3	1.4
Physical Sciences	46	12.9	9	4.1
Religion	7	2.0	1	0.5
Social Sciences	65	18.3	70	32.1
N for percentages	356		218	

The comparisons for undergraduate women are equally interesting. In fact, the woman college graduate of the gifted group differed strikingly in a number of respects from the average college woman. This will be brought out in later chapters on occupation, income, and marital status. The most radical departure of the gifted woman from the general trend was found in regard to the selection of Education both as a major field of study and as a vocation. Only 9 percent of gifted women elected Education as a major as compared with 26 percent of college women reported by Greenleaf. Approximately 37 percent of the gifted women majored in Social Sciences and 36 percent in Letters, as compared with 19 percent and 27 percent, respectively, of college women in general. Of gifted women, 6.2 percent majored in Biological Sciences as compared with 2.8 percent of all college women.

For men who took graduate work, the Greenleaf data showed Biological Sciences (20.5 percent), Social Sciences (17.3 percent), and Education (14.5 percent) in the first three places as graduate majors.

For Greenleaf's women the three most frequent graduate majors were Education (27.2 percent), Social Sciences (22.7 percent), and Letters (20.7 percent). Again, the most striking difference is in the relative unpopularity of Education as a major among men and women of the gifted group.

College Records

Table 25 shows the distribution of average academic grades separately for those who graduated and for those who remained in college two or more years but did not graduate. The average grades in this table are those reported by the subjects. We have checked a sufficient number of the reports against transcripts of records to assure ourselves that there was little tendency on the part of the subjects to report their grades too favorably; if anything, the tendency was in the opposite direction. As could have been foreseen, the grades of those who remained two years but did not graduate were on the average considerably lower than the grades of those who graduated.

TABLE 25

Average Grade in College

	Of Those Graduating				Not Graduating			
	Men		Women		Men		Women	
	N	Percent	N	Percent	N	Percent	N	Percent
Average grade								
A	64	13.09	42	11.67	7	8.64	7	9.59
B	315	64.42	255	70.83	30	37.04	41	56.16
C	108	22.08	63	17.50	39	48.15	24	32.88
D or lower	2	0.40	0	0.00	5	6.17	1	1.37
N for percentages	489		360		81		73	
Insufficient information	56		42		19		10	

The records based on average grades were superior as compared with the generality of college students, but they were perhaps less outstanding than many readers would have expected. The proportion graduating with honors, shown in Table 26, affords, in our opinion, a truer index of academic success. Here the record is quite extraordinary. We have tabulated only graduation "with honors" (*cum laude,* with distinction, *et cetera*) without discriminating between the various levels of these awards (e.g., *cum laude, magna cum laude, summa cum laude*). The only honor-society memberships we have tabulated are Phi Beta Kappa and Sigma Xi, although a great many other scholastic honor societies were reported. The proportion elected to either Phi Beta Kappa or Sigma Xi or both was 27.7 percent of the men and 21.5 percent of the women. Graduation "with honors" (of some kind) was reported by 31.3 percent of the men and 29.9 percent of the women. Three of our subjects, two women and one man, were Gold Medalists at the University of California—each the highest ranking among more than 2,000 graduating students. Three men and 8 women were valedictorians or commencement speakers, 6 of these at the University of California. Two of the gifted men were Rhodes Scholars, and 8 others were runners-up for this award. Distinguished work in law school won the Order of the Coif for 24 percent of our law graduates. Awards for advanced study included 3 National Research Council Fellowships, 3 Rockefeller Fellowships, 2 Mayo Foundation Fellowships, 2 General Education Board Fellowships, 1 Guggenheim Fellowship, and other fellowships less well known.

In considering the figures on scholastic honors and honor societies, it should be noted that the graduates of colleges where it is not the custom to award such honors were not excluded from the calculations. Thus, the percentages are smaller than they would be if based only on students who had the opportunity to compete for awards of this kind.

TABLE 26

GRADUATION HONORS*

	Men (N=512) %	Women (N=391) %
Election to Phi Beta Kappa	17.2†	19.4‡
Election to Sigma Xi	15.0†	4.4‡
Graduation "with honors"	31.3	29.9
Total winning one or more of above distinctions	39.8	32.5

* Percentages based on college graduates for whom information regarding honors was available.

† Of men, 4.5 percent were elected to both Phi Beta Kappa and Sigma Xi.

‡ Of women, 2.3 percent were elected to both Phi Beta Kappa and Sigma Xi.

Considering the superiority of the above records the reader may be surprised to learn that 53 men and 10 women flunked out of college in the undergraduate years, and that 5 men and 2 women were disqualified in the graduate years. The intelligence of these 70 did not average any lower than that of the group as a whole; their IQ's ranged from 135 to 179 with a mean of 151.3. In fact, some of the very ablest of our subjects were among the disqualified. Of the 53 men who failed in their undergraduate years, 24 later secured the Bachelor's degree and 15 continued into graduate work. Graduate degrees awarded to subjects who had been disqualified as undergraduates included four Ph.D. degrees, three degrees in law, two in medicine, and one in architecture. Only one of the 10 women who failed later completed her college course, and she graduated *cum laude*. The 5 men who were disqualified in graduate school were all studying law; 3 of them later completed their course and are practicing law, one went into business where he is very successful, and one is an invalid. Of the 2 women disqualified in graduate school, one was studying law; after leaving college, she continued to study privately, passed the bar examination, and was admitted to practice. The other woman failed in medical school and became a laboratory technician.

Causes of Unsatisfactory Work in College

The causes of failure or low grades in college are so numerous that no two subjects present exactly the same picture. In nearly every case more than one factor appeared to have been involved. With these subjects real lack of intellectual ability to achieve satisfactorily in college was rarely the source of the trouble unless some form of definite mental breakdown had occurred. Physical illnesses were occasionally involved but for the group in general did not play a major role. More important were habits of idleness, unwillingness to do routine assigned tasks, excessive amount of work for self-support, or the deliberate choice to give preference to social and extracurricular activities. Sometimes, though not often, social maladjustment or immaturity played a part.

A majority of those whose grades in college were mediocre or below passing were interviewed regarding the cause. The most common explanation given by the subjects was that in high school they had made high marks without doing any serious work and that in college they underestimated the amount of work necessary to secure passing grades. A few stated that in high school they had developed feelings of social inferiority because of being younger than their classmates, and that on entering college they decided to make good their deficiencies in this respect by going all out for popular activities and the pursuit of leadership. Some of these cultivated an adult swagger, lied about their ages, and affected complete indifference to scholastic marks. Both in high school and college some of the subjects developed an understandable loathing for the reputation they had acquired of being intellectually high-brow, and in some cases admitted to us that they had often feigned ignorance in their classes in order to appear more like their fellow students.

A few said that they became disgusted with college because of instructors who discouraged initiative and permitted no latitude of opinion on controversial issues. There were a good many instances in which the poor record could be accounted for by lack of proper guidance in the selection of a major field. On changing their major to a field more in line with their interests such students often became outstanding in their achievement. Not infrequently the trouble could be traced back to the elementary grades where the average subject in our group was held back two or three school years below the level to which he had already mastered the curriculum. One nine-year-old with an IQ near 160 was unhappy in elementary school and especially disliked the emphasis on drill in arithmetic, and his teacher complained because the boy occasionally worked ahead of the arithmetic lessons assigned! After transfer to a school which made it a point to encourage special abilities or interests, this boy in a few weeks of work solved without help all the problems in his arithmetic text and later made a very superior record in high-school mathematics. Another boy who learned to read at the age of three years gave the appearance throughout his high-school and college career of being indolent and indifferent. In college, although he usually mastered his lessons, he was so dilatory about handing in required papers and reports that he was constantly on the verge of disqualification. In his graduate work, however, his interests were aroused and he became a research assistant, then an instructor, and finally a professor in a state university.

In appraising the academic work of the gifted group, account must be taken of the institutions of higher education which they attended. Approximately 70 percent of those graduating took their degrees from the following institutions: Stanford University, the University of California (Berkeley), and the University of California at Los Angeles, all of which maintain high standards both for admission and for graduation. These students, as well as the smaller number who attended the California Institute of Technology, Pomona College, and other first-rate colleges, were faced by keen competition.

The following case notes will illustrate some of the factors responsible for the failure of bright students to do satisfactory work in college.

M 398 (Binet IQ 144) finished high school at seventeen years with 18 units of A and B grades. He had been an outstanding football and baseball player, president of the senior class, vice-president of the student body, and prominent in numerous other activities. He attended college for four years, maintaining a C average until his last semester, when his grade-point rating fell below the minimum required for graduation, and he was disqualified. The primary cause of his failure was the fact that he had a salaried position as editor of the campus daily and was also editor of the senior annual. He has had excellent positions continuously since leaving college; in fact, his record has been so exceptional that he was classified in the A group for vocational success. He served two and a half years in the Navy and was released to take a post in the United States Department of State.

M 661 (Binet IQ 150) was slightly under seventeen years when he finished high school with scholastic honors. He entered college and was disqualified at the end of his first year. After working for six months he was reinstated, but at the end of the term had failed again. In his case the cause seems to have been absorption in his own fields of interest—radio, physics, engineering, aviation—and neglect of the required courses in English and history. After leaving college he went into business where he advanced rapidly, and was making more than $500 per month at the age of twenty-two. The business slump of the early 1930's caused him to turn to the scientific field in which he had been interested since boyhood. By the age of thirty he ranked high in his profession, had a number of publications and patents to his credit, and had been awarded various honors. His achievements are the more striking in view of the fact that he has won prestige and recognition in a field where he was competing almost entirely with college graduates, many of them holding advanced degrees. As a naval officer during the war he was entrusted with several highly confidential commissions calling for superior scientific knowledge and technical skill.

M 1582 (Binet IQ 168) entered college at the age of fifteen years and ten months. He had stayed out of school one semester between high school and college, having graduated in midyear. Although he got along satisfactorily in his social relationships in high school and had no serious personality difficulties, he had been left out of things to some extent because of his youth and studiousness. He determined to overcome this in college, with the result that his scholastic interests diminished and most of his attention was given to having a good time. He was disqualified at the end of his freshman year, but after working for a year he returned to college, got his Bachelor's degree at twenty, and entered graduate school. After completing his work for a medical degree he was appointed to an important position in a university medical school. He has published a number of papers on his research studies. He served during the war first as a medical officer in the field and later as the director of a medical research laboratory for the Army.

M 743 (IQ 148), the son of a professor, completed the eighth grade at the age of ten years eleven months and high school at the age of fourteen years eleven months. Because of his youth he was kept out of school for a year before entering college. In his junior year he was disqualified because of low grades, the only reason given by the subject being "laziness." After working for a year and a half he returned to college, graduated, and was elected to the Sigma Xi honor society. He continued for graduate work in a different field, took his Ph.D. degree, and was at once appointed to a research position in a university with the rank of assistant professor.

M 233 (Binet IQ 152) attributes his failure in college to his youth and social immaturity. He finished high school at fifteen with an excellent scholastic record and then took two years of junior college work at the same private school where he had done his preparatory work. Here his lack of maturity was not a serious handicap since he was in familiar surroundings and among faculty and students whom he had known for some years. However, when he transferred to the university as a junior at seventeen he was at a tremendous disadvantage because, in addition to his youth, he was small for his age, shy, bookish, and unable to meet college men on equal terms. Worry over these defects and over his unsuccessful attempts to compensate for them caused his grades to drop so low that he was disqualified in his senior year. He stayed out for a year, working as an office clerk, then returned to the university, made an A average, and got his Bachelor's degree at twenty. Subsequently he won a graduate professional degree and later studied abroad. During the war he served as an engineer in a vital war industry.

F 292 (Binet IQ 148) entered college at sixteen years ten months, and failed at the end of her freshman year. Her difficulty seems to have been overambition; she was carrying a heavy load of courses in a major field for which she was unprepared. She re-entered the university two years later and made a B average for one semester; then illness in the family necessitated her withdrawal. The death of her mother, home responsibilities, and financial reverses prevented her continuing her college course. With considerably more than average talent in art, she entered the field of commercial design and has been very successful.

F 560 (Binet IQ 170) entered college at seventeen years six months and, she reports, "deliberately flunked out." She had little interest in college and had entered only because of family pressure. On leaving college, she took a business course and has been successful and happy as a legal secretary.

Scholarships, Fellowships, and Assistantships

One indication of academic success is the award of scholarships, fellowships, and assistantships. Of 545 men and 402 women who graduated from college, information regarding such awards in the undergraduate years was available for 517 men and 390 women. Of these, 103 men and 76 women, or almost 20 percent of each sex, received one or more scholarships or fellowships. In addition, 2 men and 8 women who left college without graduating received such awards.

Among the same 517 men and 390 women, 5.2 percent of the men and 3.9 percent of the women held one or more undergraduate assistantships. Among those not graduating, assistantship awards were made to one man and one woman.

Our records show that a graduate scholarship or fellowship was held for one or more years by 26.2 percent of the men and by 13.2 percent of the women. Such awards were made for two years or more to 13 percent of the men and 2 percent of the women. In addition, awards of graduate assistantships were made to 27.4 percent of the men and to 15.9 percent of the women. Graduate assistantships were held for two years or more by 12.4 percent of the men and 5.3 percent of the women. These percentages are based on the 307 men and 189 women who had completed their graduate work and for whom data were available. The above are minimum figures; we are by no means certain that every scholarship and assistantship was reported.

Income from Stipends and Outside Work

For 151 men and 102 women who held graduate scholarships or fellowships, the total stipends from such awards ranged from less than $200 to $9,570. For men the median was $647 and the mean $1,013. The median for women was $465 and the mean $527. The aggregate total of scholarship and fellowship stipends, both graduate and undergraduate, amounted to approximately $153,000 for men and nearly $54,000 for women, or more than $200,000 in all.

The median of total stipends from undergraduate and graduate assistantships held by 86 men was $1,000, and the mean was $1,377. The corresponding figures for 33 women were: median $175, mean $730. The aggregate total of assistantship stipends received by men was above $118,000; by women, $24,000.

The combined aid accruing to members of our group from scholarships, fellowships, and assistantships in both the undergraduate and graduate years amounted to approximately $271,000 for the men and $78,000 for the women, or nearly $350,000 for the sexes combined.

In the General Information Blank the subjects were asked to check one of the following responses most nearly indicating the proportion of undergraduate expenses which they earned by working: "none," "less than ¼," "¼," "½," "¾," "all." Table 27 gives the results for 600 men and 458 women who attended college for two years or longer. For 45 men and 27 women this information was lacking. In the case of men, hardly more than one out of five failed to earn some part of his expenses, but the proportion of women who did not work was nearly one-half. Among those graduating, approximately 36 percent of the men and 16 percent of the women earned from one-half to all of their expenses. For those who attended college two or more years but did not graduate, the corresponding figures were 45 percent of men and 23 percent of women. The inference is that lack of financial support was probably a considerable factor in the elimination of students before graduation. Scholarships made easier the path of many, but there were not enough available to take care of more than a fraction of the members of our group who merited such help. Table 28 gives the total undergraduate earnings, exclusive of scholarship awards, of 369 men and 172 women graduates who earned some part of their expenses. Some of those who were partially or wholly self-supporting had to be omitted from these tabulations because of the difficulty of evaluating earnings in the form of board, room, and tuition.

The fact that more than two-thirds of a million dollars had to be earned by members of the group attending college is eloquent proof of the need for increasing the amount of student aid. It was particularly unfortunate that during the depression period, when so many members of the group were attending college, jobs for students were abnormally scarce and ill paid.

TABLE 27

PROPORTION OF UNDERGRADUATE EXPENSES EARNED

	MEN		WOMEN	
	College Graduates (N=509) %	2 to 4 Years but Not Graduated (N=91) %	College Graduates (N=379) %	2 to 4 Years but Not Graduated (N=79) %
All	7.5	18.7	2.1	5.1
Three-fourths	12.8	12.1	5.5	6.3
One-half	15.7	14.3	8.7	11.4
One-fourth	17.9	20.9	12.7	10.1
Less than one-fourth	23.4	16.5	26.9	16.5
None	22.8	17.6	44.1	50.6

TABLE 28

UNDERGRADUATE EARNINGS OF COLLEGE GRADUATES EXCLUSIVE OF SCHOLARSHIP AWARDS

	Men (N=369)	Women (N=172)
Range	$100–$9,500	$100–$4,500
Median	$1,168.05	$530.61
Mean	1,588.94	495.14
S.D.	1,429.73	676.60
Total earnings	$586,318.86	$85,164.08

AGE AT GRADUATING FROM COLLEGE

The distribution of ages at the time of graduating from college is shown in Table 29. The range for men was 17 to 32 years; for women 17 to 27 years. For men the median was 21.58 and the mean 21.66 (S.D. 1.53). The median for women was 21.14 and the mean 21.15 (S.D. 1.27). Thirty-eight of the men, or one in fourteen, graduated before the age of 20; of the women, there were thirty-nine, or one in ten who graduated before that age. Almost a third of the men and 45.1 percent of the women graduated before the age of 21.

TABLE 29

AGE AT GRADUATION FROM COLLEGE

	Men		Women	
	N	Percent	N	Percent
17.0–17.11	1	0.19	1	0.26
18.0–18.11	6	1.16	5	1.30
19.0–19.11	31	5.97	33	8.55
20.0–20.11	133	25.63	135	34.99
21.0–21.11	152	29.29	138	35.77
22.0–22.11	105	20.23	50	12.96
23.0–23.11	54	10.40	10	2.59
24.0–24.11	24	4.62	7	1.81
25.0–25.11	8	1.54	2	0.52
26.0–26.11	2	0.39	4	1.04
27.0–27.11	1	0.19	1	0.26
28.0–28.11	1	0.19		
...	..	....		
32.0–32.11	1	0.19		
N for percentages	519*		386†	
Median	21.58		21.14	
Mean	21.66		21.15	
S.D.	1.53		1.27	

* Twelve men who proceeded directly to a professional degree without taking a Bachelor's, and fourteen men for whom information on age at college graduation was lacking, are not included. One man who graduated at 16 is deceased and therefore not included in this table. He was the only subject who got a college degree before the age of seventeen.

† Information on age at graduation was lacking for sixteen women.

The median age at college graduation is at least a year below that of the generality of college students, a fact to be taken into account in appraising the academic success of the group on the basis of such evidence as class marks, graduation, honors, and awards of scholarships, fellowships, and assistantships.

EXTRACURRICULAR ACTIVITIES IN COLLEGE

Extracurricular activities at the college level offer valuable evidence in regard to social adjustment. Here it is sufficient to note that the records of the gifted subjects in this respect are definitely superior to those of college students in general. Close to 36 percent of the men and 39 percent of the women had engaged extensively in such activities; 1 in 12 of the men and 1 in 6 of the women had won "outstanding" or "very outstanding" recognition. This is all the more remarkable in view of the age handicap.

Correlates of Academic History

We have compared the childhood IQ's of the college graduates with the IQ's of those who had lesser amounts of education. It would be unreasonable to expect a high correlation, since all of our subjects rated in the top 1 percent of the generality in IQ. There was, however, a definite relationship. As shown in Table 30, the mean for those who graduated from college was approximately 4 points higher than for those who had no college education or less than one year, a difference that is statistically reliable. In the case of men, the difference in mean IQ of college graduates and those with no college or less than one year of college, gave a critical ratio of 4.13; the corresponding critical ratio for women was 3.38.

TABLE 30

Amount of Education versus Childhood IQ

	(1) College Graduation	(2) College 1 to 4 Years	(3) No College or Less Than 1 Year	CR (1) vs. (3)
Men	(N=357)	(N=67)	(N=100)	
Mean IQ	152.75	150.90	148.70	4.13
S.D.	11.30	10.50	7.11	
Women	(N=288)	(N=62)	(N=97)	
Mean IQ	151.30	150.30	147.72	3.38
S.D.	10.30	12.30	8.64	

A relationship between childhood IQ and average college grade was also found (Table 31). The main contrast is between those whose grades averaged A and all other students, the difference being about 7 IQ points in favor of the men with A average, and slightly less for women of A average. The respective critical ratios are 3.1 and 2.4.

TABLE 31

Average Grade in College versus Childhood IQ

	Average College Grade			
	A	B	C or Below	CR
Men	(N=46)	(N=225)	(N=108)	A vs. B or Below
Mean IQ	158.96	151.60	151.40	3.1
S.D.	15.99	10.07	11.68	
Women	(N=34)	(N=215)	(N=72)	
Mean IQ	155.97	151.35	148.04	2.4
S.D.	12.99	10.29	9.61	

A relationship was also found between educational history and the Concept Mastery score of 1940. Table 32 presents the data for Concept Mastery score against amount of education and Table 33 the data for Concept Mastery score against average college grade.

TABLE 32

AMOUNT OF EDUCATION VERSUS CONCEPT MASTERY SCORE

	AMOUNT OF EDUCATION		
	(1) College Graduation	(2) College 1 to 4 Years	(3) No College or Less Than 1 Year
Men	(N=333)	(N=106)	(N=66)
Mean C.M. score	107.2	85.4	78.7
S.D.	28.3	29.2	29.9
	CR: (1) vs. (3) = 7.1; (1) vs. (2) and (3) = 8.9		
Women	(N=268)	(N=73)	(N=72)
Mean C.M. score	100.4	86.8	79.4
S.D.	25.1	30.5	29.2
	CR: (1) vs. (3) = 5.6; (1) vs. (2) and (3) = 5.9		

TABLE 33

AVERAGE COLLEGE GRADE VERSUS CONCEPT MASTERY SCORE

	AVERAGE COLLEGE GRADE			
	A	B	C or Below	CR
Men	(N=35)	(N=225)	(N=113)	A vs. C or Below
Mean C.M. score	107.6	107.7	94.1	2.2
S.D.	31.4	28.1	30.3	
Women	(N=27)	(N=208)	(N=57)	
Mean C.M. score	110.8	99.6	94.3	2.7
S.D.	26.0	25.3	26.2	

From a comparison of Table 30 and Table 32, it will be seen that the amount of schooling is much more closely related to the Concept Mastery score of 1940 than to the childhood IQ. In part, this difference reflects the fact that a test given in childhood is less predictive of adult ability than a test given after mental growth has been completed. In part, however, it is due to the greater influence of schooling on a test of the Concept Mastery type.

Another correlate of academic history is the amount of education of the parents. Table 34 shows a reliable relationship. College graduation tends to run in families, though it is impossible to apportion the credit between genetic and environmental factors. For example, the proportion of fathers who had graduated from college was nearly four times as high for subjects who graduated from college as for subjects who had no college or less than one year.

TABLE 34

ACADEMIC HISTORY VERSUS EDUCATION OF PARENTS

	GIFTED SUBJECTS					
	College Graduates		1 to 4 Years of College but Not Graduate		No College or Less Than 1 Year	
	N	Percent	N	Percent	N	Percent
I. *Father*						
College graduate	328	41.1	36	23.4	25	11.7
Some college or professional training but not equal to Bachelor's degree	117	14.7	18	11.7	20	9.4
High-school graduation only	73	9.1	19	12.3	30	14.1
One to three years of high school or equivalent	156	19.5	37	24.0	59	27.7
Eighth grade only	87	10.9	31	20.1	45	21.1
Less than eighth grade	37	4.6	13	8.4	34	16.0
N	798		154		213	
II. *Mother*						
College graduate	165	20.2	14	8.4	10	4.3
Some college or professional training but not equal to Bachelor's degree	234	28.6	32	19.2	29	12.5
High-school graduation only	152	18.6	35	21.0	39	16.8
One to three years of high school or equivalent	176	21.5	49	29.3	80	34.5
Eighth grade only	65	8.0	28	16.8	53	22.8
Less than eighth grade	25	3.1	9	5.4	21	9.1
N	817		167		232	

SUMMARY

Approximately 90 percent of the gifted men and 86 percent of the gifted women entered college, and 70 percent of the men and 67 percent of the women graduated from college. These figures are about eight times as great as for the general population in California.

Of those graduating from college, 68 percent of men and 60 percent of women returned for graduate study. Graduate degrees were taken by 51.2 percent of men graduates and 29.3 percent of women graduates. The highest degree taken beyond the Bachelor's was most frequently a law degree; following in order were the M.A., the Ph.D., and the M.D.

In undergraduate years the Social Sciences ranked first as choice of major field with both men and women. For men, Engineering and the Physical Sciences were next; in the case of women, Letters was the second most popular major. In both undergraduate and graduate years gifted subjects, and particularly gifted men, were in marked contrast to college graduates in general in the infrequency with which they elected Education as a major. However, many who did not major in Education became teachers, including a large number who are members of college or university faculties.

The average grade in college, while superior, was not always as high as might have been expected from a group of such marked intellectual superiority. Of those graduating from college, 77.5 percent of men and 82.5 percent of women had average college grades of B or better. Graduating "with honors" were approximately 30 percent of both men and women. Elected to Phi Beta Kappa or Sigma Xi or both, were 27.7 percent of men and 21.5 percent of women. On the other hand, 53, or 7.7 percent of the men who entered college flunked out. Only 10, or 2 percent of the women were disqualified. Nearly half of the men who failed later finished college, and a number took graduate degrees, but only one woman who was disqualified finished college.

About 20 percent of men and women received one or more scholarship or fellowship awards during their undergraduate years. Graduate scholarships or fellowships were awarded to 26 percent of men and 13 percent of women taking graduate work. Graduate assistantships were held by 27 percent of the men and 16 percent of the women. The mean stipends from scholarships and fellowships for men was $1,013, for women $527. From assistantships, the mean for men was $1,377 and for women $730.

Thirty-six percent of the men graduating earned from half to all of their undergraduate expenses, as compared with 16 percent of women graduating. Less than 23 percent of the men graduates earned none of their expenses, whereas 44 percent of the women did no outside work for self-support. The total earnings of our subjects during the college years amounted to more than $670,000. This does not include stipends from scholarships or fellowships. Greater financial assistance for gifted students is obviously a pressing need.

The gifted subjects graduated from college at least a year younger than the California average. The median for men was 21.6 years; for women, 21.1 years. The means were approximately the same as the medians.

The men and women of the gifted group on the whole participated to a greater extent than the generality of college students in extra-curricular activities.

There were relatively small but statistically significant differences in childhood IQ between subjects who graduated from college and those who did not, the former being slightly higher. Somewhat greater IQ differences were found between those with an average college grade of A and those with B or C, particularly in the case of men. Much more relationship was found between the 1940 Concept Mastery test and the amount of education. There is a reliable relationship between the amount of education of the gifted subjects and that of their parents.

CHAPTER XIV

OCCUPATIONAL STATUS AND EARNED INCOME

The information on educational histories foreshadows to some extent the occupational status of the group. However, except for those entering the professions it does so only in a very general way. In a majority of cases, both the high-school and the college courses pursued have been general and cultural rather than technical and vocational. This chapter will be devoted chiefly to the occupational status and earned income as of 1940. It will be understood, of course, that the cross-section view is an ever-changing one. For many the occupational status will probably continue to improve until well past middle age.

Occupations are difficult to classify satisfactorily. Various schedules and scales are available, each with its good and bad points. After consideration of such scales as those of Barr and Taussig (both of which were used in 1921–22), the Brussel revision of the Barr scale, and the Minnesota Occupational Scale[27] the last named was selected as best suited to furnish a basis of comparison between our group and the general population. We have, however, applied this scale only to men, a less formal classification being deemed more suitable for the women. The occupational status of women will be treated separately.

Occupational Classification of Men

The Minnesota Occupational Scale is based on the United States Census classification and contains a list of about 350 occupations of adult males for the United States as a whole. These are divided into seven main groups, with the number and percentage of the total population given for each group. These groups are defined as follows:

Group I. Professional.
Group II. Semiprofessional and higher business.
Group III. Clerical, skilled trades, and retail business.
Group IV. Farming and other agricultural pursuits.

Group V. Semiskilled trades, minor clerical, and minor business.
Group VI. Slightly skilled trades and other occupations requiring little training or ability.
Group VII.* Day laborers: urban and rural.

It was necessary to adapt this scale to our particular needs, since no list can possibly include all occupations. We were guided by the group definitions in interpolating unlisted occupations. The *Dictionary of Occupational Titles*,[22] prepared by the Job Analysis and Information Section, Division of Standards and Research of the United States Department of Labor, was invaluable as an aid in assigning particular occupations to groups. Although the Minnesota classification is to some extent a socioeconomic scale, the arrangement is not strictly hierarchical. For example, Group IV includes all those engaged in agricultural pursuits. These may range from a socially and economically well-placed fruitgrower with an income of $5,000 to $10,000 or more, who serves on the board of directors of the growers' organization or is a stockholder in the distributing organization and has many other calls on his business and intellectual ability, to the foreman or manager of a large ranch down to the ranch hand. Among our gifted men, 7 of the 9 falling in Group IV were college graduates, 2 were ex-lawyers, 1 an ex-teacher, and all but one were landowners and operators. Similarly, some in Group II rank higher in socioeconomic status than some of the Group I subjects. Perhaps few would question that such Group II occupations as that of bank official, president of a manufacturing firm, economist, or executive in public-welfare work would rank at least as high in a hierarchical arrangement of occupations as the high-school teacher or small-city librarian of Group I. On the other hand, the clerical and sales occupations, retail business, and the trades and crafts are pretty well ranked from Group III to Group V, and still lower to Group VI.

The "trainees" in business and industry presented a special problem. The requirements for these positions are high, often college graduation, and, although the work usually begins on a relatively low plane, most of the trainees among our subjects were being groomed for executive positions. We placed these men in Group III, but almost all can be expected to advance to Group II in time.

* No gifted subjects fall in this classification.

Our problems in rating occupations were different from those that would be found in a less-selected population. In the case of the gifted subjects, we were classifying individuals of whom approximately 70 percent were college graduates and 83 percent had had one year or more of college education. When an occupation appeared in the list under a group heading that seemed out of keeping with the status of the individual, the scale was usually adhered to nonetheless. As a result of this policy on our part, and because of the strict interpretation of the terms "professional" and "semiprofessional" in the Minnesota classification, any errors in our ratings are likely to be in the downward direction.

Information regarding occupational status in 1940 was available for 788 men, or all but 34 of the total population of 822. Of these 788, there were 48 who were still students, 7 were unemployed (and seeking employment), and one not gainfully employed but financially independent was engaged in scientific research. Eight were physically or mentally incapacitated. Of the incapacitated, 2 were epileptic, 2 suffered from tuberculosis, 2 were recovering from mental breakdowns, 1 was a chronic invalid because of a heart condition, and 1 was temporarily hospitalized for treatment of high blood pressure. This leaves 724 who were gainfully employed at the time of the follow-up. Their classification on the Minnesota scale is shown in Table 35. This table also includes, for purposes of comparison, the percentage of all employed males in California falling in each of these groups according

TABLE 35

OCCUPATIONAL CLASSIFICATION OF GIFTED MEN AND OF ALL EMPLOYED MEN IN CALIFORNIA (1940)

Occupational Group	Percentage of Gifted Men (N=724)	Percentage of Employed Males in California (1940) (N=1,878,559)
I. Professional	45.4	5.7
II. Semiprofessional and higher business	25.7	8.1
III. Clerical, skilled trades, and retail business	20.7	24.3
IV. Farming and other agricultural pursuits	1.2	12.4
V. Semiskilled trades, minor clerical, and minor business	6.2	31.6
VI. Slightly skilled trades and other occupations requiring little training or ability	0.7	17.8*
VII. Day laborers: urban and rural	0.0	

* Groups VI and VII have been combined because of the difficulty in distinguishing them from one another in the census reports available to us.

to the 1940 United States Census.[56] Since our group was originally located in California and the majority still live there, a comparison with the occupations of California men is more appropriate than one with all United States men.

Table 36 gives a breakdown of the larger occupational groups (I, II, III, and V) and indicates for each subgroup the percentage of all employed gifted men. The 5 men in Group VI were all in occupations requiring little skill, training, or ability. Group IV is wholly agricultural.

TABLE 36

BREAKDOWN OF MAIN OCCUPATIONAL GROUPS OF GIFTED MEN

	N	Percent of Employed
Group I		
Lawyers	69	9.53
Members of college or university faculties	55	7.59
Engineers	49	6.77
Physicians	44	6.08
Chemists	26	3.59
Authors or journalists	26	3.59
Teachers below college	25	3.45
Clergymen	9	1.24
Artists or composers	7	0.97
Architects	6	0.83
Miscellaneous	13	1.80
Total, Group I	329	45.44
Group II		
Owners and executives in industry, wholesale business, transportation, *et cetera*	37	5.11
Officials and executives in banking, finance, or insurance	22	3.04
Accountants, auditors, or statisticians	17	2.35
Welfare workers, personnel directors, *et cetera*	12	1.66
Army or Navy officers	12	1.66
Officials and executives in advertising, publicity, promotion, or public relations	10	1.38
Musicians or music teachers	10	1.38
Motion-picture producers, directors, or editors	9	1.24
Radio program producers or directors	7	0.97
Economists	4	0.55
Owners or managers of higher retail business	4	0.55
Miscellaneous	42	5.80
Total, Group II	186	25.69

TABLE 36 *(Continued)*

	N	Percent of Employed
Group III		
Clerical workers (higher; includes junior accountants, statistical clerks, bookkeepers, *et cetera*)	65	8.97
Salesmen	22	3.04
Workers in skilled trades or crafts	14	1.93
Real estate or insurance agents	9	1.24
Managers of small retail business	7	0.97
Commercial artists, ceramists, photographers	5	0.69
Professional service: laboratory technicians, osteopaths, teachers of athletics, dancing, shop work, *et cetera*	3	0.41
Inspectors, foremen, overseers	3	0.41
Radio operators, announcers, or actors	2	0.28
Motion-picture technicians	1	0.14
Miscellaneous	19	2.62
Total, Group III	150	20.72
Group V		
Clerical workers (minor)	9	1.24
Policemen, firemen, sheriffs, or detectives	7	0.97
Salesmen	6	0.83
Retailers (minor)	3	0.41
Semiskilled craftsmen	3	0.41
Service-station proprietors or managers	2	0.28
Skilled trade apprentices	2	0.28
Truck drivers	1	0.14
Miscellaneous	12	1.66
Total, Group V	45	6.22

Occupational Status of Gifted Men Compared to That of Male College Graduates in General

The ratings based on the Minnesota scale have been used for cross analyses of subgroups within the gifted study as well as for comparison with parental occupation and with the general population from which our group was drawn. However, studies like those reported by Babcock[4] and Greenleaf[28] offer such interesting material on intellectually superior individuals that a comparison of the status of the gifted men, both college graduates and nongraduates, with the subjects of these two investigations is very informative. These investigations are especially pertinent since they present information regarding a college-graduate population closely approximating our data in age of subjects and time of report. Since neither of these studies utilized the Minnesota scale it was necessary to recast our classification to fit as nearly as possible the pattern used by each.

A comparison with Greenleaf's data shows that the occupational status of gifted men was clearly superior to that of college men in general. Greenleaf has classified his graduates into the following groups:

	Percent
1. Owners (includes professional men and businessmen who own and manage their businesses or have capital invested and share in the management)	20.0
2. *Employed*	
a) Proprietors or officials (includes teachers)	25.8
b) Agents	10.4
c) Clerks and skilled workers	42.4
d) Unskilled	1.4

The two classes, Owners and Proprietors or officials, which account for 45.8 percent of male college graduates, are roughly comparable to Groups I and II of the Minnesota scale into which 71 percent of all employed gifted men fall. Greenleaf's "agents" appear to correspond to our Group III, but his category of Clerks and skilled workers does not fit into any one group of the Minnesota scale. Most of the clerical workers and the more skilled craftsmen would go into Group III, although some of this class belong to Group V (minor clerical, minor business, and semiskilled trades). Since no provision has been made for what Goodenough and Anderson call "semiskilled" workers, it is assumed that they have been included in Greenleaf's *2c* class. The classification, Unskilled, as used with this college group, is considered to cover the same occupations as Groups VI and VII of the Minnesota scale. Thus, while 52.8 percent of college men in general are employed as agents, clerks, and skilled workers, only 26.9 percent of gifted men are so employed. Of the college group, 1.4 percent are engaged in semiskilled or unskilled work as compared with 0.7 percent of gifted men. This leaves our Group IV unaccounted for, but in view of the fact that 8 of our 9 men in agriculture are owners, the proportion of gifted men in the owner-proprietor category is even greater than the 71 percent given above.

Greenleaf states that the majority (53 percent) of the class of 1935

—i.e., men out of college one year—found work as clerks or skilled workers. The proportion in these occupations drops after eight years (class of 1928) to 30 percent. The next largest group finds employment as proprietors or officials. This group tends to expand with passing years, increasing in eight years from 23 percent to 30 percent. About 3 percent start out after college as unskilled workers (Groups VI and VII) and this proportion decreases to less than 1 percent after eight years.

Babcock, in addition to classifying his men into two large groups—Professions and Business, with their respective subgroups—has attempted to measure the "individuality of the male college graduate in his work." He combines into one group professional workers (except teachers),* executives and minor officials, technicians, and proprietors and partners who have achieved a degree of responsibility, either managerial or in the application of special knowledge. Opposed to these are men who work in the ranks as clerical, skilled, or unskilled workers. Leaving teachers, farmers, and salesmen as classes apart, he finds the following proportions by age groups for the two classes just described:

	Under 30 Years Percent	30–39 Years Percent
Individual and executive workers	41.8	61.2
Group workers in the ranks	33.3	16.5

When we applied this same treatment to gifted men, the proportions were as follows:

	Age Range 20–39 Years Mean 29.8 Percent
Individual and executive workers	70.6
Group workers in the ranks	17.6

Thus it would appear that the gifted men, regardless of education, are assuming responsibility and leadership in far greater proportion than college graduates in general.

Unemployment Among Gifted Men

The proportion of gifted men unemployed in 1940 was less than 1 percent. In contrast, the 1940 census shows that approximately 11 percent of experienced male workers between the ages of twenty and

* Teachers are understood here to mean teachers below the college level.

thirty-four, employable and seeking work, were unemployed in California at this same period. Babcock reports 2.1 percent of college graduates of all ages unemployed or on relief in 1940, and when we consider only those of his investigation who graduated between the years 1930–39, thus securing an age range comparable to that of the gifted group, the percentage unemployed was 3.1. Greenleaf found 3.4 percent of recent college graduates, average age twenty-five to twenty-six, to be unemployed in 1936. It should be mentioned here that our survey of the gifted group in 1936, when their average age was the same as Greenleaf's group, showed only 1 percent unemployed—slightly less than a third as many as in the generality of college men.

Occupational Status of Women

Of the gifted women, 617 out of the total number of 645 were classified according to their employment status as outlined in Table 37. Information on this item was lacking or incomplete for 28 cases.

TABLE 37

Employment Status of Gifted Women (1940)

	N	Percent
Employed full time	299	48.46
Housewife: not gainfully employed	259	41.97
Housewife and part-time work	15	2.43
Single and part-time work	1	0.16
Student	24	3.89
Single: not employed (just out of school, between jobs, getting married, seeking work, *et cetera*)	14	2.27
Physically or mentally incapacitated	5	0.81
N for percentages	617	

Approximately 48 percent were employed full time and 42 percent were housewives. The category, Housewife, here includes only those married women who had no paid employment outside the home. The married women holding full-time positions in addition to their housekeeping duties were classified in the field in which they were employed and not as housewives. A small number of wives who had part-time employment have been reported separately in Table 37. Twenty-four of the unmarried women were still attending school. Another 14 women had either just finished school or were in the process of changing jobs or getting ready to be married. The 5 women classified as incapacitated included 1 case of tuberculosis, 2 who were in mental hospitals, 1 who was recovering from surgery, and 1 who was taking an enforced rest because of a run-down physical condition, aggravated by emotional difficulties. Each of the last two expected to resume her work at an early date. The one unmarried woman employed at part-time work had responsibilities at home which made it impossible for her to carry a full-time job.

Most of the women who had taken advanced professional degrees were working. Notable exceptions were a physician, a lawyer, and a Ph.D. in biological sciences who had given up their professional work for careers as housewives. No account has been taken of the large amount of volunteer work done by those not employed full time. Many of our married women were serving on boards of charitable or community-service and welfare organizations, or assisting in office or case work for such organizations.

Table 38 lists the different occupational fields in which the women of our group were working and gives the proportion in each. Of those employed, 61.2 percent were in professions,* distributed over 17 fields. Business claimed 34.8 percent, public service 1.3 percent, and miscellaneous nonprofessional work accounted for the remaining 2.7 percent. Those in public service were either telephone or telegraph operators; the 8 women classified as miscellaneous include 4 waitresses, a printer and bookbinder, a proofreader, a factory worker (machine operator), and a car hop.

Of the women in professional work, 16 were on college or university faculties as teachers or research workers; 2 who were associated with research foundations are classified here. Three were on junior college faculties, and one held an administrative position in a secondary school. The 63 teachers below college level bring the total in the field of education to 83, or 27.8 percent of all employed. In contrast, 34.8 percent of the women were engaged in business, chiefly as office workers (usually secretary or stenographer). The third most frequent occupation was that of social worker with 7 percent. The classification Arts includes a sculptress, a painter, 2 interior decorators, 6 who were actresses, dancers, or entertainers, 2 musicians, one ceramist, one film animator, one theatrical producer and director, one illustrator, and one costume designer. Not classified here are 2 musi-

* "Profession" as used here is a much broader term than in the sense in which it is used in classifying men on the Minnesota Occupational Scale.

TABLE 38

OCCUPATIONS OF WOMEN GAINFULLY EMPLOYED FULL TIME (1940)

	N		Percent	
Professions				
Education				
College teaching and/or scientific research	16		5.4	
Junior college teaching or public-school administration	4		1.3	
Teaching below college level	63		21.1	
Social work	21		7.0	
Arts	17		5.7	
Writing	15		5.0	
Librarianship	14		4.7	
Economics, statistics, accounting	7		2.3	
Psychology	5		1.7	
Medicine	5		1.7	
Nursing	4		1.3	
Law	3		1.0	
Religious work	3		1.0	
Miscellaneous professions	6		2.0	
Total professional		183		61.2
Business				
Office work (secretary, stenographer, office manager, office clerk, *et cetera*)	92		30.8	
Owner or manager of a business, saleswoman, buyer, agent	12		4.0	
Total business		104		34.8
Public Service				
Telephone or telegraph operator	4		1.3	
Miscellaneous (nonprofessional)	8		2.7	
Total N with full-time employment	299			

cians (a pianist and a harpist), both on college music faculties, and 2 artists who were college teachers of art. These 4 appear as college teachers in the tabulations. A woman who had had considerable success as a commercial artist does not appear in Table 38 as she was temporarily not working because of home responsibilities and poor health. Thus the number of women artists and musicians was actually greater than the 5.7 percent indicated in the table.

Under Writing are classified not only those doing creative writing, such as fiction, biography, short stories or plays, but also those engaged in newspaper writing, book reviewing, advertising or publicity writing, and script writing for radio or motion pictures. One of our most outstanding writers, a poet, is not included in this classification because she was a member of a university faculty and was counted in that group.

The 7 women classified as economist, statistician, or accountant, include 2 accountants (one a C.P.A. with a Bachelor's degree in business administration), and 5 who were engaged in economic or statistical research for the government, a labor organization, or an economic research institute.

The classification Psychologist presented something of a problem. There were 8 women with advanced degrees in psychology who were active professionally, but since 1 of these was a college professor and 2 were associated with university research studies, only 5 are listed separately as psychologists. These were in clinical work or vocational counseling.

The 3 women in religious work included 1 evangelist and 2 missionaries. The latter were both attached to foreign missions, one in Africa and one in China. Not included in the category of religious workers are an ordained minister who at the time of report was studying for a Ph.D. degree, and a teacher who is a member of a religious order.

The 6 women in miscellaneous professions included an architect, a dental hygienist, a home economist, a laboratory technician, a metallurgist, and a pharmacist.

Of the 299 women employed full time, 43.5 percent were married, 48 percent single, and the remainder separated, divorced, or widowed. Both the single and married women were more often employed in office and business occupations than in any other. The proportion so engaged was approximately 35 percent for both married and unmarried. Education, including teaching at the college level, college research, and teaching below the college level, accounted for nearly 33 percent of the single women and 24 percent of the married. A larger proportion of married than of single women were engaged in social work or writing, whereas the reverse was true for the occupation of librarian.

In most of the women's occupations, particularly the professional ones, the numbers are too small to justify comparisons or cross analyses. For this reason, as well as for convenience in referring to them, the occupations of women with full-time employment have been combined into the following groups:

	N	Percent
A. University or college teaching, research, higher professions (i.e., those requiring considerable graduate training and advanced degrees, such as medicine, law, psychology)	30	10.0
B. Teaching below level of the four-year college	67	22.4
C. Other professions (social work, librarianship, writing, economics, nursing, *et cetera*)	86	28.7
D. Office and business occupations	104	34.8
E. Miscellaneous (not included in the above categories)	12	4.0

These groups differ in the amount of education they have received. As one would expect, Group A leads with 100 percent college graduation followed in all cases by one or more years of graduate study. The other occupations rank in the following order as regards college graduation: Group B, 92.5 percent; Group C, 80.5 percent; and Group D, 48.1 percent. Only one of the 12 cases in Group E was a college graduate. Among the women who were housewives without outside employment, 64.6 percent were college graduates.

Comparison with Occupations of Women College Graduates in General

Babcock[4] in 1940 found that of the younger women college graduates, those of the 1930–39 classes, 66 percent were gainfully employed and 25 percent had become housewives. Dividing college women's occupations into two broad categories, professions and business, Babcock reports that among the working women graduates, 78.6 percent of those under thirty and 83.5 percent of those aged thirty to thirty-nine were in the professions. Business occupations accounted for 21.4 percent of the younger group and 16.5 percent of the thirty- to thirty-nine-year group. Education completely overshadowed all other occupations, both professional and business, with 63 percent of those under thirty and nearly 70 percent of those thirty to thirty-nine in this field alone.

In Greenleaf's report[28] two-thirds of the employed college women were in the professional or semiprofessional occupations, 4 percent in trades such as business and merchandising, close to 8 percent in clerical work, 0.4 percent in transportation or communication, and 21 percent in general occupations including agriculture, domestic (not defined, but not housewives), manufacturing, public office, *et cetera*. The occupation attracting the largest number of women in this group, as in Babcock's, was teaching, with 48 percent of the employed so engaged. Nursing accounted for 2 percent, approximately 1.5 percent were in research, and 1 percent were in journalism. The other professions which were reported separately, law, medicine, *et cetera,* all had less than 1 percent each. Thirteen percent were in miscellaneous professional and semiprofessional occupations not listed separately by Greenleaf.

The outstanding fact in the comparison of the gifted women with the college women of these two studies is the much smaller proportion of gifted who elect teaching as a vocation, and the larger proportion who choose office work.

Comparison with Parental Occupational Status

We have compared the occupational status of gifted men with that of the fathers of all gifted subjects, both men and women. As already stated, the occupational classification of fathers in 1921–22 was based upon the Taussig scale and the Barr scale. The Taussig scale, as noted in chapter ii, includes the following five classes: (1) the professions; (2) semiprofessional and higher business groups; (3) the small business and clerical group and skilled trades; (4) semiskilled workers; (5) unskilled workers. The Barr scale involves a more detailed classification of occupations based on the rated average intelligence of persons engaged in each in the general population.

We have reclassified the occupations of fathers on the basis of the Minnesota adaptation of the census groupings, and have done this separately for the fathers as of 1922, 1928, and 1940. The percentage distributions of employed fathers among the seven census groups were not at any point reliably different at these three dates. The results shown in Table 39 are accordingly based upon the 1940 classification of fathers.

The most important difference in this comparison is the greater proportion of gifted men than of fathers of the gifted in the professions, and the smaller proportion of the former than of the latter in the business occupations of Group II. The occupational status of the fathers is very superior compared to the generality, but less superior than that of the gifted men. The incidence of professional occupations for gifted men is not far from eight times that of the generality; for fathers of all gifted subjects it is approximately six times that of the generality.

TABLE 39

OCCUPATIONAL COMPARISON OF GIFTED MEN WITH FATHERS OF GIFTED SUBJECTS

Occupational Group	Gifted Men		Fathers of Gifted Subjects	
	N	Percent	N	Percent
I. Professional	329	45.44	255	33.28
II. Semiprofessional and higher business	186	25.69	248	32.36
III. Clerical, skilled trades, and retail business	150	20.72	157	20.49
IV. Farming and agriculture	9	1.24	41	5.35
V. Semiskilled trades, minor clerical, and minor business	45	6.22	58	7.57
VI. Slightly skilled trades and other occupations requiring little training or ability	5	0.69	7	0.91
VII. Day laborers: urban and rural	0	0.00	0	0.00
N for percentages	724		766	

OCCUPATIONAL CLASSIFICATION AS RELATED TO INTELLIGENCE

We have compared both the mean childhood Binet IQ and the mean 1940 Concept Mastery score of the men with occupational classification on the Minnesota scale. These comparisons are shown in Table 40. Because of the small number of cases, Groups IV, V, and VI have been combined.

TABLE 40

INTELLIGENCE SCORES OF GIFTED MEN BY OCCUPATIONAL GROUPS

Census Groups	CHILDHOOD BINET IQ			CONCEPT MASTERY SCORE		
	N	Mean	S.D.	N	Mean	S.D.
I	201	153.24	12.13	215	110.36	26.99
II	127	152.63	10.12	114	96.34	32.67
III	109	150.26	9.90	107	82.63	26.44
IV–VI	43	146.77	7.07	44	82.68	31.64

CR: Group I vs. Groups IV–VI = 4.7

CR: Group I vs. Group II = 3.9
Group I vs. Groups III–VI = 9.5
Group I vs. Groups IV–VI = 5.4
Group II vs. Groups III–VI = 3.6

It will be seen that although the difference in Binet IQ between Group I and Groups IV–VI was not great in the absolute sense, it was highly reliable, having a critical ratio of 4.7. The 1940 Concept Mastery score was more closely related to occupational classification; here the professional group was reliably higher than Group II, and the latter was reliably higher than the groups below II.

The relationship of women's occupations to childhood Binet IQ and the 1940 Concept Mastery is given in Table 41. The mean Binet IQ's of the four main occupational classes and of housewives were practically the same. However, it is an interesting fact that two-thirds of the women in our group with IQ's 170 and above were office workers or housewives (see chapter xxi). The mean Concept Mastery score was highest for the women in college teaching and the higher professions. Miscellaneous professions ranked second, teaching below the college level ranked third, and the office workers and housewives were lowest. Again the question arises whether the Concept Mastery scores may not be considerably influenced by the amount of education a subject has had.

TABLE 41

INTELLIGENCE SCORES OF GIFTED WOMEN BY OCCUPATIONAL CLASSIFICATION

Occupational Classification*	Childhood Binet IQ			Concept Mastery Score		
	N	Mean	S.D.	N	Mean	S.D.
A. Higher professions, college teaching, research	20	149.5	5.4	16	116.4	15.1
B. Teaching below level of 4-year college	42	150.3	7.2	50	97.9	24.8
C. Other professions (social work, librarianship, nursing, writing, *et cetera*)	59	151.6	10.9	50	104.3	27.8
D. Office and business occupations	82	151.3	11.6	77	91.1	28.5
Housewife: not gainfully employed	188	149.5	10.3	176	91.8	27.3

* Classification E omitted here because of small N.

It is of interest to know how the various professional fields compare with each other in respect to the intelligence of those whom they attract. This question cannot be answered with any finality in the case of women because of the small number of cases in the professional subgroups. For the men we have computed the mean Concept Mastery scores for each of the professions in which there were 10 or more for whom scores were available. In this comparison (Table 42) we have separated the junior college teachers from the members of college or university faculties. Most of the differences in this table are rather small and not very reliable. However, the mean of college and junior college teachers was significantly higher than the mean of engineers

(CR = 3.34), and was slightly higher than the mean of high-school teachers. The means for physicians, lawyers, chemists, and author-journalists were almost identical.

TABLE 42

MEAN CONCEPT MASTERY SCORES OF PROFESSIONAL SUBGROUPS (MEN)

Subgroups	N	Mean	S.D.
College or university teachers	21	128.16	25.14
Junior college teachers	11	117.73	.....
Authors and journalists	14	113.57	.....
Physicians	23	112.50	25.99
Lawyers	57	111.49	23.39
Chemists	20	110.00	21.10
High-school teachers	19	107.63	30.41
Engineers	32	102.19	23.62

CR: College and junior college teachers vs. high-school teachers = 1.94
CR: College and junior college teachers vs. engineers = 3.34

EARNED INCOME (1940)

The following data on earned income were obtained in the latter part of 1939 and the first half of 1940. As will be seen later, there has been a sharp rise in income since 1940.

Table 43 shows the distribution of monthly earned incomes of 577 men and 203 women employed full time, together with medians, means, and standard deviations. Information on income was lacking or in-

TABLE 43

DISTRIBUTION OF MONTHLY EARNED INCOMES OF SUBJECTS WITH FULL-TIME EMPLOYMENT (1940)

Salary per Month	Men	Women
$1,451–1,500	1	..
....	..	..
1,151–1,200	3	..
1,101–1,150	..	..
1,051–1,100	1	..
1,001–1,050	..	..
951–1,000	3	..
901–950	..	..
851–900	1	..
801–850	1	..
751–800	2	..
701–750	2	..
651–700	6	..
601–650	2	..

TABLE 43 *(Continued)*

Salary per Month	Men	Women
551–600	6	..
501–550	3	..
451–500	4	1
401–450	9	..
351–400	27	1
301–350	45	1
251–300	64	3
201–250	97	18
151–200	178	56
101–150	102	85
51–100	20	38
N	577	203
Median	$197.77	$138.35
Mean	241.62	144.96
S.D.	157.10	55.74

adequate for the 147 employed men and 96 employed women not included in these tabulations. Table 44 gives the median and mean earnings by age groups. It will be noted that there is a fairly steep rise in income with age for both men and women.

In terms of annual income, there were 2.4 percent of men earning $10,000 or more and 7.5 percent earning $5,000 or more. Only 0.5 percent of women earned $5,000 per year or more. For the sexes combined the proportion at these high income levels was several times that of the generality.

TABLE 44

INCOME AS RELATED TO AGE

	MEN			
Age	20–24	25–29	30–34	35–39
	(N=32)	(N=272)	(N=207)	(N=66)
Median salary per month	$147.92	$184.13	$230.95	$243.75
Mean salary per month	159.37	218.70	272.60	283.08
S.D.	66.47	145.33	169.59	183.86
	WOMEN			
Age	20–24	25–29	30–34	35–39
	(N=16)	(N=108)	(N=72)	(N=7)
Median salary per month	$ 92.50	$126.30	$165.52	$181.25
Mean salary per month	101.97	133.30	167.86	182.64
S.D.	41.18	54.26	51.81	......

INCOME AS RELATED TO OCCUPATION

There was a marked relationship between income of men and occupational grouping as shown in Table 45. Excluding those in agriculture, only three of whose incomes could be evaluated in terms of monthly earnings, the ranking of the male groups, in descending occupational classes, is II, I, III, V, and VI. There is nothing especially surprising about this order. Group II is composed chiefly of men at the upper business levels where incomes are relatively high, whereas those in professional groups are poorly rewarded in the beginning. Considering that a great majority of our subjects in Group I were still young and far below the peak of their earning capacity, their record can be regarded as definitely superior.

The mean incomes for men in the professional subgroups of Group I, numbering 10 or more subjects in the age range of twenty-five to thirty-nine inclusive, are given in Table 46.

TABLE 45

INCOME OF MEN BY OCCUPATIONAL GROUPS (1940)

Occupational Group		Salary per Month		
	N	Median	Mean	S.D.
I. Professional	262	$220.54	$264.62	$172.28
II. Semiprofessional and higher business	154	245.54	290.11	171.13
III. Clerical, skilled trades, and retail business	119	156.50	165.42	65.97
V and VI. Semiskilled and slightly skilled trades, minor clerical, minor business, *et cetera*	39	131.67	134.47	45.12

TABLE 46

INCOME OF MEN IN GROUP I OCCUPATIONS (AGE 25 YEARS AND ABOVE)

Profession		Salary per Month		
	N	Median	Mean	S.D.
Physician	26	$326.00	$396.65	$260.50
Author-journalist	18	226.00	333.84	337.06
Lawyer	56	251.00	293.36	162.41
Engineer	40	251.00	260.50	110.14
Chemist	21	221.00	217.17	64.24
University teacher or research worker	29	217.67	216.02	60.31
Junior college teacher or school administrator	14	211.00	214.79	.....
Teachers below junior college level	22	183.14	191.40	57.68

The income of women is also related to their occupation, the higher professions and college teaching ranking first, followed by teachers below the college level, other professions, and lastly the business occupations. Table 47 gives median and mean salary per month according to occupational classification for the 196 women for whom information on this item was available. The public service and miscellaneous occupations were not included in the table because the number of cases was so small.

TABLE 47

INCOME OF WOMEN BY OCCUPATIONAL CLASSIFICATION (1940)

Classification	SALARY PER MONTH			
	N	Median	Mean	S.D.
A. Higher professions, college teaching, research	12	$201.00	$215.63	.....
B. Teaching, below level of four-year college	54	171.54	167.59	37.77
C. Other professions (social work, librarianship, nursing, writing, *et cetera*)	51	145.44	159.31	57.30
D. Office and business occupations	79	116.56	113.61	30.76

INCOME AS RELATED TO EDUCATION

College graduates in the gifted group, both men and women, earn more than nongraduates (see Table 48). It is necessary to emphasize, however, that the extent to which increased education exerts a causative effect on income is a matter of inference. It is well known that to a considerable extent education acts as a selective agent.

TABLE 48

INCOME VERSUS AMOUNT OF EDUCATION

	COLLEGE GRADUATES		NOT COLLEGE GRADUATES	
	Men (N=398)	Women (N=142)	Men (N=179)	Women (N=61)
Median income	$216.50	$153.50	$170.34	$108.41
Mean income	253.75	159.30	208.04	111.57
S.D.	154.05	54.56	164.73	42.59

CR of means: Men college graduates vs. nongraduates = 3.15
Women college graduates vs. nongraduates = 6.72

COMPARATIVE DATA ON INCOME

Comparative data are available on earned income in 1939 for two groups: (1) the total population as reported in the 1940 United States

Census,[56] and (2) college graduates in general as reported by Babcock.[4] Both of these reports are in terms of annual earned income. Accordingly, the yearly income of the gifted subjects has been computed from the salary per month reported in the 1939–40 Information Blank.

The 1940 Census report gives the income for various breakdowns of the total population. For comparison with our subjects, we have selected the most favored group in the general population, namely, urban residents who were employed 12 months in 1939, exclusive of those on public emergency work.

The median annual income from wages and salaries for United States males in this category was $1,389 for those of ages 25–34 as compared with $2,373 for all gifted men (ages 20–39) with full-time employment. The corresponding medians for women are $916 for the census group and $1,660 for gifted subjects.

The median for employed gifted men was therefore nearly 70 percent above that of the generality of employed males, and the median of employed gifted women was nearly 82 percent above that of employed women in the generality.

In the case of Babcock's United States college graduates the differences are, as would be expected, much less striking. However, they still favor the gifted subjects in spite of the fact that 30 percent of gifted men and 33 percent of gifted women had not graduated from college. Median annual earnings for the two groups by age and sex are as follows:

	Under 30 Years		30–39 Years	
	Men	Women	Men	Women
Gifted subjects	$2,177	$1,493	$2,814	$2,021
College graduates (Babcock)	1,690	1,380	2,590	1,610

Following are the proportions earning $5,000 or more per year:

	Under 30 Years		30–39 Years	
	Men %	Women %	Men %	Women %
Gifted subjects	4.3	0.5	9.5	...
College graduates (Babcock)	0.7	...	9.1	0.1

Income as Related to Intelligence

Table 49 shows a peculiar trend of mean Concept Mastery scores for men with increase of earned income. The mean score rises with increase of income up to $200 a month then drops beyond salaries of $400 a month. However, the N's are small in the extreme salary ranges, and the downward trend for incomes above $400 monthly is not very reliable. There is little relationship between income and childhood IQ in the range above 135, though the trend is similar to that observed in Concept Mastery scores. The Binet IQ's rise slightly with income to $300 then drop slightly as income increases beyond that point. These differences are too small to be reliable.

TABLE 49

INCOME OF MEN VERSUS INTELLIGENCE SCORES
(AGE 25 YEARS AND OVER)

Earned Monthly Income	Childhood Binet IQ			Concept Mastery Score		
	N	Mean	S.D.	N	Mean	S.D.
$100 or less	14	147.7	...	15	92.5	22.0
101–200	176	151.6	10.1	210	94.6	31.1
201–300	98	155.1	12.5	105	102.0	29.8
301–400	37	152.5	10.1	42	102.8	30.9
401–700	13	152.8	...	22	96.3	27.9
701 and above	10	149.5	...	14	85.6	...

The Binet IQ's of the women vary little with increases in earned income, the mean of those earning $200 a month and above being almost identical with that of women earning $100 or less. Concept Mastery scores show a fairly reliable increase up to $200. Table 50 gives the means and standard deviations of both Concept Mastery scores and Binet IQ's for women at the various income levels.

TABLE 50

INCOME OF WOMEN VERSUS INTELLIGENCE SCORES

Earned Monthly Income	Childhood Binet IQ			Concept Mastery Score		
	N	Mean	S.D.	N	Mean	S.D.
$100 or less	35	150.4	9.9	33	86.3	29.3
101–150	65	152.8	10.4	70	93.2	27.2
151–200	32	147.4	7.8	40	100.0	23.9
201 and above	13	150.1	...	20	100.0	19.6

THE 1945 REPORTS ON OCCUPATION

The Information Blank sent to the subjects in 1945 called for information on occupation and income for the calendar years 1941, 1942, 1943, and 1944. The data on occupation and income will be summarized separately for men and women.

The 760 men reporting account for 93.6 percent of the number of men living in 1945. The figures on occupational status for 1941 are approximately the same as those shown in Table 35 for 1940, as the war had not yet had any marked effect. By 1944, however, the picture had changed considerably. Before the end of that year a total of 323, or 42.5 percent, of the men had entered military service. The student group of 1940 had completed or discontinued its work, and those of its members who did not go into service had entered upon professional or business careers. Changes in occupation of those employed in 1940 are also apparent. As would be expected, the shift is toward greater representation in Groups I and II, the expected advances and promotions having been accelerated by wartime opportunities. No one was in Group VI in 1944, and at that date only 1.9 percent were in Group V as compared with the 6.2 percent who were given this classification in 1940.

Among the 760 men reporting in 1945, the number who were civilians in 1944 was 477. This includes 19 who had been discharged from military service before 1944 as well as 19 who entered service during 1944. Of these 477, there was one who was a graduate student and teaching assistant, two were incapacitated through ill health, and one, discharged from the Army as psychoneurotic, was having serious adjustment difficulties and was not regularly employed. The 473 men gainfully employed in civilian occupations in 1944 were distributed as follows on the Minnesota scale:

Group I .... 48.3 percent
Group II .... 32.0 percent
Group III .... 15.7 percent
Group IV .... 2.2 percent
Group V .... 1.9 percent

The differences between these figures and those for 1940 are especially marked when account is taken of the discrepancies in the proportions who entered military service from the various occupational groups. Group I contributed 41.4 percent to the armed forces; Group II, 44.1 percent; Group III, 40.6 percent; Group IV, 30.0 percent; and Group V, 28.0 percent. No one was in Group VI at the time of entering the service.

The 591 women reporting in 1945 represent 92.1 percent of the total. The proportion employed full time decreased from the 48.5

percent of 1940 (see Table 37) to 36.0 percent in 1944. Apparently the decrease was due about equally to marriage of those who were single in 1940, and the increasing number of children to be cared for. The proportion of married women employed decreased from 31.9 percent in 1940 to 23.0 percent in 1944. College teaching or professions such as law, medicine, and psychology accounted for 12.4 percent of the women with full-time employment. The remainder were employed as follows: teaching below the college level, 23.6 percent; professions such as social work, librarianship, writing, economics, *et cetera,* 25.8 percent; office and business, 32.6 percent; war industries, 5.6 percent.

The 1945 Reports on Income

Information on income was available for 445 men and 199 women not in military service. In line with the general trend there was a marked increase in the earnings of the gifted subjects during the war years. Among men, the 1944 median earned income for those in civilian life was $392.77 per month or $4,713 per year, an increase of 98.6 percent over the 1940 median annual income of $2,373. Earning $5,000 per year or more were 45.4 percent; $10,000 per year or more, 13.5 percent; $15,000 per year or more, 7.9 percent; $20,000 per year or more, 4.7 percent; and $25,000 per year or more, 3.6 percent. The range of earned income per year for men in 1944 was from $1,500 to $84,000. There were four men with earned incomes of $50,000 or over. By age group the median earned income per year for men was as follows: under thirty years, $4,094; thirty to thirty-four years, $4,375; thirty-five to thirty-nine years, $4,893; forty to forty-four years, $4,600.

There was also a marked increase in earned income for women between the years 1940–44. The median in 1944 was $2,550, an increase of 52.4 percent over the 1940 median of $1,660. The maximum of $6,000 in 1940 has since been exceeded by 6 women, the highest income reported being $9,200.

We do not have figures for 1944 on earned income for the United States generality of employed men and women, but the Alexander Hamilton Institute reported in 1947 the proportions of United States families having annual incomes of specified amounts. Although the Alexander Hamilton Institute data are not strictly comparable to our own since they are for families and not individuals, and since they are for 1946 when incomes were higher than in 1944, the following figures are of considerable interest:

Income levels:	Generality of United States Families (1946) (Percent)	Civilian Gifted Men (1944) (Percent)
$7,500 or over	2.6	20.4
$5,000 or over	7.4	45.4

That is, the proportion of gifted men with incomes of $7,500 or over was in 1944 about eight times as great as the 1946 figure for United States families of this income level. The corresponding proportion earning $5,000 or over was approximately six times as great for gifted men as for the generality of United States families.

Summary

The gifted men were classified as of 1940 according to the Minnesota Occupational Scale into seven groups, and the percentage in each group has been compared with that in the total employed male population of California in 1940. Of the gifted men, 45 percent were in professions as compared with 5.7 percent of all California males, giving a ratio of about 8 to 1. Approximately 71 percent of the gifted men were in either Group I (professional) or Group II (semiprofessional or higher business occupations) as compared with 13.8 percent of California men in general. This ratio is more than 5 to 1.

Gifted subjects compared very favorably with two groups of college graduates, one reported by Greenleaf and one by Babcock. Approximately 55 percent of college men in general were in the professions or were owners, officials, or executives, whereas 71 percent of the gifted men were in such occupations. The conclusion is that the gifted men, both college graduates and nongraduates, were filling positions of responsibility and exercising leadership to a reliably greater extent than the generality of college graduates.

In the matter of unemployment, gifted men not only had a record far superior to that of California men in general, as reported in the United States Census reports for 1940, but also made a better showing than the college graduates reported by Greenleaf and by Babcock. Less than 1 percent of the gifted men were unemployed in 1940 as compared with 11 percent of employable California males, 3.1 percent of Babcock's 1930–39 college graduates, 2.1 percent of men in the same study who graduated in 1920–29 (1940 status), and 3.4 percent of Greenleaf's college graduates of 1928–35 (1936 status).

Of 617 women, 48.5 percent were employed full time, 42.0 percent were housewives without employment outside the home. Of the 299 women with full-time employment, 43.5 percent were married, 48 percent single, and the remainder separated, divorced, or widowed. Sixty-one percent of the employed women were in professional work, 34.8 percent in business occupations, chiefly secretarial and clerical, 1.3 percent in public service occupations, and 2.7 percent in miscellaneous nonprofessional work. Only 27.8 percent of the employed were teachers, chiefly in colleges or secondary schools, while 34.8 percent were office workers or in business. The third most frequent occupation was social work, with 7 percent. The most notable thing about women's occupations was the relative infrequency with which education was the chosen field.

The occupational classification of the gifted men according to the Minnesota Occupational Scale has been compared with that of the fathers of the gifted (both sexes) on the same scale. The occupational status of the fathers was found to be very superior compared to the generality, but less superior than that of the gifted men. The incidence of professional occupations among gifted men is about eight times that for the generality; for fathers of gifted subjects it is about six times that of the generality.

The men in the occupational groups of the Minnesota scale have been compared on childhood Binet IQ and on the 1940 Concept Mastery score. Group I ranked first in IQ, Group II second, and Group III third. Although these differences were not great in absolute score, they were statistically reliable. The occupations below Group III averaged about 6.5 points lower in IQ than Group I, and 5.9 points lower than Group II. The differences in Concept Mastery according to occupational classification showed the same trend. When professions were compared on mean Concept Mastery score, college and university teachers ranked first and other leading professions in the following order: junior college teachers, author-journalists, physicians, lawyers, chemists, high-school teachers, and engineers.

Women's occupational status was not significantly related to childhood IQ. There was more relationship between Concept Mastery score and occupational status, the women in the higher professions and college teaching being markedly superior. Other professions, such as social work, librarianship, nursing, writing, *et cetera,* were second; teaching below the college level, third; and office workers and housewives lowest on this test.

Earned income of the gifted group was higher than that reported for the generality of college graduates of corresponding age, whose earnings, in turn, were considerably greater than those of unselected men and women. In 1940 the median earned annual income of the gifted men under thirty years of age was $2,177; of those thirty to thirty-nine it was $2,814. Babcock reports medians of $1,690 and $2,590 for the college men of corresponding ages investigated by him. The gifted women under thirty years earned a median annual income of $1,493 and those thirty to thirty-nine a median of $2,021 as compared with medians of $1,380 and $1,610, respectively, reported by Babcock for college women of the same age. The data from Greenleaf substantiate the evidence for higher earnings by the gifted subjects than by college graduates in general.

Men in occupational Group II (semiprofessional and higher business) had the largest earnings, the professions came next, and the clerical, sales, retail-business and skilled-trade occupations ranked third. Among the professions, the highest median incomes were earned by physicians, and the next in order were lawyers and engineers (both with a median of $3,012 per year), author-journalists, chemists, and university teachers.

Income increased with age within the limits of our group, but the rise is more marked for men than for women.

Although the gifted group as a whole was superior in earning power to college graduates in general, income was also related to amount of education within the group. The 70 percent of men who were college graduates had a median income of $216 per month as compared with $170 per month for the 30 percent who were not college graduates. For the women graduating from college, the median salary per month was $154; for the nongraduates it was $108.

By 1945 there had occurred a marked improvement both in occupational status as rated by the Minnesota scale and in earned income. The median earned income of men for 1944 was $4,713, or 98.6 percent above that of 1940. In the same period the median for women increased by 52.4 percent. The proportion of gifted men with 1944 income of $7,500 or over was about eight times as great as the proportion of American families at that income level in 1946.

CHAPTER XV

VOCATIONAL INTEREST TESTS

One of the most valuable psychometric techniques thus far devised is Strong's test of occupational interests.[59] The test is especially useful in vocational counseling of college students, and it is also helpful in dealing with problems of occupational adjustment among older persons. The scores it yields tell us to what extent a given person's interests, attitudes, likes, and dislikes resemble or differ from those that characterize persons who are successful in given occupations. Retests of the same subjects over a ten-year period have shown that interests of the kind measured by the test are relatively permanent, and that the scores yielded for various occupations have a fairly high degree of reliability. Since the test measures factors which are largely independent of intelligence, it was hoped that it would throw light on the vocational success or failure of our gifted subjects.

The test was given in 1940 to 627 men and 200 women. It was given only to those women who expressed a desire to take it. Apart from the fact that not many of our women were interested in occupational careers, the test is less satisfactory for women than for men. For one thing, it is much more difficult to secure valid norms for women because the woman's choice of an occupation is so likely to be determined by other factors than her interest patterns. Our summary of occupational interest scores will accordingly be limited to those for men.

As a measure of economy we had the Strong blanks scored for only 26 items, including, besides occupational level and masculinity-femininity, the following 24 occupations:

Artist	Mathematics-science teacher
Psychologist	Personnel
Architect	Y.M.C.A. general secretary
Physician	Social science teacher
Engineer	City school superintendent
Chemist	Minister
Production manager	Musician

Certified public accountant	Sales manager
Accountant	Life insurance salesman
Office worker	Lawyer
Purchasing agent	Author-journalist
Banker	President of manufacturing concern

The decision not to score the test for all the occupations for which norms were available was unfortunate in view of the fact that only about half of the subjects who took the test were in the 24 occupations scored.

Scores in Own Occupation

Strong has furnished abundant evidence of the relationship between occupational success and a subject's interest score in his own occupation. Although the predictive value of the score differs from occupation to occupation, in a majority of cases a score below B+ is relatively unfavorable to success. It will, therefore, be interesting to see what proportion of gifted men fall within the "success area."

Of 360 men who were scored in their own occupations, 64.7 percent rated A, 13.6 percent B+, 11.6 percent B, and only 10.1 percent below B. As shown in Table 51 the proportion of high interest ratings was greatest in the upper census groups.

TABLE 51

Distribution of Interest Ratings in Own Occupation by Census Groups

	Census Groups					
	Group I		Group II		Group III or Lower	
Interest rating	N	Percent	N	Percent	N	Percent
A	155	72.1	46	62.2	32	45.1
B+	20	9.3	13	17.6	16	22.5
B	25	11.6	10	13.5	7	9.8
Below B	15	6.9	5	6.8	16	22.5
A and B+	175	81.4	59	79.8	48	67.6

The drop in A ratings is very marked below Census Group I. When we combine A and B+ ratings the drop is found only in Census Group III or lower. The B ratings remain fairly level, but ratings below B are nearly three and a half times as frequent in Census Group III or below as in Census Groups I or II.

We have broken down Census Group I for the vocations in which our men numbered 20 or more. This gave six professional groups in which the proportion of A and B+ ratings combined was as follows:

	N	Percentage A or B+
Chemists	23	100.0
Author-journalists	21	95.2
Engineers	44	93.2
Teachers	20	80.0
Physicians	35	74.3
Lawyers	53	66.0

The proportions of high ratings for chemists, author-journalists, and engineers were in marked contrast to those for teachers, physicians, and lawyers. Only two-thirds of the lawyers, three-fourths of the physicians, and four-fifths of the teachers received a rating of A or B+ in their own professions. The relatively low proportion of high ratings made by these three groups is not caused by lower reliability of the scales for their respective professions. Conceivably it could be due either to the presence of an excessive number of vocational misfits or to less marked channelization of interest patterns among men who become lawyers, doctors, or teachers. Both of these factors may be involved, but the latter explanation seems to be the more probable.

When ratings "in own occupation" were broken down by age, the proportion of A and B+ scores was found to remain practically constant for age groups 25 or below, 26–28, 29–31, 32–34, and 35–39. No difference even approached reliability. Nor was there a very significant difference between college graduates and nongraduates in the proportion of high ratings in their own occupations. For 272 graduates the proportion of A and B+ ratings was 77.8 percent; for 88 nongraduates it was 80.7 percent.

Mean Number of High Ratings per Subject

Table 52 summarizes the data on the mean number of occupations (among the 24 occupations scored) in which the individual subjects obtained a rating of A or B+. The material was broken down for Census Groups I, II, III, IV to VI, and for a student group. It will be seen that the mean number of high ratings in both Census Groups I and II was about one greater than in Groups III and IV or lower. The mean for students was close to that of Census Groups I and II. The drop from Groups I and II to Group III or lower is statistically significant, the critical ratio of the difference between Group I and Group III being 3.8.

TABLE 52

NUMBER OF COMBINED A AND B+ INTEREST RATINGS BY OCCUPATIONAL STATUS

	N	Mean	S.D.
Census Group I	274	6.34	2.22
Census Group II	145	6.20	2.13
Census Group III	121	5.38	2.33
Census Groups IV–VI	44	5.14	2.16
Students	31	6.29	2.08
Above groups combined	615	6.03	2.25

For men in those professional vocations which include 20 or more of our gifted subjects, we find the following mean numbers of A and B+ scores combined:

	N	Mean	S.D.
Teachers	68	6.94	2.00
Author-journalists	21	6.76	2.31
Chemists	23	6.52	1.91
Physicians	35	6.37	2.37
Lawyers	53	5.98	2.51
Engineers	45	5.78	1.56

The critical ratio of the drop in mean from teachers to lawyers is 2.3; from teachers to engineers, 3.4.

The mean number of high ratings remained almost constant from age to age. The lowest mean for any age was 5.9; the highest, 6.1. The mean does vary, however, with the amount of education. For 426 who had graduated from college it was 6.3; for 181 nongraduates, 5.4. The latter difference is highly reliable (CR = 4.2). It is not easy to interpret this relationship of high scores to the amount of education, especially as no difference was found between graduates and nongraduates in the proportion rating high *in their own occupations*.

We have compared the monthly earned incomes of 38 men, who received from 0 to 2 ratings of A or B+, with the incomes of 24 men who received 10 or more such ratings. The respective means were $242.60 and $271.33.

OCCUPATIONAL INTEREST LEVEL

The score on occupational interest level (OL) is a measure of the extent to which one's interests diverge from those of the typical unskilled laborer. It is an index of how aristocratic one's interests are.

Strong has reported that in a given occupation it usually tends to be higher for men whose work is managerial in character, and he quotes[59]* with approval Darley's definition of occupational level as "a quantitative statement of the eventual adult 'level of aspiration,' representing the degree to which the individual's total background has prepared him to seek the prestige and discharge the social responsibilities growing out of high income, professional status, recognition, or leadership in the community. . . . ."

Occupational level scores were available for 627 gifted men, who gave a mean standard score of 56.9, with S.D. of 6.8. The mean did not vary significantly with age, and was only slightly higher for college graduates (57.8) than for nongraduates (55.3). It was expected that the interest level score would be related to occupational status, and this was found to be the case. The mean for Census Groups I and II was 58.2; for Groups III and below, 54.2.

Strong reports a mean OL score of 61.7 for professional groups which is 3.8 points above the mean of our gifted men in the professions. His data show a mean of about 45 for semiskilled and unskilled laborers, but the overlap is great between any two occupations compared—even between professional and semiskilled occupations. He finds, however, that a score as low as 40 is usually indicative of less than skilled-trade level. Of 627 gifted men, only 7 (1.1 percent) had OL scores below 40, and only 20 (3.2 percent) had scores below 45. Below score 50 were 81, or 13 percent. A score of 60 or higher was made by 234, or 37 percent.

Masculinity-Femininity of Interests

The Strong M-F score is not to be confused with the M-F score based on the test devised by Terman and Miles.[66] The two tests correlate in fact only to the extent of about .50 for members of a given sex. Strong's M-F score measures the extent to which one's attitudes, likes, and dislikes, as disclosed by his occupational interest test, diverge from the average for the generality of the same sex. Strong's data indicate that the score has a fairly high reliability and that it is not greatly influenced by age between the late teens and middle life.

The mean M-F standard score of our 627 gifted men was 46.9. For the different age groups the means were all in the narrow range between 45.5 and 49.3. The mean for college graduates was 46.1;

* See page 204 of the reference.

for nongraduates, 48.4. The mean M-F scores were as follows for the subgroups in Census Group I which included 20 or more subjects:

	M-F Scores Mean		M-F Scores Mean
Engineers	55.7	College teachers	43.3
Chemists	52.5	Teachers below college level	41.7
Physicians	45.3		
Lawyers	43.7	Author-journalists	36.5

Strong reports a mean M-F score of 47.7 for a miscellaneous population of adult men, almost exactly the same as that for our gifted men, and a mean of 49.5 for college students. His data show a mean decrease of 4.6 points from age sixteen to thirty-seven, whereas for our gifted men there is a slight increase from the age group below twenty-five to the age group thirty-five to thirty-nine. Strong reports the following mean M-F scores for certain occupations: engineers, 61.9; chemists, 57.1; physicists, 55.7; psychologists, 47.9; lawyers, 47.0; physicians, 46.4; city school superintendents, 44.6; musicians, 40.6; ministers, 35.1; artists, 33.0; author-journalists, 31.8. These means agree fairly closely with the means of gifted subjects in the professional subgroups. Both on the Strong test and the Terman-Miles test, the mean M-F score is especially low for male musicians, artists, ministers, and author-journalists.

Of our 627 gifted men, 37, or about 6 percent, tested below 30; and 86, or 13.7 percent, tested below 35. The masculinity scores of men in our group who are known to be homosexuals tend to run low, while, for the few women who are known to have had a record of homosexuality, they tend to run high. However, it would be a grave error to assume that any M-F score approaching the mean of the opposite sex justifies in itself a diagnosis of homosexuality. One may be a fairly pronounced invert in sex temperament without being at all a sex invert in the usual sense. In this connection it is interesting to note that Strong finds his M-F scores to be negatively correlated with occupational level ($r = -.41$). In other words, the farther one's interests are from those of unskilled laborers, the lower the M-F score is likely to be.

Value of the Strong Test

Our use of the Strong test with gifted subjects has provided considerable evidence, both direct and indirect, of its value as a tool in vocational counseling. As we have shown in chapter xxiii (pp. 311 ff.), scores of B— or lower on the occupation in which the subject is engaged are nearly five times as numerous among the least successful men as among the most successful. The most successful also differ from the least successful in the greater number of occupations on which high interest scores are obtained, the average number being twice as great for the former as for the latter. Men who drift from job to job (vocational floaters) in many cases have few if any high scores on the Strong test. A good many who, in 1940, scored low on the occupation they were following, have since changed to an occupation in which they scored high, and almost every such change has led to greater success. Some of these were in the process of shifting their occupation at the time the test was taken. One of them was a chemist with a low score in chemistry and high scores in occupations having to do with human relationships; he had already entered a graduate school of business and has since made a brilliant record in the field of labor relations. Another was an engineer in a leading airplane factory who was beginning to find himself much more interested in management than in engineering; his score of C— in engineering and his high score in business management confirmed the wisdom of the shift he had begun to make. The situation was analogous in the case of a rather unsuccessful insurance salesman who was considering a shift to advertising. The scores of a college professor of music were particularly interesting: C for musician and A's for lawyer, psychologist, and author-journalist. This man, after teaching music for six years in college, had already decided that he was vocationally misplaced, for, although interested in musical theory and musicology, he was clearly not primarily a musician. He had considered changing to law and would have done so but for his age (thirty-four years). Instead, he accepted a graduate fellowship which would permit him to take his Doctor of Philosophy degree in musical history and theory. The high score in psychology was confirmed by his long-time interest in experimental musicology, and his high score for author-journalist by the fact that he has just been awarded the Bowdoin Prize in literature at Harvard.

Summary

The Strong Vocational Interest Test, revised edition, was given in 1940 to 627 gifted men and 200 gifted women. We have statisticized the scores made by the men on 24 occupations, on occupational level and on masculinity-femininity.

Of the scores on the occupation in which the men were engaged, 64.7 percent were A, 13.6 percent were B+, 11.6 percent were B, and only 10.1 percent were below B. From these figures it appears that not over 10 or 20 percent of the gifted men are following a vocation which is markedly out of line with their interest patterns. However, the proportion of low ratings in own vocation is nearly five times as great among the vocationally least successful as among the most successful.

The data were sorted according to number of occupations (out of the 24 occupations scored) in which a rating of A or B+ was made. The mean number of A or B+ scores per man dropped from 6.34 for those in Census Group I to 5.14 for those below Census Group III. For men in the professions, the mean was highest for teachers and author-journalists, somewhat lower for chemists and physicians, and lowest of all for lawyers and engineers. It appears that in this group of subjects the interest patterns of lawyers and engineers are definitely more specialized than those of teachers and author-journalists. The mean number of high ratings per man was unrelated to age and only moderately related to income; however, it was reliably higher for college graduates than for nongraduates.

The mean score on occupational interest level was, as would be expected, higher for men in Census Groups I and II than for those in Census Group III or below, but the difference was not great. For only a very small proportion of the group was it as low as Strong's norms for men in the skilled or semiskilled occupations.

The mean masculinity score of our men on the Strong test was almost exactly the same as that reported by Strong for a miscellaneous population of adult males. The mean was only slightly related to age or to amount of education. Among gifted men in the professions, the mean masculinity score was highest for engineers and chemists. Below these, in order of decreasing score, were physicians, lawyers, college teachers, teachers below college level, and author-journalists. The artists and musicians also averaged low in M-F score.

Our results show that the Strong test is an extremely valuable aid in the educational and vocational guidance of gifted subjects. Few men are very successful who score low on the occupation in which they are engaged.

CHAPTER XVI

AVOCATIONAL AND OTHER INTERESTS

Avocational interests are a valuable index of the extent to which an individual has developed a well-rounded personality. Historical geniuses afford numerous examples of the one-track mind that results from the lack of such interests, but among them are still more numerous examples of the breadth of interests and richness of personality that a one-track mind can never achieve. One thinks in this connection of such geniuses as da Vinci, Copernicus, Benjamin Franklin, and Thomas Jefferson.

All who have studied gifted children agree that the vast majority of them are characterized by their spontaneous interests in many fields. Only rarely does one concentrate all his attention upon a single line of mental activity. This does sometimes happen in the case of lightning calculators, chess players, or musicians, but the interests of the typical gifted child are usually many sided. It is possible that school life may occasionally starve out some of the gifted child's spontaneous enthusiasm for things in general, or it may be that maturation itself tends to produce such a result. At any rate, it seemed important to investigate the extent to which our adult gifted subjects have continued to cultivate interests not directly connected with their vocational pursuits. In the attempt to find at least a partial answer to this question we included in the General Information Blank of 1940 questions calling for information on avocational activities, reading habits, and amount of interest in twelve specific areas.*

Number and Kind of Avocational Interests

Part 25*a* of the blank asked subjects to list their avocational activities and hobbies and to indicate the degree of interest in each. The percentage of men and women listing various numbers of activities is shown in Table 53, while Table 54 gives the frequency with which the leading avocational interests were mentioned. Responses on the

* See Appendix, page 407.

number of avocational interests were received from 661 men and 535 women.

TABLE 53

NUMBER OF AVOCATIONAL INTERESTS

	Men (N=661) Percent	Women (N=535) Percent	CR
None	10.9	14.9	2.1
One	22.8	21.9	..
Two	31.9	23.2	..
Three	19.7	18.7	..
Four or more	14.7	21.3	3.0

No norms are available with which to compare the data of Table 53, but we should be greatly surprised if an unselected population would be found to have as many avocational interests as these subjects. Nearly two-thirds reported 2 or more such interests, and better than one-third reported 3 or more. Women showed greater variability than men; more women reported that they had no avocational interests, while at the other extreme a reliably greater number of them reported 4 or more. The critical ratios of these sex differences are 2.1 and 3.0, respectively.

In Table 54 the percentage figures showing the frequency with which particular avocational interests were mentioned are based on the 589 men and 455 women who reported having one or more such interests. Here again comparative norms are lacking. It is interesting, however, that sports held first place with both sexes. Omitting the "miscellaneous" group, second place went to photography for men and

TABLE 54

INCIDENCE OF SPECIFIC AVOCATIONAL INTERESTS

	Men Percent	Women Percent	CR
Sports	61.8	46.4	5.0
Photography	30.7	13.9	6.8
Music	28.4	44.4	5.4
Gardening	16.8	33.4	6.2
Reading; study	13.1	18.9	2.5
Collections	10.7	13.9	1.5
Woodworking, shop, etc.	10.5	2.6	5.4
Writing	10.0	14.9	2.3
Arts; crafts	3.4	20.4	8.4
Miscellaneous*	40.6	41.3	0.2

* The avocations classified as miscellaneous covered a wide range of interests, and the number naming any one was smaller than in any of the above categories.

to music for women; third place to music for men and to gardening for women. Interests mentioned reliably oftener by men included sports (CR = 5.0), photography (CR = 6.8), and woodworking or shop (CR = 5.4). Mentioned more often by women were arts and crafts (CR = 8.4), music (CR = 5.4), and gardening (CR = 6.2). Making collections, which was one of the leading hobbies of these subjects in childhood, had become relatively rare by 1940.

Reading Habits

Part 25*b* of the questionnaire requested information on the kinds of books preferred and called for examples of books read during the previous year. The names of magazines read "fairly regularly" were also requested. The responses covered a wide range and involved tabulations too complex to report in full. Table 55, which summarizes the data on types of books preferred, is based on statements regarding kinds liked and on illustrations given. Table 56 lists the ten magazines

TABLE 55

Kinds of Books Preferred

	Men (N=695) Percentages		Women (N=555) Percentages	
1. Literature	77.0		91.0	
Fiction, classic or current		33.7		44.2
Detective novels		15.5		13.2
Historical and social novels		13.5		11.7
Humor and satire		4.7		2.7
Poetry		3.0		8.1
Drama		2.3		4.9
Essays		2.2		4.7
Short stories		2.0		1.6
2. History (including geography, travel, biography, and current affairs)	50.7		83.4	
3. Social sciences	17.3		11.4	
4. Pure science	16.4		8.3	
5. Philosophy (including psychology)	8.4		8.5	
6. Fine arts	7.9		8.3	
7. Useful arts	6.8		2.0	
8. Religion	1.9		1.8	
9. General works (encyclopedia, museum reports, etc.)	0.9		0.2	
10. Philology	0.6		0.4	
Unclassified responses	20.4		14.0	
"All"		4.9		4.3
"Nonfiction"		5.9		6.3
"Very little reading"		4.3		0.2
"None" or none given		5.3		3.2

most frequently mentioned as read "fairly regularly." Information on these items was available for 695 men and 555 women.

Our classification of book preferences was for the most part based on the library Dewey Decimal System, the divisions of which approximate a universal system of categories. The subheadings have been retained under "literature," since the diversity of interests among the gifted subjects shows up so strikingly in this section. To the ten Dewey headings have been added four very general and, therefore, unclassified responses: "nonfiction," "all," "very little," and "none," since some subjects phrased their responses only in these terms. The subjects who gave no response at all to this item have been combined with those who indicated that no books were read by answering "none." The figures after the various headings represent the proportion of men and women expressing interest in each type of book. Since no restriction was placed on the number of preferences which might be indicated, a single individual sometimes mentioned several kinds of preferred books.

Although the rank order of the ten Dewey categories is almost identical for the two sexes, there are interesting and striking sex differences. Literature and history overshadowed all other types of reading in popularity, with 77 percent of men and 91 percent of women giving preferences classifiable under literature, and approximately 51 percent of men and 83 percent of women naming preferences in the field of history and allied subjects. Next in order of popularity, but far below, came the social sciences with 17 percent of men and 11 percent of women. Pure science ranked fourth among men with 16 percent, but was nosed into fifth place among women by philosophy (including psychology). The proportion of either sex who reported reading books in the remaining fields ranged from less than 10 percent to less than 1 percent.

Some of the subheadings under literature outnumbered in frequency of mention any one of the six categories below social science. Fiction (classic or current) was the reading preferred by 34 percent of men and 44 percent of women. Detective novels were named by 15 percent of men and 13 percent of women. Historical and social novels were mentioned by 13 percent of men and 12 percent of women.

Magazine reading covered a wide range, each sex naming a total of more than two hundred periodicals read "fairly regularly." Table 56 gives the proportion who read each of the ten most frequently mentioned nonprofessional publications, and also the proportion who stated that they read journals devoted to their own business or professional field. *Time, Reader's Digest,* and *Life* were by far the most popular magazines with both men and women. *Time* held first place with men, claiming approximately 50 percent of those reporting, and *Reader's Digest* led with women (64 percent). *Reader's Digest* was second in popularity with men (47 percent) while *Life* held second place with women (46 percent). *Life* was in third place with men, and *Time* in third place with women. The next most popular magazine with each sex was *Saturday Evening Post,* but the proportion naming it was low compared to any of the three favorites (29 percent of men and 24 percent of women).

One-third of the men and 10 percent of the women listed as read "fairly regularly" one or more business or professional journals of the field in which they were engaged. Any professional publication named outside of the respondent's particular field of work was tabulated as avocational reading.

The data we have summarized in this section indicate a reasonably wholesome situation with respect to avocational interests. Certainly there is nothing to indicate that gifted children after they have become

TABLE 56

TEN MAGAZINES MOST FREQUENTLY MENTIONED AS READ "FAIRLY REGULARLY"

Magazine	Men (N=695) Rank	Men (N=695) Percent	Women (N=555) Rank	Women (N=555) Percent
Time	1	49.5	3	42.3
Reader's Digest	2	46.8	1	64.5
Life	3	46.3	2	46.1
Saturday Evening Post	4	28.9	4	23.8
Collier's	5	20.6	7	12.4
The New Yorker	6	11.8	5	16.7
Fortune	7	8.6	..	....
Harper's	8	8.3	..	....
American	9	8.2	8	11.7
Esquire	10	6.2	..	....
Ladies Home Journal		...	6	15.1
Good Housekeeping		...	9	11.0
McCall's		...	10	9.7
Business or professional journals in own field*		33.5		9.9

* The percentage here represents the number of persons who report reading professional journals in their own professional field. The number of publications reported by each person may range from one to any number. Some report a dozen or more.

adults tend to be particularly narrow in their interests. Just as in childhood, the opposite seems to be the case. It is important to bear in mind that the reports on avocational interests and reading are both for a period of life in which leisure is likely to be at a premium. Young men are getting started in their professional and business careers in a competitive society where success demands devotion of time and energy to the job itself. That the unmarried women who are employed are probably under less pressure than men may account for the greater number of avocational pursuits and greater amount of reading they report. The women who are married and, in addition to their duties as housewives, are employed outside the home, can have very little leisure. This is also true of the mothers of young children.

SELF-RATINGS IN TWELVE SPECIFIC INTERESTS

Part of item 25 in the General Information Blank called for self-ratings of interest in 12 specific fields: travel, outdoor sports, religion, mechanics, social life, literature, music, art, science, politics, domestic arts, and pets. The ratings were on a 5-point scale, 1 being defined as "very much," 3 as "average," and 5 as "none." A cross-on-line technique was used. Such ratings were made by 693 men and 554 women. Table 57 gives the mean ratings and the standard deviations separately for the sexes.

Mean interest in the twelve fields combined was slightly but not reliably higher for women. The five fields rated highest by men were travel, science, sports, literature, and music; the fields preferred by

TABLE 57

SELF-RATING OF INTEREST IN TWELVE SPECIFIC FIELDS

	Men (N=693)		Women (N=554)		
	Mean	S.D.	Mean	S.D.	CR
Travel	2.1	1.0	2.0	1.0	2.9
Outdoor sports	2.5	1.0	2.9	1.1	5.7
Religion	3.7	1.2	3.5	1.1	3.2
Mechanics	2.9	1.2	4.1	1.0	18.7
Social life	2.9	0.9	2.7	0.8	3.1
Literature	2.5	1.0	1.9	0.7	11.8
Music	2.5	1.1	2.1	1.0	7.0
Art	3.1	1.1	2.6	1.0	8.1
Science	2.3	1.1	2.9	1.0	10.3
Politics	2.6	1.1	2.9	1.0	5.1
Domestic arts	3.6	1.0	2.6	1.1	16.2
Pets	3.2	1.1	2.9	1.2	4.6
Average of twelve traits	2.8	0.9	2.8	0.8	1.3

women were literature, travel, music, art, and domestic arts. Three of the five highest were common to the sexes—literature, travel, and music. The two interests rated lowest by men were religion and domestic arts; for women, the two lowest ratings were mechanics and religion.

The extremely large sex differences in mechanics and domestic arts were to be expected; perhaps also the marked differences in literature and science. It may be surprising to some that the sex differences are no larger than they are in religion, outdoor sports, social life, politics, and pets. It is possible that there may have been some tendency for subjects to rate themselves in relation to a hypothetical average *for their own sex,* thus spuriously reducing the apparent amount of sex difference, but the data obtained provide no check on this possibility.

Perhaps most readers would agree that in general the fields in which mean ratings were high are desirable interests. The converse can hardly be maintained; religion, for example, was rated low in interest by both sexes, and politics and science were rated fairly low by women.

Regarding religion, a special comment is necessary. Subjects often qualified their ratings on this field by specifying that they had an objective interest in religions but that they were not religious. Others stated that they were religious in the spiritual sense but that they were not interested in formal religions. This field of interest should have been better defined in the rating scheme.

Special Abilities as Related to Vocations and Avocations

In connection with a study of the avocations of the gifted subjects, a glance at the special abilities shown by members of the group is of interest. Talent along such extracurricular lines as art, music, dramatics, and writing were reported for many of the subjects in their school days. Such special ability has often been the determiner of the individual's vocation, but in a large number of subjects these talents have found their expressions in avocational pursuits. There are some 40 professional writers (including journalists), 20 or 25 workers in dramatic arts, 18 or 20 professional musicians and 10 or 12 professional artists. Some of these have combined two vocations as, for example, the large proportion of professional musicians and artists who are full-time teachers of music or art.

We are particularly interested here in those who have pursued their specialized gifts only as avocations. Considerable recognition has been won by some of these amateurs in the arts. Special ability in music has been noted frequently, and this talent more often than others has been turned to use as a means of livelihood while preparing for another profession. One brilliant young scientist began concert orchestra work at the age of fourteen, and later became a conductor of a civic orchestra. His musical gifts enabled him to finance several years of graduate study, and now provide a satisfying avocational outlet. Another man who was taking a premedical course at the university and earning his expenses by playing in a dance orchestra, found this side line so much to his liking and so lucrative that he gave up college and became a professional musician. He has been very successful as a composer, arranger, and conductor of music.

Among those enjoying success in an avocational field are 4 school teachers—2 men and 2 women. All 4 have had paintings shown at important exhibits and have received good notices. Several who are interested in dramatics have written plays that have been produced by local theater groups; others with musical ability have had songs published or have written the musical score for operatic or theatrical productions. Still others with artistic talent have had cartoons and illustrations accepted for publication.

Writing, however, has become the most frequent outlet for special abilities in the adult years. Between 300 and 400 subjects have had material published. Only 26 men and 15 women are professional writers; for all the others literary expression is chiefly an avocational activity. Some of these would like, and hope someday, to devote all their time to writing. Besides more than a thousand professional papers, mostly on scientific and technical research, many articles have been published by members of the group on social problems, economics, political science, law, art, music, *et cetera.* Articles, critiques, essays, short stories, and poems published in magazines and literary journals number around 270 for men and 40 to 50 for women. Several subjects have edited or have written for publications of limited circulation such as union papers, bulletins for employee or employer groups, trade journals, fraternity publications, religious periodicals, the Junior League magazine, *et cetera.*

One of the most versatile subjects is a woman who by thirty has had considerable success as a professional actress in major theatrical productions, is a professional dancer, and has done the illustrations for textbooks in anatomy and physiology. Her achievements also include championship ice skating, and two unpublished novels that have received encouraging comment. One of our most versatile men is a young psychiatrist who is also well known as a psychologist, and whose avocational interests have brought him national recognition among such diverse groups as semanticists and magicians. He writes with uncommon skill both technical monographs and popular science.

Of particular interest in the discussion of special abilities are the later careers of the small group selected for intensive study because of marked literary talent shown in childhood. The literary juvenilia of this group are reported at length in Volume III of this series.[7] Of the 7 subjects (all girls) who were included in the final selection of children as showing the greatest literary promise, only one has achieved distinction as a writer. She has published two volumes of poetry and many poems, critiques, and essays in literary magazines. As for the others, one has written a great deal of advertising copy in connection with her work for an advertising agency and, as a leisure-time activity, has written several plays which have been produced by a community theater group, and many poems (not published). At present she is at work on a novel. One is a scientist who has published some 15 scientific papers. Another whose interest in writing was superseded by interest in art has won considerable reputation as a sculptor. One, employed as a press agent, has had several articles and one short story published and devotes her free time to a novel. Two are housewives who still write for their own amusement but have published little.

Summary

Nearly two-thirds of the subjects reported active interest in two or more avocational pursuits, and more than one-third reported three or more. Women showed greater variability than men, more of them stating that they engaged in no avocational activities, and also more reporting several. The absence of any norms precludes a comparison with the generality in this matter, but the data indicated a considerable breadth and diversity of interests.

Among avocational interests, sports held first place for both men and women. Photography was second in popularity with men and music second with women. Music rated third with men and gardening third with women.

Self-ratings on amount of interest in 12 specific fields were highest for men in travel and science, and for women in travel and literature. Rated lowest by men were religion and domestic arts; by women, mechanics and religion.

Data presented in another chapter* indicate that the men who were most successful vocationally tended to have greater interest in most of these 12 fields than the men who were least successful. This was especially true of politics, literature, and social life, and to a lesser degree of travel, science, and music.

Two aspects of reading habits were investigated: the kinds of books preferred, and the names of magazines read "fairly regularly." Book preferences were classified under the ten headings of the standard library Dewey Decimal System. The general classification of literature was in first place, 77 percent of men and 91 percent of women mentioning books in this category. A breakdown of the literature category into ten subheadings showed fiction to be by far the most popular reading in this classification. History (defined to include geography, travel, biography, and current affairs) was reported by 51 percent of men and 83 percent of women. Least interest for both men and women was in religion, reference works, and philology.

More than two hundred magazines were listed by the members of each sex as among those which were read "fairly regularly." *Time, Reader's Digest,* and *Life,* in the order given, were the three most popular with men; *Reader's Digest, Life,* and *Time* ranked first, second, and third, respectively, in women's interest.

Many of the subjects have displayed special abilities of various kinds which sometimes have given direction to their vocational careers, but which more often have found an outlet in avocational pursuits. Several members of the group have shown remarkable versatility in their interests and abilities.

In appraising the avocational interests of our group, it is necessary to take account of the fact that the data here summarized were secured when most of the subjects were between the ages of twenty-five and thirty-five, a period in life when men were usually preoccupied with getting established in a business or profession, and when many of the women were absorbed in household duties and the care of young children.

* Chapter xxiii.

CHAPTER XVII

POLITICAL AND SOCIAL ATTITUDES

The General Information Blank of 1940 called for three kinds of data that will here be summarized: (1) a statement of political preferences, (2) information about voting habits, and (3) a self-rating on radicalism-conservatism.*

Political Preferences

Information on political preferences was secured from 568 men and 465 women. Table 58 summarizes the responses in the terms used by the subjects to characterize their preferences. Noteworthy facts include the following:

Among the 1,033 subjects who responded to this item, we find, according to their own testimony, only one Communist. Combining those who labeled themselves as either "radical" or "socialist," we have in this composite category 4.6 percent of men and 5.4 percent of women, or about 1 in 20 of the entire group.

In both sexes and to about the same degree, "Republicans"

TABLE 58

Political Preferences of the Gifted Subjects (1940)

Preference	Men		Women	
	N	Percent	N	Percent
None or undetermined	41	7.2	45	9.7
"Independent"	16	2.8	10	2.2
"Communist"	1	0.2	0	0.0
"Radical"	6	1.1	5	1.1
"Socialist"	20	3.5	20	4.3
"Liberal"	74	13.0	58	12.5
"New Deal"	20	3.5	8	1.7
"Democrat"	133	23.4	126	27.1
"Republican"	221	38.9	176	37.9
"Conservative"	36	6.3	17	3.7
Total N	568		465	

* See Appendix, page 408.

reliably outnumbered "Democrats." If we combine "liberal," "New Deal," and "Democrat" into a single category, this will include 40.0 percent of men and 41.3 percent of women. When we similarly combine "Republican" and "conservative," the category includes 45.2 percent of men and 41.6 percent of women. These combinations, if we can assume that they are legitimate, bring about a more even division between the two main political groups. In this connection it should be noted that in California, where a majority of the subjects reside, Republicans normally outnumber Democrats.

The sex differences are small and statistically insignificant. This has also been found true of the general population, where the difference between the sexes in political alignment is rarely greater than 2 percent.

Voting Habits

The data on voting habits include information from 646 men and 508 women, or 1,154 subjects in all. The results are summarized in Table 59.

To the extent that voting is evidence of good citizenship, the record of these subjects is very superior. More than 81 percent of both sexes reported that they were accustomed to vote at all elections, and an additional 10 percent reported that they vote at least in national elections. As compared with 91 percent of the gifted group who customarily vote in national elections, Connelly and Field[17] report that only 62 percent of eligible voters in the country as a whole voted in the 1940 national election. In California the proportion was somewhat larger, with 70 percent of the electorate voting, but this too is considerably below the percentage for our subjects. At the other extreme, 9.0 percent of gifted men and 7.5 percent of gifted women said

TABLE 59

Voting Habits of Gifted Subjects

	Men		Women	
	N	Percent	N	Percent
At all elections	527	81.6	414	81.5
On national and state issues	14	2.2	6	1.2
On national issues only	46	7.1	49	9.7
On state issues only	1	0.2	1	0.2
Occasionally	21	3.3	20	3.9
Not at all	37	5.7	18	3.5
N for percentages	646		508	

that they voted only occasionally or not at all. It is unfortunate, to say the least, that even so small a minority of intellectually superior persons should fail to participate regularly in this most essential procedure of democratic government.

Sex differences were as conspicuously absent in voting habits as they were in political preferences. It is particularly interesting that gifted women equal gifted men in their voting record, whereas in the country as a whole Connelly and Field estimate that only 40 to 45 percent of the total vote is ordinarily cast by women.

Self-Ratings on Radicalism-Conservatism

The self-rating on radicalism-conservatism (hereinafter designated r-c) utilized a cross-on-line technique in which the rating bar represented a continuum ranging from "extremely radical" at one end to "very conservative" at the other. The responses were evaluated on a nine-point scale. The extreme left of the horizontal bar, defined as "extremely radical," was coded 1; "tend to be radical" was coded 3; "average," 5; "tend to be conservative," 7; and "very conservative," at the extreme right, was coded 9. The intervening even numbers, 2, 4, 6, and 8, represented the midvalues between the adjacent categories. The directions were simple: "Rate yourself on the following scale as regards your political and social viewpoint." Only very occasionally did a subject complain of ambiguity in the question, though an occasional respondent checked himself at one level on political and at another on social viewpoint. For all but a very few

TABLE 60

Distribution of Self-Ratings on Radicalism-Conservatism

	Men		Women	
	N	Percent	N	Percent
1. Extremely radical	11	1.65	4	.74
2.	21	3.15	15	2.76
3. Tend to be radical	120	17.99	83	15.29
4.	116	17.39	83	15.29
5. Average	141	21.14	168	30.94
6.	59	8.85	55	10.13
7. Tend to be conservative	155	23.24	109	20.07
8.	23	3.45	17	3.13
9. Very conservative	21	3.15	9	1.66
N	667		543	
Mean rating	5.09		5.09	
S.D.	1.81		1.61	

subjects the ratings presumably represented a composite of their general attitude on political and social issues based, of courses, on their concept of the term "political and social viewpoint" and of what constitutes the "average" in this regard.

The distributions, means, and standard deviations of r-c ratings from 667 men and 543 women, a total of 1,210 subjects, are given in Table 60.

Although the mean was exactly the same for men and women, the dispersion was reliably greater for men (CR = 3.0). When the ratings are thrown into three categories by combining (*a*) 1, 2, and 3; (*b*) 4, 5, and 6; and (*c*) 7, 8, and 9, we get the following figures:

	Men Percent	Women Percent
a) On the radical side (1, 2, 3)	22.8	18.8
b) Average or near-average (4, 5, 6)	47.4	56.4
c) On the conservative side (7, 8, 9)	29.8	24.9

For the sexes combined we find slightly more than half who rated themselves as average or near-average, more than a quarter who rated themselves on the conservative side, and not much more than a fifth who rated themselves on the radical side. There are no comparative norms, but it appears that these intellectually superior subjects are inclined to steer a middle course between radicalism and conservatism. Probably some readers will think it regrettable that the politically conservative element in the group is as large as it is.

Some Correlates of Radicalism-Conservatism

Occupational status. In the case of men we have analyzed the r-c data according to occupational classification. The mean ratings were as follows for census groups of the Minnesota Occupational Scale:*

	Group I (N=281)	Group II (N=158)	Groups III–VI (N=175)
Mean rating	4.98	5.23	5.30
S.D.	1.8	1.9	1.8

CR: I vs. II = 1.4

The professional group was slightly less conservative than the other groups. Especially surprising is the fact that men in the trades (skilled and semiskilled) small business, clerical and saleswork, as well as

* See chapter xiv for description of this scale.

those in Group IV, averaged about the same as men in the higher business occupations.

A comparison of the professions within Group I is also interesting. The mean self-ratings for the six professional groups of men which numbered 20 or more were as follows:

	N	Mean	S.D.
Author-journalists	23	3.7	1.6
Teachers	64	4.6	1.7
Chemists	24	5.2	1.4
Doctors	37	5.3	1.6
Engineers	42	5.4	1.9
Lawyers	61	5.5	1.8

Author-journalists were by far the most radical of the professional groups. Chemists, doctors, engineers, and lawyers were the most conservative, while teachers held an intermediate position slightly to left of center.*

Earned income. As in the case of occupational status, the comparison here was limited to men. The means of the r-c ratings for the various income groups were as follows:

	Earned Income per Month			
	$150 or less (N=117)	$151–250 (N=254)	$251–350 (N=101)	Above $350 (N=70)
Mean r-c rating	4.99	5.12	4.91	5.79
S.D.	1.89	1.82	1.68	1.76

The three lower income groups did not differ reliably from each other, but the mean of these three groups combined was 5.04 as compared with 5.79 for the group earning more than $350 per month. The difference is quite reliable (CR = 3.3). That is, incomes above $350 are definitely associated with conservatism as measured by our rating scale.

Amount of education. The mean of the r-c ratings was computed separately for college graduates and nongraduates. The results were as follows:

	MEN		WOMEN	
	Graduates (N=461)	Nongraduates (N=187)	Graduates (N=353)	Nongraduates (N=178)
Mean	5.07	5.16	5.12	5.09
S.D.	1.80	1.85	1.61	1.61

* The average r-c rating of the 9 clergymen in our group was 4.5, which places them next to author-journalists for radicalism.

The differences between college graduates and nongraduates were unreliable and were in opposite directions for men and women. In this group, the amount of education is practically unrelated to social and political radicalism.

Nervous and mental balance. Following are the r-c means according to 1940 ratings on mental health and general adjustment. On the latter variable the subjects were divided into three classes on the basis of rather extensive information: *1,* "satisfactory"; *2,* "some maladjustment"; *3,* "serious maladjustment."

	1 Satisfactory	*2* Some Maladjustment	*3* Serious Maladjustment	CR *1* vs. *2+3*
Men	(N=531)	(N=107)	(N=23)	
Mean r-c rating	5.20	4.74	4.35	2.8
Women	(N=445)	(N=78)	(N=21)	
Mean r-c rating	5.19	4.76	4.29	2.9

The trend in the above means is significant. In both sexes the tendency toward radicalism increased appreciably with the seriousness of nervous and mental symptoms. This finding is in line with data reported by Lasswell.[39]

Social adjustment. The 1922 ratings of social adjustment, based on numerous items of information furnished by parents, teachers, and examining physicians, showed only moderate relationship with the r-c ratings in the case of women and none in the case of men. The mean for 473 women whose social adjustment was rated as "satisfactory" on the 1922 data was 5.12. The mean for 21 women rated on the 1922 data as having "some" or "serious" difficulty in social adjustment was 4.57. The difference in absolute terms is considerable, but because of the small N of 21 is not statistically reliable (CR = 1.3). Similar data on social adjustment in 1928 showed somewhat greater relationship with r-c ratings for men than for women, but again the relationship for neither sex was reliable. In the category, "satisfactory," 413 men had a mean of 5.18 on the r-c ratings, and 34 men with "some" to "serious" maladjustment had a mean of 4.62. The critical ratio of this difference is 1.5. The mean for 383 women rated "satisfactory" was 5.12, as compared with 4.95 for 20 with "some" or "serious" maladjustment. This difference is entirely unreliable.

Interest in religion, science, and politics. Of the 12 fields in which the subjects were asked in 1940 to rate themselves as to degree of interest (see chapter xvi), 3 were selected for comparison with r-c ratings. These were religion, science, and politics. In the case of men, those who rated themselves as having "more than average" or "very much" interest in religion were a little more conservative than those who professed no interest. The means were 4.95 and 4.57 respectively, and the critical ratio 1.7. However, the women with more than average interest in religion were very much more conservative than those with no interest in religion. The mean for the former was 5.49, for the latter 4.38. The difference is highly reliable (CR = 5.3).

Subjects with "very much" interest in science were compared with those rating this interest as "slight" or "none." For both sexes, those with very much scientific interest tended to be less conservative than those with slight or no scientific interest. In the former category, the mean r-c rating for men was 4.87 and for women 4.95. The mean for slight interest or none was 5.51 for men and 5.44 for women. The critical ratio of the difference between means is 2.6 for men and 2.0 for women.

Interest in politics was significantly correlated with radicalism for both men and women. Men with very much interest in politics had a mean of 4.70 on r-c ratings; those with slight or none, a mean of 5.66. The difference is reliable (CR = 3.7). The women with top rating on interest in politics had a mean of 4.09 as compared with 5.67 for those with slight or none (CR = 4.9).

It should be pointed out that none of the groups in the foregoing comparisons rated either extremely radical or extremely conservative, for in no instance did the mean deviate as much as one sigma of the distribution from the middle point of the scale designated as "average." However, the tendencies toward radicalism or toward conservatism, as the case may be, were sufficiently characteristic of each interest group to suggest genuine relationships.

R-C ratings of Jewish subjects. The literature of race prejudice is filled with allegations about the part played by Jews in radical and revolutionary movements of many kinds. The Jewish subjects who rated themselves on this trait numbered 66 men and 51 women, and the means of these have been compared with the self-ratings of 601 men and 492 women who were non-Jewish. For Jewish and non-Jewish men the respective means were 4.56 and 5.15 (the middle point of the scale being 5). The difference, with a critical ratio of 2.68, approaches reliability. The means for Jewish and non-Jewish women were 4.25 and 5.16, respectively. This difference has a critical ratio of 4.50 and is therefore highly reliable. In other words, among Jewish subjects it is chiefly the women who rate themselves significantly more radical than do non-Jewish. On the other hand, there is less tendency among Jewish than among the non-Jewish subjects to rate themselves at either extreme of the r-c scale. Only one Jewish man rated himself as "extremely radical," and one as "extremely conservative," and not a single Jewish woman rated herself at either of these extremes. Of non-Jewish subjects, 10 men and 4 women rated themselves as "extremely radical," and 20 men and 9 women as "extremely conservative." Actually, the Jewish subjects averaged no more radical than the teacher group (5 percent Jewish), and not nearly so radical as the author-journalists (less than 20 percent Jewish). Of doctors and lawyers, our two most conservative professional groups, 23 percent are Jewish.

Correlation with Binet IQ and with vocational success. As shown in chapter xxi the subjects whose Binet IQ in childhood was 170 or over tended to rate themselves slightly to the left of center on the r-c scale rather than slightly to the right as did the gifted group as a whole. The r-c mean for this selected group of highest IQ was 4.83 for men and 4.90 for women. The number of cases with IQ's above 170 is too small to warrant conclusions, but the data indicate a tendency for the brightest among our group to be more liberal in their attitudes.

Data summarized in chapter xxiii show that among men there was a tendency for the vocationally most successful to rate themselves as a little more radical than did the least successful. The respective means were 4.96 and 5.11, a difference too small to be statistically reliable. The significant fact is that the least successful were not, as some would have expected, more radical than the most successful.

Marital adjustment. There was very little difference in the mean marital happiness score of subjects at the three levels of the r-c scale. In the case of men, the "radicals" (ratings 1–3) and the "conservatives" (ratings 7–9) were almost identical in mean marital happiness score, but the "average" group (ratings 4–6) was very slightly higher in happiness score than the other two. The women showed a small but unreliable trend toward higher happiness score with increased conservatism.

Summary

Statements as to political preferences showed 45.2 percent of the men and 41.6 percent of the women to be "Republicans" or "conservatives," and 40.0 percent of the men and 41.3 percent of the women to classify themselves as "liberal," "New Deal," or "Democrat" in political alignment. There was only one professed "Communist" in the group, and only about one subject in twenty was either a "radical" or "socialist" in political belief. Sex differences were negligible.

In the proportion who vote regularly, the gifted group apparently excels the electorate in general. Ninety-one percent reported themselves as voting in national elections, as against less than 65 percent of the United States electorate who voted in the 1940 presidential election. Contrary to the pattern in the general population, women in our group vote in as large proportion as the men.

Self-ratings on radicalism-conservatism placed men and women at the same point, and almost exactly at the center of the scale in this regard. However, the dispersion was reliably greater for men.

An examination of the men's self-ratings on radicalism according to occupation showed the professional group to be the most liberal in political and social viewpoint, the average falling very slightly to the left of center. Men in the semiprofessional and managerial occupations were more conservative; farmers, retail dealers, clerks, salesmen, technicians, and those engaged in skilled or semiskilled trades were the most conservative of all. Among the professions, author-journalists were the most radical, lawyers the most conservative.

A comparison of r-c ratings with income showed those men earning above $350 per month to average reliably more conservative than those earning less than this amount.

College graduates did not differ from nongraduates in radicalism-conservatism either in mean rating or in variability.

The 1940 rating on mental health and general adjustment showed for both sexes a reliable increase in tendency toward radicalism with increase in symptoms of nervousness and mental maladjustment.

Childhood ratings on social adjustment (1922) showed only slight relationship with 1940 r-c ratings in the case of women and none in the case of men. Social adjustment ratings of 1928 showed some relationship between adult radicalism and adolescent maladjustment for men, but practically none in the case of women.

The r-c ratings were compared with self-ratings obtained at the same time (1940) on the amount of interest in religion, science, and politics. Men with more than average or very much interest in religion were slightly more conservative than those with no interest, and women with above-average interest in religion were significantly more conservative than those without religious interest. Both men and women with marked scientific interest tended to be less conservative than those with little or no interest in science. There was a marked increase in the tendency to radicalism with greater interest in politics among both men and women.

Jewish subjects on the average showed somewhat more radical tendencies than the non-Jewish, the difference being statistically significant only for women. On the other hand, there were fewer extreme scores, either radical or conservative, among the Jewish subjects than among the non-Jewish.

Subjects of IQ 170 and above rated themselves on the average slightly to the left of center, but the number of cases in this intellectual category is too small to permit conclusions.

Marital happiness as measured by our test is not appreciably related to self-rating on political and social viewpoint.

CHAPTER XVIII

MARRIAGE, DIVORCE, MARITAL SELECTION, AND OFFSPRING

By the middle of 1940, information was available on the marital history of 800 men and 624 women. Of the men, 69.5 percent had been married one or more times; of the women, 71.6 percent. These figures must be considered in relation to the age of the subjects at that time. As we shall see later, the incidence of marriage in the group increased considerably between 1940 and 1946, and further increase, may, of course, be expected. Table 61 shows the incidence of marriage to 1940.

TABLE 61

INCIDENCE OF MARRIAGE TO 1940

	N		PERCENTAGE WHO HAD MARRIED	
Age Groups	Men	Women	Men	Women
Under 20	4	6	0.0	0.0
20–24	72	66	30.5	54.7
25–29	369	311	62.3	73.0
30–34	268	212	86.2	76.9
35–39	87	29	83.8	72.4
Ages 20–39	796	618	69.8	72.3
Ages combined	800	624	69.5	71.6

The mean age at marriage (first marriage if more than one) was 25.2 for men and 23.4 for women. The medians were 24.4 years and 22.4 years for men and women respectively. The S.D. of the age distribution was 3.1 years for each sex. Men ranged in age at marriage from 18 to 36 years and women from 16 to 34 years, with 1.7 percent of men and 9.8 percent of women marrying before the age of 20.

Comparative data on the marriage rate in the general population are available from the United States Census reports.[56] The 1940 Census gives the following figures on incidence of marriage for the

United States total population, and for California population in the age range 20 to 39 years.

PERCENTAGE WHO HAVE MARRIED

Age	Total United States Population		Total California Population	
	Male %	Female %	Male %	Female %
20–24	27.8	52.8	27.3	59.5
25–29	64.0	77.2	62.8	81.9
30–34	79.3	85.3	76.9	88.6
35–39	84.7	88.8	81.9	91.2
20–39	63.0	75.1	62.2	80.2

The incidence of marriage among gifted men to 1940 was reliably above that of the generality, either in the United States as a whole or in California. However, a slightly smaller proportion of gifted women had married than of the generality of women in the United States, and a reliably smaller proportion of the gifted than of the generality of California women. Perhaps the fairest comparison is that with the California population. For the age range 20–39 the figures are as follows: gifted men, 69.8 percent as compared with 62.2 percent of all California men; gifted women, 72.3 percent as compared with 80.2 percent of all California women.

Since our group resembles the college population more than the general population in such respects as intelligence, socioeconomic status, education, and occupation, a comparison of marital status with that of college graduates is of particular interest. Babcock's *The U.S. College Graduate*[4] furnishes data for comparison with college graduates by age groups. His report is based on 10,146 cases, a cross section of all living college graduates of the United States "so distributed as to age, sex, geography and other factors as to be faithfully representative of the whole body." Table 62 shows the incidence of marriage in two age ranges (below 30, and 30 to 39) for (1) Babcock's college graduates, (2) college graduates in the gifted group, and (3) the total gifted group.

It will be seen from the table that the incidence of marriage for Babcock's college graduates is far below that for the total gifted group or for the gifted college graduates. For example, the percentage of women college graduates in the gifted group below the age of 30 who have married is more than twice that for Babcock's generality of women graduates; for women in the age range 30 to 39, the dif-

TABLE 62

INCIDENCE OF MARRIAGE FOR BABCOCK'S COLLEGE GRADUATES, GIFTED COLLEGE GRADUATES, AND TOTAL GIFTED GROUP

	Those who are, or have been, married			
	Under 30 Years		30–39 Years	
	Men %	Women %	Men %	Women %
1. Babcock's college graduates	35.0	33.6	77.4	59.9
2. Gifted college graduates	58.5	68.8	84.3	71.5
3. Total gifted group	56.6	68.7	85.6	76.3

ference is much less marked but is statistically quite reliable. In the case of male college graduates, the proportion below the age of 30 who have married is nearly 1.7 times as high for the gifted as for Babcock's group, but the difference is relatively small for the age group 30 to 39. The incidence of marriage in the total gifted group differs little from the incidence for the gifted college graduates; however, in the case of women aged 30 to 39, the incidence is somewhat lower for the gifted college graduates than for the total of the gifted women.

Keys, in his monograph, *The Underage Student in High School and College,*[35] points out the negative relationship between marriage and higher education for college women and cites several studies as evidence. Regarding University of California women he says: "Of nine thousand alumnae reached in compiling the 1934 directory, only one in ten was married before the age of 25 and even by age 35 barely three-fourths were married." The accelerated group studied by Keys, however, presents a picture more closely resembling our own data, 59 percent of his accelerated girls having been married by the age of 25.

INCIDENCE OF MARRIAGE TO 1946

Our information on marriages between 1940 and the end of 1945 is not complete, but it is estimated that the known marriages constitute at least 93 percent of all that occurred in this five-year period. If we count only known marriages, the proportion of men who were or had been married increased from 69.5 percent in 1940 to 84.4 percent in 1945, and the proportion of women from 71.6 percent to 84.2 percent. At the end of 1945 the average age of the gifted group was approximately 35 years and the age range was from 20 to 44 years. As we have seen earlier in this chapter, the marriage rate of our group to 1940 was somewhat greater for men than for the generality of men either in the United States as a whole or in California, and somewhat less in the case of women. A comparison of the marital status of our group as of 1945, ranging in age from 20 to 44, with the generality in that age range as reported in the 1940 Census gives the following figures:

	1940 CENSUS Total United States Population Ages 20–44		1940 CENSUS California Population Ages 20–44		1945 FOLLOW-UP Gifted Subjects Ages 20–44	
	Men	Women	Men	Women	Men	Women
Percentage who have married	66.7	77.7	66.5	83.6	84.4	84.2

That is, by 1945 the proportion of gifted women who had married was reliably higher than that for the generality of women in the United States, and almost exactly the same as for the generality of California women, whereas the proportion of gifted men who had married by that date was about one-fourth higher than for the generality of men either in the United States as a whole or in California.

Divorce and Separation

By 1940, of the 556 men who had married, 51 had been divorced once and 6 had been divorced more than once, making 57 in all, or 10.25 percent. Five others were separated from their wives at the time of the 1940 follow-up. The proportion with a history of divorce or separation was 11.15 percent of the men who had married. Corresponding figures for 447 women were as follows: Divorced once, 48; divorced more than once, 5; total number of divorced, 53, or 11.85 percent. Adding 4 cases of separation brings the proportion of women with history of divorce or separation to 12.75 percent.

Our information on divorce and separation after 1940 is incomplete, but it is estimated that, as in the case of marriage, the known cases are probably not less than 93 percent of all that have occurred. Among the 1,003 gifted subjects who were or had been married by 1940, the number of those divorced or separated during the five-year period following 1940 was 30 men and 25 women. This increased the rate of marital fatalities for men from 11.15 percent to 16.54 percent, and for women from 12.75 percent to 18.30 percent. These figures, it should be noted, are for subjects who had married by 1940.

Among the 197 known marriages that occurred during the five-year period following 1940, there have been 7 cases (3.55 percent) of divorce or separation that have come to our knowledge. By 1945 the total score on divorce and separation was as follows for the 1,207 subjects (680 men and 527 women) who at that time were or had been married:*

Number of Times	Divorced or Separated			
	Men		Women	
	N	Percent	N	Percent
Once	88*	12.94	76†	14.42
Twice	8	1.18	8	1.52
Three or more times	2	0.29	2	0.38
Total	98	14.41	86	16.32

* Includes 11 separations and 5 cases in which remarriage to the same spouse followed the divorce.

† Includes 4 separations and 2 cases in which remarriage to the same spouse followed the divorce.

Comparisons with the general population on the rate of divorce are made difficult by various sources of error in the available statistical reports. In figuring the number of divorces for the gifted group all individuals who had been divorced, whether remarried or not, were counted among the divorced. We were able to do this because of our individual case-history records. In surveys such as those conducted by Babcock, and also in census reports, the item asked for is marital status at a particular time, *not* marital history, so that the divorced who had remarried were not counted among the divorced. The proportion of divorced persons in the general population who later remarry is unknown but has been estimated all the way from 25 percent to 80 percent. The latter figure by Rubinow[52] has been criticized by Cahen[9] as spuriously high, but Cahen's own estimate of 33 percent is probably too low. Of our divorced gifted subjects, 73 percent of the men and 64 percent of the women have already remarried. This means that a census on marital status in our group by the usual method would reveal less than a third of the cases with a divorce history.

Separations also complicate the problem of comparison. We have combined divorces and separations, but our separations were very few in number, and with one or two exceptions were undoubtedly a prelude to divorce. In the general population the proportion of

* These figures include 7 subjects (5 men and 2 women) for whom information on marital status was not obtained in 1940 and who, therefore, do not appear in Tables 61 and 62. Subsequent reports showed 4 of the men to be married and without history of separation or divorce; 1 man has been divorced twice; and both women have been married, divorced, and remarried.

couples separated but not divorced is much higher; according to Stouffer and Spencer[58]* "there is some evidence that at any given time more couples are separated, but not divorced, than are living in a state of divorce."

Back of the above sources of error, all of unknown magnitude, is another equally unknown and perhaps no less serious; namely, the fact that in the census many persons living in a state of divorce report themselves as single or married or widowed. As stated by Cahen, "every census editor has admitted that the number of divorced persons stated in the decennial census is woefully inadequate." That such is the case is clearly evident when the census data are checked against court records of divorces granted. The upshot of the matter is that, however accurate our data for the gifted subjects may be (and it is certain that the check-ups afforded by our methods of field work insure more valid data than the census reports), no accurate comparison can be made between divorce rate in the general population and in the gifted group.

Marriage as Related to Intelligence and Education

We have computed mean childhood IQ's on the Stanford-Binet tests for subjects who in 1940 had not been married, for subjects who had been married but not divorced or separated, and for subjects who had been divorced or separated. In the case of men, the mean IQ was within 1 point the same for the three groups, and for women the three means were the same within 2 IQ points. Among these subjects neither marriage rate nor divorce rate is correlated with childhood IQ.

We have already seen in the comparative data presented earlier in this chapter that the incidence of marriage among college graduates of our group was greater than has been found for college graduates in general, and also that the subjects of our group tended to marry at a younger age than do most college graduates. Within the gifted group there was no relationship between marital status and amount of education in the case of men, the proportion who had married being 70.7 percent of college graduates and 71.9 percent of nongraduates. In the case of women the marriage rate was somewhat lower for graduates than for nongraduates, the proportions being 70.1 percent and 79.1 percent respectively. The critical ratio of this difference is

* See page 68 of reference.

2.5. The highest incidence of marriage (81.5 percent) was among women who attended college for one or more years but left before graduating. The majority of these discontinued college to be married. Table 63 summarizes the relation of education to marital status as of 1940.

TABLE 63

MARITAL STATUS (1940) VERSUS AMOUNT OF EDUCATION

	Percentage*	
	Men (N=540) %	Women (N=402) %
I. *College graduates*		
Single	29.3	29.8
Are, or have been, married	70.7	70.1
Separated or divorced (includes remarried)	8.4	8.2
II. *More than one year of college but not college graduate*	(N=100)	(N=81)
Single	31.0	18.5
Are, or have been, married	69.0	81.5
Separated or divorced (includes remarried)	17.4	16.7
III. *One year of college or less*	(N=135)	(N=120)
Single	25.9	22.5
Are, or have been, married	74.1	77.5
Separated or divorced (includes remarried)	19.0	22.5
II and III. *Noncollege graduates*	(N=235)	(N=201)
Single	28.1	20.9
Are, or have been, married	71.9	79.1
Separated or divorced (includes remarried)	18.3	20.1

* The percentages of those separated or divorced are based on the N who had married.

The proportion of those married who had been divorced or separated by 1940 was 8.4 percent for men graduated from college and 18.3 percent for nongraduates. The difference is quite reliable (CR = 3.5). For women, the proportion divorced or separated was 8.2 percent for college graduates and 20.1 percent for nongraduates, again a statistically reliable difference (CR = 3.8). Babcock's figures on divorce among the generality of college graduates in the United States are much lower than our own, but because of the method used in his survey no comparison with the gifted group is possible; the questions asked failed, presumably, to reveal divorce histories of those who had remarried.

Marital Selection

Education of spouses. Investigations agree in showing education to be an important factor in marital selection. Husband-wife correlations of .40 to .50 in years of schooling are not unusual. It will not be surprising, therefore, to find that many of our gifted subjects have married college graduates. Table 64 gives the percentages of spouses with various amounts of schooling.

TABLE 64

Amount of Schooling of Spouses

	Husbands (N=425) %	Wives (N=529) %
College graduate	54.3	42.7
College 1–4 years (no degree)	19.1	25.1
High-school graduation	16.5	26.3
Less than high-school graduation	10.1	5.9

The proportion of college graduates was 54.3 percent for the husbands of gifted women and 42.7 percent for the wives of gifted men. The proportion of spouses who either had taken a graduate degree, or had two or more years of graduate work without a degree, was 24.7 percent for husbands and 5.9 percent for wives. Having had one or more years of college work without graduating were 19.1 percent of the husbands and 25.1 percent of the wives. Only 26.6 percent of the husbands of gifted women, and 32.2 percent of the wives of gifted men, had no college work or less than one year. Of the husbands who graduated from college, 46 percent took one or more years of graduate work; of the wives graduating, 14 percent returned for one or more years of graduate study. Superior as these records are, they do not approach the records of the gifted subjects themselves. As we have shown in chapter xiii, about 70 percent of the gifted men and 67 percent of the gifted women graduated from college. Only 3 men and 9 women failed to graduate from high school.

Occupational status of spouses. Husbands of the gifted women rated as high in occupational status as in education; 35.2 percent were in Census Group I, 24.6 percent in Group II, 29.3 percent in Group III, and only 10.9 percent were below Group III. These figures do not compare badly with those for our gifted men, of whom (in 1940) 45.4 percent were in Group I, 25.6 percent in Group II, 20.7 percent in Group III, and 8.0 percent below Group III.

The parental occupational status of the spouses of gifted subjects approaches but does not quite equal that of the fathers of the gifted subjects themselves. Of the fathers-in-law of gifted men, 57.5 percent were in Census Group I or II, and 22.7 percent were below Group III. Of the fathers-in-law of gifted women, 52.1 percent were in Group I or II, and 24.7 percent were below Group III. Of own fathers of gifted men, 64.5 percent were in Group I or II, and 15.9 percent were below Group III. The corresponding figures for own fathers of gifted women were 67.1 percent in Group I or II, and 11.3 percent below Group III.

The proportion of wives of gifted men who were employed full time was only 18.0 percent, as compared with 31.9 percent of our married gifted women. The difference is completely reliable (CR = 4.9). Since the proportion of offspring per marriage is about the same for both gifted men and women, this greater tendency among the gifted wives to engage in work outside the home cannot be attributed to more freedom from the responsibilities of child care.

Intelligence scores of spouses. The Concept Mastery test was given to 527 spouses, including 305 wives of gifted men and 222 husbands of gifted women. The mean point score of the wives was 58.9; of the husbands, 64.3. The critical ratio of the difference between means is 1.7. The variability of the husbands and wives of the gifted was practically identical, the S.D. for both distributions being approximately 35. Scores above 99 were made by one husband in eight and by one wife in nine. Scores below 20 were made by one husband in six and by one wife in five. As was shown in chapter xi the mean score of the gifted subjects was 98.1 for men and 93.9 for women, with only two scores as low as 20.

Distributions were made of the difference scores between spouses. Gifted men ranged from 135 points higher than their wives to 65 points lower, the mean difference score being 39.3 points in favor of the gifted husbands (S.D. 34.9). Gifted women ranged from 115 points higher than their husbands to 105 points lower, the mean difference score being 29.7 points in favor of the gifted wives (S.D. 37.6). One gifted man in nine scored lower than his wife; one gifted women in five scored lower than her husband. These figures reflect the fact that gifted women, somewhat oftener than gifted men, marry "upward."

There is only a slight relationship between the childhood IQ of the gifted subjects and the 1940 Concept Mastery scores made by their spouses. Men with childhood IQ between 135 and 150, had wives who averaged 9.7 points lower on the Concept Mastery test than did the wives of men who as children tested between 150 and 200. The difference is not entirely reliable (CR = 1.8). In the case of women, the relationship is in the same direction but less marked and less consistent.

Age difference between spouses. This information was available in 1940 for 513 gifted men and 414 gifted women. Gifted men ranged from 17 years older to 9 years younger than their wives. The mean age difference was 1.4 years in favor of the husband (S.D. 3.1 years). Gifted wives ranged from 26 years younger to 9 years older than their husbands. The mean difference was 4.0 years in favor of the husband (S.D. 4.0 years). Of the gifted men, approximately 20 percent were younger than their wives by a year or more. Of the husbands of gifted women, only 11 percent were a year or more younger than their wives.

Ratings of spouses by field workers. Field workers rated 526 spouses of the gifted subjects on 12 traits. The spouses who were rated included 312 wives of gifted men and 214 husbands of gifted women. Table 65 gives the proportion of spouses with high ratings on each trait (1 or 2 on a scale of 5), and for comparison includes the proportion of gifted subjects so rated. It will be seen that the impression made by the spouses on the field workers compares favorably with that made by the gifted subjects. The field workers' reports abound

TABLE 65

PROPORTION OF SPOUSES AND OF GIFTED SUBJECTS RATED HIGH ON PERSONALITY TRAITS BY FIELD WORKERS

	Percentages Rated 1 or 2 on a Scale of 5			
	Gifted Men	Husbands of Gifted Women	Gifted Women	Wives of Gifted Men
1. Appearance	53.1	46.3	60.6	59.9
2. Attractiveness	58.0	56.0	66.8	61.5
3. Poise	55.6	57.0	62.0	62.3
4. Speech	61.2	57.6	68.4	61.0
5. Freedom from vanity	15.4	14.6	24.4	21.2
6. Alertness	80.0	73.7	75.4	62.5
7. Friendliness	58.1	56.9	64.2	58.8
8. Talkativeness	40.6	31.3	47.0	39.5
9. Frankness	53.8	52.4	61.1	53.4
10. Attentiveness	76.1	80.5	72.9	62.4
11. Curiosity	50.8	58.5	46.6	42.5
12. Originality	54.2	38.3	45.7	38.2

with comments on the interest, cordiality, and co-operation of the husbands and wives of our subjects. Certainly, far from the least of the achievements of the gifted group has been their choice of spouses.*

Fertility

It is impossible at this time to estimate what the ultimate fertility of the gifted group will be. Up to 1940 we have practically complete information on the number of subjects who had married, the age of marriage, and the number of living and deceased offspring, but at that time the average age of subjects was not quite thirty years. We have obtained similar information to 1945, when the average age of the subjects was about thirty-five years, but this is complete for only about 93 percent of the group. The data as of 1940 are summarized in Table 66.

TABLE 66

Fertility of Married Gifted Subjects to 1940

Number of Children Per Family	Number of Families	Number of Children
One	298	298
Two	157	314
Three	41	123
Four	8	32
Five	2	10
Six	1	6
Total, one or more	507	783
Married, no children	496	..
Total marriages	1,003	..

The 783 children to 1940 include 412 boys and 371 girls, giving the rather high sex ratio of 111.05 to 100. Of the 783 children, 12 boys (2.9 percent) and 6 girls (1.6 percent) were deceased. The mean number of children in the fruitful marriages was 1.54 per family. For total marriages—fruitful and nonfruitful—the mean number of children was 0.78 per family.

In 1945, when the average age of the subjects was approximately thirty-five years, the number of offspring (of the 93 percent of subjects contacted) was 1,551 : 817 boys and 734 girls. This included 20 boys and 16 girls who were deceased. The mortality rate of 2.3 percent for the offspring is far below that in the general population. The sex

* There were 10 marriages in which both spouses were members of the gifted group and 6 others in which a gifted subject married the sibling of a gifted subject.

ratio for offspring was 111.31 boys to 100 girls. The mean number of offspring for subjects married one or more years was 1.39 for men, 1.38 for women, and 1.39 for the total. For the gifted who by 1945 had been married five years or longer, the average number of offspring per family was 1.52. We have no reason to suppose that the average of 1.52 per family would have been materially altered had all the subjects been contacted at this date instead of 93 percent of them.

Considering the marriage rate among the subjects and the number of offspring for those married five years or longer, what is the outlook for the future of the gifted group? Folsom[25] estimates that where the marriage rate is up to normal for the generality, those who marry will have to produce an average of 2.62 live births per family in order to maintain the stock. He further estimates that since about 17 percent of marriages are infertile, the necessary average number of children that must be born in fertile families must be about 3.17 if the stock is to be maintained. As we have seen, the marriage rate for our gifted subjects is a little above that for the general population, but it is still too early to predict whether they will produce enough additional offspring to bring the average to 2.62 for those who marry, or to 3.17 for those who have children. In view of the fact that the mean age of the subjects was approximately thirty-five years at the time of the last report, it is very doubtful whether their ultimate fertility will be sufficient to maintain the stock. Another fifteen years will have to pass before an accurate estimate of fertility will be possible.

Differential Fertility Within the Group

When the subjects are older, it will be interesting to check the data for evidence of differential fertility within the group. This would involve detailed comparisons between males and females, between college graduates and nongraduates, between those with superior and those with mediocre scholastic records, between subjects of higher and lower childhood IQ, between the less successful and the more successful vocationally, *et cetera.* Also to be investigated are the relationships between fertility and such variables as parental fertility, age at marriage, and general mental adjustment. Because many of the breakdowns necessary for these comparisons would yield relatively small N's, it has seemed best to postpone the treatment of this entire problem until ultimate fertility can be more accurately estimated than is now possible.

Intelligence Tests of Offspring

In connection with the follow-up of 1940, the 1937 Stanford-Binet (Form L) was administered to 384 members of the second generation: 192 boys and 192 girls. Those tested included nearly all the children aged two and one-half or above who could be conveniently reached by the field assistants and are believed to be fairly representative of the entire second generation. The results are summarized in Table 67.

TABLE 67

Stanford-Binet IQ's of Offspring Tested

IQ	Boys	Girls	Boys and Girls
180–189	..	2	2
170–179	5	..	5
160–169	8	10	18
150–159	18	16	34
140–149	23	26	49
130–139	35	44	79
120–129	44	39	83
110–119	21	21	42
100–109	24	20	44
90– 99	6	6	12
80– 89	3	5	8
70– 79	2	1	3
60– 69	1	2	3
50– 59	1	..	1
40– 49	1	..	1
N	192	192	384
Mean	127.23	128.17	127.70
S.D.	22.13	20.70	21.43

The mean IQ of 127.7 for the sexes combined is about 24 IQ points below the mean childhood IQ of their parents, and represents a regression of somewhat less than half the distance of their parents from the mean of the generality. This is fairly close to the amount that would be expected from Galton's law of filial regression. Such regression is not to be attributed to the fact that spouses marrying into the group averaged a little below the gifted subjects in intelligence, but to the fact that only half of one's heredity comes from the two parents while the other half is from more remote ancestry. The regression is about the same as that found for height of offspring from exceptionally tall parents.

The sex difference of less than one point in mean IQ is not statistically significant. The difference of 1.43 IQ points in S.D. of distribution is in the direction of greater variability of the boys, but this difference is not reliable (CR = 0.93). Contrary to expectation, the variability of both sexes is definitely greater than that found for the 3,000 unselected subjects on whom the 1937 Stanford-Binet was standardized.

Below 100 IQ were 14 of each sex or approximately 7.3 percent. Below 80 were 5 boys (2.6 percent) and 3 girls (1.5 percent). The proportion of the total below 80 was 2.1 percent, as compared with 4.7 percent of the standardization group. Those testing below 70 IQ make up 1.3 percent of the offspring tested. Of the 2,350 subjects in the standardization group between the ages of two and one-half and thirteen years, 2.1 percent tested below 70 on the same scale (Form L). The latter percentage would have been higher but for the fact that extreme cases of mental deficiency do not attend school and so were not caught in the Binet standardization group. The proportion in the generality who test below 70 is as great as the proportion of gifted offspring who test below 80. These figures suggest that the incidence of feeble-minded and border-zone cases among the offspring of the gifted subjects is far below that in the general population.

At the opposite extreme of the distribution, the proportion of offspring with IQ's of 150 or higher is 16.1 percent of boys, 14.6 percent of girls, and approximately 15.4 percent of all. The proportion of 2,350 subjects between two and one-half and thirteen years of age in the unselected standardization group who tested this high was only .55 of 1 percent. That is, the incidence of IQ's of 150 or above among offspring of the gifted subjects is about twenty-eight times as high as in the generality of corresponding age. A part of this huge excess could, of course, be due to the superior environment in the homes of the gifted subjects.

Summary

The incidence of marriage and the age at marriage in the gifted group are approximately the same as for the general population. However, the incidence of marriage is markedly higher and the age at marriage lower among college graduates of our group than among college graduates in general. This difference is particularly striking in the case of gifted women. By 1945 approximately 84 percent of both men and women were or had been married.

Of the subjects married by 1940, approximately 11.1 percent of the men and 12.7 percent of the women had been divorced or separated. By 1945, the proportion divorced or separated had increased to 14.4 percent for the men and 16.3 percent for the women. There is no correlation between divorce and childhood IQ, but the divorce rate is less than half as high among our college graduates as among our non-graduates.

Marital selection is indicated by the fact that the gifted subjects have chosen spouses whose average intelligence is equal to that of the average college graduate. Nearly three-fourths of the husbands and over two-thirds of the wives have attended college one or more years. The occupations of 60 percent of the husbands are in Census Groups I and II, and only 11 percent are below Group III. Gifted men average about one and one-half years older than their wives, and gifted women about four years younger than their husbands. Ratings of spouses by the field workers on traits of personality compare favorably with similar ratings of the gifted subjects.

By 1940, when the average age of subjects was a little below thirty years, the number of children born to the group was 783. By the end of 1945, the number had increased to 1,551. At the latter date the mean number of offspring for subjects who had been married five years or longer was 1.52. It is too early to predict whether the ultimate fertility of the group will be sufficient to maintain the stock. The sex ratio of offspring in 1945 was approximately 111 boys to 100 girls.

The mean IQ of 384 offspring given the Stanford-Binet test was 127.70. This figure conforms fairly closely to Galton's law of filial regression. The proportion of offspring who test below 80 IQ is no higher than the proportion in the generality who test below 70. This indicates a relatively low incidence of feeble-mindedness and border-zone mentality among offspring of the gifted group. At the opposite extreme of the distribution, the proportion of offspring with IQ's of 150 or higher is about twenty-eight times as great as that found for the unselected children on whom the 1937 revision of the Stanford-Binet was based.

The proportion of deceased among offspring of the gifted subjects to 1945 was 2.3 percent, which is far below the rate for the general population.

CHAPTER XIX

MARITAL ADJUSTMENT*

Three aspects of marital adjustment in the gifted group have been investigated: marital happiness, specific sexual adjustments, and marital aptitude.

1. The Test of Marital Happiness

In a study of marital adjustment it is necessary to adopt some method of estimating the degree of satisfaction or dissatisfaction that is present. Davis, in one of the earliest scientific investigations of marriage,[19] merely asked the subjects to rate their marital happiness on a 5-point scale. Hamilton[29] improved the technique by using a numerical index based upon the answers to thirteen questions. This index was the forerunner of the more elaborate tests of marital happiness devised by Burgess and Cottrell,[6] and by Terman.[63]

The test used with the gifted subjects is a modification and extension of the one used by Terman with a group of 792 married couples of more nearly average intelligence than the gifted subjects. The test calls for information on 15 aspects of the marriage, as follows:†

1. Number of outside interests in common.
2. Rated amount of agreement in ten fields.
3. Method of settling disagreements.
4. In a list of 40 specific activities respondent
   a) checks once those he (or she) enjoys doing, and
   b) double checks those enjoyed with spouse.
5. Regret of marriage.
6. Choice of spouse if life were to be lived over.
7. Contemplation of separation or divorce.
8. Admission or denial of present unhappiness.
9. Preference for spending leisure with spouse.

* The investigation of marital adjustments in the gifted group was made possible by grants from the National Research Council on the recommendation of its Committee for Research on Problems of Sex.

† The test items are reproduced in Part II of the blank entitled "Your Present Marriage," Appendix, pages 431 ff.

10. Gaiety and happiness when spouses are alone together.
11. Extent to which spouse irritates or bores respondent.
12. Rated satisfactoriness of the spouse's personality.
13. Degree of certainty that no other spouse would have been so satisfactory.
14. Subjective rating of happiness of the marriage, on a 7-point scale.
15. In a list of 38 common faults respondent
    a) checks once those that the spouse has, and
    b) double checks those that have made the marriage less happy.

A score weight was assigned to each of the various possible responses to each test item. The score weights were arrived at empirically after several sets of tentative weights had been tried out. An important consideration was the correlation of each item with the total score of the entire test, since it was regarded as essential that the test as a whole should have a considerable amount of internal consistency, and that the various items should get at the same general factor from different angles. Another factor taken into account was the variability of response permitted by the individual items. Other things equal, the item which calls for a graded response is more desirable than the item which permits only an all-or-none answer. Both in the earlier investigations of Terman and in that of Burgess and Cottrell, the marital happiness scores were bunched heavily toward the high end of the scale. The explanation of this lies in the natural tendency of subjects who are not positively unhappy to give overly optimistic answers to the questions asked. Most persons who are reasonably well satisfied with their marriage do not like to admit, even to themselves, that in some respects it is not as satisfactory as it might be. In order to counteract this tendency so far as possible, we have departed at times from the criterion of internal consistency by giving more weight or less weight to certain items than would have been given them had the criterion been rigidly adhered to. The effect of this was to give a more nearly normal distribution of scores.

Our empirical approach to the problem is illustrated by the experimental work that was done on alternative methods of scoring Item 4 (activities enjoyed in common). Three kinds of scores were tried out: (1) the absolute number of activities enjoyed by the respondent; (2) the absolute number the respondent enjoys doing with the spouse; and (3) the ratio between these two numbers. The results showed clearly that the third was superior to either of the others, both with respect to correlation with the total happiness score and with respect to the resulting score distribution.

Among those who took the marital happiness test in 1940 were 636 gifted subjects whose spouses also took the test. The data analyzed are based upon the first 567 couples who filled out the marriage blank, including 317 gifted men and their wives, and 250 gifted women and their husbands. In all but a few cases the test was taken in the presence and under the supervision of a field assistant who brought the subjects together in small groups for this and other tests. The purpose of this precaution was to avoid the possibility of collaboration between husband and wife in answering the questions.

Table 68 gives the score distributions for 556 couples who had filled out the blanks completely. These include 310 gifted husbands and their wives, 243 gifted wives and their husbands, and 3 couples in which both spouses belonged to the gifted group. Three distributions are shown: (1) that for all husbands, (2) that for all wives, and (3) the distribution of husband-wife composite scores. The composite

TABLE 68

Happiness Score Distributions of 556 Couples

Score	Husbands (N=556)	Wives (N=556)	Husband-Wife Composite (556 Couples)
96–100	11	9	4
91–95	29	26	8
86–90	24	51	39
81–85	51	56	51
76–80	55	61	65
71–75	57	63	62
66–70	50	49	70
61–65	44	56	50
56–60	52	45	61
51–55	45	33	42
46–50	31	27	29
41–45	29	23	19
36–40	22	16	19
31–35	19	11	16
26–30	12	9	10
21–25	10	9	4
16–20	6	5	2
11–15	6	5	4
6–10	2	..	..
0–5	1	2	1
Mean	63.15	66.34	64.74
S.D.	19.76	18.90	16.97

score is the average of the two scores made by husband and wife, and can be regarded as an index of success of the marriage.

The possible score range is 0 to 100, and the scores of each sex extend over practically the entire range. The mean for husbands was 63.15, and for wives 66.34, with respective S.D.'s of 19.76 and 18.90. Although this difference between means is small, it is statistically reliable (CR = 3.8) and is in line with Terman's data for a less-selected group. Whether it represents a real sex difference in happiness, or only a greater willingness of wives to give verbal expression to their satisfactions, it is impossible to say. The fact that marriage is more of a career for women than for men may tend to sensitize the wife to the satisfactions that derive from it.

The reliability of the test computed by the split-half method was found to be .89 both for husbands and for wives. This figure compares favorably with reliabilities commonly found for leading personality tests. It will be understood that the reliability coefficient does not indicate what correlation would be obtained between two applications of the test several months or years apart; it means only that the test gives a fairly consistent measure of the marital happiness at a given time. Everyone knows that some marriages become less happy with the passing of time, and that others, which start out with considerable maladjustment, later improve. There are various kinds of lightning that can blast the happiness of any but the most stable marriage, and there are various therapeutic measures that can sometimes in some measure repair the damage. One of the main purposes of the test is to enable investigators and clinicians to follow the ups and downs of a marriage.

The internal consistency of the test is reflected in the mean total happiness scores of subjects who check particular responses to the individual items. In the case of nearly all the items, the mean total score of those giving the most favorable response is in the range 70 to 90, while the mean of those giving the least favorable response usually falls in the range 20 to 40. This drop in mean happiness for less and less favorable responses on given items ran closely parallel for all four groups of spouses (gifted husbands, husbands of gifted women, gifted wives, and wives of gifted men).

The correlation between the scores of husbands and wives cannot be taken as a measure of the reliability of the test. This correlation is relatively low—only .52 for the gifted group, and only .60 for Terman's earlier nongifted group. The husband-wife difference amounted to 30 points or more in nearly 12 percent of the gifted marriages, and was 25 points or more in 20 percent. Evidently marriage is a venture in which the principals cannot be guaranteed an equal share of the proceeds. The predictive significance of such differences can only be determined by continued follow-up of the marriages.

One would like to know how the marital happiness of the gifted subjects compares with that of husbands and wives in the general population. No such comparison can be made at this time because the test has not been given to a random sample. However, there are seven items included in the present test which were also used in the test administered to 792 less-selected couples in an earlier study. Table 69 gives the percentage distribution of responses to each of these seven items both for 567 couples of the gifted group and for the nongifted group.

TABLE 69

COMPARISON OF GIFTED GROUP WITH A LESS-SELECTED GROUP ON DISTRIBUTION OF RESPONSES TO SEVEN ITEMS IN THE MARITAL HAPPINESS TEST

Items as Numbered in the Test	GIFTED GROUP Husbands (N=567) %	GIFTED GROUP Wives (N=567) %	LESS-SELECTED GROUP Husbands (N=792) %	LESS-SELECTED GROUP Wives (N=792) %
1. *Outside activities together*				
All of them	14.0	20.2	13.7	19.8
Most of them	61.1	60.5	54.6	55.9
Some of them	18.2	12.7	26.7	18.7
Very few of them	5.6	5.3	4.9	4.4
None of them	0.7	1.2	0.1	1.2
3. *How disagreements settled*				
Mutual give and take	84.9	87.1	81.3	79.3
Respondent gives in	8.3	9.8	14.9	16.0
Spouse gives in	6.7	3.0	3.8	4.7
5. *Regret of marriage*				
Never	63.3	69.1	55.3	58.4
Rarely	24.9	20.3	28.9	25.3
Occasionally	8.7	9.0	12.4	12.8
Frequently	2.6	1.1	3.4	3.5
6. *If life to live over would*				
Marry the same person	87.3	93.5	82.7	86.1
Marry a different person	6.7	4.5	10.1	10.4
Not marry at all	5.8	2.0	7.2	3.5

TABLE 69 (*Continued*)

	GIFTED GROUP		LESS-SELECTED GROUP	
	Husbands (N=567) %	Wives (N=567) %	Husbands (N=792) %	Wives (N=792) %
7. *Consideration of separation or divorce*				
Separation				
Yes	12.9	18.1	16.3	21.0
No	87.1	81.8	83.7	79.0
Divorce				
Yes	8.1	9.2	8.8	11.5
No	91.9	90.7	91.2	88.5
8. *Admission of unhappiness*				
Not admitted	95.1	95.8	92.1	90.6
Admitted	4.9	4.2	7.9	9.4
14. *Rated happiness of the marriage*				
Extraordinarily happy	34.0	43.0	29.5	34.6
Decidedly more than average	39.8	37.6	36.8	35.9
Somewhat more than average	14.1	10.9	16.3	14.7
About average	7.4	3.7	12.9	9.2
A little below average	2.6	2.1	2.9	3.0
Definitely below average	1.1	2.1	1.6	1.8
Extremely unhappy	0.2	0.0	0.1	0.8

There is a striking similarity in the response distributions for the gifted group and the less-selected group on every one of the seven items. On all of them, however, the gifted group gives a slightly larger proportion of "happy" answers. The only conclusion possible is that the average marital happiness in the present group is higher than that found in the less-selected group. There is no reason to believe that the results would have been otherwise if all fifteen items of the test had been used with both groups.

One can also evaluate the happiness of the gifted subjects by comparing their scores with scores made by the spouses who have married into the group, although this comparison is less significant than that just given, since the spouses are also rather highly selected for intelligence and education. Table 70 gives the means and S.D.'s separately for gifted husbands, husbands of gifted women, gifted wives, and wives of gifted men.

The table shows that gifted wives and wives of gifted husbands differ in mean score by only 1.8 points, the small difference favoring the latter group. The mean for gifted husbands is 7.4 points below

TABLE 70

MEAN HAPPINESS SCORES OF GIFTED SUBJECTS AND SPOUSES OF GIFTED

	Gifted Husbands (N=317)	Husbands of Gifted Women (N=250)	Gifted Wives (N=250)	Wives of Gifted Men (N=317)
Mean	59.50	66.90	64.86	66.66
S.D.	20.36	18.80	18.71	19.30

that for husbands of gifted wives, a difference that is statistically quite reliable. If taken at its face value, it means that gifted husbands are appreciably less happy, on the average, than any of the other three groups. It is conceivable, however, that the difference could be due in part to a tendency of gifted men to be a little more realistic and objective-minded in their responses to the test items; that is, less given to unconscious exaggeration in expressing their satisfactions with the marriage.

To what extent are happiness scores at a given time predictive of later marital success or failure? We can now give a tentative answer to this very important question. Between 1940 and 1946 there were 88 marriages of gifted subjects that ended in divorce (N = 74) or separation (N = 14). In 46 of these cases either the husband (N = 41) or the wife (N = 45), or both (N = 39), had taken the marital happiness test in 1940. All of the 530 unbroken and 37 of the broken marriages of Table 71 were included in the N of 567 in Table 70.

TABLE 71

MARITAL HAPPINESS SCORES AS PREDICTIVE OF DIVORCE OR SEPARATION

	Husbands' Scores			Wives' Scores			Husband-Wife Average		
Marriage	N	Mean	S.D.	N	Mean	S.D.	N	Mean	S.D.
Broken	41	50.32	19.97	45	49.67	20.71	39	48.59	16.98
Not broken	530	63.57	19.76	530	66.88	18.52	530	65.21	19.46
CR of difference between means		4.10			5.39			5.84	

Although the 1940 happiness scores of these subjects were scattered over almost the entire range of the scale, the means for marriages later broken were far lower than the means for those that remained intact. For husbands, the difference was 13.25 points; for wives, 17.21 points. The respective critical ratios are 4.10 and 5.39. The husband-wife composite score proved slightly more predictive than the score of either spouse alone (CR of the difference on this score, 5.84). Of the 41 divorced or separated husbands, only 8, or less than 20 percent, had scored in the upper half of the happiness range in 1940; of 45 wives, only 12, or 26.6 percent, had scored in the upper half. These figures offer the first substantial proof that marital happiness scores have genuine predictive value.

In view of the fact that the marital happiness scores are predictive of marital adjustment during the ensuing six years, it would be reasonable to expect them to show some correlation with case-history data obtained prior to the time when the test was given. A few moderately significant relationships of this kind were found.

There was no correlation with the IQ's or the achievement quotients of 1922, but a slightly negative correlation was found between happiness scores and the Concept Mastery scores of 1940. On masculinity of play interests in childhood, there was no relationship for husbands, but wives of more than average masculinity on the play test tend to have a lower happiness score (CR = 2.82). Husbands, who in 1922 had rated low in sociability as indicated by play interests, averaged lower in marital happiness than others (CR = 2.23); for wives there was no appreciable relationship on this variable. Only one significant relationship was found between happiness scores and scores on the seven parts of the character test described in chapter v. This was for the Woodworth-Cady Test of Emotional Stability. "Good" scores on this test tend to be somewhat associated with superior happiness for both husbands and wives. The biserial correlation was approximately .25. On the Wyman Interest Test, given in 1923, it was found that a medium score for social interests, rather than an extreme score, is associated with greater happiness of husbands, and that wives who had scored high in intellectual interests averaged slightly below other wives in happiness (biserial correlation = — .17).

The ratings on 25 traits by parents and teachers in 1922, and similar ratings on 12 traits in 1928, yielded no statistically reliable correlation with marital happiness scores. The same is true of the 1922 and 1928 data on nervous symptoms and social adjustment. On the other hand, general adjustment of the subjects as rated by field workers in 1940 was appreciably correlated with happiness scores. Husbands rated as "satisfactory" in general adjustment averaged 9.7 points higher in happiness than those rated as showing "some" or "serious" maladjustment (CR = 2.26).

Little or no correlation was found between marital happiness scores and birth order, number of opposite-sex sibs, attachment to sibs, childhood residence, history of sex shock, adolescent "petting," amount of religious training, rated adequacy of sex instruction, and many other variables having to do with childhood and family situations.

2. Sex Adjustments in Marriage

The purpose in obtaining information on the sex adjustments was threefold: (1) to check the validity of the rather widespread opinion that highly intellectual and much-educated persons are more likely than others to be sexually maladjusted; (2) to secure data on the role of sex as a factor in marital success or failure; and (3) to investigate the relationships between sex adjustments and various aspects of personality and life history.

The information was obtained by questions included in the marriage blank (Part III). There were 5 questions to be answered by both husband and wife, and 3 to be answered by the wife only. All but one of the items included were selected from a much larger number that had been used with a group of 792 less-selected couples, and were the only ones which in that study showed appreciable correlation with marital happiness. The information sought from both spouses included: usual frequency of intercourse per month, the preferred frequency; usual duration of intercourse; a 5-point rating on relative passionateness of the spouses; and a 5-point rating on how well mated (sexually) the spouses were. Additional questions to be answered by the wife called for information on her experience of the sexual orgasm, degree of satisfaction (release) which she derives from intercourse, and amount of enjoyment, disgust, or pain experienced at first intercourse.

The material on sex adjustment could logically have been included as a part of the test of marital happiness, but it seemed better to treat separately the psychological factors that make for marital success and the specific sexual factors.

Data were analyzed for the 544 couples who had responded to all items on sex adjustment, to all in the test of marital happiness, and to all in the test of marital aptitude. These included 307 gifted husbands and their wives, and 237 gifted wives and their husbands.

The items on sex adjustments were in all but a few cases filled out in the presence of a field assistant, thus ruling out the possibility of collaboration between husband and wife. Moreover, because of the intimate nature of the information called for, the subjects were assured that their names would be cut from the blanks, and that the blanks would thereafter be identifiable only by case numbers stamped upon them. They were further assured that the blanks and the numbered key to the names would be kept in a confidential file separate from all other case histories. These assurances brought a high degree of co-operation, although a few of the subjects failed to respond to one or more of the questions. The number of omissions was less for the gifted subjects than for their spouses, perhaps because of the confidence built up among them over so many years of follow-up.

Can one expect that the answers to such questions would be sufficiently truthful to warrant their being taken seriously? There are two lines of evidence regarding their validity. One is the fact that in most cases the two spouses agree fairly closely on the questions they are both asked to answer. A second is that the reports by gifted subjects agree so closely with those previously obtained from a less-selected group. The internal evidence is such as to rule out the likelihood of any great amount of deliberate falsification.

How "normal" are the gifted men and women in their sex adjustments? Sexologists have often asserted that higher education and much preoccupation with things intellectual tend to unfit one for a normal sex life. This effect is popularly supposed to be much worse for women than for men. In order to answer this question, the data were coded and punched on Hollerith cards, which were then sorted to bring out all the significant relationships that might exist. The result was several hundred statistical tables showing separately for gifted husbands, gifted wives, husbands of gifted wives, and wives of gifted husbands such facts as: (1) the distributions of responses to each item, (2) central tendencies of responses as indicated by means or medians, (3) agreement or disagreement in the testimony of husband and wife, (4) resemblance of gifted husbands to husbands of gifted wives, and of gifted wives to wives of gifted husbands, (5) the relation of each possible type of response both to the marital happiness score and the marital aptitude score, and (6) relationships to such other variables as childhood IQ, Concept Mastery score, family background, amount of education, ratings on personality traits, and case-history data bearing on mental and social maladjustment.

The resulting statistical material is too bulky to include in the present report, which is concerned primarily with the bearing of the data on the sexual normality or abnormality of the gifted group. The conclusions on this point can be briefly stated in two paragraphs:

1. There is not a single item relating to sex adjustment on which the distribution of responses for gifted husbands differed reliably from the responses of men who had married into the group, and not one on which the responses of gifted wives differed reliably from those of women who had married into the group. That is, the gifted subjects in general are exactly as normal as the spouse group, who, on the average, are somewhat less highly selected for intelligence and education.

2. Similarly, there is not a single item on which the responses of the gifted subjects differed reliably from those of 792 nongifted subjects of the same sex. The results for the two groups are so nearly identical that the reader who wants to know what gifted men and women are like with respect to such things as frequency, preferred frequency, and estimated duration of intercourse, relative passionateness of spouses, or orgasm adequacy of wives, can get the essential facts from Terman's already published statistics for nongifted subjects.[63]

The conclusion is unavoidable that the gifted group is just as normal in its sexual adjustments as is the less-selected group. We do not know, however, how either of these groups would compare with a strictly random sample of married couples in the general population. One characteristic of every group that has been studied is the wide range always found with respect to any phase of specific sexual behavior. As we have stated, this range was almost exactly the same for the gifted subjects as for less-selected subjects.

Moreover, the gifted and less-selected subjects resemble each other not only in range, means, and variability of responses given to the individual items, but also (and this is particularly significant) in amount and direction of relationship between a given response and the marital happiness score. That is, in both groups particular responses are indicative of happiness or unhappiness to much the same degree. Factors little correlated with happiness in one group are almost equally uncorrelated with happiness in the other group. For example, in both sexes of both groups the happiness score is highest when the ratio of actual intercourse frequency to preferred frequency is close to unity. In both groups the happiness score is positively correlated with orgasm adequacy of wife, and in both groups the association with the wife's happiness is closer than with the husband's.

A total score on sex adjustment has been computed for each subject who filled out the marriage blank. Score weights were assigned to the various possible responses on a given item in proportion to the mean marital happiness score of subjects giving a particular response. The method of weighting was essentially the same as that used in weighting items of the marital aptitude test, as described in a later section of this chapter. The total score for a given subject is the sum of all the weights carried by the responses the subject has made. The greater the correlation between a particular response and marital happiness, the greater the weight assigned.

The maximum total score possible is 23 for husbands and 30 for wives. (The higher maximum for wives is accounted for chiefly by the fact that three of the items are answered only by the wives.) Besides the total score as just defined, we have also computed what has been designated as a "subtotal," the only difference being that the subtotal does not include the item which calls for a rating on how well mated (sexually) the couple is. This rating is highly subjective and probably reflects chiefly the general happiness of the marriage, whereas the other items call for information of a more factual kind. Table 72 gives the distributions of both total and subtotal scores for husbands and wives.

The husband-wife correlation on subtotal scores was .59, which is slightly higher than the husband-wife correlation on marital happiness (.52). A correlation as low as .59 means, of course, that one spouse is often much better satisfied with the sexual aspects of the marriage than is the other. The predictive significance of such spouse differences is still unknown.

Consider next the relationship between sex score and happiness score. In computing this relationship we have used the subtotal sex score, which excludes the subjective rating on how well mated husband and wife were. The subtotal score of the husband correlates .40 with his happiness score; that of the wife correlates .43 with her happiness. The composite subtotal of husband and wife correlates .47 with their composite happiness score. These correlations run somewhat lower than the correlations of marital aptitude with happiness.

TABLE 72

DISTRIBUTIONS OF TOTAL AND SUBTOTAL SCORES ON SEXUAL ADJUSTMENTS

	SCORE FREQUENCIES			
	Total Scores		Subtotal Scores	
Score Intervals	Husbands	Wives	Husbands	Wives
29–30	..	10	..	..
27–28	..	26	..	..
25–26	..	87	..	..
23–24	..	100	..	2
21–22	15	81	..	51
19–20	68	79	..	126
17–18	121	50	..	124
15–16	121	40	25	90
13–14	90	22	144	63
11–12	48	16	179	40
9–10	30	16	92	23
7–8	24	9	54	16
5–6	11	4	28	4
3–4	13	4	19	5
1–2	3	..	3	..
N	544	544	544	544
Mean*	14.66	20.40	10.83	16.28
S.D.	4.06	5.16	2.83	3.82

* Computed from ungrouped data.

One's sex score correlates not only with one's own happiness but also with the spouse's happiness. The husband's sex score correlates .37 with the happiness of his wife, and the wife's correlates .27 with the happiness of her husband. In other words, one's sex adjustment in marriage reflects not only one's own happiness but also the spouse's happiness. The causal influence probably works in both directions, but there is ground for believing that the sex satisfactions are less a cause of happiness than its result. Couples who are psychologically well mated show a surprising tolerance for the things that are not entirely satisfactory in their sexual relationships. The psychologically ill-mated show no such tolerance but are prone to exaggerate the amount of sexual incompatibility that may be present. Analysis of the sexual complaints expressed by the less-selected group of 792 couples points clearly to the conclusion that sexual complaints are often just a convenient peg on which to hang psychological discontent.[63] This conclusion is supported by data on the relative value of sex adjustment scores, marital happiness scores, and marital aptitude scores in predicting later divorce or separation in our gifted group.

Among the 88 couples divorced between 1940 and 1946 are 42 husbands and 46 wives for whom sex adjustment scores are available. For 40 of these marriages the composite husband-wife sex scores are also available. Only the 37 divorced couples who were included in the 544 reported in Table 72 have been deducted in the figures for "not broken" marriages given in Table 73.

TABLE 73

TOTAL SEX ADJUSTMENT SCORES AS PREDICTIVE OF DIVORCE OR SEPARATION

	Husbands' Scores			Wives' Scores			Husband-Wife Average		
Marriage	N	Mean	S.D.	N	Mean	S.D.	N	Mean	S.D.
Broken	42	12.93	5.19	46	18.87	5.71	40	15.85	4.98
Not broken	507	14.76	3.97	507	20.55	5.09	507	17.63	4.12
CR of difference between means		2.23			1.93			2.20	

The comparison here is between the total (not the subtotal) scores. From the table it will be noted that, although the differences between means are in the direction that indicates some predictive value of the sex scores, they are not large enough to be statistically very reliable. The critical ratio is 2.23 for husbands, 1.93 for wives, and 2.20 for the husband-wife average. This suggests that the strictly sexual factors have played only a minor role in the breakup of these marriages.

3. The Test of Marital Aptitude

On the theory that some persons have more aptitute for marriage than others, several attempts have been made to identify the personality factors and the factors in childhood and family background that contribute to one's chances of marital success or failure. Among the earlier studies of this kind, those of Davis,[19] Hamilton,[29] and Dickinson and Beam[21] did much to prepare the way for the more elaborate statistical approaches to the problem. Burgess and Cottrell,[6] using chiefly items of information relating to childhood and family background, and to the general background of the marriage, found a correlation of approximately .50 between the sum total of their prediction items and their index of marital adjustment. Terman, in his study of 792 couples,[63] used a prediction test which included numerous items relating to personality in addition to the kinds of information used by Burgess and Cottrell. He found on the whole somewhat less correlation between background items and marital adjustment than Burgess and Cottrell had found, but this was more than offset by the predictive value of the items testing personality and temperament.

The test of marital aptitude used with the gifted subjects included all of the items which had shown some evidence of validity in Terman's earlier study, and a number of additional items which were believed to be promising; in all, 150 items.* These may be classified in the following categories:

1. Relating to personality, 117 items including
   a) 53 of the Bernreuter type,
   b) 34 from the Strong Vocational Interest Test,
   c) 16 expressions of opinion about the ideal marriage,
   d) 14 self-ratings on personality traits.
2. Relating to childhood, family background, age, education, and occupation, 33 items.
3. Relating to background of the marriage, 30 items.

Items in the first and second categories are usable with any adult person, whether married or single. Those in the third category are usable only with married subjects, since they have to do with the background of a particular marriage.

The 150 items usable with either married or unmarried subjects were printed as an eight-page booklet. The purpose of the test was disguised by giving it the title "Personality and Temperament."† The 30 items designed for use only with married subjects constituted Part I of the marriage blank which is reproduced in the Appendix, pages 429 f.

All three parts of the test were given in 1940 to 636 married gifted subjects and their spouses. Among these were 317 gifted men and their wives, and 250 gifted women and their husbands, all of whom took *both* the test of marital aptitude and the test of marital happiness. In addition, the first two parts of the test were given to 371 gifted subjects who were not married. A majority of the blanks were filled out in the presence of a field worker, although this precaution was hardly necessary. Statistical treatment was limited to data on 567 couples, whose blanks were used in the item selection for the test of marital happiness. Among these are four couples with both spouses gifted.

The validity of each test item was figured on the basis of its rela-

* In the formulation of the entire test of marital aptitude, the senior author was greatly assisted by Dr. Winifred B. Johnson.

† See Appendix, pages 418 ff.

tionship to score on the marital happiness test. Items which discriminated between high-scoring and low-scoring subjects on the happiness test were deemed valid, and were assigned response weights in proportion to the discrimination shown. The discriminative value of each item was checked in two ways: (1) by comparing the responses given by the 150 most happily married couples with the responses given by the 150 couples least happily married; (2) by comparing the mean happiness score of subjects giving a particular response with the mean score of subjects giving a different response to the same item. The comparisons of means were based on the scores of 317 gifted men and their wives, and 250 gifted women and their husbands. The following examples will make clear the nature of the evidence used in the high-low comparison and in the comparison of means.

Do you usually try to get your own way even if you have to fight for it?

COMPARISON OF HIGH AND LOW GROUPS

Response	Husbands High Percent	Husbands Low Percent	Husbands CR	Wives High Percent	Wives Low Percent	Wives CR
Yes	30.6	43.3	2.30	18.0	41.3	4.57
No	59.3	41.3	3.19	76.7	47.9	5.40
?	10.0	15.4		5.3	10.8	

MEAN HAPPINESS SCORE BY RESPONSE

Response	Husbands	Wives
Yes	61.54	61.26
No	65.00	68.41
?	57.09	61.89
CR: No vs. Yes or ?	2.81	4.21

Conflict with mother

COMPARISON OF HIGH AND LOW GROUPS

Response	Husbands High Percent	Husbands Low Percent	Husbands CR	Wives High Percent	Wives Low Percent	Wives CR
None	51.8	30.6	3.71	44.4	25.0	3.53
Any other response	48.2	69.4		55.6	75.0	

MEAN HAPPINESS SCORE BY RESPONSE

Response	Husbands	Wives
None	67.19	69.91
Any other response	59.70	63.50
CR of difference	4.00	3.00

In general, a critical ratio between 2.00 and 3.00 was regarded as justifying a weight of 1 point; a critical ratio as high as 3.00 but less than 4.00, a weight of 2 points; a critical ratio of 4.00 or more, a weight of 3 points. However, this system could not be followed rigidly, because the comparison of high-low groups and the comparison based on mean happiness scores did not yield exactly the same critical ratios.

As previously stated, most of the items used in the present test had shown predictive value with Terman's 792 less-selected couples. However, about a fourth of the items that had predictive value in the earlier study showed little or none with gifted subjects. Some of the items that were predictive of happiness in both of these groups were more predictive for one group than for the other. Despite such differences, it is highly significant that many items have behaved similarly in the Burgess-Cottrell group, Terman's earlier group, and the present group. Agreement of this kind is evidence of the essential soundness of the methods used.

The score weights give a composite picture of what constitutes a "happy" or an "unhappy" temperament. For a detailed description of the personalities of happily married and of unhappily married persons, the reader is referred to Terman's earlier study.[63]* The composite pictures for the present group closely resemble those for the earlier group.

The total score of a subject is the sum of the score weights carried by the individual responses the subject has given. The maximum possible scores are as follows for the three parts of the tests:

	Men	Women
1. Personality and temperament	118	94
2. Childhood and family background	37	23
3. Background of the marriage	38	36
Grand total	193	153

Excluding the items on background of the marriage (category 3), which can be used only with married subjects, the maximum total for the other two categories is 155 for men and 117 for women. Since the greatest potential value of the test is in the evaluation of marital aptitude prior to marriage, nearly all of the following statistical data are based on total scores that do not include the items of category 3.

* See pages 110–41 of reference.

The reliability of the test (exclusive of category 3), computed by the split-half method, was found to be .86 for 567 husbands and .82 for their wives. The test-retest reliabilities have not been computed, but they probably would not differ greatly from the above values.

Table 74 gives the score distributions separately for gifted husbands, husbands of gifted wives, gifted wives, and wives of gifted husbands. These distributions are for total score exclusive of the items on background of the marriage. The sex differences in the mean score and in the upper range of scores are due to the fact that more items were predictive of the marital happiness of men than of women.

The table shows that gifted husbands average lower than the husbands of gifted wives, but that gifted wives are about on a par with the wives of gifted husbands. The difference between the husband groups is fairly significant, the critical ratio being 2.63. It will

TABLE 74

DISTRIBUTION OF SCORES OF GIFTED SUBJECTS AND THEIR SPOUSES ON THE TEST OF APTITUDE FOR MARRIAGE

Aptitude Score	Gifted Husbands	Husbands of Gifted Wives	Gifted Wives	Wives of Gifted Husbands
130–134	..	1	..	..
125–129	5	2	..	..
120–124	9	5	..	..
115–119	14	10	..	..
110–114	14	17	..	..
105–109	29	26	2	1
100–104	26	31	5	11
95–99	27	30	14	26
90–94	34	34	38	37
85–89	30	17	31	47
80–84	32	15	39	44
75–79	24	21	29	42
70–74	22	8	24	32
65–69	12	10	22	29
60–64	12	8	23	19
55–59	13	1	8	7
50–54	4	1	7	6
45–49	2	4	3	7
40–44	2	1	1	1
35–39	2	..	..	..
30–34	1	..	..	1
N	314	242	246	310
Mean	88.82	92.81	78.61	79.44
S.D.	18.94	16.75	13.06	13.28

be recalled that on the marital happiness test, also, the gifted husbands averaged below the husbands of gifted women, whereas the two groups of wives were very close together. This suggests that if either sex is handicapped for marriage by very superior intelligence it is the man and not the woman (as popular opinion would have it).

We are unable to compare the marital aptitude scores of these subjects with the scores made by the less-selected group of 792 couples, since the measuring instruments used in the two studies were not identical. However, as we have already noted, the items that were common to the two tests gave much the same results for both groups.

The scores of gifted subjects in Table 74 are for those who had married by 1940. The question arises whether marriage tends to be selective in terms of marital aptitude. To answer this question we have compared, for the sexes separately, the aptitude scores of those who had married with those who had not married. In the case of women the means for the married and the unmarried were practically identical. In the case of men, however, the mean of the unmarried was 7 points lower than that of the married. The difference is highly reliable (CR = 4.77). It cannot be due to the lower age of the unmarried subjects, for the aptitude scores are uncorrelated with age. It appears, therefore, that men who postpone marriage are often the ones who have less than average aptitude for marriage.

On validity of the marital aptitude scores, evidence of two kinds is available: (1) the correlation of aptitude scores with scores on the marital happiness test which was also given in 1940, and (2) the extent to which the aptitude scores are predictive of later divorce or separation. The second of these two lines of evidence is the more crucial. One might argue that any correlation found between the aptitude and happiness scores could result from halo effects operating in the two tests taken near the same time.

The correlation between marital aptitude scores and marital happiness scores in this group of subjects is .53 for men and .48 for women. In computing this correlation we excluded from the aptitude test the items on background of the marriage. Table 75 shows the correlations of the happiness score with the separate parts of the aptitude test, and the multiple correlation with certain combinations of the latter. The first part of the table gives for husbands and wives separately the zero correlations between the happiness score and each of the three groups of prediction items. The second part of the table gives the multiple correlations between the happiness score and combinations of the prediction categories.

TABLE 75

CORRELATIONS OF MARITAL HAPPINESS SCORES WITH SEPARATE PARTS OF THE APTITUDE TEST

	Husband	Wife
Correlations of happiness score with		
1. Total of personality items	.52	.45
2. Childhood and family background	.35	.32
3. Background of marriage	.51	.43
Multiple correlation of		
1 plus 2	.53	.48
1 plus 2 plus 3	.62	.55

Attention is called to the fact that the correlation of the happiness score with the total of personality items is .52 for husband, and .45 for wife, and that when we add in the items on childhood and family background, these correlations are raised only to .53 and .48. That is, the effects of childhood and family background are nearly all contained in the personality items themselves. However, when we add by multiple correlation the score on background of the marriage to the items of the first two categories, the correlation is raised to .62 for husbands and to .55 for wives. This means that the items on background of the marriage add something not contained in the personality items.

The correlations support the hypothesis that one's marital happiness is, to a considerable extent, determined by all-round happiness of temperament and personality. There are persons of such happy temperament that they could live comfortably with almost any kind of mate, and there are others of such unhappy temperament that they would find no happiness in any marriage. The truth of the latter statement, at least, could be supported by several case histories of gifted subjects who have gone through three or four marriages and as many divorces. Our conclusion regarding the role of personality in marital adjustment is further supported by the low correlation that is found between the happiness scores of husbands and their wives. As we have stated elsewhere, this correlation was .52 for these subjects and .60 for Terman's 792 less-selected couples. The husband-wife correlation could hardly be so low were there not a strong tendency for each individual to go through life in his own happy or unhappy way. This, of course, is not to say that neither spouse is ever to blame for the unhappiness of the other.

The above evidence on validity of the marital aptitude scores is circumstantial, or at least indirect. For incontrovertible proof of their validity we must examine their efficiency in predicting later marital success or failure. Evidence on this is now available. Of the gifted subjects who took the marital aptitude test in 1940, there were 41 men and 45 women who became divorced or separated by 1946. In the case of 39 marriages which ended in divorce or separation between 1940 and 1946, both spouses had taken the marital aptitude test. Table 76 gives the means and S.D.'s of marital aptitude scores for broken and unbroken marriages. All three comparisons of means show highly reliable differences in the expected direction. In the case of husbands the difference of about 8 points between failures and nonfailures has a critical ratio of 3.04. The corresponding difference for wives is close to 11 points (CR = 5.03). The difference between failures and nonfailures on the husband-wife composite score is more than 10 points (CR = 5.20). For husbands, the difference in means between failures and nonfailures is equal to about half the sigma of the distribution of the husbands' scores; for wives the difference almost equals the sigma of the wives' scores. Of the 45 wives divorced or separated, 33 (73 percent) had scored below the average of all wives as compared with only 12 (27 percent) who had scored above average. In the case of wives, the chances of marital breakup within six years were two and three-quarter times as great for those with scores below average as for those with scores above average. Of the 41 men who became divorced or separated, 26 had scored below the husband average and 15 above. That is, the odds against men who scored below average are one and three-quarter times as great as for men scoring above average.

We are now in position to compare the relative predictive value

TABLE 76

MARITAL APTITUDE SCORES AS PREDICTIVE OF DIVORCE OR SEPARATION

Marriage	Husbands' Scores N	Mean	S.D.	Wives' Scores N	Mean	S.D.	Husband-Wife Average N	Mean	S.D.
Broken	41	83.22	15.88	45	68.89	14.07	39	75.21	11.73
Not broken	519	91.13	18.14	519	79.81	12.81	519	85.38	12.46
CR of difference between means		3.04			5.03			5.20	

of the marital happiness scores, the sex adjustment scores, and the marital aptitude scores in forecasting the breakup of marriages. We can do this roughly by bringing together the three sets of critical ratios indicating reliability of differences between the means for broken and unbroken marriages. These are as follows:

	Husbands' Scores	Wives' Scores	Husband-Wife Average
Marital happiness	4.10	5.39	5.84
Sex adjustment	2.23	1.93	2.20
Marital aptitude	3.04	5.03	5.20

The figures show that the marital happiness scores and the marital aptitude scores are both definitely predictive of later divorce or separation and to much the same degree, although for husbands the prediction from happiness scores is a little better than from aptitude scores. The sex adjustment scores have comparatively little predictive value for either spouse. In the case of marital happiness and sex adjustment, the husband-wife average scores are not appreciably more predictive than the individual spouse scores; in the case of marital aptitude, however, the prediction from husband-wife average is much better than from the husband's score.

Since the aptitude scores are predictive of later maladjustment in marriage, one might expect them to show appreciable correlation with some of the earlier case-history data. A check of the aptitude scores against numerous case-history variables has revealed a number of significant relationships.

Although there is no relationship between aptitude scores and either the amount of education or the childhood IQ, there is a *negative* correlation between aptitude scores and Concept Mastery scores of 1940. This amounts to —.28 for husbands and —.26 for wives. Women who had been rated as having "some" or "marked" nervous symptoms in 1928 averaged, a dozen years later, 8.5 points lower in marital aptitude than women without such symptoms. The difference is quite reliable (CR = 4.18). Ratings on social adjustment as far back as 1922 showed a fairly significant correlation with marital aptitude as measured eighteen years later. Both men and women who were rated as showing "some" or "marked" social maladjustment in 1922 averaged about 6 points lower in aptitude score than those whose 1922 social adjustment was "satisfactory." The social-adjustment ratings of 1928 showed even a higher correlation with the marital aptitude score. Men with "satisfactory" social adjustment in 1928 averaged 12.6 points higher in aptitude than those with "some" or "marked" maladjustment (CR = 4.53). The corresponding difference for women was 8.9 points (CR = 2.96).

An all-round rating on "general adjustment" was made of each subject on the basis of all information obtained throughout many years. Men rated "satisfactory" on general adjustment in 1940 had a mean marital aptitude score of 89.5; those with "some" or "serious" maladjustment had a mean of 73.7. The difference of 15.8 points has a critical ratio of 9.62. Women rated "satisfactory" average 79.5 in marital aptitude, as compared with 69.6 for those with "some" or "serious" maladjustment. The difference of 9.9 points has a critical ratio of 6.96. From such data it is evident that aptitude for marriage, as here measured, depends in very considerable degree on aptitude for all-round adjustment.

Summary

In 1940 a test of marital happiness and a test of marital aptitude were given to more than 600 gifted subjects and their spouses. The latter was also given to 371 gifted subjects who were not married. The married gifted subjects and their spouses answered, in addition, a list of questions regarding the sexual aspects of their marriage, the responses to which permitted the computation of a score on sex adjustment. All three sets of test items were revisions of similar tests used by Terman in an earlier study.

The marital happiness test is characterized by a high degree of internal consistency as indicated by a split-half reliability of .89 for each sex. The reliability of the marital aptitude test is only slightly less; namely, .86 for men and .82 for women. Both tests permit a wide range of total scores, and give score distributions more nearly approximating the normal curve than those yielded by earlier tests of similar type.

The validity of each item in the test of marital aptitude was estimated by the extent to which the responses were associated with scores on the happiness test. On this basis a score weight from 0 to 3 was assigned to each possible response to each of the individual items. A similar method was used in assigning weights to each type of response to individual items on sex adjustment; that is, a response was regarded as indicative of "good" sexual adjustment if it was given more often by subjects with high happiness score than by subjects with low happiness score. About three-fourths of the items used in the marital aptitude test, and all the items in the test of sex adjustment were predictive of marital happiness in greater or less degree.

How the scores of gifted subjects on these three tests would compare with those that might be found in a strictly random population is unknown, since the tests have not been given to an unselected group. We are able, however, to compare the gifted subjects with two groups less selected for intelligence and education: (1) the men and women who are spouses of gifted subjects, and (2) a group of 792 less-gifted couples who were given a similar battery of tests. These comparisons indicate a slightly higher level of marital happiness, and a no less satisfactory sexual adjustment among gifted subjects than among less-gifted subjects.

As could be expected from the method used in assigning response weights, the total scores on marital aptitude and on sex adjustment show a positive correlation with marital happiness scores. This correlation is around .50 to .60* for the test of marital happiness, and around .40 for the score on sex adjustment. That is, both of these tests are predictive of marital happiness as measured at a given time by the happiness test. The correlations are to be regarded as presumptive evidence of the validity of both the aptitude scores and the sex adjustment scores.

Crucial evidence on the validity of all three tests can best be gauged by the extent to which they are predictive of later marital failure or success. Such evidence is now for the first time available from a comparison of the 1940 scores of subjects who became divorced or separated between 1940 and the end of 1946 with the scores of subjects whose marriages at the latter date were still intact. The comparison shows that the best prediction is afforded by the test of marital aptitude, that the marital happiness test is only slightly less predictive, and that the sex adjustment test ranks as a poor third. As a tentative conclusion we estimate that the test of marital aptitude predicts later marital failure or success about as well as a good scholastic aptitude test predicts later scholastic grades.

The data, in general, confirm the hypothesis that one's happiness in marriage is largely determined by one's all-round happiness of temper-

* About .60 when items on "background of the marriage" are included in the aptitude test, and about .50 when these items (usable only with married subjects) are excluded.

ament, and that this trait can be at least roughly measured by a pencil-and-paper test. Evidence to this effect is brought to light by analysis of the test items most predictive of happiness scores, and by examination of the case-history records back to 1922. Additional evidence is found in the moderately low husband-wife correlation for happiness scores, and in the fact that divorce or separation can be almost as well predicted from the score of the individual spouse as from the composite score of husband and wife.

Follow-up of the marriages for another ten or twenty years will establish more accurately the predictive value of the tests of marital happiness and marital aptitude, and will throw additional light on the role of temperament in the success or failure of a marriage.

CHAPTER XX

THE PROBLEM OF SCHOOL ACCELERATION

There has been much controversy regarding the extent to which children of high IQ should be allowed to become accelerated in school. At one extreme is the opinion that the gifted child should be given a grade placement corresponding to his mental age; at the other extreme are those who would base promotions on the calendar without regard to mental ability. Neither of these extreme views has many advocates, though the latter is perhaps more commonly held than the former. The fact remains, however, that many educators believe considerable acceleration is desirable, whereas many others are opposed to it.

An alternative is to provide special classes with an enriched curriculum for the gifted. Such classes have been established in many cities during the last two decades and have thoroughly demonstrated their value. In view of the fact that at present special classes are available to only a small minority of gifted children, we are usually faced by the choice between acceleration and nonacceleration in grading systems designed primarily for the average child. Attempts are often made to enrich the program for especially bright children in the ordinary classroom, and such programs at their best can be very helpful. Unfortunately, the so-called enrichment often amounts to little more than a quantitative increase of work on the usual level. This may keep the gifted child out of mischief, but it is hardly educational. Since only a very few of our California subjects had enjoyed any special educational opportunities in the elementary or secondary schools—beyond the opportunity to skip an occasional grade or half-grade—this chapter will be devoted to an examination of the evidence which bears on the advantages and disadvantages of acceleration.

The most common arguments in favor of acceleration are that it improves the child's motivation, prevents him from developing habits of dawdling, allows earlier completion of professional training, and makes earlier marriage possible. The total cost of the child's education would be somewhat reduced, but this is hardly a major consideration. On the other side it is argued that grade skipping aggravates the child's problem of social adjustment, promotes bookishness and one-sided development, is dangerous to physical or mental health, and leaves gaps in the child's academic knowledge and skills. Although our data do not afford an accurate measure of all these alleged effects, they do furnish evidence of considerable value with respect to some of them.

As an index of degree of acceleration, we have used the age at high-school graduation and have divided our subjects into three groups: (1) those who graduated below the age of 15 years 6 months; (2) those graduating between 15 years 6 months and 16 years 6 months; and (3) those graduating at or above the age of 16 years 6 months. The distribution of ages for the three groups at high-school graduation is shown in Table 77. If age 18 plus or minus 6 months is considered the normal age for completing high school, those in Group I are accelerated from 2 to 4 years, those in Group II from 1 to 2 years, and those in Group III from 0 to 1 year. Only 6.8 percent of men and less than 2 percent of women graduated above the upper limit of normal age as above defined; that is, above 18 years 6 months. The mean ages at completing high school were as follows for Groups I, II, and III respectively: 14.9, 16.0, and 17.3 years.

When in the following passages the groups are referred to as "accelerates" and "nonaccelerates," the former includes Groups I and II—i.e., those graduating from high school before the age of 16 years 6 months (average 15.9)—and the latter term includes all graduating at 16 years 6 months or over (average age 17.4).

TABLE 77

GROUPING BY AGE AT HIGH-SCHOOL GRADUATION

Group I	Men		Women	
	N	Percent	N	Percent
13-6 to 13-11	..	..	1	0.2
14-0 to 14-5	6	0.8	3	0.5
14-6 to 14-11	10	1.3	7	1.1
15-0 to 15-5	20	2.5	15	2.5
Total, Group I	36	4.6	26	4.3

TABLE 77 (*Continued*)

	Men N	Men Percent	Women N	Women Percent
Group II				
15-6 to 15-11	71	9.0	61	10.1
16-0 to 16-5	110	14.0	90	14.8
Total, Group II	181	23.0	151	24.9
Group III				
16-6 to 16-11	170	21.7	184	30.3
17-0 to 17-5	192	24.5	136	22.4
17-6 to 17-11	95	12.1	69	11.4
18-0 to 18-5	58	7.4	30	4.9
18-6 and above	53	6.8	11	1.8
Total, Group III	568	72.5	430	70.8
Total, all groups	785		607	
Mean ages (years)				
Group I	14.93		14.90	
Group II	16.00		16.00	
Group III	17.43		17.22	
Groups I and II	15.87		15.89	
Groups I, II, and III	16.99		16.78	

Our data regarding the above groups will be presented under six heads: (1) intelligence, (2) educational history, (3) vocational status and avocational interests, (4) social adjustment, (5) marital status, and (6) physical and mental health.

Acceleration as Related to Intelligence

The data here include the childhood IQ's of those qualifying for the gifted group on the Stanford-Binet test, 1940 scores on a group intelligence test (the Concept Mastery), and 1940 self-ratings on the extent to which early mental superiority had been maintained. The information is summarized in Table 78. In this and the following tables, the N's for which data are available *both* on acceleration and on the item in question are given in parentheses. Means and percentages are given to the nearest first decimal.

The reader is reminded that not all the items in the case-history record were available for every subject. In the first place, there are 37 men and 38 women not included in any of the acceleration groups because their education had been irregular, because they had not completed high school, or because the exact age at completion could not be obtained from our records. Furthermore, the Stanford-Binet had been given only to those subjects who were 13 years or younger when located. These numbered 1,030 cases.* The Concept Mastery test of 1940 required supervision for its administration and so was given only at group meetings or during a personal interview with subjects; those living at too great a distance for personal contacts were not given this test. There were in all 954 Concept Mastery tests given, without regard to whether the subjects had originally qualified for the gifted study on a Binet or a group test. The subjective report on maintenance of mental superiority was available for 1,252 subjects who responded to this item on the General Information Blank of 1940. Thus the populations in Parts 1, 2, and 3 of Table 78, though overlapping, are not identical.

TABLE 78

ACCELERATION VERSUS INTELLIGENCE

	Acceleration Groups			
	I	II	I + II	III
1. Childhood IQ (Binet)				
Mean for men	161.1	155.1	156.1	149.7
	(27)	(130)	(157)	(365)
	CR: I + II vs. III = 5.6			
Mean for women	155.3	152.8	153.1	149.2
	(20)	(125)	(145)	(300)
	CR: I + II vs. III = 3.5			
2. Concept Mastery point score (1940)				
Mean for men	118.9	102.7	105.1	96.1
	(18)	(108)	(126)	(387)
	CR: I vs. III = 3.4; CR: I + II vs. III = 2.8			
Mean for women	105.2	93.6	95.1	93.7
	(15)	(96)	(111)	(303)
	CR: I vs. III = 1.9			
3. Subjective report on present mental superiority: now "less marked"				
Men	43.3%	35.0%	36.5%	31.0%
	(30)	(140)	(170)	(455)
	CR: I vs. III = 1.3			
Women	54.5%	41.7%	43.8%	46.8%
	(22)	(115)	(137)	(342)
	CR: I vs. II = 1.1			

* Of the original 1,070 Binet-tested subjects, 40 were deceased by 1940.

The table shows a significant relationship between the degree of acceleration and childhood IQ. Although the IQ difference between the accelerates (Groups I and II) and the nonaccelerates (Group III) is not great in the absolute sense, being only 6.4 points for men and 3.9 points for women, it is statistically reliable. The respective critical ratios are 5.6 and 3.5. Even so, the correlation between acceleration and IQ is very low, for among the nonaccelerates are 50 men and 39 women in the IQ range 160 to 190. In the schools these subjects attended, IQ's played little part in grade placement.

The 1940 Concept Mastery scores show much the same trends as the childhood IQ's. Again the differences are more marked for men. For both sexes, Group I rates well above Group III, the critical ratio being 3.4 for men and 1.9 for women. However, when the total accelerates (Groups I and II) are compared with Group III, the difference, though still in favor of the accelerates, is not striking. For men it is fairly reliable, with a critical ratio of 2.8, but in the case of women the average score is as high for Group III as for Group II.

The subjective reports in the table on the extent to which early mental superiority had been maintained are contradicted by the test scores. The latter indicate that the highly accelerated have maintained their ability as well as the nonaccelerates, whereas the subjective reports indicate a greater tendency among the accelerates for mental superiority to become less marked. One must accept the evidence of the test scores. The reports are probably influenced by the natural tendency of an accelerated child to become more conscious of his early superiority than does the equally bright child who is not accelerated.

Acceleration as Related to Educational History

Table 79 presents data on the relationship of acceleration to the proportion graduating from college, the proportion completing one or more years of graduate work, age at college graduation, average grade in college, the winning of graduation honors, and the high-school scholastic record. At the end of the table are the mean achievement quotients for those given the Stanford Achievement Test battery in 1922, though here the N's are relatively small because this test was given only to members of the Main Experimental Group enrolled in the second school grade or above.

TABLE 79

ACCELERATION VERSUS EDUCATIONAL HISTORY

	ACCELERATION GROUPS			
	I	II	I + II	III
1. Graduated from college				
Men	86.1% (31)	76.0% (136)	77.7% (167)	68.8% (373)
	CR: I vs. III = 2.8; I + II vs. III = 2.6			
Women	79.1% (19)	71.6% (106)	72.7% (125)	66.3% (272)
	CR: I vs. III = 1.5; I + II vs. III = 1.5			
2. Mean age at college graduation (years)				
Men	19.9 (29)	21.1 (131)	20.9 (160)	22.1 (354)
Women	19.8 (19)	20.6 (105)	20.5 (124)	21.6 (261)
3. Average college grade of B or better				
Men	75.8% (33)	77.1% (144)	76.8% (177)	71.5% (390)
	CR: I + II vs. III = 1.3			
Women	78.9% (19)	86.9% (115)	85.8% (134)	77.4% (297)
	CR: I + II vs. III = 2.2			
4. One or more graduation honors				
Men	40.0% (30)	41.9% (136)	42.2% (166)	39.0% (346)
Women	47.4% (19)	33.7% (104)	35.8% (123)	30.9% (265)
5. One or more years of graduate work				
Men	58.3% (21)	54.8% (98)	55.3% (119)	43.4% (235)
	CR: I + II vs. III = 3.0			
Women	58.3% (14)	41.9% (62)	44.2% (76)	34.4% (141)
	CR: I + II vs. III = 2.2			
6. Earning 15 or more recommending units in high school				
Men	93.9% (31)	87.0% (140)	88.1% (171)	82.4% (417)
	CR: I + II vs. III = 1.8			
Women	95.2% (21)	92.6% (135)	92.9% (156)	93.2% (381)

TABLE 79 (*Continued*)

	ACCELERATION GROUPS			
	I	II	I + II	III
7. Mean achievement test quotient (1922)				
Men	155.5	150.8	151.5	144.7
	(16)	(94)	(110)	(278)
	CR: I + II vs. III = 4.9			
Women	154.2	145.6	146.5	139.6
	(12)	(102)	(114)	(211)
	CR: I + II vs. III = 5.3			

Table 79 shows that the greater the degree of acceleration, the greater is the likelihood of graduation from college and of remaining for one or more years of graduate work. In the case of men both trends are statistically significant. However, the relationship may not be entirely one of cause and effect, since the accelerates had also a little advantage in IQ.

A slightly larger proportion of accelerates than nonaccelerates made an average grade of B or better in college, and the accelerates did a trifle better in winning graduation honors, despite the fact that for men the mean age of graduation was 2.5 years younger in Group I than in Group III, and for women 2.3 years younger.

Turning to the high-school record we find in the case of men a fairly definite trend toward better scholastic achievement by the accelerates. There is no such relationship between high-school achievement and acceleration in the case of women.

The last section of the table shows that the accelerates greatly excelled nonaccelerates in achievement as measured by a three-hour battery of objective tests given in 1922 when the subjects were in the elementary grades. The difference is highly reliable, the critical ratio being 4.9 for men and 5.3 for women. In the main, however, promotions were only very loosely correlated with the amount of curriculum material the child had mastered. Probably the question of promotion or nonpromotion was usually decided on the whims of individual classroom teachers or school principals.

Acceleration as Related to Vocational History and Avocational Interests

Table 80 gives for men the occupational classification by census groups, and the proportion of each acceleration group in the A and C classifications for vocational success to be described in chapter xxiii. These groups include, respectively, the most and least successful 20 percent of men.

TABLE 80

ACCELERATION VERSUS OCCUPATIONAL CLASSIFICATION AND VOCATIONAL SUCCESS (MEN)

	ACCELERATION GROUPS			
	I Percent	II Percent	I + II Percent	III Percent
1. *Census occupational grouping of men*				
Census Group I	51.5	51.2	51.3	44.4
		CR: I + II vs. III = 1.6		
Census Group II	36.4	28.3	29.7	24.2
		CR: I vs. III = 1.4		
Census Groups III to VI	12.1	20.5	19.0	31.4
		CR: I + II vs. III = 3.6		
2. *In class A for vocational success (A, B, C grouping)*	42.2	22.2	25.6	19.4
		CR: I vs. III = 2.6		
N for percentages	33	166	199	509

The table shows that among men the accelerates more often than nonaccelerates are in the professional and higher business occupations, and less often in occupational Groups III to VI. The data do not tell to what extent acceleration in itself has caused subjects to choose a profession who would not otherwise have done so, but we know of individual cases who believe that acceleration was a factor in such choice. Especially in such professions as medicine, law, or university teaching, an early entrance into graduate study is a real advantage to the gifted student. Part 2 of the table gives additional evidence on the greater vocational success of men who were accelerated. Of the most highly accelerated men, 42.2 percent are in the A group for vocational success as compared with 19.4 percent of the nonaccelerates. In the case of women there was no significant relation between acceleration and occupational status.

Finally, we have compared the acceleration groups with respect to their avocational interests and their interest in 12 specific fields. One question in the 1940 General Information Blank asked the subjects to indicate their avocational interests. Another item in the same blank called for ratings of amount of interest in travel, outdoor sports, religion, mechanics, social life, literature, music, art, science, politics, domestic arts, and pets. The results of these inquiries showed no significant difference between accelerates and nonaccelerates in the frequency with which any given avocational activity was mentioned, in the number of avocational activities engaged in, or in the average rating of interest in the 12 specific fields named. The figures for accelerates and nonaccelerates were almost identical with respect to these variables. The conclusion is that even marked school acceleration has little if any effect upon either the kind or the number of avocational activities, and that it has no narrowing effect upon such interests as are represented in the 12 fields mentioned.

Acceleration as Related to Social Adjustment

The data on social adjustment given in Table 81 include the following items: (1) a social adjustment rating based on information from parents and teachers in 1922; (2) a rating on social adjustment by field workers in 1928; (3) another rating on social adjustment in 1928 based on reports from parents; (4) preferred age of companions as reported by the subjects when in high school; (5) and (6) extracurricular activities of the subjects in high school and college; (7) 1940 scores on a test of aptitude for marital adjustment; (8) opinions of the subjects themselves on the advantages and disadvantages of any acceleration they had experienced.

TABLE 81

Acceleration versus Social Adjustment

	Acceleration Groups			
	I	II	I + II	III
1. Social adjustment (1922) : parent-teacher rating "satisfactory"				
Men	88.2%	88.0%	88.1%	90.4%
	(34)	(167)	(201)	(518)
Women	95.7%	95.8%	95.8%	95.1%
	(23)	(142)	(165)	(388)
2. Social adjustment (1928) : rated as "satisfactory" by field workers				
Men	70.0%	76.7%	75.7%	82.8%
	(20)	(95)	(115)	(268)
	CR: I vs. III = 1.5			
Women	100.0%	81.7%	83.3%	85.9%
	(8)	(88)	(96)	(235)

TABLE 81 (*Continued*)

	ACCELERATION GROUPS			
	I	II	I + II	III
3. Social adjustment (1928): rated as "satisfactory" by parents				
Men	81.5%	96.2%	93.7%	92.1%
	(27)	(132)	(159)	(356)
		CR: I vs. II = 1.9		
Women	90.5%	92.2%	92.0%	97.4%
	(21)	(128)	(149)	(303)
4. Preferred older companions in high-school years				
Men	71.4%	64.5%	65.7%	49.7%
	(28)	(138)	(166)	(364)
	CR: I vs. III = 2.4; I + II vs. III = 3.5			
Women	77.3%	72.3%	73.0%	50.5%
	(22)	(130)	(152)	(313)
	CR: I vs. III = 2.9; I + II vs. III = 4.9			
5. Extracurricular activities in high school: "several" to "outstanding"				
Men	32.4%	54.7%	50.8%	57.5%
	(34)	(159)	(193)	(497)
	CR: I vs. III = 3.0; I + II vs. III = 1.6			
Women	65.0%	59.3%	60.0%	62.3%
	(20)	(135)	(155)	(363)
6. Extracurricular activities in college: "several" to "outstanding"				
Men	33.3%	32.3%	32.5%	37.6%
	(30)	(130)	(160)	(343)
Women	22.2%	41.1%	38.2%	39.2%
	(18)	(102)	(120)	(257)
		CR: I vs. II + III = 1.7		
7. Mean score on test of aptitude for marital adjustment (1940)				
Men	84.18	86.72	86.29	86.28
	(31)	(153)	(184)	(499)
Women	69.09	78.87	77.27	77.67
	(24)	(124)	(148)	(375)
		CR: I vs. III = 2.2		
8. Proportion mentioning only disadvantages of acceleration				
Men	76.7%	58.8%	62.1%	61.0%
	(30)	(136)	(166)	(195)
		CR: I vs. II + III = 2.0		
Women	52.2%	63.3%	61.4%	59.1%
	(23)	(109)	(132)	(159)
		CR: I vs. II + III = 0.8		

The social adjustment rating of 1922 was a composite based on 12 items in the School Information Blank and 6 items in the Home Information Blank. The information called for related to such matters as the following: amount of play with other children, sex of playmates, relationships with other children (companionship sought or avoided, teased, considered queer or different), unusual or abnormal sex interests or behavior, *et cetera.* The information thus supplied was evaluated as indicating "satisfactory adjustment," "some difficulty in adjustment," or "serious maladjustment." Table 81 shows that for each sex the proportion rated in 1922 as "satisfactory" was almost exactly the same for all the acceleration groups.

The field workers' adjustment ratings of 1928 were for men slightly less favorable to the accelerates than to the nonaccelerates, but for women there was no consistent trend. The 1928 ratings based on information from parents indicated a slight tendency to less-satisfactory adjustment among the most highly accelerated, but for neither sex was this trend statistically significant.

Part 4 of the table shows a marked relationship between degree of acceleration and preference expressed during adolescent years for older companions, the trend being about the same for boys and girls. The reader will have to judge for himself the significance of this fact for social adjustment. Our opinion is that at the high-school age a preference for older companions is a favorable rather than an unfavorable sign.

The ratings on extracurricular activities in high school showed no relationship to acceleration in the case of women. The one significant relationship in the case of men was in the smaller proportion of high ratings among those graduating from high school before the age of 15 years 6 months. This sex difference may reflect the difference between boys and girls in the age of reaching physical maturation. The high-school girl who is greatly accelerated is usually more mature physically than the high-school boy equally accelerated. In college, however, the participation in extracurricular activities by men was about the same for all the acceleration groups. The highly accelerated women made a poor showing on extracurricular activities in college, but the N of 18 here is too small to warrant any generalization.

The mean scores on the 1940 test of aptitude for marital adjustment were, in the case of men, about the same for all the acceleration groups. In the case of women the mean for the highly accelerated was somewhat lower than for the other groups, but the difference was not entirely reliable (CR = 2.2). The nature of this test is described in chapter xix.

In the last section of the table we have summarized the opinions expressed by the subjects regarding the advantages and disadvantages of acceleration they had experienced. In the General Information Blank the statement was worded as follows: "Were you greatly accelerated in school? If so to what extent do you consider this was an advantage or disadvantage?" It turned out that there were subjects in all the groups who did not regard themselves as having been accelerated; in fact there were 64 men and 53 women graduated from high school before 17 who said they were not accelerated. Eight of these were under 16 at high-school graduation. On the other hand, there were a number of nonaccelerates (according to our definition) who considered themselves accelerated. Ninety-two men and 60 women who finished high school at 17 years or over felt that they had been "greatly accelerated" in school. We have omitted those who did not consider themselves accelerated from our computation of the percentages given in Part 8 of Table 81. The responses were classified into three categories: those which mentioned advantages only, those mentioning disadvantages only, and those mentioning neither or both; but we have included in the table only the percentages alleging disadvantages. The figures for Group II and Group III did not differ appreciably for either sex. Among the highly accelerated (Group I) there was a marked sex difference, a larger proportion of men than of women stressing its disadvantages. This is probably another reflection of the fact that boys are retarded in their physical and social maturation as compared with girls.

Our conclusion from the evidence of Table 81 is that the influence of school acceleration in causing social maladjustment has been greatly exaggerated. There is no doubt that maladjustment does result in individual cases, but our data indicate that in a majority of subjects the maladjustment consists of a temporary feeling of inferiority which is later overcome. The important thing is to consider each child as a special case.

Acceleration as Related to Marriage

Table 82 gives the data on 4 items relating to marriage: the proportion who have married, mean age at marriage (first marriage if more than one), proportion separated or divorced, and mean score on a test of marital happiness.

TABLE 82

ACCELERATION VERSUS MARRIAGE

	ACCELERATION GROUPS			
	I	II	I + II	III
1. Are, or have been married				
Men	72.7% (36)	68.2% (179)	68.9% (215)	70.5% (559)
Women	60.0% (25)	74.0% (150)	72.0% (175)	71.5% (425)
	CR: I vs. II = 1.3			
2. Mean age at marriage				
Men	24.8 (26)	25.5 (115)	25.4 (141)	26.1 (358)
	CR: I vs. III = 2.1; I + II vs. III = 2.1			
Women	22.8 (15)	23.5 (108)	23.4 (123)	24.1 (290)
	CR: I vs. II = 2.1; I + II vs. III = 1.8			
3. Separated or divorced (percentage of number married)				
Men	(1 case) (26)	10.7% (122)	9.5% (148)	11.9% (394)
Women	(1 case) (15)	12.6% (111)	11.9% (126)	12.8% (304)
4. Mean score on test of marital happiness				
Men	56.6 (18)	62.8 (82)	61.7 (100)	58.8 (274)
Women	64.7 (13)	63.6 (68)	63.8 (81)	62.0 (213)

The differences in the marriage rate are not statistically reliable. For men, the highest incidence was among the most accelerated, whereas women in this group had the lowest marriage rate. Separations and divorces occurred less often among the highly accelerated.

The mean age at marriage was appreciably lower for the accelerated group. For each sex, Group I was 1.3 years and Group II was 0.6 of a year below the mean of Group III. This trend is significant from the point of view of eugenics.

The test of marital happiness showed no reliable differences in mean score between accelerates and nonaccelerates. Among the women, both accelerated groups averaged a trifle higher than the non-accelerates. On the whole, the data suggest that marital adjustment is not appreciably correlated with degree of acceleration.

Acceleration as Related to Physical and Mental Health

Our information on this topic includes the following items: (1) a health rating based on information secured from medical examinations and from several questions in the Home Information Blank and the School Information Blank of 1922 (our ratings of these data being in terms of "very good," "good," "fair," "poor," and "very poor"); (2) a rating on nervous tendencies based upon the responses to several questions in the Home Information Blank and the School Information Blank of 1922; (3) a 1928 health rating made by parents; (4) a 1928 rating on information furnished by parents regarding nervous tendencies; (5) age of puberty as reported by the parents, based upon first menstruation of girls and on voice change in the case of boys; (6) a self-rating on health made by the subjects in 1940 on a 5-point scale from "very good" to "very poor"; (7) a rating by us on all-round adjustment in 1940 based upon field workers' conferences with subjects, reports by parents or other relatives, and information which came to us through letters or conferences.

TABLE 83

Acceleration versus Physical and Mental Health

	Acceleration Groups			
	I	II	I + II	III
1. Health rating (1922) "good" to "very good"				
Men	78.1% (25)	75.5% (117)	75.9% (142)	74.3% (359)
Women	90.9% (20)	83.2% (114)	84.3% (134)	83.1% (304)
	CR: I vs. III = 1.2			
2. Rating on nervous tendencies (1922) "satisfactory"				
Men	96.9% (31)	84.2% (139)	86.3% (170)	82.6% (409)
	CR: I vs. III = 4.1; I + II vs. III = 1.2			
Women	95.7% (22)	93.6% (131)	93.9% (153)	90.1% (345)
	CR: I vs. III = 1.2			

TABLE 83 (*Continued*)

	ACCELERATION GROUPS			
	I	II	I + II	III
3. Parents' rating on health (1928) "good"				
Men	100.0% (33)	89.2% (140)	91.1% (173)	84.3% (398)
	CR: I + II vs. III = 2.5			
Women	100.0% (24)	89.6% (120)	91.1% (144)	86.8% (302)
	CR: I + II vs. III = 1.5			
4. Parents' rating on nervous tendencies (1928) "satisfactory"				
Men	96.9% (31)	89.8% (131)	91.0% (162)	87.4% (368)
	CR: I vs. III = 2.7; I + II vs. III = 1.3			
Women	85.7% (18)	91.5% (119)	90.7% (137)	88.2% (292)
5. Mean age at puberty				
Men	14.2 yrs. (21)	14.5 yrs. (100)	14.5 yrs. (121)	14.8 yrs. (358)
	CR: I + II vs. III = 2.4			
Women	12.7 yrs. (25)	12.8 yrs. (142)	12.8 yrs. (167)	13.1 yrs. (414)
	CR: I + II vs. III = 2.5			
6. Self-rating on health (1940) "good" to "very good"				
Men	90.6% (32)	89.9% (158)	90.0% (190)	91.2% (497)
Women	92.0% (25)	82.8% (134)	84.3% (159)	83.3% (389)
	CR: I vs. III = 1.5			
7. Composite of 1940 data on all-round mental adjustment "satisfactory"				
Men	74.3% (35)	83.2% (167)	81.7% (202)	79.5% (537)
	CR: I vs. II = 1.1			
Women	79.2% (24)	83.6% (147)	83.0% (171)	82.0% (411)

The outstanding facts given in Table 83 can be briefly summarized. The proportion whose health was rated "good" or "very good" on the 1922 evidence was highest in Group I, but for neither sex was the difference reliable. It is possible that good health was regarded by some of the teachers as a necessary condition for granting extra promotions. The rating on nervous tendencies based on 1922 evidence was best for the most accelerated, as was also the 1928 health rating by parents. In the case of men the same was true of parents' rating on nervous tendencies in 1928, but on this rating women did not show any consistent trend.

The mean age of puberty of Group III was for men 0.6 of a year later than for Group I; for Group II it was 0.3 of a year later than for Group I. The trend for women was the same as that for men, the figures corresponding to those just given being 0.4 of a year and 0.3 of a year. The differences for both sexes between the accelerates (Groups I and II) and nonaccelerates (Group III) in the age at puberty are fairly reliable, the critical ratio being 2.4 for men and 2.5 for women.

The 1940 self-ratings on health by men averaged almost exactly the same for all three groups; in the case of women, the self-ratings were highest for Group I (CR = 1.5).

Ratings on the all-round adjustment of men in 1940 were lower for Group I than for the other groups, but the difference is not reliable. In the case of women, the percentages rated "satisfactory" were almost identical in the three groups.

The data reviewed give no support to the fairly widespread opinion that rapid promotion in school is likely to be detrimental to physical or mental health, though one must bear in mind the possibility that physical health and good general adjustment may sometimes have been regarded by teachers as necessary conditions for extra promotion.

Section 5 of the table suggests that children most accelerated in school were on the average also accelerated in physical maturation as indicated by the age of puberty. The relationship verges on reliability. Here again it is possible that teachers are sometimes influenced by the child's apparent physical maturity in permitting rapid advancement.

Conclusions

The controversy on the advantages and disadvantages of acceleration hinges on the relative weight that should be given to intellectual and social values in the educative process. If the child's intellectual welfare were the sole criterion, then promotion ought to be based primarily on mental age, since it is this factor that chiefly determines the intellectual difficulty of the school tasks one is able to master. The child who starts to school at the age of 6 and a half years with a mental age of 10 years, can be brought to fourth-grade achievement before the end of his first school year. We know this as fact because it has happened over and over among the subjects of this group. Others in the group equally capable of making such progress—and this includes half or more of the subjects—have been caught in the lock step and held to school work two or three full grades below the level on which they could have functioned successfully.

Fortunately, this forced retardation does not slow up school achievement as much as one might expect. The gifted child may get bored, but, promoted or not, he manages somehow to achieve far more rapidly than his classmates. We have seen in chapter iii that in a majority of school subjects the achievement quotient almost keeps pace with the intelligence quotient; or, stated in another way, the child's achievement in the school subjects closely parallels his mental age, although this is somewhat less true in such drill subjects as spelling and arithmetical computations than in the "thought" subjects. It is a fact of extraordinary significance that among our ten-year-olds there was almost no correlation between achievement test scores and the number of years and months they had attended school. Heilman's notable study[30] shows that this is also largely true of the general school population at age ten. Achievement tests administered by Learned and Wood[40] in 49 colleges and numerous high schools show that even at the upper educational levels there is only a mild correlation between achievement attained in a given subject and the months or years of formal study devoted to it. Incredible as it may seem, they discovered high-school seniors who knew more science than some university seniors who had majored in science and were about to begin their careers as high-school teachers of that subject.

Although children can and often do achieve remarkably in spite of being denied the special promotions they have earned, a considerable proportion of those in our gifted group languished in idleness throughout the grades and high school and failed to develop the ambition or habits of work necessary to make them successful in college. The question is, how much risk of social maladjustment one can afford to take in order to keep the gifted child at school tasks difficult enough to command his attention and respect. The data here reviewed indicate that the risk of maladjustment is less than is commonly believed. Our case histories indicate that the disadvantages of acceleration so frequently mentioned by our subjects (see Table 81) are usually temporary. Moreover, the handicaps of social immaturity among the accelerated would not be so great if a larger proportion of the gifted were promoted rapidly, since in that case the under-age child would not feel so conspicuous.

Sometimes, however, the choice between acceleration and nonacceleration is unavoidably a choice between evils, each of which needs to be weighed against the background of the individual child's personality. No universal rule can be laid down governing the amount of acceleration that is desirable. Some gifted children are less injured by acceleration of three or four years than are others by one or two years. Important factors are the child's social experience and his natural aptitude for social adjustment. So far as physique is concerned, perfect health is probably less crucial than physical maturity or even mere size. The oversized, physically mature, and socially experienced child of twelve may be at less disadvantage in high school than the undersized, immature, and socially inexperienced child of fourteen.

It is our opinion that children of 135 IQ or higher should be promoted sufficiently to permit college entrance by the age of seventeen at latest, and that a majority in this group would be better off to enter at sixteen. Acceleration to this extent is especially desirable for those who plan to complete two or more years of graduate study in preparation for a professional career.

For a carefully controlled study of acceleration at the college level the reader is referred to the excellent monograph by Keys[35] whose findings support the conclusions of this chapter at almost every point. Keys's study is particularly valuable because of his use of a control technique that enabled him to compare accelerates in college with a group of nonaccelerates who were equally intelligent. Several recent studies by Pressey and his associates present equally striking evidence on the advantages of acceleration for bright students.[48]

CHAPTER XXI

SUBJECTS OF IQ 170 OR ABOVE

In the literature on gifted children much has been written about the unfavorable correlates of exceptionally high IQ. As we have pointed out in chapter i, there was a period in the history of child psychology when precocity of any degree was regarded as an evil omen. Later, when studies of gifted children showed this view to be contrary to fact, the child of moderately superior IQ (120 to 140) came to be looked upon more favorably, but the old prejudices persisted with respect to children testing in the higher levels of the IQ range.

Among our living gifted subjects (1940) are 47 men and 34 women who as children tested on the Stanford-Binet at IQ 170 or above.* It is doubtful whether more than 3 children in 10,000 of the general population would score this high.† The mean IQ of the men who had tested at or above IQ 170 was 177.7; of the women, 177.6. These means are about 25 points above the mean of the total group. The IQ's of this upper level group ranged from 170 to 194 for men, and from 170 to 200 for women.

The men of highest IQ averaged two and one-half years younger than the total 822 men, and the women of highest IQ averaged nearly three years younger than the 645 women.

In a search for correlates of exceptionally high IQ we have compared the high-testing subjects with the total group on a large number of variables. The subjects of 170 or above will be referred to as the "high" group. The variables on which comparisons were made fall into the following categories: physical and scholastic acceleration, physical health, nervous and mental health, social adjustment, educa-

* Six subjects (4 boys and 2 girls) included in this group had IQ's of less than 170 in 1922, but earned scores above that level in the follow-up Binet tests of 1928. In all of these cases the first test had been given before the age of five years, and it was believed that the second test was a more valid measure. Not included are 2 boys with IQ above 170 who had died.

† Of 2,970 unselected children, aged two and one-half to eighteen years, on whom the 1937 revision of the Stanford-Binet was based, only one scored as high as 170 IQ on Form L, and on Form M none reached this level.

tional history, occupational status and income, marriage and offspring, and a few other items.

Physical and Scholastic Acceleration

The most important findings in this category are summarized in Table 84. It will be seen that on age at walking, age at talking, and age at puberty, neither sex shows a statistically significant difference between the high group and the total group. On the proportion learning to read before the age of five or four, both sexes show a greater precocity of the high group. Of males, 42.8 percent in the high group learned to read before five, as compared with 18.4 percent in the

TABLE 84

Physical and Scholastic Acceleration:
High Group versus Total Group

	Men			Women		
	High Group	Total Group	CR	High Group	Total Group	CR
I. *Age at walking*	(N=44)	(N=690)		(N=29)	(N=539)	
Mean in months	13.4	13.9	1.2	13.6	13.6	
S.D.	2.54	2.82		1.85	2.53	
II. *Age at talking*	(N=35)	(N=545)		(N=20)	(N=428)	
Mean in months	17.6	17.5		15.4	16.3	0.9
S.D.	5.76	5.11		4.52	4.66	
III. *Age at puberty*	(N=24)	(N=489)		(N=31)	(N=603)	
Mean in years	14.7	14.7		13.1	13.0	
S.D.	1.19	1.17		1.16	1.25	
IV. *Learning to read*	(N=42)	(N=684)		(N=28)	(N=540)	
Before age 5 (percent)	42.8	18.4	4.2	25.0	18.5	0.9
Before age 4 (percent)	13.3	5.4	2.3	14.3	5.7	2.0
V. *Completing eighth grade*	(N=47)	(N=798)		(N=29)	(N=621)	
Mean in years	12.2	12.9	5.3	12.4	12.8	2.9
S.D.	0.88	0.93		0.60	0.76	
VI. *Completing high school*	(N=45)	(N=785)		(N=31)	(N=607)	
Mean in years	16.2	17.0	6.0	16.3	16.8	3.6
S.D.	0.94	0.92		0.77	0.80	
VII. *College graduation*	(N=39)	(N=519)		(N=19)	(N=386)	
Mean in years	20.9	21.7	3.4	21.0	21.1	
S.D.	1.46	1.53		1.43	1.27	

total group. The critical ratio of the difference is 4.2.* For females the proportions were 25.0 percent of the high group and 18.5 percent of the total group, a difference that is not reliable (CR = 0.9). The proportion reading before the age of four years was for both sexes about two and a half times as great for the high group as for the total group.

In the matter of school acceleration there was a highly significant difference between the male groups throughout their school careers, and between the female groups at all levels except college graduation. The high men completed the eighth grade 8.4 months younger on the average than the total group, and both high school and college 9.6 months younger. The women of the high group completed the eighth grade 4.8 months younger than gifted women as a whole, and high school 6 months younger, but they averaged only 1.2 months younger at college graduation.

Physical Health

Health ratings are available as of 1922–23, 1928, and 1940. Those of 1922–23 were based partly on medical examinations and partly on information secured from parents and teachers. The ratings of 1928 were based entirely on information furnished by parents, and the 1940 ratings were made by the subjects themselves.

No very high reliability can be claimed so far as these individual ratings are concerned, except for those of 1922–23, which were supplemented by medical examinations. However, even moderate reliability is sufficient to reveal any considerable differences that may exist between groups. If children of highest IQ tend to be significantly less healthy than children whose IQ's average 25 points lower, this certainly ought to be reflected in our data.

Of the six comparisons in Table 85, only two show any appreciable divergence of the high group from the total group. Among males, the 1922–23 ratings favored the high group; among females, the 1940 ratings favored the total group. However, neither difference is reliable, the respective critical ratios being 1.6 and 1.8. The conclusion sug-

* Since the values compared in this chapter are in all cases differences between a total population and a subgroup of that population, instead of between mutually exclusive groups, the CR's have not been computed in the usual way. The method used involves dividing the deviation of the mean (or percentage) for the high group from that for the total group by the standard error of the value for the subgroup obtained by the formulas for finite sampling. The resulting CR's closely approximate those which would result from comparing the high group with the remainder of the population. For formulas, see reference number 44, p. 334.

gested is that the subjects of IQ 170 or above are not significantly different from the total group, either in childhood or adult life, so far as physical health is concerned.

TABLE 85

PHYSICAL HEALTH: HIGH GROUP VERSUS TOTAL GROUP

	MEN			WOMEN		
	High Group	Total Group	CR	High Group	Total Group	CR
I. *Health ratings, 1922–23*	(N=41)	(N=699)		(N=30)	(N=554)	
"Very good" or "good" (percent)	85.3	74.5	1.6	80.0	83.2	
II. *Health ratings, 1928*	(N=44)	(N=683)		(N=27)	(N=524)	
"Very good" or "good" (percent)	88.5	86.1		92.5	88.0	
III. *Health ratings, 1940*	(N=43)	(N=700)		(N=31)	(N=562)	
"Very good" or "good" (percent)	93.0	90.8		71.9	83.6	1.8

NERVOUS SYMPTOMS AND MENTAL ADJUSTMENT

We also have ratings of 1922–23, 1928, and 1940, on nervous symptoms and mental adjustment. The 1922–23 ratings were based on fairly extensive information furnished by the medical examiners, parents, and teachers; those of 1928 were based on information chiefly from parents, but supplemented in a majority of cases by reports from schools and field workers. The ratings of 1940 were based on all the case-history data obtained by the field assistants from the parents, the subjects themselves, and other sources during the follow-up period. The results, summarized in Table 86, are probably more reliable and valid than the material on physical health.

The figures in Table 86 are almost identical for the two groups, with one exception: in 1940 the general mental adjustment was rated as "satisfactory" for 81.8 percent of women in the total group, but for only 65.6 percent of the high group. The difference is fairly reliable (CR = 2.5). Women rated in 1940 as having "some" or "serious" maladjustment included 18.2 percent of the total group and 34.4 percent of the high group. However, in view of the fact that the 34.4 percent represents an N of only 11, it would be hazardous to conclude from the data that there was any true difference between the high women and total group of women on the variable in question.

TABLE 86

NERVOUS SYMPTOMS AND MENTAL ADJUSTMENT: HIGH GROUP VERSUS TOTAL GROUP

	MEN			WOMEN		
	High Group	Total Group	CR	High Group	Total Group	CR
I. *Ratings of 1922–23*	(N=43)	(N=719)		(N=33)	(N=575)	
Difficulty: "little" or "none" (percent) ...	81.5	83.4		87.9	90.8	
II. *Ratings of 1928*	(N=41)	(N=618)		(N=26)	(N=496)	
Difficulty: "little" or "none" (percent) ...	85.4	88.3		88.5	88.5	
III. *Ratings of 1940*	(N=41)	(N=605)		(N=32)	(N=493)	
"Satisfactory" (percent)	82.9	79.6		65.6	81.8	2.5

SOCIAL ADJUSTMENT

The data on social adjustment include ratings of 1922 and 1928 based on several items of information furnished us by parents and teachers, testimony of the subjects themselves in 1922 and 1928 on preferred age of companions, information on amount of participation in extracurricular activities in school, mean total scores on the Cady-Raubenheimer character tests of 1922, and mean scores on aptitude for marital adjustment as measured in 1940. All of this material is summarized in Table 87.

The 1922 ratings on social adjustment showed no difference between the two groups. The 1928 ratings, however, gave a smaller proportion of both sexes in the high group rated as "satisfactory." For males the difference is moderately reliable (CR = 2.0), but for females it is highly significant (CR = 4.5).

The male groups did not differ on the proportion who preferred older companions; among females the proportion was slightly greater for the high group (CR = 1.4).

On extracurricular activities in high school, the high group of neither sex showed up as well as the total group, though the differences were quite unreliable. In college activities there was no difference that approached significance.

The 1922 character tests devised by Cady and Raubenheimer yielded almost identical scores for the two male groups. Among females the high group tested better on the average than the total group.

The test of aptitude for marital adjustment gave about the same mean score for the two groups of males. Among females the mean for the high group was a trifle below that for the total group (CR = 1.1). This difference, however, is out of line with the scores on the test of marital happiness in which the women of high IQ scored slightly higher (see Table 90).

TABLE 87

SOCIAL ADJUSTMENT: HIGH GROUP VERSUS TOTAL GROUP

	MEN			WOMEN		
	High Group	Total Group	CR	High Group	Total Group	CR
I. *Ratings of 1922*	(N=45)	(N=749)		(N=29)	(N=586)	
Percent "satisfactory"	88.9	89.6		93.1	95.2	
II. *Ratings of 1928*	(N=39)	(N=535)		(N=28)	(N=465)	
Percent "satisfactory"	84.5	92.5	2.0	78.5	95.5	4.5
III. *Companion preference*	(N=39)	(N=548)		(N=23)	(N=483)	
Percent preferring older	41.0	39.2		56.5	42.6	1.4
IV. *High-school activities*	(N=45)	(N=703)		(N=27)	(N=526)	
"Several" to "outstanding" percent	51.1	55.6	0.6	55.5	61.2	0.6
V. *College activities*	(N=40)	(N=520)		(N=19)	(N=388)	
"Several" to "outstanding" percent	35.0	35.6		47.4	38.7	0.8
VI. *Character test, 1922*	(N=17)	(N=268)		(N=16)	(N=226)	
Mean, total score	−1.1	−1.1		−1.4	−1.0	2.0
S.D.	0.91	0.89		0.68	0.84	
VII. *Aptitude for marital adjustment*	(N=39)	(N=697)		(N=28)	(N=538)	
Mean	87.1	86.6		74.9	77.6	1.1
S.D.	18.91	18.03		13.18	13.91	

Except for the ratings of 1928, the data give little support to the belief that children of extremely high IQ develop a greater amount of social maladjustment than do bright children of considerably lower IQ. That the ratings secured in 1928 were somewhat unfavorable to the high groups may possibly mean that for a period around the middle teens the child of IQ 170 or above is especially likely to show some maladjustment. If this is true, the condition is one which appears to correct itself later.

That the child of very high IQ faces a more difficult problem in social adjustment than does the less precocious child cannot be denied. Consider, for example, the seven-year-old boy in our group whose mental age at the time was thirteen years, and whose favorite reading was Gibbon's *Rise and Fall of the Roman Empire!* A large part of this boy's vocabulary was utterly unintelligible to the average boy of his age; it was almost as though he spoke a different language. For a time he had difficulties galore in social adjustment, but in ten years he seemed to have won out over all of them. Many other subjects in our group have had a similar history. The point is that, although children of this type are faced by difficult problems of adjustment, they have very superior intelligence with which to meet them. "Social" intelligence correlates positively rather than negatively with "verbal" intelligence. Although among gifted children and also among historical geniuses there are individual cases of what might be called social imbecility, these are rare exceptions to the rule.

Scholastic History

Table 88 summarizes our data on amount of education and quality of work done both in high school and college. Among men, significantly more of the high group than of the total group graduated from college, and somewhat fewer of the high group stopped with high-school graduation or less; in fact, only one man in the high group failed to attend college for at least a year. Slightly more men of the high group took graduate work beyond the Bachelor's degree. Among women, a slightly lower proportion of the high group than of the total group graduated from college, and a smaller proportion of the high group took one or more years of graduate work, but neither of these differences is reliable.

With respect to the quality of high-school work, men of the high group did a trifle better than men of the total group, but there was no difference in the case of women. In college there was a significantly greater proportion of men in the high group than in the total group who made an average of A. This was true to a less-marked degree of women also. In the proportion whose average grade was below B, there was no difference for the men, but among women the high group made a slightly better showing. The proportion elected to Phi Beta Kappa or Sigma Xi was greater for the high groups of both sexes, but for neither sex was the difference statistically significant.

Considering that in mean IQ the two groups differed by about

25 points, it is surprising that the superiority of the high group in scholastic record was not greater. The fact is that a good many of the most highly gifted did not achieve (as achievement is here measured) in proportion to their scholastic abilities.

Everyone will have his own explanation for this enormously important finding. In our opinion two factors are largely responsible: (1) our present educational methods are unsuited to the needs of extreme deviates in intelligence; and (2) the actual educational achievement of our high group is not adequately measured by school marks. The influence of the first of these factors is all but universally admitted. The presence of the second factor seems almost equally certain in the light of the studies by Learned and Wood[40] showing the low correlation between school marks and achievement as measured by objective tests.

TABLE 88

SCHOLASTIC HISTORY: HIGH GROUP VERSUS TOTAL GROUP

	MEN			WOMEN		
	High Group	Total Group	CR	High Group	Total Group	CR
I. *Amount of education*	(N=47)	(N=781)		(N=30)	(N=605)	
Graduated from college (percent)	85.1	69.8	2.7	63.3	66.4	
One or more years of graduate work (percent)	55.3	47.6	1.1	30.0	39.8	1.0
High-school graduation or less (percent)	2.2	7.9	1.5	6.6	11.5	1.0
II. *High-school grades*	(N=47)	(N=710)		(N=34)	(N=543)	
Percent with 15 recommending units	88.4	83.8		93.1	93.2	
III. *College grades*	(N=43)	(N=545)		(N=28)	(N=402)	
Average grade A (percent)	30.2	12.4	3.7	21.4	11.5	1.8
Average grade B (percent)	41.8	60.5	2.6	64.3	68.9	
Average grade below B (percent)	27.9	27.0		14.3	20.5	0.8
IV. *Graduation honors*	(N=39)	(N=512)		(N=19)	(N=391)	
Percent of graduates elected to Phi Beta Kappa or Sigma Xi	35.9	27.7	1.2	31.6	21.5	1.1

Occupational Status and Earned Income (1940)

It will be seen in Table 89 that the men of highest IQ excelled the total group of men in occupational status as of 1940. This was especially true in respect to the proportion in the professional class, 61.6 percent as against 45.4 percent. The critical ratio of the difference is 2.2. There was a somewhat smaller proportion of the high group than of the total group in the second census classification (semiprofessional and managerial), and notably fewer in occupations below Group II. Average income was almost the same for the high group and the total group, but it is necessary to remember that the high men averaged about two and a half years younger than the total group, and were more often in professions that require considerable time to establish oneself. Of the 27 high men in the professions, there were 7 members of college or university faculties, 5 engineers, 4 lawyers, 4 author-journalists, 2 chemists, 2 clergymen, and 1 architect.

In the comparison of the 150 most successful A men and 150 least successful C men, representing approximately the top and bottom 20 percent of those aged 25 and over (see chapter xxiii), it was found that 33 percent of the men of IQ 170 or above in this age range were in the A group, while only 12.8 percent were in the C group.

TABLE 89

Occupational Status and Earned Income of Men: High Group versus Total Group

	High Group	Total Group	CR
I. *Census classification*	(N=44)	(N=724)	
Group I (percent)	61.6	45.4	2.2
Group II (percent)	20.5	25.7	
Groups III to VI (percent)	18.0	28.9	1.7
II. *Earned income per month (men, age 25 or over)*	(N=35)	(N=545)	
Mean	$244.79	$246.97	
S.D.	135.11	162.08	

Among women, the occupational status of the high group did not differ significantly from that of the total group. Of the high group, 50 percent were in 1940 engaged in full-time employment as compared with 48.5 percent of the total group. Of those so employed, more than half were office workers as compared with 34.8 percent of those employed in the total group. The high group includes a talented sculptor and several writers, but no college teacher, physician, lawyer, or full-fledged scientist (although there were two with strong scientific interests who discontinued their work with a Master's degree in order to raise families). Regardless of intellectual level, women as a rule accept whatever employment is at hand to bridge the gap between school and marriage.

Marriage and Offspring (1940)

Table 90 summarizes the data for the marriage rate, the reproductive rate, the incidence of separation or divorce, and the marital happiness score.

TABLE 90

Marriage and Offspring (1940): High Group versus Total Group

	Men			Women		
	High Group	Total Group	CR	High Group	Total Group	CR
I. *Marriage rate*	(N=47)	(N=800)		(N=32)	(N=624)	
Percent having married	59.6	69.5	1.5	71.9	71.6	
Percent of married who have separated or divorced	7.1	11.2	0.9	13.0	12.7	
II. *Fertility rate*						
Mean offspring per marriage	0.7	0.8		0.3	0.8	
III. *Marital happiness test**	(N=19)	(N=383)		(N=14)	(N=302)	
Mean score	66.5	59.4	1.6	66.2	62.4	
S.D.	19.4	20.3		20.9	20.4	

* Among the total 697 tests taken were 12 received too late for inclusion.

The age difference between the high group and the total group probably accounts for the smaller proportion of men in the high group who had married by 1940. This factor may also account for the small discrepancy in the divorce rate among the men, since, being younger, they have not been married so long. There was little difference in the marriage or divorce rate among women of the two groups. For these selected subjects of both sexes the average age at marriage was almost exactly the same as that for the total group.

In the test of marital happiness, the high group of both sexes scored above the total group, but the differences are not reliable.

The 51 marriages in the two high groups had resulted in 26 offspring by 1940. Eleven of these children who were old enough to test had a mean Binet IQ of 129.5 as compared with a mean IQ of 127.7 for the total number of offspring tested. The difference is negligible for this small sampling.

The men of the high group married better from the standpoint of education of spouses than did the men as a whole. Sixty percent of their wives were college graduates as compared with 42.7 percent of all wives of gifted men (CR = 2.4). The husbands of high women did not differ appreciably in education from husbands of all women.

On the Concept Mastery test the differences between the spouses of the high group and of the total group were especially striking. Husbands of the gifted women with IQ of 170 or over averaged 98.8, as compared with a mean of 64.3 for all husbands of gifted women. The mean of the wives of high men was 71.5, as compared with a mean of 58.9 for all wives of gifted men. Critical ratios of these two differences were 2.6 and 1.2, respectively.

Other Variables

Comparison of the high group with the total group on several additional items from our case-history records will serve to round out the picture of these highly gifted individuals. The 1940 Information Blank called for self-appraisals on several points, and it is interesting to see to what extent the high group differed from the group as a whole on these variables.

Opinions regarding maintenance of their early mental superiority were almost exactly the same for the high groups as for the total group. Self-ratings on feelings of inferiority showed no relationship whatever with IQ in the case of women. Men of the high group rated themselves on the average as slightly more subject to inferiority feelings than did the total group, but the difference was not reliable. Men of the high and total groups agreed closely in their opinions about the advantages and disadvantages of the school acceleration they had experienced. Somewhat fewer of the high women than of all women were inclined to regard their acceleration as an advantage, but, on the other hand, more of them believed there had been no effect or that the advantages and disadvantages were about equal.

Self-ratings on radicalism-conservatism gave means a trifle more in the radical direction for the high groups of both sexes than for the total groups.

About 1.2 percent of the total group reported excessive drinking as against none in the high group of either sex, but the proportions of total abstainers did not differ.

Comparisons of parental background revealed some interesting differences between the two groups. The proportion of high-group fathers who were college graduates was 51.4 percent as against 33.4 percent of all fathers. The corresponding percentages for mothers were 24.7 (high) as compared with 15.5 (all). Although 42.8 percent of all fathers and 41.6 percent of all mothers failed to complete high school, only 27.1 percent of the high fathers and 19.2 percent of the high mothers fell within this category.

Ratings on occupational status in 1940 showed 33.3 percent of all fathers to be in professional occupations. In contrast, 56 percent of the high-group fathers were professional men. The difference is reduced when the professional group is combined with the semiprofessional and higher business group. Of all fathers, 65.7 percent are in these two census groups, as compared with 76 percent of the high-group fathers. In number of parents deceased, and in number of homes broken by separation or divorce, there was no difference between the high and total groups.

Summary

Many comparisons were made to discover how the subjects of 170 IQ or above differed from the gifted group as a whole. The results of these comparisons were more often negative than positive. Variables on which the high group and the total group of neither sex differed significantly included age at walking, age at talking, and age at puberty; health as rated in 1922, 1928, and 1940; age at marriage, marriage rate, divorce rate, and fertility.

The ratings on nervous symptoms and mental adjustment as of 1922, 1928, and 1940 were almost identical for the high group and total group with one exception: in 1940 a somewhat smaller proportion of women in the high group than in the total group were rated as "satisfactory."

Ratings on social adjustment in 1922 showed no difference between the high group and the total group of either sex. On the social adjustment ratings of 1928, the high-testing subjects of both sexes made a less satisfactory record than the total group, the difference in the case of women being statistically reliable. However, in extracurricular activities both in high school and college there was no appreciable difference between the high group and the total group of either sex. Moreover, the 1940 test of marital aptitude (which is largely a test of aptitude for general social adjustment) also failed to differentiate the high group of either sex from the total group. Everything considered, it appears that the subjects of highest IQ have been, on the average, about as successful as lower-testing subjects in their social adjustments.

The high group more often learned to read at an early age and were more accelerated in school. Reliably more of the high men than of total men graduated from college; among women there was a slight (though unreliable) trend toward *less* schooling for the high group. A large proportion of the high subjects of both sexes received much less schooling than they should have had.

In school grades there was no appreciable difference between the high group and the total group in the four years of high school. In college, however, the proportion making an A average was more than twice as great for the high group as for the total group, and Phi Beta Kappa or Sigma Xi honors were about 40 percent more common in the high group than in the total group. The most challenging fact in regard to scholarship is that about 25 percent of the most gifted subjects have college records than are only fair to poor.

Men in the high group made a better showing in occupational status than did men of the total group; relatively more of them were in the professional class, and relatively more were rated in the top 20 percent for vocational success. However, women in the high group did not differ appreciably from the total group of women in occupational status. Among both men and women of highest IQ there were individual subjects whose occupational histories were much less satisfactory than might have been expected from their intelligence ratings.

The parental background of subjects of highest IQ was superior to that of the total group, especially with respect to educational and occupational status. Moreover, the spouses of high subjects made a reliably better showing on the Concept Mastery test than did the spouses of the total group. It is possible that these two factors may have contributed to the greater success of the high group.

The characteristics of the subjects of IQ 170 and above would probably have stood out a little more clearly if the high group had been compared with subjects of 140 or 145 IQ instead of with the total group. Two additional circumstances have tended to blur the picture: (1) the fact that the high group averaged more than two and a half years younger than the total group, and (2) the fact that some subjects who deserved an IQ of 170 or higher were rated below this level because of inadequate top in the measuring instruments used in the original survey. However, even when generous allowance is made for these factors, it is obvious that subjects of highest childhood IQ are not sharply differentiated in adult life from subjects who tested considerably lower. On the average, those of highest IQ accomplish more and are equally well adjusted, but one cannot anywhere draw an arbitrary IQ line that will set off potential genius from relative mediocrity. Some of our subjects who have achieved most notably did not, either in childhood or in adult life, rate above the average of the total group in tested intelligence.

CHAPTER XXII

SUBJECTS OF JEWISH DESCENT

It would be interesting to know what differences exist, if any, between gifted subjects of various racial descent. However, our only ethnic subgroup large enough to warrant such a comparison was the Jewish. Among our 1,467 living subjects are 152 (88 men and 64 women) whose parents were both of Jewish descent. The proportion is 10.36 percent.* In the Main Experimental Group, located chiefly in the larger cities of California, the proportion of Jewish subjects is 14.8 percent; in the Outside Binet group and the High School Group, both recruited chiefly from the smaller cities, the proportion is 7.0 percent. In making this classification we have arbitrarily excluded from the Jewish group all who were reported as having a non-Jewish parent or grandparent.

The question arises whether the number of Jewish subjects is disproportionate to the Jewish school population in the areas canvassed by the original survey. Unfortunately, there are no statistical data on which a reliable estimate of this kind can be based. However, from the rough estimates we have been able to obtain regarding the urban Jewish population of California at the time of our original survey, it seems probable that the number of Jewish subjects is considerably greater than would be expected from the number of Jews then living in the areas canvassed.

Intelligence Scores

Childhood IQ's (Binet) were available for 71 men and 51 women of Jewish descent. The mean was 1.2 points higher for Jewish than for non-Jewish boys; that for Jewish girls was .9 of a point lower than for non-Jewish. Both differences are quite insignificant.

The Concept Mastery test was given in 1940 to 56 Jewish men and 45 Jewish women. The mean of Jewish women differed by only

* Of the 61 deceased subjects, 7 were Jewish. Thus, in the original group of 1,528, the proportion of Jewish subjects was 10.41 percent.

.4 of a point from that of the non-Jewish, but Jewish men averaged 5.3 points higher than non-Jewish. Even the latter difference is not reliable. Any significant difference in achievement of Jewish and non-Jewish subjects will therefore have to be accounted for by nonintellectual factors.

Occupational Status and Income

The comparisons on occupational status and income are limited to the men. In Census Group I, which includes the professions, the proportion in 1940 was 57.5 percent for Jewish men as against 43.9 percent for non-Jewish. The critical ratio of this difference is 2.32. In Census Group II, the upper business level, the respective proportions were nearly the same: 27.5 percent and 25.4 percent. In Groups III to VI combined the proportion was 15.0 percent for Jewish men as against 30.6 percent for non-Jewish. The latter difference is highly reliable (CR = 3.59).

There are a few rather significant differences in some of the professional subgroups. For example, physicians account for 26.1 percent of Jewish professional men and for only 10.9 percent of the non-Jewish men in the professions (CR = 2.24). Lawyers account for 30.4 percent of Jewish professional men and for 19.8 percent of non-Jewish (CR = 1.24). In contrast, the proportion teaching in colleges or universities is 8.7 percent of the Jewish professionals and 18.0 percent of the non-Jewish (CR = 1.64). For engineering, the corresponding percentages are 8.7 and 15.9 (CR = 1.32). These figures no doubt reflect to some degree the amount of antisemitic prejudice encountered in the different professional fields. Probably medicine and law, once the professional degree has been obtained, are the professions in which success is most likely to depend upon merit rather than upon the favors of others.

The monthly earned income of 55 employed Jewish men aged twenty to thirty-nine, reporting in 1940, averaged nearly 25 percent above that reported by the non-Jewish men. Earned income for 1944 reported by 40 Jewish men in civilian employment rose to approximately 42 percent above that of the non-Jewish for the same year. This is in line with the superiority of Jewish men in occupational status. We have noted elsewhere (p. 350), that the Jewish element among the 150 most successful men in the gifted group is considerably greater than in the gifted group as a whole.

Occupational Status of Fathers

Table 91 gives the 1940 occupational classification of 79 fathers of Jewish and 687 fathers of non-Jewish subjects. The figures are confined to fathers still living and actively employed at that date. When we compare these data with the occupational classification of our Jewish male subjects, as shown in the preceding section, it will be seen that the Jewish men, far oftener than the non-Jewish, have moved above their fathers in occupational status. For example, in the professional class were 57.5 percent of Jewish male subjects but only 15.2 percent of Jewish fathers, whereas the corresponding percentages for the non-Jewish were 43.9 and 35.4.

TABLE 91

Occupational Status of Jewish and Non-Jewish Fathers

Census Group	Jewish N	Jewish Percent	Non-Jewish N	Non-Jewish Percent
I	12	15.2	243	35.4
II	44	55.7	204	29.7
III and below	23	29.1	240	34.9

Educational Histories

School acceleration. Mean ages at graduation from the eighth grade, high school, and college were computed. No consistent difference was found for women, but the Jewish men averaged younger than the non-Jewish at all levels. The mean difference was 1.7 months at the end of the eighth grade, 3.4 months at high-school graduation, and 7.9 months at college graduation. This probably reflects the special concern shown by Jewish parents for the educational progress of their sons.

Amount of education. Of Jewish men, 75.3 percent graduated from college; of non-Jewish men, 69.1 percent. The difference is not reliable (CR = 1.09). Those with only high-school education or less included 2.3 percent of Jewish men as compared with 8.6 percent of non-Jewish. For women, the proportions were as follows: college graduation, 75.0 percent of the Jewish and 65.7 percent of the non-Jewish (CR = 1.52); high-school graduation or less, 14.3 percent of the Jewish and 11.3 percent of the non-Jewish. No Jewish women but 9 non-Jewish failed to complete high school. The proportion taking one or more graduate degrees was 62.5 percent of the Jewish men who completed college, as against 46.2 percent of the non-Jewish.

The difference is fairly reliable (CR = 2.52). The corresponding figures were 31.0 percent of the Jewish women as against 23.3 percent of the non-Jewish (CR = 1.03). The trend is consistent in the direction of more education for Jewish subjects.

Scholastic records. The proportion who graduated from high school with fifteen or more recommending units was almost exactly the same for Jewish and non-Jewish subjects. In college the proportion with average grades of A or B was 84.2 percent of Jewish men as against 76.6 percent of non-Jewish. Averaging C or lower were 15.8 percent of Jewish men as against 23.4 percent of non-Jewish. The corresponding figures showed no significant difference in the case of women. For neither sex was there any appreciable difference between Jewish and non-Jewish in the proportion elected to Phi Beta Kappa or Sigma Xi.

The proportion awarded one or more undergraduate scholarships or fellowships showed no difference for men. Of the non-Jewish women, 20.0 percent received such an award, but only 12.5 percent of the Jewish women. Graduate scholarships or fellowships were awarded to 20 percent of the Jewish men and to 27.1 percent of the non-Jewish. The corresponding figures for women were 20.8 percent for the Jewish and 12.1 percent for the non-Jewish. That is, among graduate students, Jewish men were less favored than were other men, whereas Jewish women were more favored than other women. For neither sex, however, was the difference very reliable.

Among those who attended college four years, the proportion reporting that they earned half or more of their expenses was 32.1 percent of the Jewish men as against 36.4 percent of the non-Jewish. For women the proportions were 8.1 percent of the Jewish as against 17.3 percent of the non-Jewish (CR = 1.9). The mean of reported total earnings in the undergraduate years was almost exactly the same for Jewish and non-Jewish men. The number of Jewish women reporting total earnings was too small to permit a meaningful comparison.

Extracurricular activities. Rating high ("several" to "outstanding") on extracurricular activities in high school were 54.3 percent of the Jewish men and 55.8 percent of the non-Jewish. For Jewish women the proportion was 56.5 percent as compared with 61.7 percent for the non-Jewish. For both sexes the difference is insignificant. In college the proportions for Jewish and non-Jewish men were 31.6

percent and 36.6 percent; for Jewish and non-Jewish women, 23.7 percent and 37.6 percent. The latter difference has a critical ratio of 1.9. It appears that both in high school and college our Jewish men have held their own fairly well in the competition involved in extracurricular activities, but that the Jewish women either have labored under a handicap or have been less interested than the non-Jewish in this field of endeavor.

Marriage and Offspring

A larger proportion of Jewish than of non-Jewish subjects of both sexes had married by 1940. For men the respective percentages were 77.8 and 68.5 (CR = 1.9). In the case of women the difference was very small: 73.7 percent of the Jewish women had married as against 71.4 percent of the non-Jewish. By 1945 the difference had decreased in the case of men, the proportion married by that time being 88.5 percent of the Jewish men and 84.4 percent of non-Jewish men. In the case of women the direction of the difference had changed, with 82.8 percent of the Jewish women and 84.2 percent of the non-Jewish women married. The 1945 figures for the sexes combined showed 86.1 percent of the Jewish and 84.3 percent of the non-Jewish subjects to have married.

The proportion of those married who had been separated or divorced by 1940 was 4.5 percent for Jewish men and 12.1 percent for the non-Jewish. This difference is fairly reliable (CR = 2.6). The percentages for Jewish and non-Jewish women who had separated or divorced were 8.9 and 13.2 (CR = 0.9). For the sexes combined the percentage was 6.3 for Jewish subjects and 12.6 for non-Jewish (CR = 2.5). The 1945 reports indicated a less marked difference in the number separated or divorced. For the sexes combined the percentages had risen to 12.3 for Jewish subjects as compared with 15.6 for the non-Jewish. This difference is not statistically significant (CR = 1.2).

It is surprising to find the above trend reversed for the parents of the two groups. The parents of 18.4 percent of Jewish subjects had been separated or divorced, as compared with only 13.4 percent of the non-Jewish parents. This difference, although suggestive, is not statistically reliable (CR = 1.5).

The mean Concept Mastery score of 40 wives of Jewish men was 2.6 points above that of 265 wives of non-Jewish men. The difference is not significant. The mean for 24 husbands of Jewish women was 71.2 as against 63.5 for 198 husbands of non-Jewish women. Although the latter difference is not entirely reliable, it is large enough to suggest a trend.

The test of marital happiness was given to 42 Jewish men and 28 Jewish women of the gifted group; it was also given to 24 Jewish husbands and 39 Jewish wives who had married Jewish subjects. For neither sex did the mean happiness score of the Jewish subjects differ at all significantly from that of the non-Jewish, nor did the Jewish spouses of either sex differ very significantly from spouses of the non-Jewish. The largest difference was between wives of Jewish and wives of non-Jewish men, the respective happiness means being 73.35 and 66.39 (CR = 2.3). The difference indicates a fairly reliable trend toward greater happiness among wives of Jewish subjects.

The test of marital aptitude was given to 69 Jewish men and to 53 Jewish women of the gifted group; it was also given to 24 Jewish husbands and 39 Jewish wives who had married Jewish subjects. There was no difference in the means on this test that even approached significance.

Ninety-one of the 124 Jewish marriages of one year's duration or longer had proved fruitful by 1945, the total number of children being 155, or 1.2 per marriage. By this date the non-Jewish subjects had produced an average of 1.4 children per marriage. It is impossible on the basis of facts thus far available to predict the ultimate fertility of the two groups.

Nervous Symptoms and Mental Adjustment

It is a common belief that people of Jewish descent are especially prone to nervous and mental maladjustment. However, as has been pointed out by Landis and Page,[37] studies by various investigators have shown that there is little or no difference between Jews and non-Jews in the incidence of mental disease as determined by hospital admissions. For the functional psychoses, the admission rates are about the same, and for such disorders as old-age psychoses, general paresis, and alcoholic psychoses the incidence is lower for Jews than for non-Jews. There is no evidence that such differences as do exist are racial in the biological sense.

Ratings on nervous symptoms were made for 75 Jewish and 644 non-Jewish boys, and for 54 Jewish and 521 non-Jewish girls. The proportion with "some" or "marked" symptoms in 1922 showed no difference between Jewish and non-Jewish girls. For Jewish boys the proportion was 18.6 percent as against 16.2 percent for the non-Jewish, a difference that is quite unreliable.

Ratings on general mental adjustment in 1940 were available for 82 Jewish and 678 non-Jewish men, and for 60 Jewish and 543 non-Jewish women. The percentages with "some" or "serious" difficulties in these ratings were as follows:

	Jewish	Non-Jewish
Men	21.9	20.2
Women	15.0	18.6

Of 7 suicides in the gifted group, 2 were Jewish subjects. Of 13 psychotics who became hospitalized, 2 were Jewish. Of 17 known cases of homosexuality in the gifted group (11 male and 6 female), none was of Jewish descent. The Jewish element was also entirely lacking among the known cases of delinquency. The differences mentioned in this paragraph are too small to be statistically significant.

Social and Political Attitudes

Our information on the political attitudes of the Jewish subjects includes three items: (1) a self-rating on radicalism-conservatism using the technique described in chapter xvii, (2) a statement as to political preferences, and (3) responses to questions about voting habits. Table 92 summarizes the self-ratings on radicalism-conservatism, and Table 93 the reports on political preferences and voting habits. In Table 93 the sexes have been combined, as the data in question did not bring to light any significant sex differences.

The ratings on radicalism and conservatism were made on a scale

TABLE 92

Comparison of Jewish and Non-Jewish Subjects on Self-Ratings of Radicalism-Conservatism

	Jewish	Non-Jewish	CR
Men	(N=66)	(N=601)	
Mean	4.6	5.2	2.7
S.D.	1.7	1.8	
Women	(N=51)	(N=492)	
Mean	4.3	5.2	4.5
S.D.	1.4	1.6	

of nine intervals from "extremely radical" (rated 1) to "very conservative" (rated 9). Table 92 shows that Jewish subjects rated themselves on the average somewhat more radical than did the non-Jewish. The difference is fairly reliable for men and highly reliable for women. There was no sex difference in the self-ratings of the non-Jewish subjects.

The information summarized in Table 93 is of a more objective kind. In Part I of this table there are several striking facts. One is the very small proportion in both groups who classified themselves as Communists, radicals, or even Socialists. In these three classes combined are only 6.2 percent of Jewish and 5.0 percent of non-Jewish subjects. The proportions who classified themselves as "independent" or "conservative" are low and about equal for Jewish and non-Jewish. "Liberals" are more numerous in the Jewish group, but by far the greatest difference is in the way the groups divide between Republicans and Democrats. Of Jewish subjects, 12.2 percent are Republicans; of the non-Jewish, 41.2 percent. Of Jewish subjects, 42.9

TABLE 93

COMPARISON OF JEWISH AND NON-JEWISH SUBJECTS ON POLITICAL PREFERENCES AND VOTING HABITS (SEXES COMBINED)

	Jewish (N=98) Percent		Non-Jewish (N=935) Percent		CR
I. *Political preference*					
None or undetermined	8.2		8.3		
Independent	3.1		2.5		
Communist	0.0	6.2	0.1	5.0	
Radical	3.1		0.9		
Socialist	3.1		4.0		
Liberal	17.3	65.3	12.3	38.0	5.4
New Deal	5.1		2.5		
Democrat	42.9		23.2		
Republican	12.2	17.3	41.2	46.3	6.9
Conservative	5.1		5.1		
	(N=115) Percent		(N=1,039) Percent		
II. *Voting habits*					
At all elections	84.3		81.2		
On national and state issues	2.6		1.6		
On national issues only	7.0		8.4		
On state issues only	...		0.2		
Occasionally or not at all	6.1		8.5		

percent are Democrats; of non-Jewish, 23.2 percent. The critical ratios of these differences are extremely high. About three-fourths of the subjects were living in California, a state which prior to 1930 was heavily Republican. This greater tendency to political liberalism on the part of Jewish subjects is not due to lack of vocational success, for on the average they have done better vocationally than the non-Jewish.

Part II of Table 93 discloses no reliable differences between Jewish and non-Jewish subjects, though there is a slight trend indicating that more of the Jewish vote at all elections, and more of the non-Jewish only occasionally or not at all.

It is not our purpose to evaluate the merits of radicalism as against conservatism, or of being a Democrat rather than a Republican. It is sufficient to note that these two lines of evidence are in agreement in indicating that conservatism on current political issues is less common among the Jewish subjects. In regard to voting habits, all will agree that the trend of difference found, even if too small to be statistically reliable, is in the direction of better citizenship on the part of the Jewish group.

The self-ratings on radicalism-conservatism take on a different color if we substitute the term liberalism for radicalism. There is ground for this substitution in the fact that the central tendency of the Jewish group is only moderately more radical than the mean of the non-Jewish. Actually, only a small proportion of the Jews rated themselves anywhere near the "extremely radical" end of the scale. Moreover, it is a matter of fact that the liberalism of the Jewish group is in line with the historical trend of political thinking of the last century.

Trait Ratings

Ratings by parents and teachers in 1922. These are ratings of the 25 traits referred to in chapter v. For the present purpose we have averaged the ratings by parents and teachers on each individual trait, and have computed the composite parent-teacher rating of each child for the 25 traits combined. This procedure increases the reliability of rating scores and provides a fairly good index of how favorably the child's personality had impressed the raters. The mean of the 25 ratings was obtained for 78 Jewish and 667 non-Jewish boys, and for 57 Jewish and 538 non-Jewish girls. For both sexes the mean of the

Jewish subjects was slightly but not significantly below the mean of the non-Jewish.

Ratings by parents and teachers in 1928. In the follow-up of 1928, ratings were secured from parents and teachers on 12 of the 25 traits rated in 1922. The traits selected for rating at that time were chosen on the basis of the reliability and objectivity with which they could be rated as indicated by the 1922 data. They included Perseverance, Fondness for groups, Leadership, Popularity, Desire to excel, Freedom from vanity, Sympathy, Conscientiousness, Desire to know, Originality, Common sense, and General intelligence. The ratings of parents and teachers were combined, as was done for the 25 traits rated in 1922. The 1928 data were available for 64 Jewish and 426 non-Jewish boys, and for 43 Jewish and 378 non-Jewish girls. The result was that the means were almost identical for the Jewish and non-Jewish subjects of each sex.

For two reasons the 1928 ratings are more significant than those obtained in 1922: (1) the reliability of the ratings was higher, and (2) the subjects in 1928 averaged about six years older than in 1922. It is well known that personality traits can be more objectively assessed at the teen age than in childhood.

*Self-ratings on personality in 1940.** These ratings were secured for 68 Jewish men and 53 Jewish women, and for 621 non-Jewish men and 488 non-Jewish women. The differences between the Jewish and non-Jewish means were for most of the traits small and unreliable. On Emotionality, Good nature, Sociability, Integration toward goals, Inferiority feelings, and Exclusiveness of friendships, the two groups gave almost identical means in the case of each sex. On Happiness of temperament, the Jewish subjects, both men and women, rated themselves slightly lower than did the non-Jewish, but the difference was not reliable. On Moodiness, the means for men were practically identical. The mean for Jewish women was slightly lower (more moody) than for non-Jewish, but again the difference was unreliable. On Self-confidence, the mean for Jewish men was slightly lower than for non-Jewish, but for women there was a small difference in the reverse direction. On Conformity, men showed no difference, but Jewish women were a trifle less conformist than the non-Jewish. On Perseverance, the mean for Jewish men was slightly but not reliably lower than for the non-Jewish (CR = 1.3); for women the difference

* See Appendix, pages 427 f.

was about the same in amount, but in the reverse direction. The only traits showing differences approaching reliability were Impulsiveness and Sensitiveness (in the case of women), and Egotism (in the case of men). The Jewish women rated themselves more impulsive and more sensitive than did the non-Jewish, the respective critical ratios being 3.0 and 2.3. Jewish men rated themselves as more egotistical than did the non-Jewish (CR = 2.2).

About the only conclusion one can draw from these self-ratings is that the Jewish and non-Jewish subjects probably do not differ greatly on the traits in question, or that any differences which may exist were obscured by some tendency on the part of those in each racial group to rate themselves in comparison with the general population of that group.

Ratings by parents on personality in 1940. The ratings made by parents in 1940 included all but 4 of the traits on which the subjects rated themselves: Impulsiveness, Self-confidence, Emotionality, Conformity, Sociability, Perseverance, Integration, Sensitiveness, Inferiority feelings, and Egotism. They included also 3 traits on which the subjects were not asked to give self-ratings: Talkativeness, Common sense, and Popularity. These ratings, like the preceding, utilized a cross-on-line technique and were scored on a scale of 1 to 11, where 6 was defined as "average." They were obtained for 75 Jewish subjects (45 men, 30 women), and for 684 non-Jewish (383 men, 301 women).

Traits on which mean ratings were almost exactly the same for the two groups included Impulsiveness, Self-confidence, Sensitiveness, Emotionality, and Talkativeness. The Jewish subjects, both men and women, were rated on the average as somewhat more vain than the non-Jewish, as more popular, as less conformist in their attitude toward authority, and as more integrated toward their goals; but in no case was the difference reliable. Jewish men were rated lower than the non-Jewish men on Common sense, but were rated higher than the non-Jewish on Sociability and on Perseverance. The very slight difference in rating on Inferiority feelings favored the Jewish men. In the case of women, the two groups did not differ on Inferiority feelings, Common sense, or Sociability. On Perseverance, Jewish women, unlike the Jewish men, were rated slightly below the non-Jewish.

Personality ratings by field workers (1940). The ratings by field workers are more significant than the self-ratings by subjects or the ratings made by parents because they are probably less biased. The traits to be rated by field workers were selected so as not to overlap too greatly the traits rated by the parents and by the subjects themselves. They were intended to provide an index of the impressions the subject made on the field worker in one or more personal conferences. Traits included were Appearance, Attractiveness, Poise, Speech, Vanity (freedom from), Alertness, Friendliness, Talkativeness, Frankness, Attention, Curiosity, and Originality.

The ratings were made on a 5-point scale on which 1 was high, 5 low, and 3 average. The ratings were made by Dr. Bayley, Dr. Marshall, and Dr. Sullivan. Ratings were secured for 62 Jewish and 488 non-Jewish men, and for 46 Jewish and 410 non-Jewish women.

TABLE 94

PERCENTAGES OF JEWISH AND NON-JEWISH SUBJECTS RATED HIGH ON PERSONALITY TRAITS BY FIELD WORKERS

	MEN		WOMEN	
	Jewish (N=62)	Non-Jewish (N=488)	Jewish (N=46)	Non-Jewish (N=410)
1. Appearance	56.4	52.7	56.5	61.0
2. Attractiveness	58.1	58.0	69.6	66.1
3. Poise	48.4	56.5	54.3	62.8
4. Speech	60.7	61.3	58.7	69.4
5. Vanity (freedom from)	19.3	14.9	19.6	24.9
6. Alertness	82.3	79.7	78.3	75.1
7. Friendliness	62.9	57.5	71.7	63.3
8. Talkativeness	30.6	41.9	54.3	46.0
9. Frankness	46.8	54.6	67.4	60.4
10. Attention	82.2	75.3	73.9	72.8
11. Curiosity	48.7	51.1	50.8	45.0
12. Originality	51.8	54.4	51.1	45.1

Table 94, showing the percentages rated 1 or 2 (above "average"), reveals no very significant differences. Slightly fewer Jewish than non-Jewish of each sex were rated high on Poise, the critical ratio being 1.2 for men and 1.1 for women. On Speech, Jewish women rated lower than non-Jewish (CR = 1.4), but for the men there was no difference on this trait. The Jewish subjects of both sexes rated a little higher than the non-Jewish on Friendliness, the critical ratio for men being 0.8 and for women 1.2. Jewish men were a bit more talkative than non-Jewish (CR=1.8), but this difference was reversed for the women (CR = 1.1). Frankness yielded similar results: Jewish men slightly lower (CR = 1.2), and Jewish women slightly higher (CR = 1.0). On Attention, Jewish men were rated higher than non-Jewish (CR = 1.3). Evidently the Jewish and non-Jewish subjects made, by and large, an equally favorable impression on our non-Jewish raters.

Summary

There are 152 Jewish subjects in the gifted group—a proportion that exceeds the proportion of Jews in the school population canvassed in the search for gifted subjects. Our data have been examined in considerable detail to discover in what respects these subjects tend to differ from the non-Jewish.

Neither in childhood IQ nor in score on the 1940 intelligence test was there a reliable difference between the two groups.

A larger proportion of Jewish men than of the non-Jewish were in professional occupations, and correspondingly fewer were in the middle and lower occupational levels. More than twice as large a proportion of Jewish men as of non-Jewish became physicians or lawyers, but only half as many Jewish as non-Jewish entered college teaching or engineering. The average earned income reported for 1944 was reliably higher for Jewish than for non-Jewish men.

The occupational status of fathers of Jewish and non-Jewish subjects differed in two respects: reliably more of the Jewish fathers were in the higher business occupations, and reliably fewer were in the professions.

A comparison of educational histories brought out a number of differences of varying amounts. School acceleration was a little more common among Jewish than among non-Jewish men, the average difference in age at college graduation being nearly two-thirds of a year. The proportion of college graduates was a little higher for the Jewish subjects of both sexes, and the proportion who completed one or more years of graduate work was considerably higher.

Scholastic records of the two groups in high school did not differ, but in college the Jewish men averaged a little better than the non-Jewish. Undergraduate scholarships were awarded about equally to Jewish and non-Jewish men, but less frequently to Jewish than to non-Jewish women. At the graduate level, Jewish men received less than their proportionate share of scholarships, and the Jewish women more. The proportion of college expenses earned was about the same for Jewish and non-Jewish men, but was considerably lower for Jewish than for non-Jewish women.

Both in high school and college the Jewish men held their own fairly well in the competition involved in extracurricular activities, but Jewish women participated less than the non-Jewish in this field of endeavor.

The marriage rate is slightly higher for Jewish than for non-Jewish men, and a trifle lower for Jewish than for non-Jewish women. The divorce rate among the Jewish subjects to 1945 is somewhat lower than that for the non-Jewish. The spouses of Jewish subjects averaged a little higher on an intelligence test than the spouses of the non-Jewish. Relative fertility of the two groups cannot yet be accurately assessed.

In the test of marital happiness, the average score did not differ for men, but was somewhat higher for Jewish than for non-Jewish women. For neither sex was there any appreciable difference between the groups in the test of aptitude for marriage.

Ratings on nervous symptoms and general adjustment in 1922, and again in 1940, failed to show any significant difference between the two groups. Because of the small number of Jewish subjects, it is impossible to judge the significance of the fact that among them there has been no known case of delinquency or homosexuality.

In self-ratings on radicalism-conservatism the Jewish subjects averaged significantly less conservative than the non-Jewish. A similar trend toward liberalism on the part of Jewish subjects was evidenced in their expressed political preferences.

The groups were compared on five sets of personality ratings. The average of parent-and-teacher ratings on 25 traits in 1922, was slightly lower for Jewish than for non-Jewish subjects. However, parent-and-teacher ratings secured on 12 of the same traits in 1928, when the mean age of the subjects was sixteen years, showed no difference between the two groups.

Self-ratings by the subjects on 14 traits of personality in 1940 showed only the following differences that approached reliability: Jewish women rated themselves as more impulsive and more sensitive than did non-Jewish women, and Jewish men rated themselves as more egotistical than did the non-Jewish.

Ratings of the subjects in 1940 were made by parents on 10 of the

14 traits just referred to, and also on 3 additional traits. Differences found indicated that the Jewish subjects of both sexes, as compared with the non-Jewish, were a little more vain, more popular, less conformist, and more integrated toward their goals.

The conclusion suggested by these detailed comparisons is that the Jewish subjects in this group differ little from the non-Jewish except in their greater drive for vocational success, their somewhat greater tendency toward liberalism in political attitudes, and somewhat lower divorce rate.

CHAPTER XXIII

FACTORS IN THE ACHIEVEMENT OF GIFTED MEN

Our group offers a unique opportunity for investigating the factors that make for vocational success or failure. Although as children all were above the 99th percentile of the generality in IQ, twenty years later they ranged in vocational success all the way from international eminence to semiskilled labor. What is here proposed is to read their careers backwards, so to speak, and to discover what factors and circumstances are correlated with adult achievement. In this connection it is important to remember that correlates are not necessarily causal. Nevertheless, once the correlates are known we shall be in a better position to draw reasonable inferences about causes.

The method of approach will be to compare the most successful with the least successful in order to discover what variables discriminate between these two extreme groups. The study has been limited to men because of the lack of a yardstick by which to estimate the success of women. By means of rating techniques, it is possible to identify fairly accurately outstanding chemists, astronomers, mathematicians, or psychologists, but no one has yet devised a method for identifying the best housewives and mothers, and this is what the vast majority of women aspire to be. The few women who go out for a professional career do so with one eye on the preferred alternative. Those who make no pretense of wanting a career are willing to accept any reasonably pleasant and respectable employment that will bridge the gap between school and marriage. For some the gap will never be bridged, and the result is that there are highly gifted women working as secretaries, filing clerks, elementary teachers, and telephone operators.

The Evaluation of Success

How shall success be evaluated? Among the criteria which almost everyone would want to consider are status on the vocational ladder, earned income, amount of education, moral character, marriage, social adjustment, and health; but it goes without saying that no one of these can be made the sole criterion. History affords numberless examples of great creative achievement by individuals who starved in garrets, had little or no formal education, were guilty of moral transgressions, failed miserably in their domestic and social adjustments, went through life as physical invalids, or skirted the border zone of insanity. Even the failure to rise above the lowest rungs of the occupational ladder does not necessarily mean that achievement in the truest sense has been trivial. There may have been heroic sacrifices, uncommon judgment in handling the little things of daily life, countless acts of kindness, loyal friendships won, and conscientious discharge of social and civic responsibilities.

Greatness of achievement is relative both to the prevailing patterns of culture and to the individual's personal philosophy of life; there neither exists nor can be devised a universal yardstick for its measurement. It must remain a matter of personal opinion whether the highest meed for accomplishment should go to the Napoleons, Newtons, and Miltons, or instead to missionaries, industrial entrepreneurs, teachers, and nurses. The standard we have used in the experiment to be described reflects both the present-day social ideology in this country, and an avowed bias in favor of achievement that demands the use of intelligence. It is concerned chiefly with vocational accomplishment rather than with the attainment of personal happiness.

Method of Rating Vocational Success

The primary criterion of success was the extent to which a subject had made use of his superior intellectual ability. Although this criterion is admittedly subjective, the three judges who made the ratings agreed upon certain general principles. In the case of subjects who had completed a graduate university course and had entered one of the professions, academic marks and professional recognition counted heavily. Earned income was given little weight except where it seemed clearly indicative of success as above defined. For example, young lawyers or college instructors with a brilliant academic record, but small salary, were not penalized for low income. Earnings could not be ignored in the case of those who had gone into business or into certain of the semiprofessional pursuits, but the judges were warned against overweighting this factor even in business occupations.

With these instructions in mind, the judges examined the records of 730 men who were twenty-five years of age or older for whom information on vocational status in 1940 was available, and from these they selected the 150 most successful (A group) and the 150 least successful (C group). These represented roughly the top and bottom 20 percent. Among the remaining three-fifths (the B group) were some who had made a very promising start but had not had time to prove themselves, and many more who were doing satisfactorily but were not quite up to the high standard of accomplishment required for an A rating. The three judges made their ratings independently, but after this was done they discussed each case on which there had been disagreement, and disposed of it by majority vote. The judges included, besides the present authors, Barbara Mayer, formerly research assistant in psychology, Stanford University, and later supervisor of counseling of the San Francisco office of the United States Employment Service. Miss Mayer's long experience in vocational counseling and her practical knowledge of occupational fields and their requirements were extremely helpful.

It was not possible to set up in advance any absolute standards for classifying subjects in the A, B, and C groups. The procedure followed was to begin with the most successful and work downward until the A quota was filled; and, at the other extreme, to begin with the least successful and work upward until the C quota was filled. There was no way of knowing a priori what degree of achievement would be found at the lowest level of A's or at the highest level of C's.

In the classification that resulted, the A's included all the men listed in *Who's Who*[73] or *American Men of Science*,[11] a large majority of those who were teachers above the rank of instructor in universities or superior colleges, the men who were outstandingly successful in law, medicine, engineering, or business, and a few who had achieved most in literature, art, motion pictures, or radio. Other information on the achievement of the A group will be found in chapter xxv.

The reader must not assume that the C group is composed almost entirely of failures. It does include a half-dozen who have been more or less chronically unemployed, and many others who are in occupations that do not make heavy demands on general intelligence, such as skilled or semiskilled trades, clerical and minor business positions, and civil service jobs in police or fire departments. But it also includes

25 men in occupations classified as professional, semiprofessional, and managerial whose records of accomplishment were among the least impressive found among our gifted subjects in such occupations. A number of the C group are in relatively humble vocations as a matter of deliberate choice. Some men like to work with their hands, some enjoy saleswork, bookkeeping, farming, or obscure civil service jobs that leave them free of responsibility out of work hours. In a few of these cases, leisure time is devoted to writing or to scientific pursuits of doubtful promise; in other cases it is devoted entirely to hobbies. Although more C's than A's are mentally or socially maladjusted, many of them are well adjusted and contented. Often the difference between a C and an A is little more than a difference in level of aspiration.

It will be understood that our classification of the men is cross-sectional and therefore highly tentative. On the basis of the evidence available when the ratings were made, the judges agreed that not only was there no overlapping between group A and group C in vocational success, but that the two groups were separated by a considerable gap. That the future will bring many changes can be taken for granted. Ill health, personal maladjustment, unhappy marriage, or other misfortune may affect some of the now promising careers unfavorably. Others who have been relatively unsuccessful may "find" themselves and move upward. As we shall see later, a few shifts in each direction have occurred since the 1940 classification was made.*

Age Comparability of the Groups

As we have previously stated, it was decided in the present classification to limit the comparison to subjects who were 25 years of age or older in order to give reasonable time for success to become evident. However, two men of 23 years and one of 24 were so outstanding in achievement that they were included in the A group. Except for these, all of both groups were 25 years of age or older. The A and C

* A somewhat similar classification of our gifted men was made in 1937, based on rather inadequate data secured chiefly by mail. This will account for the fact that some of the figures to be presented in this chapter differ from the published report of the 1937 study.[67] The more detailed information obtained in 1940 made possible the classification of some subjects whose status was indeterminate at the earlier date, and the arbitrary reduction of the A group from the earlier N of 167 to the present N of 150 also disturbs the comparison. There were other shifts in rank between 1937 and 1940 that were due to actual changes in success status, but these were not numerous.

groups to be compared were, as shown in Table 95, well matched for range of age, median and mean age, and age variability.

TABLE 95

AGES OF A AND C GROUPS (1940)

Ages	Group A (N=150)	Group C (N=150)
Range	23–39 years	25–38 years
Median	30.7	30.4
Mean	30.8	31.0
S.D.	2.9	3.3

COMPARATIVE DATA EXAMINED

We have compared the A and C groups on some 200 items of information secured between 1921 and 1941. The results will be presented under the following heads: occupational classification and earned income; amount of education and educational histories; intellectual differences; vocational and avocational interests; early development; childhood tests of interest and personality; family background; physical health; mental health; social adjustment and activities; marriage; special trait ratings. The most important data in each of these categories will be summarized in the above order.

As usually happens in investigations of this kind, it was not possible to secure all the needed information on every item to be considered. In some comparisons the N's are severely limited by the fact that in 1922 certain kinds of data were secured only for the Main Experimental Group of 643 subjects, which is less than half the total number of subjects in our files. In the follow-up study the N's on a good many items were further reduced by the fact that subjects outside California could not be visited by field assistants. In other cases, information was lacking merely for the reason that the subject failed to respond to certain items when filling out the General Information Blank. The question arises whether those failing to respond form a selected group and so distort our results. In the case of a majority of the items of information we think no such distortion has occurred, but in the case of certain others it may have entered to some extent.

OCCUPATIONAL CLASSIFICATION

Table 96 gives the occupational classification of all the A and C subjects in terms of the Minnesota Occupational Scale.

TABLE 96

OCCUPATIONAL CLASSIFICATION OF A AND C GROUPS (1940)

Occupational Group	Group A (N=150)		Group C (N=150)	
	N	Percent	N	Percent
I. Professional	103	68.67	14	9.33
II. Semiprofessional and managerial	46	30.67	11	7.33
III. Clerical, skilled trades, retail business	..	....	73	48.67
IV. Agriculture	..	....	2	1.33
V. Semiskilled occupations, minor clerical positions, and minor business	..	....	33	22.00
VI. Slightly skilled trades or occupations requiring little training or ability	..	....	6	4.00
Student	1	0.67	3	2.00
Unemployed	..	....	6	4.00
Incapacitated	..	....	1	0.67
Unclassified	..	....	1	0.67

Of the A's, more than two-thirds were in the professions, and the remainder, except for one who was still a student, were all in Group II—the higher business or semiprofessional occupations. Only 17 percent of the C's were in the two highest occupational classes, close to 49 percent were in Group III, and 22 percent in Group V. Two C men (1.3 percent) were in the agricultural occupations of Group IV, and 6 were unemployed.

The 103 A's in the professional group included 27 members of college or university faculties, 24 lawyers, 16 physicians, 11 engineers, 10 writers or journalists, 7 chemists, 2 architects, an artist, a clergyman, and 4 others in miscellaneous professions. The 14 C's in the professional group included 3 writers, 2 teachers, 3 engineers, 3 chemists, 1 clergyman, 1 lawyer, and 1 artist.

Among 46 A's in occupational Group II were 12 economists, investment counselors, or executives in the banking, brokerage, or insurance business; 11 A's were owners or managers in business or industry; 8 were in radio or motion-picture work (director, editor, or producer); 5 were in personnel, social, or welfare work; 4 were in advertising or public relations; one was a naval officer, one a musician, and 4 were in miscellaneous executive or managerial positions. Among the 11 C's in Group II were 3 musicians, 2 owners and managers of a brokerage business, 1 radio program producer, 1 factory department manager, 1 welfare worker, 1 draftsman, 1 personnel man, and 1 pharmacist.

Close to half of the 73 C men in Group III were in clerical work, and the remainder were distributed among such occupations as sales work, skilled trades, technical work, retail business and jobs as foremen or inspectors in industry.

Seven of the 33 men in Group V were in protective service occupations (members of police or fire departments), 7 in minor clerical positions, 4 in semiskilled trades, 3 in minor retail business, 2 were salesmen of retail goods, and the remainder held jobs as baker, cook, letter carrier, streetcar conductor, *et cetera.* The 6 C men in Group VI included 2 laborers, 1 porter, 1 delivery man, 1 bartender, and 1 seaman.

One student was admitted to the A group because his record was so outstanding and his future so promising. Three men of student status were placed in the C group; all three continued schooling because of reluctance to enter the working world or because of limited success in jobs previously held. The ages of these men were twenty-eight, thirty, and thirty-one. All had taken a Bachelor's degree; two had been engaged unsuccessfully in several occupations and returned to college for special certificates, and one had been studying intermittently for ten years for an advanced degree, working at relatively menial jobs when not in college.

The 6 unemployed in the C group had been out of work a considerable part of the time since leaving school. Two of them were engaged in independent projects, one as a free-lance salesman, and one as manager of his father's estate, but neither of these enterprises was a full-time occupation. In all cases the unemployment could be attributed to personality quirks resulting in dissatisfaction on the part of both employer and employee, rather than to inability to secure and execute a job. The man classed as incapacitated was one who, having failed to get a job he considered suited to his talents, developed hypochondriacal tendencies and decided he was not strong enough to work, although he was able to do a great many other things. One man in the C group (see page 118) could not be classified vocationally because he was serving a prison term.

Earned Income

Information on earned income (Table 97) was available in 1940 for 130 A's and 104 C's. Information was either lacking or could not be evaluated for 20 of the A's, and for 46 of the C's. These include the students, the unemployed, the incapacitated, and those whose income was derived chiefly from independent means.

TABLE 97

MONTHLY EARNED INCOME OF A AND C GROUPS (1940)
(UNEMPLOYED OMITTED)

	Group A	Group C
Range	$150 to $1,500	$ 50 to $300
Median	315.81	143.05
Mean	387.04	144.25
S.D.	236.44	43.96

In view of the fact that earned income was purposely given relatively little weight in classifying the subjects in the A, B, and C groups, the contrast between the A's and C's in this respect is much greater than was expected. There were 73 A's but no C's with an earned income above $300 a month, and the mean of $387.04 for A's is more than 2.6 times that of the C's.

AMOUNT OF EDUCATION

Table 98 shows the striking contrast between the A and C groups in amount of education; the differences are so great that the computation of critical ratios would be senseless. Of the A's, 90 percent graduated from college and 76 percent have done one or more years of graduate work. For the C's, the corresponding figures were 37.2 percent and 14.7 percent. Four of the A's (2.7 percent) and 47 of the C's (31.4 percent) failed to attend college at all.

Graduate degrees taken by members of the two groups to 1940 were as follows:

	A's	C's
Doctor of Philosophy	33	1
Master's	25	3
Law degree	23	4
Doctor of Medicine	16	0
Bachelor of Theology	1	0
Total	98	8

The reader may feel that the differences in amount of education were largely a corollary of the method used in classifying the subjects; that is, setting as the chief criterion the extent to which the individual had made use of his intellectual abilities. It is possible that this rule may have led the raters to overstress educational achievement as contrasted with achievement of other kinds, for the part played by intelligence in academic success is more obvious than the part it plays in success of other kinds. However, we believe that the procedure of classification used is on the whole defensible.

TABLE 98

AMOUNT OF EDUCATION OF THE A AND C GROUPS

	Group A (N=150) Percent	Group C (N=150) Percent
Graduation from college	90.0	37.2
One or more years of graduate work	76.0	14.7
One to four years of college work without graduation	7.3	31.3
High-school graduation plus special courses	2.7	12.7
High-school graduation only	...	16.7
Less than high-school graduation	...	2.0

EDUCATIONAL HISTORIES

Other information on educational histories included Stanford Achievement Test scores of 1922 for those in the Main Experimental Group enrolled in grades two to eight inclusive, age of learning to read as reported by parent, a composite of parent and teacher estimates of amount of reading in 1922, a reading record kept by the child over a period of two months in 1922, a report by the parent in 1922 on amount of home instruction, age at graduation from the eighth grade and high school, the subject's personal reaction to any acceleration that he may have experienced, scholastic achievement in high school and college, awards of scholarships, fellowships, and assistantships and the stipends therefrom, and the total extent of self-support in college.

The Stanford Achievement Test was given in 1922 to 101 boys who were later classified as A's and to 117 classified as C's. We have computed for those who took the test the separate achievement scores in reading, arithmetic, language usage, spelling, science, literature, history and civics, art, and total of the achievement test battery. As it turned out, the scores of 37 A's and 34 C's were so high that they went beyond the available norms and so could not be used in the computation of achievement quotients. The proportion of A's falling in this category was 36.6 percent; of C's, 29.1 percent. Comparison of the remaining 64 A's and 83 C's gave almost identical mean achievement quotients in every school subject except language usage and art information, in both of which the A's averaged slightly higher. Even if one makes reasonable allowance for the larger proportion of A's who scored above the norms, it appears that during the elementary school years the C's were only slightly below the A's in all-round mastery of the curriculum. However, the C's averaged nearly a third of a year older at completion of the eighth grade.

It was not until the high-school period that the two groups began to fall apart with respect to achievement. By the end of high school the difference had become very marked, for 95 percent of the A's earned 15 or more recommended units as compared with 67 percent of C's. At the college level the difference was still greater; fewer C's went to college, and the average grades of those who did were relatively low. We have information regarding the grades of 125 A's who graduated from college, and 52 C's. An average of "A" was made by 29.6 percent of the A's and by only 5.8 percent of C's. Only 7.2 percent of the A group averaged "C" or lower as compared with 30.8 percent of the C group. Both differences are highly reliable. A similar comparison of those who attended college two or more years but did not graduate, was equally unfavorable to the C's.

Of graduates in the A group, 37.8 percent were elected to Phi Beta Kappa and 26.7 percent to Sigma Xi. The corresponding proportions for graduates in the C group were 1.8 percent and 3.6 percent. Both of these honors were won by 11.9 percent of the A's, but by only 1.8 percent of the C's. The proportion who graduated from college with honors (*cum laude,* with distinction, *et cetera*) was 51.9 percent of the A's and 14.3 percent of the C's.

Of those attending college two years or more, 29.7 percent of A's were awarded scholarships and 7.7 percent assistantships. The corresponding figures for C's were 10.0 percent and 0.0 percent. Graduate scholarships or fellowships were awarded to 57.9 percent of the A's but to only 4.3 percent of the C's; assistantships to 46.8 percent of the A's and to 20.0 percent of the C's. For those who held scholarships, fellowships, or assistantships, the average total of stipends from all these sources was $1,517.14 for the A's and $277.28 for the C's. Many of the A's held such awards for two to four years, the C's usually for one year or less.

Comparison of responses on the proportion of total college expenses earned showed no difference between the A and C groups, either for those graduating or for those attending two or more years without graduating. Reliable differences were also lacking in estimates of total undergraduate earnings of those who attended college for four years. The mean was $1,529.50 for the A's (S.D. $1,153.95) and $1,606.50 for the C's (S.D. $1,180.61). In the graduate years the advantage was with the A's, of whom 53.4 percent had to earn half or more of their expenses as compared with 73.3 percent of the C's. However, the number of C's who did graduate work is so small that this difference is not reliable. The economic pressure on the A's was considerably alleviated during the graduate years by awards of scholarships, fellowships, and assistantships.

Analysis of major fields of study selected by 142 A's and 79 C's attending college two years or more yielded no significant differences between the groups. Similar data at the graduate level for 114 A's and 22 C's showed 21 A's as against 1 C majoring in the Biological Sciences, and 2 A's as against 5 C's majoring in Letters. However, it would be hazardous to base any conclusions on N's so small.

Table 99 gives means and standard deviations of ages at graduating from the eighth grade, high school, and college. Where the N's are less than the number who graduated, information on exact date of graduation was not available.

TABLE 99

COMPARISON OF A AND C GROUPS ON SCHOOL ACCELERATION

	Group A	Group C	CR
Age at completing eighth grade	(N=150)	(N=147)	
Mean in years	12.8	13.2	4.0
S.D.	0.9	0.8	
Age at high-school graduation	(N=150)	(N=142)	
Mean in years	16.8	17.6	7.9
S.D.	1.0	0.8	
Age at college graduation	(N=134)	(N=51)	
Mean in years	21.2	22.5	4.9
S.D.	1.3	1.8	

At all educational levels the A's were reliably more accelerated than the C's. On the average they completed the eighth grade 4.8 months earlier, high school 9.6 months earlier, and college 15.6 months earlier.

The groups also differed in their reaction to the acceleration they had experienced. There were 91 A's and 46 C's who considered themselves to have been accelerated and who expressed an opinion regarding its advantages and disadvantages. Advantages only were mentioned by 26.4 percent of the 91 A's and by 10.9 percent of the 46 C's; disadvantages only by 45.1 percent of the A's and 73.9 percent of the C's. There were 28.6 percent of the A's and 15.2 percent of the C's who regarded their acceleration as both an advantage and a disadvantage, or neither. The outstanding fact here is that although the C's were actually less accelerated than the A's, they were more inclined to stress disadvantages. It is possible that the harsher opinions expressed by the C's on the evils of acceleration were to some extent a rationalization of their lack of scholastic success.

Intelligence as of 1922, 1928, and 1940

Since all the subjects rated in childhood within the highest 1 percent of the school population for IQ, one would hardly expect to find a very large difference between the A and C groups in intelligence test scores. The differences shown in Table 100 were, in fact, even less than we had expected.

Information on intelligence in 1922 included IQ's of 96 A's and 92 C's who qualified on the Stanford-Binet, and IQ's of 52 A's and 55 C's who qualified on the Terman Group Test. Not included in the table were 2 A's and 3 C's who qualified on the Army Alpha. Forty-one A's and 50 C's who had earlier been given the Stanford-Binet, were retested in 1928 on the Terman Group Test. In 1940 the Concept Mastery test described in chapter xi was administered to 79 of the A group and to 116 of the C group. The relatively small number of A's given this test is in large part explained by the fact that more of them lived outside of California in 1940 and could not be reached by field assistants.

In addition to the intelligence test scores, we have included in Table 100 the composite of the parent-and-teacher ratings of 1922 and also of 1928 on four traits classified as intellectual in the sense that all of them involved to a greater or less degree the factor Spearman would call *g*. The four traits in question were labeled "General intelligence," "Desire to know," "Originality," and "Common sense." Because of the well-known fact that the reliability of ratings on such individual traits is relatively low, we have thrown the four traits together and secured the average rating by the parent and the average rating by the teacher. The composite we have used is the average of these two averages. Finally, we have included with the data on intelligence the self-ratings made by the subjects on how fully their early superiority had been maintained.

TABLE 100

INTELLECTUAL DIFFERENCES BETWEEN THE A AND C GROUPS

	Group A	Group C	CR
Binet IQ, 1922	(N=96)	(N=92)	
Mean	155.0	150.0	3.0
S.D.	13.3	9.1	
T.G.T. IQ, 1922	(N=52)	(N=55)	
Mean	143.2	142.3	
S.D.	5.2	9.2	
Parent and teacher ratings of intellectual traits, 1922	(N=139)	(N=141)	
Mean	3.5	3.8	1.9
S.D.	1.3	1.2	
Parent and teacher ratings of intellectual traits, 1928	(N=87)	(N=78)	
Mean	3.5	4.7	5.0
S.D.	1.4	1.8	
T.G.T. IQ, 1928	(N=41)	(N=50)	
Mean	141.0	139.2	
S.D.	4.2	3.8	
Concept Mastery Score, 1940	(N=79)	(N=116)	
Mean	112.4	94.1	4.2
S.D.	28.4	31.3	
Self-rating on maintenance of superior ability, 1940	(N=127)	(N=120)	
More marked	11.8%	4.2%	
Unchanged	65.4%	52.5%	
Less marked	22.8%	43.3%	3.5

The differences between the A and C groups in Table 100 are all in favor of the A's, and are statistically significant except for the scores on the Terman Group Test and the parent-teacher ratings of 1922. In the absolute sense, however, the differences are not large. On the Stanford-Binet, for example, it is only 5 points in terms of IQ. The most significant difference is in the parent-teacher composite ratings in 1928 on four aspects of intelligence. The critical ratio of this difference is 5.0 as compared with 1.9 for similar ratings of

1922. The intellectual differences between the groups were evidently more discernible in youth than in childhood.

Most impressive is the great amount of overlapping between the groups in tested intelligence at all ages. Although the 1940 mean of the Concept Mastery scores of the A's was reliably higher than that of the C's, the mean of even the C's was so high as to be equaled by only 15 percent of students in superior universities. The Concept Mastery mean of the A's was not far below that of Doctor of Philosophy candidates in leading universities. Notwithstanding the reliable difference between mean C.M. scores, it can hardly be claimed that this accounts for the striking contrast between the groups in adult achievement. Where all are so intelligent, it follows necessarily that differences in success must be due largely to nonintellectual factors.

The last section of the table shows that the C's more often than the A's believed that their early superiority in intelligence had not been maintained. In some cases this opinion was borne out by the intelligence test scores, but in many cases it was not. The responses on this item probably tended to be influenced by the degree of vocational success experienced.

Vocational Interests

The Strong Vocational Interest Test was administered to 131 A's and 121 C's. The blanks were scored for 26 items, including 24 occupations, occupational level, and masculinity-femininity.* It was thought that these scores would cover most of the occupations in which gifted men were engaged, but, as it turned out, only 83 A's and 48 C's were employed in the occupations scored. Even these small N's provide some evidence that a greater proportion of A's than of C's were in vocations suited to their interests. Of the 83 A's, 72.3 percent received an interest rating of "A" in their own vocation, as against 52.1 percent of the 48 C's. The critical ratio of the difference is 2.32. Ratings of "B—" or less in their own vocations were received by only 4.8 percent of A's as against 22.9 percent of the C's (CR = 2.78). Strong has found that few men are successful in a vocation in which they have scored "B—" or lower. These differences suggest that one factor in the relative lack of success of the C group, though possibly not a major one, is that more of them are vocationally misplaced.

* See pages 196 f. for a list of the occupations scored.

We have found a considerable number of men in the gifted group who seemed to have no genuine interest in any particular vocation, and whose employment records indicated that they were drifters. Some of these on being given the Strong test failed to get a high interest score in a single occupation. This raised the question whether the tendency to drift, as so many of the C's do, may not be caused by interests so generalized that they fail to match any of the patterns characteristic of specific occupational groups. To test this hypothesis we have sorted the A and C vocational interest scores to show the number of scores as high as "B+" or better. The mean number of scores meeting this criterion per individual was 6.37 for A's and 5.59 for C's. The difference is fairly reliable (CR = 2.79). The proportion with 3 or fewer high scores was 9.9 percent of the A's and 19.8 percent of the C's; the proportion with 8 or more high scores was 32.1 percent of the A's and 22.3 percent of the C's.

Still better discrimination between the groups was yielded by the score for "occupational level," a score intended as a measure of the extent to which an individual's interests are, at one extreme, like those of unskilled men, or, at the other extreme, like those of higher business and professional men. In standard score units the mean occupational interest level of the A's was 59.52; that of the C's, 54.13. The difference is completely reliable (CR = 6.54). The proportion of A's with O.L. scores below 55 was 22.1 percent; of C's below this level, 50.0 percent. The proportion of A's above 59 was 54.2 percent; of C's, 21.7 percent. This difference parallels the difference in occupational classification by census groups as presented earlier in this chapter.

Finally, the A and C groups were scored for masculinity-femininity of interests as measured by the Strong test, but the groups did not prove to be reliably different in this trait. At most there was a slight tendency for C's to be more masculine in their interests. This small difference is fully accounted for by the stronger cultural interests of the A's, a factor which tends to reduce the score in mental masculinity as measured by tests of interests and attitudes.[66]

In the light of the above differences in vocational interest scores, the expressed attitudes of A's and C's regarding the work they were engaged in are very significant. There were 96 A's and 76 C's who stated categorically whether they liked, disliked, or were indifferent toward the kind of work they were doing. Of the A respondents, all but two, or 97.9 percent, said they liked their work; of C respondents, 75.0 percent so stated. The critical ratio of the difference is 10.7. No A's but 5 C's expressed positive dislike of their work.

There were 142 A's and 118 C's who indicated whether their occupation had been "definitely chosen" or "drifted into." Of A's responding, 74.6 percent said it had been definitely chosen; of C's, 31.4 percent. The critical ratio of this difference is 7.7. Asked whether they would prefer some other kind of work, 9.0 percent of the A's and 43.4 percent of the C's replied definitely in the affirmative (CR = 6.8). However, one must be cautious in interpreting this greater dissatisfaction of C's with their work. To some extent it no doubt does reflect vocational misplacement, but in some cases it may be a method of rationalizing lack of vocational success.

Avocational Interests

In the General Information Blank of 1940, subjects were asked to indicate their chief avocational interests. Of 145 A's who responded, 26.3 percent mentioned only one avocational interest or indicated that they had no such interest. Of 126 C's who responded, 42.1 percent were in the "one" or "none" category. The critical ratio of the difference is 2.8. Listing three or more avocational interests were 39.2 percent of A's and 27.8 percent of C's (CR = 2.00).

There were a few differences, none very reliable, in the proportion of A's and C's mentioning specific avocational interests. For example, sports were mentioned by 57.9 percent of the A's and by 50.0 percent of the C's; photography by 32.4 percent of the A's and by only 19.8 percent of the C's; reading or study by 17.2 percent of the A's and by 7.9 percent of the C's; gardening by 20.0 percent of the A's and by 13.5 percent of the C's.

In order to secure information on the catholicity of interests among intellectually superior persons, our subjects were asked to rate the strength of their interests in each of 12 specific areas. The rating was on a 5-point scale from "very much" to "more than average," "average," "slight," or "none." We have compared the A and C groups with respect to mean rating on each of the 12 interests. Ratings were secured from 144 A's and 127 C's.

For 3 of the 12 areas, the A and C means were practically identical: outdoor sports, religion, and domestic arts. Higher mean ratings were given by A's on travel (CR = 2.3), science (CR = 2.0), music (CR = 1.8), and art (CR = 1.4). The means were slightly higher for the C's on mechanics (CR = 0.9) and pets (CR = 1.7). There was no field in which the mean was reliably higher for the C group, but the means of A's were reliably higher for politics (CR = 4.5), social life (CR = 3.5), and literature (CR = 3.4). These ratings strongly suggest a greater breadth of interest among A subjects, and particularly more interest in politics, social life, and literature.

Some Aspects of Early Development

Table 101 summarizes the reports by parents on age at walking, talking, and pubescence, the latter defined as the age at change of voice. The reports on walking and talking were secured in 1922, those on pubescence chiefly in 1928. According to these reports, the mean age of learning to walk was nearly a month lower, and that of learning to talk one-half month lower, for the C's. The first of these differences approaches statistical reliability. The difference in the age of pubescence, however, is in the other direction, being nearly a half-year lower for the A's, and yielding a critical ratio of 2.8. These differences may or may not represent the real facts. One reason for regarding them with some suspicion is that the direction of differences is not consistent. Data of the kind in question are subject both to errors of observation and of memory and are notorious for their low reliability. It is conceivable that the differences here found could reflect merely the difference between A and C parents in ability to report accurately. The A parents averaged much above C parents in education, vocational status, and cultural background.

TABLE 101

Comparison of A and C Groups on Age at Walking, Talking, and Pubescence

	Group A	Group C	CR
Age at walking	(N=130)	(N=131)	
Mean in months	13.6	12.8	2.4
S.D.	3.1	2.7	
Age at talking	(N=110)	(N=97)	
Mean in months	17.3	16.8	0.7
S.D.	5.0	5.2	
Age at puberty	(N=104)	(N=97)	
Mean in years	14.5	14.9	2.8
S.D.	1.1	1.2	

Data of four kinds were available on childhood reading. These include: age at learning to read as reported by parents, composite of parent-and-teacher estimates on the amount of reading indulged in (rated on a 5-point scale), reading records kept by the subjects on books read during a period of two months, and reports by parents on the interest shown in dictionaries, atlases, and encyclopedias. All these data were secured in 1922.

Reports on age of learning to read were available for 130 A's and 132 C's. The differences, though not reliable, show a trend toward earlier reading by the A's. For example, reading before four and one-half years was reported for 27.6 percent of the A's and for only 13.7 percent of the C's. Learning to read after starting to school was reported for 45.4 percent of the A's and 51.5 percent of the C's.

The composite parent-teacher estimates of amount of reading were almost identical for the two groups. However, the records kept by the children themselves over a two months' period show a moderately reliable trend toward more reading by the C's. For example, 10 books per month or fewer were recorded by 57.2 percent of the A's and by 43.1 percent of the C's. At the other extreme, the proportion reading 15 books per month or more was 21.4 percent of the A's and 37.3 percent of the C's. This difference in reading interest is in line with the differences reported by parents on interest in dictionaries, atlases, and encyclopedias. This item of information was available for 124 A's and 129 C's. Interest in all three was reported for 25.0 percent of the A's and 34.9 percent of the C's. Interest in none or only one of the three was reported for 56.4 percent of the A's and for 44.9 percent of the C's.

The Home Information Blank of 1922 called for reports on special abilities the child had shown as evidenced by interest in music, arithmetic, science, art, dramatics, and collections. The N's for whom reports on these special abilities were available ranged from 126 to 132 A's, and from 127 to 129 C's. The reports were in terms of "no special ability," "more than average," "marked ability." The figures on music ability, ability in science, and ability in art showed no differences between the A and C groups. In the case of arithmetic, "more than average" or "marked" ability was reported for 65.9 percent of the A's and 55.8 percent of the C's ($CR = 1.68$). The corresponding figures for "more than average" or "marked" ability in dramatics were 29.7 percent of the A's and 21.3 percent of the

C's (CR = 1.57). Parents' reports also show the A's to have made a greater number of collections. The proportion making four or more was 31.7 percent of the A's and 20.3 percent of the C's, giving a critical ratio of 2.09.

In general, the data we have summarized in this section on early development have not brought out many differences large enough to be very significant statistically, but the trends are of considerable psychological interest.

Childhood Tests of Interests and Personality

The material to be summarized in this section was all secured in 1922 or 1923 and includes the data afforded by three tests: a test of interest in and knowledge of plays, games, and amusements (described in chapter iv) the Cady-Raubenheimer tests of character traits (described in chapter v), and the Wyman Test of Intellectual, Social, and Activity Interest (described in chapter iv). As these tests were given only to the Main Experimental Group, the N's for the men here classified as A's and C's are small, ranging from 45 to 64 for the A's and from 54 to 67 for the C's. Partly because of the small N's, most of the A-C differences on the tests in question lack statistical reliability.

On the amount of play information, 57.4 percent of the A's scored in the highest range attained by any in the control group of unselected children, as compared with 45.5 percent of the C's (CR = 1.44). The scores for sociability and masculinity derived from the test of play interest did not differ reliably for the two groups.

The Wyman test yielded no significant difference on any of the three interests scored, though there was a small but unreliable trend toward stronger intellectual and social interests among the A's, and stronger activity interests among the C's.

The Cady-Raubenheimer character tests yielded no difference that approached significance on the subtests for overstatement or trustworthiness (honesty when under temptation to cheat). Emotional stability as measured by Cady's modification of the Woodworth test showed the A's slightly but not reliably more stable. The Raubenheimer tests of social attitudes (moral wholesomeness of attitudes and interests) yielded the most nearly significant difference: 45.3 percent of the A's and 31.3 percent of the C's were in the highest interval of scores made by a control group (CR = 1.66).

FAMILY BACKGROUND

In this section we shall review the data on age of parents at birth of the child, birth order, number of sibs, occupational classification of fathers, schooling of fathers and mothers, size of the home library, amount of home instruction given the child, marital status of parents, ratings of homes on the Whittier scale, and number of abnormal relatives reported by the parents or known from other sources of information.

Much has been said by psychoanalytically inclined writers about the influence on personality of such factors as age of parents, birth order, and size of family, but there was no evidence in our data that these things have had any influence on the vocational success of intellectually gifted men. For the A and C groups, respectively, the mean age of fathers was 33.10 and 33.35 years; of mothers, 29.10 and 29.75 years. Birth order was equally unrelated to success, as was also the mean size of sibships. However, there was a fairly reliable difference in the proportion of subjects who were "only" children: 12.0 percent in the A group as against 22.0 percent in the C group (CR = 2.33). This was counterbalanced by the fact that 26.7 percent of the C's had 3 or more sibs as against 20.0 percent of the A's. The mean number of children in the family was 2.79 for A's and 2.83 for C's, a difference that is quite insignificant.

However, in childhood IQ and adult occupational status the differences between siblings of the A's and C's were striking. We secured childhood IQ's of 87 A and 39 C siblings. The means were 135 and 120 respectively. Of the A sibs, 19 percent had IQ's of 150 or above and 8.3 percent of 170 or above. Only one C sib tested above 150.

In 1940 we secured considerable information on 211 A and 204 C siblings. More than two-thirds of the brothers of A subjects were in occupational Groups I and II (professional and higher business) as compared with 37.9 percent of C brothers. In the professions alone there were 34.8 percent of A and 21.8 percent of C brothers. On the other hand, 10 percent of A and 20.6 percent of C brothers were in semiskilled or slightly skilled occupations. The differences were not so marked for the sisters, although there was a definite tendency for more A sisters to go into occupations requiring advanced professional training.

The difference in amount of schooling was equally striking. The following percentages bring out the contrast between the siblings of the two groups.

	BROTHERS		SISTERS	
	A Percent	C Percent	A Percent	C Percent
College graduation	62.2	31.1	60.4	28.1
One to four years of college, no degree	17.6	12.2	20.8	18.8
High-school graduation only	14.8	37.8	16.0	43.8
Less than high school	5.4	18.9	2.8	9.3

Furthermore, 35 percent of A brothers had two or more years of graduate study, usually with an advanced degree, while only 7.8 percent of C brothers had done this much advanced work. The proportion of A sisters with two or more years of graduate study was 15.1 percent; of C sisters, 5.2 percent.

About 60 percent of the brothers of both A's and C's had married. Only one A brother had been divorced, but six C brothers had a history of separation or divorce. Considerably fewer of the A sisters than of C sisters had married, the proportions being 54 percent for the former and 71 percent for the latter. The divorce rate did not differ for the A and C sisters.

The occupational status of fathers shows a marked contrast between the A and C groups. The proportion of fathers in the professional class in 1922 was 38.0 percent for the A's and 18.5 percent for the C's. The difference is highly reliable (CR = 3.63). The proportion of fathers in the Census Groups IV to VII was 25.3 percent for the A's and 33.1 percent for the C's (CR = 3.46). The difference was even greater in 1928 and 1940.

The proportion of deceased fathers was considerably larger for the C group: 38.0 percent as against 23.0 percent for the A's (CR = 2.8). It is possible that death of the father may have had an unfavorable effect on the vocational success of some of the C subjects.

The difference in parental education was even greater than in occupational classification. Adequate information on amount of schooling was available for 130 fathers and 135 mothers of the A group, and for 134 fathers and 135 mothers of the C group. The figures are summarized in Table 102.

The proportion of A fathers who graduated from college was more than three times that of C fathers, and the proportion with eighth-grade education or less was only half as great. Mothers showed less difference than fathers in college graduation.

TABLE 102

COMPARISON OF A AND C GROUPS ON PARENTAL EDUCATION

	Group A Percent	Group C Percent	CR
I. *Fathers*			
College graduation or beyond	50.4	15.5	6.3
Less than high-school graduation	32.2	57.4	4.1
Eighth grade or less	15.7	29.5	2.7
II. *Mothers*			
College graduation or beyond	18.4	11.0	1.7
Less than high-school graduation	38.4	60.6	3.6
Eighth grade or less	10.4	26.8	3.4

Other information on the family background of these subjects included field workers' ratings of home conditions, parents' estimates of the number of books in the home library, marital status of the parents, and the incidence of abnormalities among relatives. The home ratings on the Whittier scale (described in chapter ii) were made in 1922 and were available for the homes of only 55 A's and 54 C's. Of A's, 58.2 percent were from homes rated as "very superior" or "outstandingly superior" as against 50.0 percent of the C's. The difference is not reliable.

The more extensive education of A parents is reflected in their 1922 estimates of the number of books in the home library. Data were secured for 124 A's and 121 C's. The mean for A's was 427 books as against 290 for the C's. The difference is quite reliable (CR = 3.37).

The amount of home instruction in childhood was reported in 1922 by parents of 122 A's and 111 C's. The responses were classified in three categories, indicating "none," "some," or "considerable." Subjects falling in the "none" category included 49.2 percent of the A's and 54.1 percent of the C's; in the "considerable" category, 24.6 percent of the A's and 19.0 percent of the C's. The differences are at most suggestive of a very slight trend in the direction of more home instruction for the A's.

Table 103 summarizes data on the marital status of parents as of 1922, 1928, and 1940.

The incidence of separation or divorce was in 1922 and 1928 about twice as high for C parents as for A parents. For both groups the incidence almost doubled between 1922 and 1928, and in 1940 was still much higher for C than for A parents. The trend toward better marital adjustment of A parents is too consistent to be a result of chance factors.

TABLE 103

COMPARISON OF A AND C GROUPS ON MARITAL STATUS OF PARENTS

	Group A Percent	Group C Percent	CR
I. *As of 1922*	(N=148)	(N=148)	
Home unbroken	85.1	77.7	1.6
Father deceased	6.8	9.4	
Mother deceased	4.1	4.0	
Parents separated or divorced (includes deceased)	4.7	8.9	1.4
II. *As of 1928*	(N=148)	(N=148)	
Home unbroken	75.0	67.1	1.5
Father deceased	10.9	11.2	
Mother deceased	8.2	5.6	
Parents separated or divorced (includes deceased)	7.5	16.1	2.3
III. *As of 1940*	(N=150)	(N=150)	
Home unbroken	56.0	38.0	3.2
Father deceased	23.3	38.0	2.8
Mother deceased	16.7	18.7	
Parents separated or divorced (includes deceased)	14.0	20.0	1.4

The question arises whether the greater success of A subjects is in part caused by the lower incidence of broken homes. We are very skeptical about the existence of such a causal relationship. As will later be shown, a similar difference has been found in the marital status of the A and C subjects themselves, from which one might infer that in the case of both subjects and parents, the unstable marriage may be largely a symptom of ineffective social adjustment in general.

Our data on abnormal relatives are almost certainly far from complete. However, we have pooled such information as was secured from field workers, parents, and other relatives between 1922 and 1940. The results showed no appreciable difference between the A and C groups on the total number of abnormal relatives reported, and no appreciable difference on the incidence of any specific kind of abnormality except feeble-mindedness. Ten cases of this defect were reported for A relatives as compared with 20 for C relatives. The difference is not certainly reliable (CR = 1.8).

The outstanding fact in regard to family background is that the greatest differences for both the subjects and parents of A and C groups are in occupational classification and amount of education. Another parallel between subjects and their parents is found in the higher incidence of separation and divorce in the C group. Our data do not enable us to appraise the relative influence of heredity and environment in causing these parallels, but the lower IQ's of the C siblings indicate that heredity may enter into the picture.

Physique and Health

Information here includes the medical examinations and anthropometric measurements of the Main Experimental Group in 1922–23, responses to several questions in the Home and School blanks of 1922, parent and teacher ratings of health in 1922, parent ratings of health in 1928, a self-rating on health by the subjects in 1940, and height and weight as reported by the subjects in 1940. Information on the age of pubescence has been reported in an earlier section of this chapter.

The medical examinations and the parent and teacher reports of 1922–23 were pooled and used to derive a health rating in terms of "very good," "good," "fair," "poor," and "very poor." Such a rating was available for 132 A's and 131 C's. Rated as "very good" or "good" were 78.8 percent of A's and 72.5 percent of C's. The difference is not reliable. Health ratings by parents in 1928 were almost exactly the same for the two groups, as were also self-ratings on health by the subjects in 1940. The only reliable or near-reliable differences we have found in physique were in height and weight as reported by the subjects. If these reports can be accepted at their face value, the mean height of 144 A's in 1940 was 5 feet 10.83 inches; of 130 C's, 5 feet 10.12 inches. The difference is approximately 0.7 of an inch in favor of the A's, and the critical ratio of the difference is 2.21. The respective means for weight were 164.85 and 160.91 pounds. The weight difference of almost 4 pounds has a critical ratio of 3.09. It bears repeating that these differences are based upon figures reported by the subjects. It seems unreasonable that there would be a constant tendency for A's to overstate, or for C's to understate the facts in reporting height and weight, but in the absence of more exact information the possibility of such a tendency cannot be altogether dismissed. If the differences found are real they could be variously interpreted. Since the A parents are on the average better educated, the better physical development of the A subjects might be the result of superior diet in childhood.

MENTAL HEALTH

A rating on nervous symptoms was made on 1922–23 data furnished by parents and teachers in response to several questions in the Home and School information blanks, and on observations recorded by the examining physicians. The ratings based on the above data were made in terms of three categories, "little or none," "some but not severe," or "marked symptoms." A similar rating was made on data furnished by parents and teachers in 1928. The 1922–23 ratings from this source showed no difference whatever between the A and C groups. The 1928 data, however, showed a fairly reliable difference: rated as having either "some" or "marked" nervous symptoms were 7.2 percent of 124 A's and 19.0 percent of 105 C's (CR = 2.61).

Not included in the 1922–23 data just referred to were special ratings by parents and teachers on three traits that may be classed as emotional: "Sense of humor," "Cheerfulness or optimism," and "Permanency of moods." The mean of the parent-teacher ratings on the three traits combined was almost exactly the same for 139 A's and 141 C's.

Ratings were also secured in 1922 from parents and teachers on four traits which we have classified as volitional: "Prudence and forethought," "Self confidence," "Will power and perseverance," and "Desire to excel." We have computed a parent-teacher composite on average ratings of the four traits combined. The composite mean for A's was reliably higher than for C's (CR = 3.96). In 1928, only two of the volitional traits were rated, "Perseverance" and "Desire to excel," and the subjects then rated included only 63 A's and 71 C's. Again the parent-teacher mean was very much higher for the A's (CR = 5.23).

More extensive and, we believe, much more dependable information was secured in 1940. Part of this was furnished by the subjects themselves in response to questions in the General Information Blank, and part by parents in response to questions in the Home Information Blank. The most important sources of recent information were the field workers' conferences with the subjects, their spouses, and their parents. Additional information came from our correspondence and conferences with the subjects over a period of many years. On the basis of information from all these sources, we have been able to rate the all-round mental adjustment of every one in the A group and of 144 in the C group.* The ratings were as follows:

Adjustment	Group A (N=150) Percent	Group C (N=144) Percent	CR
1. Satisfactory	84.0	62.7	4.21
2. Some maladjustment	14.7	26.0	4.21
3. Serious maladjustment	1.3	11.3	

The group differences here are extremely significant; there can be no doubt that serious difficulties of mental adjustment have been far more prevalent among the C's.

A not infrequent symptom of mental maladjustment is the excessive use of liquor. The question on this in the General Information Blank was answered by 143 A's and 126 C's. That excessive drinking was a problem was admitted by 5 C's, but by none of the A's. However, teetotalers were also more numerous among the C's: 11.9 percent of the C's as against 7.0 percent of the A's.

Social Adjustment

Both in 1922 and 1928 the subjects were rated by us for social adjustment on the basis of responses to several questions in the Home and School information blanks. The ratings based on these responses are in terms of "satisfactory," "some maladjustment," "serious maladjustment." Ratings were secured in 1922 for 139 A's and 146 C's. Of the A's, 92.8 percent were rated as "satisfactory," as compared with 83.6 percent of the C's (CR = 2.44). The 1928 ratings also discriminated fairly reliably between the two groups; the number rated "satisfactory" was 94.9 percent of the A's as against 84.6 percent of the C's (CR = 2.35).

Among the 25 traits rated by parents and teachers in 1922 were 5 which we have classed as having a bearing on social adjustment: Fondness for large groups, Leadership, Popularity, Sensitiveness to approval and disapproval, and Freedom from vanity. Subjects rated included 139 A's and 141 C's. The mean of parent-teacher ratings

* See chapter x for a description of the categories used.

for the 5 traits combined was higher for the A group, though the difference did not reach statistical significance (CR = 1.51). The 12 traits rated by parents and teachers in 1928 included 4 which we have classed as related to social adjustment: Fondness for large groups, Leadership, Popularity, and Freedom from vanity. In this case the respective N's of A's and C's were only 87 and 78. On these traits the composite mean for the A's was again higher (CR = 2.59).

In 1928 the subjects were asked to report their preferences regarding age of companions. The data for 107 A's and 88 C's showed a fairly reliable difference in the direction of greater preference for older companions on the part of the A's: 44.9 percent as against 29.5 percent (CR = 2.25).

Another indication of social adjustment is afforded by the ratings of 144 A's and 123 C's on extracurricular activities in high school. In making this rating we have used the following categories: "little or none," "slight," "several," "considerable," and "outstanding." Of the A's, 65.3 percent were in the three highest categories, "several" to "outstanding," as compared with 44.7 percent of the C's (CR = 3.09). A similar rating on extracurricular activities in college for subjects with four years of college work showed 49.6 percent of the A's and only 22.2 percent of the C's in the three highest categories. Again the difference is quite reliable (CR = 3.85). In this case, ratings were available for 133 A's, but for only 54 C's, because so many of the latter did not attend college four years.

In 1940 the married subjects who were given the test of marital happiness were asked to report information on the various kinds of clubs or social organizations to which they belonged. We have responses to this item from 78 A's and 69 C's. The greatest difference was in the proportion who were members of a labor union: 6.4 percent of the A's and 42.0 percent of the C's (CR = 5.43). Another reliable difference, though not so great, was in the proportion belonging to a social club: 48.7 percent of the A's and 29.0 percent of the C's (CR = 2.50). There were 43.6 percent of the A's as compared with 30.4 percent of the C's who belonged to a church club, and 19.2 percent of the A's as against 11.6 percent of the C's who belonged to a luncheon club. Neither of these two differences is very reliable.

Our test of personality and temperament was taken by 138 A's and 132 C's. This is the test described in chapter xix, which was devised primarily as a measure of aptitude for marital adjustment. As it turned out, the differences between the A and C groups in mean score, although in the expected direction, were not large: 86.02 for the A's and 82.53 for the C's (CR = 1.52).

Social Attitudes

Our information on social attitudes includes data on voting habits, political preferences, and self-ratings on radicalism-conservatism. Voting habits were reported by 135 A's and 124 C's. Of the A's, 81.5 percent said they voted at all elections as against 86.3 percent of the C's. The difference, while suggestive, is not reliable. At the other extreme were 7.4 percent of the A's and 10.3 percent of the C's who said that they voted not at all or only occasionally. Political preferences were reported by 116 A's and 96 C's. Here the only difference approaching significance was in the proportion who labeled themselves as Democrats: 20.7 percent of the A's and 32.3 percent of the C's (CR = 1.91). Classifying themselves as Republicans were 38.8 percent of the A's and 33.3 percent of the C's.

The self-rating on radicalism-conservatism was made by 140 A's and 120 C's. The means were surprisingly close together for the two groups: 4.96 for the A's and 5.11 for the C's, a difference which is quite insignificant.* We had expected that one of the characteristics of the less successful C group would be a greater tendency toward political radicalism, but about the only indication pointing in this direction was the somewhat larger proportion of C's who classified themselves as Democrats.

Marriage and Marital Adjustments

Information was secured on the marital status of all members of both the A and C groups. The number who had been married by 1940 was 121 A's, or 80.7 percent, and 100 C's, or 66.7 percent. The critical ratio of this difference is 2.79. The mean age at marriage (first marriage, if more than one) was approximately the same for the two groups—25.4 years for the A's and 25.2 for the C's. If the larger average income of the A's has influenced the proportion of marriages, it does not seem to have influenced age at marriage.

The maladjustment of the C's was reflected in their greater divorce rate. The proportion who had been divorced, or in 1940 were

* A rating of 1 is extremely radical, a rating of 9 extremely conservative.

separated from their wives, was 14.0 percent of the C's as against 6.7 percent of the A's. Because of the small N's, the difference is only moderately reliable (CR = 2.09). As was shown in an earlier section of this chapter, parents of the C's had a higher incidence of divorce or separation than parents of the A's.

One reason for the difference in divorce rate may be the fact that the A's married better. The proportion of A wives who had graduated from college was 53.8 percent as against 24.5 percent of C wives (CR = 4.6). With high-school education or less were 14.6 percent of A wives and 52.0 percent of C wives. This critical ratio is 6.2. The occupational classification of the wife's father is known for 99 A's and 70 C's. Among these the proportion of wives who were daughters of professional men was 40.4 percent for the A group and only 14.5 percent for the C group (CR = 3.98). The proportion who were daughters of men in Census Groups IV to VII was 8.0 percent for the A's and 40.5 percent for the C's (CR = 4.99).

Wives of 58 A's and 60 C's were given the Concept Mastery test in 1940. The respective means were 66.40 for the A wives and 47.17 for the C wives (CR = 3.04). The mean of A wives approximates that of Stanford students; the mean of C wives is about 0.5 S.D. lower.

The test of marital happiness was given to 78 A's and 69 C's, also to 77 A wives and 64 C wives. The description of this test will be found in chapter xix. Table 104 summarizes the results of the test for men and for their wives.

TABLE 104

COMPARISON OF A AND C MEN AND OF A AND C WIVES ON THE TEST OF MARITAL HAPPINESS

	Group A	Group C	CR
Gifted men	(N=78)	(N=69)	
Mean happiness score	60.8	56.7	1.2
S.D.	19.7	21.1	
Wives of gifted men	(N=77)	(N=64)	
Mean happiness score	70.2	61.4	2.6
S.D.	15.7	23.3	3.1

The means of the A and C groups in Table 104 should be compared not only with each other, but also with the means of all gifted subjects of both sexes, and of all the spouses of gifted subjects who were given the test. The data for such comparisons will be found in chapter xix. Table 104 shows that A men had a mean marital happiness score 4 points higher than C men, a difference that falls short of statistical reliability. The mean of the A men was close to that of the entire group of gifted men who took the test. The means for wives of A and C men differed by nearly 9 points (CR = 2.6).

The N's for the ratings of personality traits in Table 105 were as follows: self-ratings, A's 132 and C's 129; wife's ratings, A's 76 and C's 66; parents' ratings, A's 87 and C's 72. These ratings indicate that adult success, as here defined, is significantly related to several of the traits in question. Attention is called to the marked agreement among the three sets of raters on the various individual traits. There is, in fact, almost perfect agreement between the subjects, their wives, and their parents on the characteristics which best differentiate between the A and C men.

TABLE 105

PERSONALITY TRAITS OF A AND C MEN AS RATED BY THEMSELVES, THEIR WIVES, AND THEIR PARENTS (1940)

	Group A	Group C	CR
1. *Happiness of temperament*			
Mean of self-ratings	5.17	5.21	...
S.D. of self-ratings	1.61	1.98	2.3
Mean of ratings by wives	4.96	5.42	1.5
S.D. of ratings by wives	1.76	1.74	...
2. *Absence of moodiness*			
Mean of self-ratings	5.99	5.79	...
S.D. of self-ratings	1.91	2.09	...
Mean of ratings by wives	5.25	5.67	1.1
S.D. of ratings by wives	2.12	2.30	...
3. *Cautiousness-impulsiveness*			
Mean of self-ratings	5.42	5.33	...
S.D. of self-ratings	1.73	1.87	...
Mean of ratings by wives	4.80	4.94	...
S.D. of ratings by wives	1.91	2.14	1.0
Mean of ratings by parents	4.33	4.65	1.0
S.D. of ratings by parents	2.08	1.96	...
4. *Self-confidence*			
Mean of self-ratings	4.68	5.64	4.2
S.D. of self-ratings	1.66	2.06	2.5
Mean of ratings by wives	3.95	5.02	3.3
S.D. of ratings by wives	1.51	2.22	3.1
Mean of ratings by parents	3.96	4.99	3.7
S.D. of ratings by parents	1.45	1.92	2.4

TABLE 105 (*Continued*)

	Group A	Group C	CR
5. *Freedom from emotionality*			
Mean of self-ratings	5.74	5.71	...
S.D. of self-ratings	1.68	1.95	1.7
Mean of ratings by wives	5.80	5.67	...
S.D. of ratings by wives	1.36	1.65	1.6
Mean of ratings by parents	5.60	5.19	1.6
S.D. of ratings by parents	1.21	1.68	2.8
6. *Conformity, or acceptance of authority*			
Mean of self-ratings	6.85	6.43	1.9
S.D. of self-ratings	1.74	1.91	1.1
Mean of ratings by wives	6.26	6.14	...
S.D. of ratings by wives	1.80	2.23	1.8
Mean of ratings by parents	5.22	5.39	...
S.D. of ratings by parents	2.06	2.43	1.0
7. *Good nature*			
Mean of self-ratings	4.67	4.81	...
S.D. of self-ratings	1.46	1.87	2.7
Mean of ratings by wives	4.25	4.83	1.7
S.D. of ratings by wives	1.84	2.18	1.4
8. *Sociability*			
Mean of self-ratings	5.81	6.13	1.3
S.D. of self-ratings	1.81	2.18	2.1
Mean of ratings by wives	6.03	6.27	...
S.D. of ratings by wives	1.88	2.25	1.5
Mean of ratings by parents	5.23	6.11	2.7
S.D. of ratings by parents	1.92	2.15	1.0
9. *Perseverance*			
Mean of self-ratings	4.04	5.23	5.4
S.D. of self-ratings	1.60	1.92	2.1
Mean of ratings by wives	3.39	5.11	5.4
S.D. of ratings by wives	1.61	2.15	2.3
Mean of ratings by parents	3.14	4.56	5.5
S.D. of ratings by parents	1.06	2.03	5.1
10. *Integration toward goals*			
Mean of self-ratings	4.72	6.05	6.7
S.D. of self-ratings	1.34	1.79	3.2
Mean of ratings by wives	4.21	5.36	4.0
S.D. of ratings by wives	1.60	1.84	1.1
Mean of ratings by parents	3.87	5.48	6.2
S.D. of ratings by parents	1.12	1.89	4.3
11. *Freedom from sensitiveness*			
Mean of self-ratings	6.78	6.81	...
S.D. of self-ratings	1.65	1.86	...
Mean of ratings by wives	6.57	6.79	...
S.D. of ratings by wives	1.63	1.71	...
Mean of ratings by parents	6.55	6.75	...
S.D. of ratings by parents	1.67	1.60	...

TABLE 105 (*Concluded*)

	Group A	Group C	CR
12. *Absence of inferiority feelings*			
Mean of self-ratings	5.69	6.41	3.0
S.D. of self-ratings	1.95	1.97	...
Mean of ratings by wives	4.76	5.70	2.7
S.D. of ratings by wives	1.90	2.16	1.0
Mean of ratings by parents	4.39	5.51	3.7
S.D. of ratings by parents	1.77	1.91	...
13. *Freedom from egotism*			
Mean of self-ratings	6.54	6.35	...
S.D. of self-ratings	1.39	1.54	...
Mean of ratings by wives	5.76	5.89	...
S.D. of ratings by wives	1.90	1.83	...
Mean of ratings by parents	4.73	5.00	...
S.D. of ratings by parents	2.07	1.92	...
14. *Number of friendships*			
Mean of self-ratings	4.73	5.05	1.4
S.D. of self-ratings	1.66	2.03	2.3

THE FOLLOWING TRAITS WERE RATED BY PARENTS BUT NOT BY THE MEN OR THEIR WIVES

	Group A	Group C	CR
Talkativeness			
Mean of ratings by parents	6.26	6.78	1.8
S.D. of ratings by parents	1.77	1.85	...
Common sense			
Mean of ratings by parents	3.52	4.54	3.9
S.D. of ratings by parents	1.33	1.88	2.9
Popularity			
Mean of ratings by parents	4.32	4.97	2.3
S.D. of ratings by parents	1.61	1.78	...

The three traits showing the highest A-C differences were Integration toward goals, Perseverance, and Self-confidence. These three traits were rated by all three sets of judges, with resultant critical ratios of differences ranging from 3.3 to 6.7. The members of this triad of traits undoubtedly have much in common, and it would have been surprising if they had not shown clear differences between the A and C groups.

Just below these three traits in amount of discrimination is Absence of inferiority feelings. Here, too, the differences are reliable and yield almost the same critical ratio for the three sets of ratings.

Happiness of temperament and Good nature were rated only by the subjects and their wives. The self-ratings on these two traits did not differ for the A and C groups, but on both traits the A men were rated somewhat higher by their wives than were C men, though the differences were not very reliable. Sociability was rated by all three sets of raters: ratings by wives were about the same for the A and C groups; self-ratings and ratings by parents were higher for the A group, the latter difference having a critical ratio of 2.7. Exclusiveness of friendships was rated only by the subjects, the A's rating themselves as slightly less exclusive though not reliably so. On Conformity to authority, C men rated themselves as more conformist than did the A's (CR = 1.9). Ratings by wives and parents showed no difference between the A's and C's on this trait. On Freedom from emotionality, the A's and C's did not differ appreciably on self-ratings or on ratings by wives, but on ratings by parents the C's appeared to be somewhat less emotional than the A's (CR = 1.6). A difference in this direction was not expected, and may have been due to the fact that extreme lack of emotionality was defined in such a way that it could have been interpreted as meaning emotional coldness or hardness. Sensitiveness and Egotism were rated by all three sets of judges with no appreciable difference between the A and C groups on either trait.

At the end of Table 105 there are three traits which were rated by parents but not by the subjects themselves or by their wives. These are Talkativeness, Common sense, and Popularity. The largest difference in mean rating is for Common sense, the critical ratio being 3.9 in favor of the A's. The superiority of the A's is moderately reliable in the case of Popularity, the critical ratio here being 2.3.

When we compare the self-ratings of these men with the ratings of them by their wives, the question arises whether the ratings by A wives are more favorable than those by C wives. In such a comparison one may take as a point of departure either the mean of self-ratings or the mean of ratings by wives. The tendency in the case of most of the traits is for both A and C men to be rated higher by their wives than they rate themselves, although there are exceptions to the rule. In Happiness of temperament the A men are rated slightly higher by their wives than by themselves, whereas C men are rated appreciably lower by their wives than by themselves. In Perseverance, A men are rated by their wives reliably higher than they rate themselves, whereas C men and their wives show no such difference. On Absence of inferiority feelings, wives of both A and C men rate them higher than they rate themselves. On Absence of egotism, both A and C wives give higher ratings than the men give themselves. Emotionality, Sociability, and Sensitiveness show very little difference between self-rating and rating by wives in either the A or C group.

We may repeat that the outstanding fact in Table 105 is the marked agreement among the different sets of judges with regard to the four traits which best discriminate between A and C men. These are Integration toward goals, Perseverance, Self-confidence, and Absence of inferiority feelings.

Finally we present in Table 106 the 1940 mean ratings by field assistants on twelve personality traits. The traits in this group have been selected so as to overlap very little the trait ratings summarized above, and so as to furnish information on aspects of personality that would be most likely to evidence themselves in the field workers' conference with the subjects.

TABLE 106

PROPORTION OF A AND C SUBJECTS RATED 1 OR 2 (HIGH) ON TWELVE TRAITS BY FIELD WORKERS (1940)

	Group A (N=81) Percent	Group C (N=115) Percent	CR
1. Appearance	71.6	35.6	5.4
2. Attractiveness	76.2	45.2	4.7
3. Poise	75.3	43.5	4.8
4. Speech	79.0	53.0	3.0
5. Freedom from vanity	12.3	20.0	1.5
6. Alertness	91.4	74.8	4.9
7. Friendliness	75.3	53.0	3.0
8. Talkativeness	48.1	40.9	1.0
9. Frankness	60.5	56.5	0.6
10. Attentiveness	91.4	70.4	4.0
11. Curiosity	63.7	40.3	4.5
12. Originality	75.6	45.4	4.5

In only one of these traits were the A's rated lower than the C's, namely on Freedom from vanity, a fact which raises the question whether vanity is really an undesirable trait! On Frankness there was no difference, and on Talkativeness only a very slight difference.* There are seven traits which yielded very high critical ratios of differences between A and C men. They were in order of magnitude:

* Unfortunately, "talkativeness" was somewhat ambiguous because of the use of the word "loquacious" to designate one extreme.

Appearance, Alertness, Poise, Attractiveness, Curiosity, Originality, and Attentiveness. Traits only slightly below these in reliability of difference in favor of the A's were Speech and Friendliness.

Probably the ratings on these twelve traits by field workers were more or less influenced by halo effects, but if halo was present it did not affect equally the ratings on all the traits. The validity of the ratings of the field workers is supported by the reports they made on conferences with the individual subjects. On the whole, one gets a very different composite picture of the A men from these conference reports than of the C men.

The A and C Groups as of 1945

The follow-up data secured in 1945 furnished information on war records, occupation, income, physical and mental health, marital status, and offspring. In the years between 1940 and 1945, there were 3 deaths among the A's and 4 among the C's. A fourth man in the A group died early in 1946, a few months after sending in his 1945 Information Blank. Reports were received from all but one of the 147 living A's, and from all but ten of the 146 living C's. The A man who did not report is known to be a successful radio engineer. For 7 of the 10 C's not reporting, addresses were secured (in most cases from the subjects themselves), and it is hoped that these subjects will yet return the Information Blank.

In general, the findings of 1945 have confirmed the 1940 classification of A and C subjects. With few exceptions the A group continued to be outstanding in achievement. In one case, a top A man with a distinguished record both academically and professionally, suffered an emotional upset which caused him to throw overboard his whole way of life. He is now getting a start in a new profession, but it is yet to be seen how far he will go in it. For two A men who were of Japanese ancestry, the war brought complete disruption of their lives, including removal to a relocation center for a time, and later the establishment of new homes in the interior of the United States. Both engaged in civilian work in connection with the war effort. A third A man of Japanese ancestry entered the Army as a private a few months before war was declared and rose to the rank of major.

The 1945 information indicated improvement among a good many of the C's, but there was still a wide gap between the two groups. Vocational and salary advances had been so general throughout the gifted group that the improvement in the status of C men did not, except in a few instances, change their relative position. One man who until 1940 (aged thirty years) had held only low-paying or part-time jobs despite his A.B. and M.A. degrees, later secured a position along the line of his interests and rose rapidly to an executive position in industry. This man, without doubt, has moved out of the C group, but whether he will eventually equal the standard set by the A's is yet to be seen. Two men with graduate professional training, who had worked at low income, nonprofessional jobs, have both gone into junior college teaching. Another C man who, prior to 1941, had had difficulty in finding a job in the engineering field for which he had trained, found his talents to be in demand in a war plant and was soon holding a $5,000 position. Confidence and experience gained during the war years have enabled him to open his own office as a consultant.

War records. The war records of the two groups reveal some striking differences in ranks attained. This is not, of course, a measure of the relative contribution of the two groups, but it is interesting as further evidence of the greater ability—or, perhaps, desire—on the part of the A's to achieve positions of leadership and prestige. Some of this difference may be due to the educational advantages of the A's.

Of the A's, 40.5 percent were in active military service; of the C's, 36.4 percent. One A man and 3 C men lost their lives in the service, and one man from each group met accidental death in war work. In one case the man was overcome by fumes in the plant where he was employed as a machinist; the other case was that of a research chemist who was engaged in highly important research for the War Department when he came in contact with materials that proved fatal.

The A and C men who went into the service were divided as follows:

	A (N=60) %	C (N=51) %
Army	56.7	70.6
Navy	43.3	29.4

Of the A men in the Army, 38.2 percent entered as privates and 61.8 percent as commissioned officers. For the C's, the proportion in the Army who entered as privates was 75.0 percent; as noncommissioned officers, 5.6 percent; with commissions, 19.4 percent. The ranks at the close of the war (September 1945) or at termination of service (by death or discharge), if earlier, were as follows:

Army ranks	(N=34) %	(N=36) %
Private	2.9	13.9
Private first class	2.9	0.0
Noncommissioned officer	11.8	52.8
Commissioned officer	82.4	33.3

In the Navy the differences were even more marked. Going in as seamen were 7.7 percent of the A's and 33.3 percent of the C's; going in as petty officers were 11.5 percent of the A's and 66.7 percent of the C's; as commissioned officers, 80.8 percent of the A's and no C's. The ranks at the end of the war or at termination of service, if earlier, were as follows:

Navy ranks	A (N=26) %	C (N=15) %
Seaman first class	3.9	0.0
Petty officer	7.7	86.7
Commissioned officer	88.5	13.3

Civilian occupations. Those in civilian occupations made advances both vocationally and financially in the years between 1940 and 1945. The progress of the A group is less apparent from their status on the Minnesota Occupational Scale than is that of the C's, since all of them were already in either professional or higher business pursuits (Groups I and II). Positions of greater importance and responsibility, and increased income in the occupational fields in which they were already established are evidence of the continuing success of the A's.

In the case of C's there was a marked upward trend in occupational grouping on the Minnesota scale. The 1940 and 1944 figures for C men are as follows:

Occupational Group	1940 Percent	1944 Percent
I.	9.3	12.0
II.	7.3	26.1
III.	48.7	48.9
IV.	1.3	2.2
V.	22.0	8.7
VI.	4.0	0.0
Miscellaneous, not employed	7.4	2.1

Two men in the C group were not working in 1944. One was an

invalid of some years' standing, the other had a history of irregular employment even before the war, and a few months after being drafted was discharged as a psychoneurotic. He was still badly adjusted at the time of report and was undecided as to his future. In the meantime he was unemployed except for giving some part-time help in his father's business.

Income. Both A's and C's showed a marked increase in earned income during the war years. The annual median income of A men in 1944 was $7,187.50, an increase of 90.2 percent over the 1940 median of $3,770.60. For the C's, the percentage increase in median income was even greater; from $1,710.60 to $3,571.43, or 108.7 percent.

Physical and mental health. The 1940 self-ratings on physical health showed practically no difference between the A and C groups, but those of 1945 showed a tendency on the part of C's to rate themselves somewhat lower. The Information Blank of 1945 asked the subjects to describe their physical condition by underlining one of the following: "very good," "good," "fair," "poor," "very poor." Of the A's, 53.1 percent rated themselves in the top category (very good) as compared with 35.4 percent of the C's. Rating their physical condition as "good" were 37.2 percent of the A's and 50.4 percent of the C's; as "fair," 7.6 percent of the A's and 11.0 percent of the C's. In the "poor" or "very poor" categories were 2.1 percent of the A's and 3.1 percent of the C's.

The ratings on mental health made on the basis of case-history records show little change between 1940 and 1945. One A man who was rated 2 in 1940 now falls into the 3*a* classification (seriously maladjusted). One C man rated 3*a* has had a mental breakdown requiring hospitalization, and so now belongs in the 3*b* category. Except for the few cases showing marked change, the 1945 information did not afford a very adequate basis for rerating the subjects on degree of adjustment.

Marital status. The 1945 reports showed that 93.1 percent of the A men and 76.0 percent of the C men had married, as compared with 80.7 percent and 66.7 percent respectively in 1940. Of the C marriages, 20.7 percent had ended in divorce or separation by 1945; of the A marriages, only 10.2 percent. The mean number of offspring per marriage was 1.7 for the A men and 1.2 for the C men.

Summary and Conclusions

Because of the unique opportunity this study has afforded to investigate the correlates of success and failure in a large group of gifted subjects, we have presented so many items of detailed information that the effect upon the reader may have been confusing. It will be helpful, therefore, to close the chapter with a succinct résumé of the most important findings that have been reviewed.

The investigation has been confined to the male group, since the achievement of women is difficult to estimate and is so often the outcome of extraneous circumstances. Three judges, working independently, examined the records (to 1940) of 730 gifted men who were twenty-five years old or older, and rated each on life success. The criterion of "success" was the extent to which a subject had made use of his superior intellectual ability. On the basis of these ratings the men were classified into three groups, composing roughly the highest fifth, the middle 60 percent, and the lowest fifth. The extreme groups, designated as A and C, were composed of 150 men each and were closely matched for mean age and range of age. The two groups were then compared on some 200 items of information collected between 1922 and 1940.

The educational and occupational records of these two groups presented a vivid contrast. Of the A's, 90 percent graduated from college; of the C's, only 37 percent. Approximately 76 percent of the A's but only 15 percent of the C's completed one or more years of graduate work. Among those graduating, more than half of the A's but only 4 percent of the C's were elected to Phi Beta Kappa or Sigma Xi. None of the A's but 2 percent of the C's failed to graduate from high school. The A's were more often accelerated in school, and the difference between the groups in this respect increased greatly between the eighth grade and graduation from college.

In professional pursuits were nearly 70 percent of the A's as compared with 9 percent of the C's. Although salary had been given little weight in the success ratings, the average earned income of the A's in 1940 was more than two and a half times that of the C's. In 1944 the ratio was 2 to 1.

Turning to the childhood records and test scores of the two groups, we note first that during the elementary school years the A's and C's were almost equally successful. Their average grades were about the same, and the average scores on the achievement tests were only a trifle higher for the A group. In high school the groups began to draw apart as a result of lower grades in the C group, but it was not until the college period that the slump of this group assumed alarming proportions. The slump cannot be blamed upon extracurricular activities, for these were almost twice as common among the A's as among the C's. Nor can much of it be attributed to intellectual deterioration. Although the intelligence scores of both 1922 and 1940 averaged higher for the A's than for the C's, the difference was not great.

The family backgrounds of the two groups differed markedly. More than three times as many A fathers as C fathers had graduated from college, and a similar difference was found between the siblings of the A's and C's. More than twice as many fathers of the A's were in the professional classes. The important point here is that the educational tradition was stronger in families of the A group. In line with this is the fact that the Jewish element was three times as large among the A's as among the C's.

A number of significant differences between the groups were found in the childhood data on emotional stability, social adjustments, and various traits of personality. All the 1922 trait ratings except those for health averaged lower for the C group. That is, eighteen years prior to the classification of these subjects on the basis of adult achievement, teachers and parents had been able to discern personality differences that would later characterize the two groups. The trait ratings and case-history data secured from parents and teachers in 1928 gave even larger differences between the groups.

In physical health, no significant differences between the two groups were found in 1922, 1928, or 1940. Mental health, as indicated by symptoms of nervousness and emotional instability, differed little for the two groups in 1922, but was reliably better in the A group in 1928 and much better in 1940.

Evidence of social maladjustment in the C group increased steadily from 1922 to 1940. Both in high school and college, leadership was far more often displayed by members of the A group. By 1940 few of the C's but many of the A's held positions that made heavy demands upon social qualifications. The marriage rate for the C's was lower than for the A's, and the incidence of divorce among the C's was more than twice that of the A's. A similar but somewhat smaller difference is found in the divorce rate of parents of the A and C men. Notwithstanding the more frequent "purging" of C marriages by divorce and remarriage, the average score on the test of marital happiness was somewhat higher for A men, and significantly higher for wives of A men.

The groups differed strikingly with respect to the women they married. More than half of the A wives, but only a quarter of the C wives were college graduates. With only a high-school education or less were 15 percent of the A wives and 52 percent of the C wives. Moreover, the A wives were reliably superior to C wives in intelligence as measured by the test of Concept Mastery. The great difference in family background is indicated by the fact that 40 percent of the A wives but only 15 percent of the C wives had fathers who belonged to the professional class.

The inferior adjustment of the C's was further indicated by their more frequent unemployment and by change of jobs without improvement in their position. Three times as many C's as A's reported that they had drifted into their jobs, and an equally disproportionate number of C's said they would prefer some other work to that which they were doing. One factor here is actual vocational misplacement, for on the Strong test of occupational interests, 23 percent of the C's but only 5 percent of the A's earned a rating below B for the occupation in which they were engaged. This higher incidence of vocational misfits among the C's probably reflects in part the inferior social judgment of members of this group.

Another result of the Strong test was to show that the A men rated high in more occupations than did the C men, and particularly in occupations above the skilled-labor level. There was other evidence suggesting a greater catholicity of interests on the part of the A's: their avocational hobbies were more numerous, and their self-rated interests in twelve special fields averaged higher than those of the C's.

Some of the most interesting A-C differences were brought to light by trait ratings, including self-ratings by the subjects, ratings on the same traits by their wives and parents, and ratings on certain other traits by the field workers. These ratings were all made before the A and C groups were made up. The subjects, their wives, and their parents showed remarkable agreement in rating the A's far higher than the C's on Perseverance, Self-confidence, and Integration toward goals. The three sets of raters agreed similarly in rating the A's higher on Absence of inferiority feelings, though here the group differences were not quite so large. Only the ratings by wives yielded differences on Happiness of temperament and Good nature. Little or no difference was found in the ratings on Egotism, Sensitiveness, Moodiness, or Impulsiveness.

In another set of traits on which subjects were rated by the field workers, the A group greatly outclassed the C group in Appearance, Attractiveness, Alertness, Poise, Attentiveness, Curiosity, Originality, and, to a somewhat lesser degree, in Speech and Friendliness.

Everything considered, there is nothing in which the A and C groups present a greater contrast than in drive to achieve and in all-round social adjustment. Contrary to the theory of Lange-Eichbaum[38] that great achievement is usually associated with emotional tensions which border on the abnormal, in our gifted group success is associated with stability rather than instability, with absence rather than presence of disturbing conflicts—in short, with well-balanced temperament and with freedom from excessive frustration. The Lange-Eichbaum theory may explain a Hitler, but hardly a Churchill; a Goebbels, perhaps, but hardly a Goethe.

At any rate, we have seen that intellect and achievement are far from perfectly correlated. Why this is so, what circumstances affect the fruition of human talent, are questions of such transcendent importance that they should be investigated by every method that promises the slightest reduction of our present ignorance. So little do we know about our available supply of potential genius, the environmental factors that favor or hinder its expression, the emotional compulsions that give it dynamic quality, or the personality distortions that make it dangerous.

CHAPTER XXIV

WAR RECORDS

The war records both as to military service and civilian contribution to the war effort were compiled from the information supplied in the 1945–46 Information Blank, supplemented, in many cases, by later correspondence.

War Work of Men

Military service. Information had been secured for 760 men by late 1946 (for 648 of whom the follow-up reports had been received by September 1945), and the data showed that 323 (42.5 percent) of the 760 served in the armed forces during the war. An additional 9 men (1.2 percent) were in the Merchant Marine. There were 6 men (0.8 percent) who registered as conscientious objectors, of whom 3 were drafted and sent to Civilian Public Service camps.

The 323 men in military service were distributed among the various divisions of the service as follows: Army, 63.2 percent; Navy (including Coast Guard) 35.9 percent; Marine Corps, 0.9 percent.

Only 72 of the 760 men were under thirty at the time of reporting. Of these, 41, or 57.0 percent, went into service as compared with 41.0 percent of those aged thirty or over at the time of report. A good many of the latter, of course, were well under thirty when the war began.

Approximately one-half (49.5 percent) of the men in the Army entered as privates, and 46.1 percent entered as commissioned officers. Seven men (3.4 percent) entered as cadets or officer candidates, and 2 (1.0 percent) as noncommissioned officers. The ranks in the Army at time of report (chiefly late 1945), or at time of discharge for those who had left the service previous to reporting, were as follows: privates or privates first class, 6.9 percent; noncommissioned officers, 22.1 percent; officer candidates, 1.0 percent; and commissioned officers, 70.0 percent.

Of men in the Navy, 13.8 percent entered as seamen, 19.8 percent with a petty officer rating, 3.4 percent as cadets, and 62.9 percent as commissioned officers. Their ranks in late 1945, or at the time of their leaving the service if before reporting, were as follows: seamen, 3.4 percent; petty officer rating, 21.6 percent; commissioned officers, 75.0 percent.

The officer ranks in the Army ranged from second lieutenant to brigadier general, and in the Navy from ensign to captain. Above the rank of lieutenant in the Army were 41 captains, 33 majors, 23 lieutenant colonels, 2 colonels, and one brigadier general. Above the rank of lieutenant (junior grade) in the Navy were 40 lieutenants, 7 lieutenant commanders, 4 commanders, and one captain. The 3 men in the Marine Corps included one private first class and 2 first lieutenants.

The 204 men in the Army were distributed over a wide range of service branches. The largest proportion (25 percent) in a single branch was in the Air Forces, and the Medical Corps ranked second with 16.5 percent. The combat services combined account for 59.5 percent of those in the Army.

Three of the 204 men in the Army were graduates of West Point and were in the regular Army; 5 of the 116 Navy men were Annapolis graduates on regular duty with the Navy.

Length of time in the service for those who entered during the emergency was computed to September 1, 1945. That date was chosen because approximately 85 percent of our reports had been received by that time, and because it marked the end of the war. The mean length of time in the service to that date, including those already discharged as well as those still in the armed forces, was 35.5 months (S.D. 12.5). Inasmuch as many were kept in the service several months to a year or more after the war ended, the average length of total service would probably be a little above three years.

Occupations from which men entered service. Of the men who in 1940 were classed in the professional group on the Minnesota Occupational Scale, 41.4 percent entered the service. These included 71.4 percent of the physicians, 56.9 percent of the lawyers, 28.1 percent of the engineers, and 27.1 percent of the college teachers. Of those in other professional fields, 34.3 percent entered the service. From Group II (semiprofessional and higher business pursuits), 44.1 percent were in the service; from Group III, 40.6 percent; and from groups below III, 28.6 percent.

Casualties. Three men were taken prisoner during the war. Two of these who were in German prison camps were later liberated; one taken prisoner by the Japanese at Corregidor lost his life while being moved from a prison camp in the Philippines to one in occupied China. Four additional men were killed, 2 in the American Air Forces while on combat duty, one in the Royal Air Force when his plane crashed while on a reconnaissance flight, and one in the Navy when his ship was lost in a storm at sea. Fourteen men were wounded, one of them twice.

Awards. Our information on the award of citations and decorations is not complete since, as pointed out above, close to 85 percent of our reports were received before the end of the war. As the records stand, 70 (22 percent) of the men in military service reported receiving one or more citations, with a total of 90 citations reported. The more important decorations were as follows:

	Number
Legion of Merit	4
Silver Star	2
Distinguished Flying Cross with Oak Leaf Cluster	1
Distinguished Flying Cross	5
Bronze Star with Oak Leaf Cluster	5
Bronze Star	8
Air Medal with 9 Clusters	1
Air Medal with 6 Clusters	1
Air Medal with 3 Clusters	1
Air Medal with 2 Clusters	1
Air Medal	3
Purple Heart	15

The number of battle stars reported by individual men ranged from 1 to 10. Letters of commendation, Presidential Unit Citations, and the nonspecific "several citations" and "usual area and combat awards" were also listed.

The most often decorated man in the gifted group received the following awards: the American Defense Medal, the British General Services Medal, 10 Battle Stars, the Bronze Star Medal, the Air Medal with 9 Oak Leaf Clusters, the Distinguished Flying Cross, Pilot Wings of the Royal Canadian Air Force and of the Jugoslav Air Force.

Civilian contributions. The gifted men not in military service made their contribution toward the war effort in various civilian capacities. In many cases the prewar occupation was directly in line with war needs so that they remained in their own fields of work. This was particularly true of aircraft engineers, naval architects, chemists, and many more. Others, not called or not qualified for military duty, transferred from their regular peacetime work to civilian war work, either in industry or government.

Some took jobs as skilled workers in war plants, others were in significant scientific or technical work, and a sizeable number worked in the field of personnel, labor relations, wage standards, price control, *et cetera.* The gifted men were well represented in the activities of the Office of Scientific Research and Development, the Office of War Information, the Office of Price Administration, the State Department, the Labor Department, and various other agencies of the government.

War Work of Women

The gifted women also did their share of war work, and although their accomplishments were less spectacular than those of some of the men, they were nonetheless valuable.

Twelve women have been in the services, 4 in the WAC, 5 in the WAVES, 2 in the Women's Division of the Coast Guard, and 1 in the Women's Marine Corps. In addition, 2 women served overseas with the American Red Cross.

Between 50 and 60 women were engaged directly in war work either in government agencies or in private industry. Among the latter were engineering draftsmen, aircraft workers, radio mechanics, machine-shop workers, a supervisor of farm labor, and a truck driver. Those in government agencies served with the Department of Labor, the Office of War Information, the War Labor Board, and many other departments. They included economists, statisticians, editors, job analysts, secretaries, *et cetera.*

Summary

In view of the fact that more than half of the gifted men were above the age of thirty years when America entered the war, it is noteworthy that the proportion enrolled in the armed forces (42.5 percent) exceeded that for all males in the country aged eighteen to forty-four.

Our records are not complete on the number rejected for physical or other reasons, or on the grounds for discharge when discharge occurred before the war was over. In the country as a whole approximately 39.5 percent of all men examined by local draft boards were rejected as physically or mentally unfit. The proportion of our gifted men rejected was in all probability much below this figure.

Occupational Group II (semiprofessional and higher business pursuits) contributed the largest proportion of its total to the armed forces, namely, 44.1 percent. The proportion entering the service from the professional group was 41.4 percent; from Group III (higher clerical, skilled labor, and retail business), 40.6 percent; and from groups below III, 26.6 percent.

The proportion of those entering the service who became commissioned officers was gratifyingly large: 70 percent of those in the Army and 75 percent of those in the Navy. Approximately half of the Army men attained a rank of captain or higher, and approximately 45 percent of the Navy men attained the rank of lieutenant (senior grade) or higher.

With our records still incomplete, 90 citations have been reported by 70 men (about 22 percent of all the men who entered the service).

The 5 men who lost their lives constituted 1.6 percent of the men in the service. The 21 killed or wounded account for 6.5 percent of the men in the service.

Only 12 women served in the Army or Navy, but 50 or 60 others were engaged directly in war work either in government agencies or in private industry.

Like a majority of their fellow citizens, both the men and the women of our group participated wherever and whenever possible in various kinds of volunteer war work. Blood-bank donations were mentioned by a large proportion. Other activities frequently mentioned had to do with civilian defense, ration-board work, the Red Cross, and the U.S.O.

CHAPTER XXV

APPRAISAL OF ACHIEVEMENT

To what extent is superior IQ in childhood predictive of superior achievement in adult life? If it is uncorrelated with later achievement, then intelligence tests are a waste of time and special educational provisions for high-scoring children are unwarranted. The follow-up data on our large gifted group afford a more adequate answer to this question than has hitherto been possible. Although the subjects of the group are still too young to justify more than a rough estimate of what their total ultimate achievement will amount to by the end of another twenty or thirty years, they are old enough to indicate clearly the direction in which the truth lies. The many comparisons we have made between these subjects and the general population confirm an opinion expressed by the senior author more than thirty years ago, namely, that the IQ level is one of the most important facts that can be learned about any child. In this chapter we shall bring together the various lines of evidence which point to this conclusion.

Occupational Status

A quarter-century after the subjects were selected for study solely on the basis of a high intelligence score we find almost half of all the men and more than half of the fully employed women engaged in one or another of the professional occupations. In the case of men this is almost nine times the proportion so classifiable in the California generality of employed adults. Approximately 80 percent of the men are in the two highest occupational groups: I, the professions and II, the semiprofessional and higher business occupations. In the generality only about 14 percent are in these two groups. Occupational Groups IV to VII on the Minnesota Occupational Scale account for about half the generality of employed men, but for only 4 percent of the gifted men (of whom not one in 1945 was in either Group VI or Group VII). During the depression when 15 to 20 percent of employable males in California were unemployed, the proportion of unemployed among our gifted men was not over 1 percent.

Educational Histories

The contrast between the gifted subjects and the generality in educational histories is no less striking than the contrast in occupational status. We have seen that nearly 90 percent of the gifted subjects entered college and that nearly 70 percent are college graduates. The latter figure is about ten times as high as for the California generality of corresponding age. Probably not more than one in a hundred of the general population graduates from college with Phi Beta Kappa or Sigma Xi honors, as compared with about 16 percent of the total gifted group and 25 percent of those who completed college. The proportion of gifted subjects who have taken one or more graduate degrees from a college or university is about 29 percent, as against a possible 2 or 3 percent in the general population of comparable age. There are 73 gifted subjects who have taken a Ph.D. degree or an equivalent doctorate, and 17 others who are still working for a doctorate. The proportion of the age-comparable generality receiving such a degree is not far from one or two in a thousand. Those who have taken either the M.D. degree (52) or a graduate law degree (82) account for 134 of the total group. It is doubtful whether 1,500 school children picked at random would contribute one-twentieth as many doctors or lawyers.

Another indication of the educational achievement of the group is the large number of subjects who were awarded scholarships, fellowships, and assistantships. As we have noted in chapter xiii, 20 percent of those who completed college held one or more undergraduate scholarships. This is approximately 14 percent of the total group. One or more graduate fellowships were awarded to 105 members of the group, and one or more graduate assistantships to 114. These figures are, respectively, 7.6 percent and 8.2 percent of all gifted subjects irrespective of the amount of education, and are unquestionably many times larger than would be found for an unselected group of school children followed to the same age.

Earned Income

In earned income the contrast between the gifted group and the generality is significant but less spectacular. For the calendar year 1944 the average earned income of the gifted men was $4,700; of the employed women, $2,600. At that time the average age of the subjects was between thirty-three and thirty-four years, or probably twenty years below the age when maximum earning capacity is ordinarily attained. Yet, despite their relative youthfulness, 13.5 percent of the men reported earned incomes of $10,000 or more. Data on earned income for the generality of comparable age are not available, but it is unlikely that in 1944 the average would have been anywhere near that of the gifted subjects. The proportion of gifted men with earned income of $5,000 or over in 1944 was more than six times as great as the 1944 proportion reported by the Alexander Hamilton Institute for employed males of all ages in the United States: 45.4 percent as compared with 7.4 percent. The earnings of gifted women employed full time, although superior, are probably closer to the earnings of the generality than are the earnings of gifted men.

Publications and Patents

By the end of 1945, when the average age of the subjects was close to thirty-five years, the group had published about 90 books or monographs and approximately 1,500 articles which appeared in scientific, scholarly, or literary magazines. The publications, both major and minor, cover a wide range. The books include 8 college textbooks (4 of which have been translated into foreign languages), 14 volumes of fiction and 3 of poems, 2 medical treatises, 2 books of popular science, 5 in the social sciences, and several story books for children.

More than half of the hundreds of articles are of scientific nature and are widely distributed among the physical and engineering sciences, the medical and biological sciences, and the social sciences (including psychology). The others include articles on current events and literary topics, numerous poems, and 50 or more short stories. In addition, members of the group have written several novels and innumerable short stories which have not been published.

Patents granted to members of the group by 1945 numbered more than 100. Nearly half of these were granted to two men, one of whom is in radio engineering and the other in chemistry. We have record of only 2 patents awarded to a woman in the group, both in the field of metallurgy. Many of the patents have been sold to industrial firms, but so far as we know none of them is of epoch-making importance. The output of both publications and inventions would doubtless have been greater but for the fact that for three or four years a majority of the men were either in military service or were engaged in other kinds of war work.

Comparison with American Rhodes Scholars

A recent report by Aydelotte[3] lists the names of the American Rhodes scholars who had been appointed to 1939, and gives for nearly all of them the following information: date of scholarship award, name of the Oxford college attended, occupation (presumably as of 1945), firm or institution with which associated (if any), rank or title, and address. On the basis of Aydelotte's report we have summarized the records of those who received their appointments during the eleven-year period from 1927 to 1937, inclusive, for comparison with the records of our gifted men. If we assume that the scholarship awards were received at the average age of twenty-two years, the 1945 age range of this Rhodes group would be roughly thirty to forty years, with a mean of about thirty-five years. These figures agree fairly well with the age range and mean of our gifted men.

Of the 348 Rhodes scholars appointed during this period, 11 were deceased at the time of Aydelotte's report, 9 were still students, 12 were in the Army or Navy (not otherwise classified as to occupation),* and 7 were listed with no information other than the date of appointment and the name of the Oxford college attended. This leaves 309 for whom some occupational information is available. Table 107 gives the occupational classification of this group as compared with that of (1) all gifted men and (2) the gifted men in our A group. The classification is in terms of the Minnesota Occupational Scale.

TABLE 107

Occupational Classification of Rhodes Scholars and Gifted Men

Occupational Group	Rhodes Scholars Percent	All Gifted Men Percent	Gifted A's Percent
I	79.3	48.3	69.3
II	20.7	32.0	30.7
III	....	15.7	....
IV or below	....	4.0	....

The table shows that in occupational status the Rhodes men decisively outrank the total group of gifted men, but are only slightly superior to the 150 most successful gifted men (the A group discussed in chapter xxiii). This is not surprising in view of (1) the manner in which the Rhodes scholars and the gifted subjects were selected,

* The others who were in the Army or Navy were classified on the basis of their prewar occupations.

and (2) the greater amount of schooling of the Rhodes group. The gifted subjects were selected at the average age of eleven years and solely on the basis of IQ on an intelligence test. The Rhodes scholars were selected after college graduation at the average age of about twenty-two years and on the twofold basis of demonstrated superiority in scholastic achievement and evidence of leadership qualities. Selective factors therefore favor the Rhodes group. Whereas the gifted subjects all rated in childhood as the best in 100 of the generality (only a minority of them as the best in 300 to 500), a majority of the Rhodes men must surely have been among the best in many hundreds. The Rhodes men, by the mere fact of their scholarship appointments, are all college graduates who have had the advantage of three years of postgraduate study in one of the world's greatest universities. In contrast, only 70 percent of the gifted men have completed college, and only 45 percent of them have had one or more years of postgraduate training.

A more just comparison is that between Rhodes scholars and our gifted A's, of whom 90 percent have completed college and 76 percent have had one or more years of postgraduate study. The comparisons which follow will therefore be limited to the Rhodes men and the men of our A group.

Comparison of the proportion of Rhodes scholars and gifted A's in particular professions revealed some interesting differences. Classified in the field of education were 41.4 percent of the Rhodes men, but only 18 percent of the A men. On the other hand, journalists and other writers account for 5.8 percent of the Rhodes men as against 7.3 percent of the A men. Medicine has attracted only 4.8 percent of the Rhodes men as compared with 10 percent of the A men. Law is about equally popular with the two groups, the respective percentages being 18.7 and 16.7.

A little over one-third of the Rhodes men are teachers, as compared with one-fifth of the A men. Of Rhodes teachers, 28 percent are in the field of humanities (English, foreign language, philosophy, and the fine arts); of gifted A's who are teaching, only 16 percent are in this field. Two of the Rhodes teachers but none of the gifted A's are teaching law.* The two groups differ little in the proportion of teachers in the physical sciences (physics, chemistry, mathematics,

* Two or three practicing lawyers in the A group who lecture on the side in law schools are not classified as teachers.

and engineering), or in the proportion in the social sciences (history, political science, psychology, and economics). In biology and medicine, however, there are only 10 percent of the Rhodes teachers as against 31 percent of the gifted A teachers.

Consider next the professional ranks attained by those who are teaching. Data on this point are available for 98 Rhodes teachers and for 29 gifted A's.* From Table 108 it will be seen that gifted A's make the decidedly better showing. Holding the rank of professor or associate professor in four-year colleges or universities are 41.4 percent of the gifted A teachers and 28.6 percent of the Rhodes teachers. There is a difference of similar magnitude, and in the same direction, for the rank of assistant professor, whereas the lower ranks of instructor, lecturer, or tutor are more than twice as common in the Rhodes group. Teaching in secondary schools are four of the Rhodes men but none of the gifted A's.

TABLE 108

PROFESSIONAL RANKS ATTAINED BY RHODES AND GIFTED A TEACHERS

	Rhodes Men Percent	Gifted A's Percent
A. *Teaching in four-year colleges or universities*		
1. Professor or associate professor	28.6	41.4
2. Assistant professor	39.9	48.3
3. Instructor, lecturer, or tutor	27.4	10.3
B. *Teaching in high school*	4.1	....
N for percentages	98	29

Table 109 gives the proportion of Rhodes men and of gifted A's who have distinguished themselves in certain specified ways. It will be noted that only the Rhodes group has thus far given us any college presidents or directors of great foundations, but that the gifted A's make a trifle better showing in *Who's Who,*[73] *American Men of Science,*[11] and the National Academy of Sciences.

From the data reviewed it appears that although the Rhodes group has clearly outdistanced the total group of gifted men, it is barely on a par with the gifted men in our A group. Compared to the latter the Rhodes men are a little superior in occupational status, but this is fairly well offset by the slightly better showing of the gifted A's in several of the other comparisons. More of the Rhodes men are

* For 19 additional Rhodes teachers the professional rank could not be determined, and these were omitted from the above comparison. One might suspect that these were among the less-successful teachers.

found in important administrative positions, but probably none of them is more eminent than two or three of the gifted A's.

TABLE 109

Proportion of Rhodes Men and of Gifted A's Who Have Achieved Certain Kinds of Distinction

	Rhodes Men %	Gifted A's %
Directors of large foundations	0.6	...
College or university presidents	1.6	...
Deans or department heads	1.0	3.3
Listed in *Who's Who*	3.6	4.7
Listed in *American Men of Science*	11.3	12.7
Members of the National Academy of Sciences	...	0.7
N for percentages	309	150

A survey of this kind impresses one with the difficulty of achieving any considerable degree of national eminence. Of the 348 Americans appointed as Rhodes scholars from 1927 to 1937, there were only 5 of whom we had ever heard, and 2 of these were known to us only because they were members of our gifted group.* The names are equally unfamiliar to other university professors who have scanned the list for us.

Examples of Superior Achievement

The following examples of outstanding accomplishments will lend a touch of concreteness to our account of the group, and relieve somewhat the monotony of the statistical summary. The list of cases selected for mention could have been greatly extended without dipping into much lower achievement levels. The examples given have been chosen to illustrate the variety of fields in which exceptional achievement has been found. Men and women will be listed separately.

A physicist who is extremely gifted in administration as well as in science is director of one of the great laboratories devoted to the applications of atomic energy.

During the last year of the war, a historian served as director of a large project for the Office of Strategic Services, in which position he directed the work of more than a hundred social scientists

* Eight other members of the gifted group were runners-up for Rhodes scholarship awards.

engaged in research on the cultural, economic, political, and social conditions of the people in one of our enemy countries. He is now assistant director of a great foundation.

A professor of physiology was co-director, during the war, of what was perhaps the most important investigation that has ever been made of the physiological, biochemical, and psychological effects of prolonged semistarvation. The report of this research will run to several volumes.

A professor in one of the applied physical sciences served throughout the war as director of a government research laboratory which employed hundreds of scientists and technicians, spent millions of dollars, and created devices that so reduced the efficiency of enemy radar as definitely to shorten the war. This man has received two of the highest honors that can come to a scientist: the presidency of his national scientific society, and membership in the National Academy of Sciences.

Among the men who have taken medical degrees, several have achieved a national reputation. One is a widely known plastic surgeon. One is described by his colleagues as the most productive researcher in the medical school in which he teaches. One is head of the department of public health in a leading medical school.

One of our psychiatrists was, at the age of thirty-three, chief of psychiatric therapy in one of the great combat areas of the war, and later served as psychiatrist at the Nuremberg prison. In the latter position he had the unique responsibility of making official psychiatric and psychological examinations of all the top-ranking Nazis. He has published one book, is the coauthor of another, and has published about a dozen articles in professional journals.

A professor of pharmacology in a medical school has published more than a hundred research contributions before the age of thirty-five, and is the executive head of his department.

One of our men is director of a psychological research organization, is prominent in the activities of the American Psychological Association, and is generally regarded as among the country's ablest psychologists of the younger generation.

One of our scientists is an oceanographer who was chief of one of the technical staffs at the Bikini atomic bomb explosions. Another member of the group participated in this event, and a third was invited to be present but was unable to accept.

One of our men, a graduate of Annapolis, was commander of a destroyer; another, who graduated from West Point, served in the Air Forces and before the end of the war became one of the youngest brigadier generals in the Army.

A member of the State Department has been promoted to the position of chief for one of the critical areas of the Western Hemisphere. Another is a rising member of the foreign diplomatic service.

Our most accomplished linguist is a lawyer who, just for the fun of it, has acquired a mastery of some fifteen languages, including Japanese, French, Spanish, Russian, Croatian, Norwegian, Danish, Hawaiian, Greek, Latin, and several Celtic languages.

Two of our men have won national recognition as writers of fiction. One of these has published seven detective novels. The other, a graduate in engineering, has published dozens of articles and short stories based upon technological themes, three novels—one of which has been compared favorably with the best of its genre—and a book on inventions. His *magnum opus* to date, a scholarly book on witchcraft and magic, has just been completed.

One of our men is a relatively young motion-picture director who is rapidly becoming known as among the most talented in the country.

In the group are four professional writers for screen and radio whose work is paid for to the tune of $20,000 to $40,000 a year.

Several of the men have risen to positions of importance in the aircraft industry, one as chief structural engineer for a leading airplane manufacturing firm, the other as chief legal counsel for another firm.*

Far fewer women than men in our group have made records of outstanding achievement. This is hardly surprising in view of the fact that only a small minority of them have gone out wholeheartedly for

* As an addendum to these case notes on men it is fitting that reference be made to one of my subjects of rare creative genius who was not included in the statistics of this report because his intelligence level was not definitely established in childhood. He is several years older than anyone included in the group, and when he was a child no satisfactory IQ test had been devised. However, I have followed his development since 1910, when he was 13 years old, and know him about as intimately as any gifted subject I have ever observed. He is an eminent musician who has produced hundreds of musical compositions, authored two books and scores of articles on musical theory, invented new musical techniques, given recitals throughout the United States and Europe, lectured in leading American universities, founded and edited a musical magazine, and won recognition as an authority on musicology and primitive music. His compositions cover a wide range with respect to type, theme, and technique. Many of his productions have been recorded; several of his orchestral selections are played by leading conductors; and some of his briefer compositions are famous among musicians because of their originality.—L. M. T.

a career. Two, however, are nationally known writers. One of these is a university teacher of English who has published two books of poems that have been highly praised by critics, a scholarly monograph, and a number of articles in literary journals. The other is a journalist and the author of a successful wartime novel. Another woman is a talented actress who is also the author of a successful Broadway play; still another has shown considerable promise as a writer of storybooks for children.

Two women are artists of more than ordinary talent and some regional reputation. One of these as a child produced remarkable juvenilia, both prose and poetry, and graduated from college at the early age of seventeen. A third woman artist is a concert pianist and composer, as well as a housewife and the mother of three children.

Two women are missionaries, one in the Far East, the other in Africa. The latter has translated a volume of religious literature into an African language. Two other women are successful ministers in this country.

Several of our women have taken a doctorate in science and have done creditable research. One is a metallurgist who holds a very responsible research position in an industrial firm. One is a bacteriologist who holds the rank of assistant professor in a leading medical school. Another, an M.D., is also on the faculty of a medical school. All of these have authored a number of technical research publications. Five women are having successful careers as professional psychologists.

A good many of the women have made their most notable achievement in the selection of a mate. Two of the husbands are eminent musicians, and several others have won national recognition in the physical, biological, or social sciences.

The Outlook for Future Achievement

Only a professed seer would venture at this time a statistical forecast of the probable future achievements of the group. Nearly half of the subjects are below the age of thirty-five years, an age when a considerable number of the most eminent persons of history were still unknown to fame. One can recall the names of famous writers, generals, and industrial or political leaders who lived to the age of forty or fifty years in relative obscurity. As Lehman[42] has shown, the median age at which positions of leadership are attained in America has greatly increased in the last 150 years. In field after field the increase has amounted to 8, 10, or even 12 years. This is true not only of Presidents, Congressmen, United States Supreme Court justices, chief state justices, cabinet members, foreign diplomats, heads of federal services and bureaus, and top-ranking Army and Navy officers, but also of college presidents, religious leaders, and scientists.

Yet Lehman has also presented[41] incontrovertible evidence that in nearly all fields of intellectual achievement the most creative period is between the ages of thirty and forty-five years. The peak of creativity, defined as the age when the most important work of one's life is accomplished, is more often reached between thirty-five and forty than in any other five-year period. Particularly in almost every field of science, art, and literature the *best* work of one's life is more likely to be produced before rather than after the age of forty. In mathematics the peak is most frequently attained before thirty. In individual cases, creative productivity of high order continues into the late seventies or even into the eighties, but these are exceptions to the rule.

Lehman's data, it bears repeating, are concerned primarily with the *quality of* achievement. Productivity as measured by quantity is often greater in the second forty years than in the first forty. And however meritorious one's early output of work may have been, the peak of recognition, honors, and earned income is usually not reached until the fifties, and often not until the sixties. Reputation and fame continue to mount long after one's best work has been done. This is especially noticeable in *Who's Who* listings, relatively few of which occur for the first time before the age of thirty-five years. The time lag in popular recognition is to be expected, but it is surprising to find a similar lag in scientific recognition. Of 81 persons elected to membership in the National Academy of Sciences in 1943, 1944, and 1945, only 3.7 percent were under forty years of age. In contrast, among the 95 persons elected to membership in this organization from 1864 to 1883, there were 45.5 percent below the age of forty. The increasing lag is probably due in part to the growing complexity of science, the multiplication of special fields of investigation, and the rapid increase in the number of scientific workers. It is becoming ever more difficult to follow the progress of research even in areas that are fairly closely related to one's own.

What does all this mean in terms of the outlook for future achievement in our gifted group? The following tentative conclusions appear to be warranted.

1. The majority of the group have reached or have closely approached what is normally the most creative period of life, and few if any have passed through this period. The best work of some has perhaps been done, but for a majority the peak of accomplishment will probably not be reached for another five years or more. Interruptions caused by the war may delay the peak for our group by three or four years beyond this normal expectation. As a rough guess we would estimate that between half and two-thirds of the total ultimate achievement of the group lies ahead.

2. The peak of *recognition* for achievement will come much later, probably not before another fifteen or twenty years have elapsed. Listings in *American Men of Science* may well be doubled by 1960, and listings in *Who's Who* may be trebled or quadrupled by 1970. In the decade 1960 to 1970 there should be several times as many holding positions of high responsibility as in 1945, and several times as many of national or international reputation in their special fields of accomplishment.

3. Despite conclusions (1) and (2), it is possible even now to estimate, at least roughly, what the probable ultimate limits of accomplishment will be for many of the subjects. It is possible because statistics have shown that high achievement of almost every kind is usually foreshadowed by earlier promise of achievement. There are, of course, exceptions. The soldier, the politician, or the man of business may be catapulted to eminence after mid-life largely by the whims of chance, but not the scientist or musician, and only rarely the painter, the poet, or the novelist. In no one of these fields is a person likely to achieve notably if he has not shown more than ordinary promise by the age of thirty or thirty-five years.

The group includes 20 or 25 scientists who have either achieved, or appear likely to achieve, a national reputation among their kind. A randomly selected group of 1,500 persons could hardly be expected to produce one-tenth as many. The number of talented writers in the group is several times the normal expectation. Among the best candidates for outstanding achievement are a dozen or more of the men who have gone into medicine. The group contains many able and successful lawyers, but whether they will continue their competent legal practice in relative obscurity or get into the limelight through judicial appointments or entrance into public affairs it is too early to hazard even a guess. Lawyers have an advantage over most other men in the fact that age seems to add to their professional dignity and reputation; if they live they have a long time in which to increase their eminence. Perhaps the most unpredictable of the subgroups is that made up of business men. A high order of financial success for many of these seems fairly certain. Several have shown exceptional talent in the managerial field; whether any of them will ever become nationally prominent as industrial or financial leaders no one can say.

The Difficult Road to Eminence

That the group contains no one who shows promise of matching the eminence of Shakespeare, Goethe, Tolstoy, da Vinci, Newton, Galileo, Darwin, or Napoleon is not surprising in view of the fact that the entire population of America since the Jamestown settlement has not produced the like of one of these. Such eminence in a given field is usually possible only at a given stage of cultural progress and can never be very closely paralleled in a different era. For one thing, science and scholarship are growing so highly specialized that eminence is becoming progressively more difficult to attain. Conceivably, if Darwin were living today he might be just another specialist in a restricted field of biology, and a present-day Newton might be just another high-class mathematician, astronomer, or nuclear physicist.

Fame, moreover, is a poor measure of creative genius. Every student of biography knows that eminence and intellect are not very highly correlated. All of our United States Presidents have a more or less permanent niche in history, yet a few of them were anything but intellectual giants. Even Washington, the nineteenth most eminent person of history in Cattell's list, was less gifted intellectually than many of his less eminent contemporaries.

Much depends upon the myriad factors of chance and circumstance. But for the colonial policy of George III and his cabinet, Washington might have remained only a respected planter, moderately prominent in the affairs of the Virginia colony. We should probably never have heard of Newton if his uncle had not made it possible for him to enter Cambridge University. We might never have heard of Faraday, the untutored apprentice bookbinder, if Humphry Davy had not discovered his talent and made him his protégé and assistant. Darwin's chance for fame may have been decided by his opportunity to join the

Beagle expedition. Even when the potential genius finds what for him is the right road, his way is often made difficult by ill health, other misfortunes, or limited opportunity for his talent to flower. Especially by limited opportunity, though in America today this difficulty is more easily surmounted than in other cultures and other times.

One of the most difficult bars to real eminence is the narrow span of human memory and attention. To be eminent means to stand out above the crowd in the minds of others. It is impossible to imagine a million or even a hundred thousand truly eminent persons living at a given time. There are probably few college professors who could identify more than one name in a hundred of the 35,000 listed in the last edition of *Who's Who*.[73] It is doubtful whether the average man-on-the-street could identify more than one out of a thousand. Let the reader try to recall the names of even five living chemists or physicists, five living mathematicians, five living biologists, or five living philosophers or historians.

If our memories are capable of registering so few of our living contemporaries, how infinitesimal must be the chance that a name picked at random from the pages of *Who's Who* or *American Men of Science* will live on through the ages! Cattell[12] based his selection of the thousand most eminent persons of history on the total number of words devoted to each in leading biographical dictionaries and encyclopedias, yet in this highly selected list the names of several hundred will ring no bell in the memory of the average professor of history. Castle[10] undertook to make a statistical study of the thousand most eminent women of history, similarly selected, but found that in recorded history there were not that many women who could be considered eminent in any reasonable sense of the term. The chances that a single one of our gifted group will ever be included in a future list of the thousand most illustrious men and women of all time must be small indeed.

Achievements in Contentment

Our discussion so far has been concerned with the achievement of eminence, professional status, and recognized position in the world of human affairs. But these are goals for which a large proportion of highly intelligent men and women do not consciously strive. Many of them ask nothing more of life than happiness and contentment in comparative obscurity. Nor can they be blamed for not enlisting in the battle for "success" in the worldly sense. Everyone must be conceded the right to tailor his own personal philosophy.

We have no yardstick for measuring the intangible achievements that make for contentment, and we venture no estimate of the success of our gifted subjects in this quest. We do not even know whether they are more happy or less happy than the average person in the generality. We do know that they are better fed, better housed, and better doctored than the average person, that they are in a position to care better for their children, and that they have less reason generally to be anxious about the future. Such things cannot insure happiness, but they would seem to favor it.

CHAPTER XXVI

LOOKING BACKWARD AND FORWARD

Viewed in retrospect, not many scientific researches are wholly satisfactory. This is especially true when the investigator is working in a relatively uncharted field of an immature science. Even in the more exact sciences new techniques are continually being developed, and new problems emerge that could not have been foreseen a decade in advance. Physics, electronics, genetics, and medical science have been revolutionized within recent decades. Psychology, in which the present investigation chiefly falls, is also evolving rapidly. In the light of what is now known it will be obvious that our study of gifted children has many imperfections. The plan of the study as formulated a quarter of a century ago and the methods employed at each of its later stages can be fairly evaluated only with reference to the insights then possible and the techniques then available.

Although a definitive appraisal of the undertaking and of its accomplishments will only be possible in the perspective afforded by the lapse of another twenty or thirty years, we nevertheless venture to record what seem to us some of the merits and shortcomings of the investigation. In such an evaluation one must, of course, take account of what was feasible within the rigid limitations imposed by the modest research funds it was possible to secure. We shall mention first those aspects of the study to date with which we are reasonably well satisfied, in view of the circumstances that prevailed when important decisions had to be made.

On choice of the problem for prolonged investigation there is not the slightest regret. We still believe that a nation's resources of human talent are the most valuable it possesses, and that any contribution whatever to our knowledge regarding the characteristic traits and potentialities of intellectually gifted children is bound to be worth far more than it costs in labor and money. For the same reasons we are equally well satisfied with the decision to concentrate on the follow-up of the original group of subjects in preference to making cross-section studies of additional groups.

The decision in regard to the size of the group to be selected for study was one of the most difficult to make, and it was only after long consideration that the goal was finally set at 1,000 rather than at a half or a third of that number. The relative advantages and disadvantages of the larger N are obvious enough, but how they are to be weighed one against the other is a matter of subjective judgment as to the type of study that will be most useful at a given time. As it turned out, the goal of 1,000 was considerably exceeded. Had the number been rigidly limited to 500 it would have been possible to secure much more data regarding each subject, and the follow-up would have been correspondingly less cumbersome and expensive. On the other hand, a group so limited in size would have yielded such small subgroups when broken down by age, sex, and other variables that it would often have been impossible to evaluate the significance of numerical comparisons. In this connection one thinks especially of statistical data on nervous and mental disorders, physical defects, mortality, delinquency, personality maladjustment, fertility, marital adjustment, correlates of scholastic and vocational success, and the effects of school acceleration. We were also influenced by the belief that, regardless of the theoretical issues viewed from a strictly scientific angle, the study of a large group would more effectively open up the field for future research than a more intensive study of a small group. The relative merits of the two possible courses are at least debatable, and we are unable to assert dogmatically that the choice made was the better one, though we believe it was. In psychology, as in archaeology, it is often desirable that large-scale reconnaissance should precede the intensive digging of a restricted area.

The methods used in selecting subjects, although not ideal, provided a fairly representative population of high IQ's. This is especially true of the Main Experimental Group, and we have since learned that this group does not differ significantly from the other groups obtained by less systematic procedures. Fewer potential subjects would have been missed if group tests could have been given to the entire school enrollment prior to the final sifting by individual testing, but the slight improvement that this would have made in the representativeness of the sample would hardly have justified the vastly greater cost. Errors of measurement in establishing the original IQ's would have been reduced if the study had been confined to an age range of six to twelve years. They would have been further reduced had it been possible to give two forms of the Stanford-Binet scale to subjects who rated high on the preliminary group test. As the reader probably knows, a second form of this scale was not available until 1937. Because of lack of top in the 1916 Stanford-Binet, the Terman Group Test was devised for the selection of older gifted subjects.

Considering the scope of the investigation, the limited funds, and the status of psychological methodology at various stages of the research, we find little to regret regarding the choice of devices, rating schemes, case-history procedures, and other techniques employed. For our purpose there were no better intelligence tests or achievement tests available than those used in the original survey. When the investigation was being planned there did not exist a battery of achievement tests so standardized that it would give strictly comparable achievement quotients in the several school subjects, and the need for such a battery in the gifted study gave rise to the Stanford Achievement Tests, since so widely used in revised editions. Other psychometric devices that were developed to meet specific needs in the gifted study were the Raubenheimer tests of character, the Wyman test of interests, and the test of play interests and play information. The play test in turn gave rise to the Terman-Miles test of mental masculinity and femininity later given to many of our subjects.

The intelligence tests used in 1928 were among the best then available, but the rest of the 1928 testing program would perhaps have been more fruitful if a smaller variety of tests had been used, and if each had been given to all the subjects of suitable age instead of (in some instances) to random samples of the group. It is unfortunate that so few satisfactory instruments for measuring achievement at the high-school level were available when the follow-up of 1927–28 was planned. Even so, the job done could have been better if adequate funds had been at our command. As for the testing program of 1940, there is little if anything we would change, costs considered. Many will regret that the half-hour intelligence test could not have been extended to at least two or three hours so as to yield a more valid and reliable measure of the adult intellectual status of the group, but if this had been done it would have been necessary to omit both the test of marital aptitude and the test of marital happiness. One's choice between alternatives so qualitatively different as to be incommensurable must be decided on the basis of personal interests, and the reader is entitled to his own opinion as to the wisdom or unwisdom of the choice made.

The anthropometric measurements and the medical examinations of 1922–23 were expertly done. The various information schedules filled out by parents and teachers in 1922 and 1928, and by the subjects and their parents in 1928 and 1940, might have been better in certain respects, but on the whole were almost as satisfactory as any we could formulate now in the light of our experience.

No aspect of the study has been more satisfactory throughout than the quality of the field work, for on this the success of the entire project was constantly dependent. Assistants of less competence than Florence Goodenough, Helen Marshall, Dorothy Yates, Barbara Burks, Alice Leahy, Ellen Sullivan, and Nancy Bayley could have wrecked the investigation at any stage. It is much to be regretted that two assistants of this rank could not have been kept in the field through all the years since 1922.

In reflecting upon what could have been accomplished in a long-range study of this kind with unlimited funds, it is difficult not to become obsessed by thoughts of the might-have-beens. The abilities of the group when located should have been more thoroughly explored. Ideally, the physical measurements should have been repeated annually throughout the period of growth in order to provide accurate data on the rate of physical maturation. The medical examinations should have been repeated from time to time and they should have been extensively supplemented by physiological and biochemical tests. Every subject should have been examined periodically by one or more psychiatrists. Personality adjustment and parent-child relationships should have been studied intensively and continuously by field assistants. Tests of mechanical, musical, and artistic ability should have been given. More detailed and more accurate genealogical data, of kinds suitable for statistical analysis by a geneticist, should have been obtained. A battery of mental tests should have been given to the parents and to all the siblings of the subjects, and the careers of low-testing siblings should have been followed as closely as the careers of subjects who qualified for the group. Marital selection, fertility, and mortality among parents and grandparents should have been more thoroughly investigated. All the marriages of the subjects should have been followed up year after year by field assistants.

Although all of the above data would have been scientifically valuable, such intensive and continuous investigation of the group would also have involved certain risks: (1) Under constant observation, the subjects might have grown unduly self-conscious about the experiment, and some of them might have become "fed up" and less cooperative; (2) the more intensive follow-up would inevitably have led to remedial treatment of various kinds, making hazardous definite conclusions regarding the development of gifted children under normal conditions.

Despite the limitations of the study, many facts have been more or less firmly established, some of them in line with the results of earlier but less conclusive investigations, some of them in direct contradiction to the traditional beliefs of both laymen and educators. For example:

We now know that in physique and general health, children of high IQ are on the average superior to the general child population, and that the later mortality rate for such a group to the age of thirty-five is lower than for the generality; but we do not yet know how much of this is to be credited to superiority of home environment.

That the achievement quotients of gifted children in the pre-high-school grades average nearly as high as their IQ's; that, as a rule, achievement continues to be very superior in the high school, but that on entering college a good many subjects lose interest and make poor or mediocre records.

That versatility rather than one-sidedness is the rule with gifted children is demonstrated by the fact that their achievement quotients are usually high in all the school subjects.

That the typical gifted child is customarily held to a grade location two or three years below the level to which normal mastery of the curriculum has already been attained, and that school retardation (defined as grade placement below achievement) is almost universal among the gifted.

That gifted children who have been promoted more rapidly than is customary are as a group equal or superior to gifted nonaccelerates in health and general adjustment, do better schoolwork, continue their education further, marry a little earlier, and are more successful in their later careers.

That in character and personality, as evidenced both by tests and by trait ratings, gifted children average above the general child population, but that the degree of superiority is less marked for traits indicative of emotional stability and social adjustment than for intellectual and volitional traits.

That to near mid-life such a group may be expected to show a normal or below-normal incidence of serious personality maladjustment, insanity, delinquency, alcoholism, and homosexuality.

That, as a rule, those who as children tested above 170 IQ were more often accelerated in school, got better grades, and received more schooling than lower-testing members of the group; that they are not appreciably more prone to serious maladjustment; and that vocationally they are more successful.

That the intellectual status of the average member of the group at the mean age of thirty years was close to the 98th or 99th percentile of the general adult population, and was far above the average level of ability of graduates from superior colleges and universities.

That in vocational achievement the gifted group rates well above the average of college graduates, and as compared with the general population is represented in the higher professions by eight or nine times its proportionate share.

That the vocational success of subjects all of whom as children tested in the top 1 percent of the child population is, as one would expect, greatly influenced by motivational factors and personality adjustment.

That the incidence of marriage in the group to 1945 is above that for the generality of college graduates of comparable age in the United States, and about equal to that in the general population.

That marital adjustment of the gifted, as measured by the marital happiness test, is equal or superior to that found in groups less highly selected for intelligence, and that the divorce rate is no higher than that of the generality of comparable age.

That the sexual adjustment of these subjects in marriage is in all respects as normal as that found in a less gifted and less educated group of 792 married couples.

That the test of marital aptitude predicts later marital success or failure in this group a little better than the test of marital happiness, much better than the index of sexual adjustment, and almost as well as scholastic aptitude tests predict success or failure in college.

That offspring of gifted subjects show almost exactly the same degree of filial regression as is predicated by Galton's law.

That the fertility rate of the group to 1945 is probably below that necessary for the continuation of the stock from which the subjects come, and that this stock is greatly superior to the generality.

That Jewish subjects in the group differ very little from the non-Jewish in ability, character, and personality traits, as measured either by tests or by ratings, but that they display somewhat stronger drive to achieve, form more stable marriages, and are a little less conservative in their political and social attitudes.

The investigation is now only at its half-way point, and it is possible that some of the above generalizations may have to be modified when the group has been followed another twenty-five years. It is still too early to estimate accurately the ultimate contribution of the group to science, scholarship, literature, and social welfare, or its ultimate fertility, longevity, insanity rate, and divorce incidence. Of the more than 1,500 children born to the group by 1946, less than 400 have been given an intelligence test. By 1950 all of the second generation aged three or above should be tested by the Stanford-Binet scale, and those of eight or above by the Stanford Achievement Tests. From the genetic point of view it is to be hoped that the Binet tests, at least, will be continued to the third or even the fourth generation in order to determine whether and to what extent Galton's law of regression operates in successive generations beyond the second.

It is extremely important that the original subjects themselves should in the near future be given a more thorough test of general intelligence than they have yet had as adults, so as to provide the basis for a more accurate estimate than is now possible of the degree to which early intellectual status has been maintained. If at all possible this test should be repeated at five- or ten-year intervals, in order to establish the normal rate of mental decline in gifted subjects during the period of later maturity, and the range of individual differences in such decline. The problem of mental aging is important not only from the theoretical and biological point of view; now that the average span of human life has been lengthened to almost seventy years, it is equally important from the economic and social angle. A group of superior individuals who are so test-willing, and whose case histories are so well documented by test scores and specific records of achievement, presents an incomparable opportunity for research in this field of gerontology.

High on the agenda for future research are the problems of personality and general adjustment. (1) All marriages should be followed by repeated administration of the marital happiness test and by keeping up to date the records on domestic maladjustment and divorce. Here as elsewhere in our study the data already garnered become increasingly valuable with the passage of time. As the case histories lengthen, the significance of new facts increases in geometrical rather than arithmetical ratio. (2) Psychiatric examinations should be given if possible to all the members of the group, and these should be supplemented by tests designed to reveal basic patterns of personality structure. Psychometric techniques to be considered for this purpose are the Rorschach test, Murray's Thematic Apperception Test, and Raymond Cattell's tests of primary personality traits. (3) The subjects, or at least the male subjects, should be somatotyped by the Sheldon method, so that personality data and case histories could be correlated with body build.

That personality and temperament are somehow related to body build has been remarked by many observers since the days of the famous Greek physician, Galen, but the problem has been little investigated by objective methods. Although Sheldon's scheme of measuring and expressing the body build is a great improvement over earlier methods,[54] this author's published account of the relationship between personality and somatotype is largely subjective and speculative.[55] The correlations found in the Grant study of 258 Harvard students appear to rest upon a more substantial basis and to give some support to Sheldon's claims regarding the importance of somatotype for the understanding of personality structure. Particularly interesting are the relationships reported in that study between personality traits and (1) masculinity of physique, and (2) number of bodily disproportions.[31] Our gifted group, because of the detailed case histories available for the individual subjects, is probably capable of throwing more light on this problem than any other group in the world.

The above program for future research is, of course, subject to modifications in the light of results obtained at successive stages. The program may seem ambitious, but it is in fact minimal rather than ideal. It cannot be too strongly emphasized that the data already at hand become more valuable as the lives and careers of the subjects take final form. Follow-up of the group for another twenty-five years can hardly fail to yield more significant results than the first twenty-five years, for it would bring the pay-off. With few exceptions the subjects are genuinely interested in the outcome and can be counted on for continued co-operation under appropriate guaranty that the confidential nature of the records will be safeguarded in the future as they have been in the past.

The program of field work realizable will, of course, depend on the financial support that can be obtained, and when it is obtained. An idea of the magnitude of the financial problem can be gained from the fact that one field study comparable in scope to that of 1940 will cost at least $40,000 by the time the data have been collected, statisticized, and summarized for publication. Three such studies might well run to $120,000 over and above the modest sum now in prospect for continued contact with the subjects by correspondence. An even greater sum could be profitably expended in the next thirty years. Costs, after all, are relative. It is conceivable and probable that the outcome of the research, if it is carried to its conclusion, could repay the cost of the entire study by enhancing the contribution of a single gifted individual to science or social welfare. The fruits of potential genius are indeed beyond price. The task ahead is not simply that of finding how gifted children turn out; it is the problem rather of utilizing the rare opportunities afforded by this group to increase our knowledge of the dynamics of human behavior, with special reference to the factors that determine degree and direction of creative achievement.

REFERENCES CITED

1. ANDERSON, E. E., *et al.* "Wilson College Studies in Psychology: I. A Comparison of the Wechsler-Bellevue, Revised Stanford-Binet, and American Council on Education Tests at the College Level." *Journal of Psychology* (1942), **14**, 317–26.
2. ANDERSON, J. E. "The Prediction of Terminal Intelligence from Infant and Preschool Tests." *Yearbook of the National Society for the Study of Education* (1940), **39 (I)**, 385–403.
3. AYDELOTTE, FRANK. *The American Rhodes Scholarships.* Princeton: Princeton University Press (1946). 208 pages.
4. BABCOCK, F. L. *The U.S. College Graduate.* New York: The Macmillan Company (1941). 112 pages.
5. BRIMHALL, D. R. "Family Resemblances among American Men of Science." *American Naturalist* (1922), **56**, 504–47; (1923), **57**, 74–88; 137–52; 326–44.
6. BURGESS, E. W., and COTTRELL, L. S. *Predicting Success or Failure in Marriage.* New York: Prentice-Hall, Inc., (1939). 472 pages.
7. BURKS, BARBARA S., JENSEN, DORTHA W., and TERMAN, L. M. *Genetic Studies of Genius, III. The Promise of Youth.* Stanford University: Stanford University Press (1930). 508 pages.
8. CADY, V. M. *The Estimation of Juvenile Incorrigibility. Journal of Delinquency* Monograph Series (1923), No. 2. 140 pages.
9. CAHEN, ALFRED. *Statistical Analysis of American Divorce.* New York: Columbia University Press (1932). 149 pages.
10. CASTLE, CORA S. *A Statistical Study of Eminent Women.* New York: Science Press (1913). 90 pages.
11. CATTELL, JACQUES (editor). *American Men of Science* (7th edition). Lancaster, Pennsylvania: Science Press (1944). 2,706 pages.
12. CATTELL, J. M. "A Statistical Study of Eminent Men." *Popular Science Monthly* (1903), **53**, 359–78.
13. CATTELL, J. M., and BRIMHALL, D. R. "Families of American Men of Science." In *American Men of Science* (3d edition). New York: Science Press (1921), 781–808.
14. CHASSELL, CLARA F. *The Relation Between Morality and Intellect.* Teachers College Contributions to Education (1935), No. 607. 556 pages.
15. CIOCCO, ANTONIO. "Sex Differences in Morbidity and Mortality." *Quarterly Review of Biology* (1940), **15**, 59–73; 192–210.
16. CLARKE, E. L. "American Men of Letters: Their Nature and Nurture." *Columbia University Studies in History, Economics, and Public Law* (1916), **72**, 1–169.

17. Connelly, G. M., and Field, H. H. "The Non Voter—Who He Is, What He Thinks." *Public Opinion Quarterly* (1944), **8**, 175–87.

18. Cox, Catharine M. *Genetic Studies of Genius, II. The Early Mental Traits of Three Hundred Geniuses.* Stanford University: Stanford University Press (1926). 842 pages.

19. Davis, Katherine B. *Factors in the Sex Life of Twenty-two Hundred Women.* New York: Harper & Brothers (1929). 430 pages.

20. Dennis, Wayne. "The Adolescent." In L. Carmichael (editor), *Manual of Child Psychology.* New York: John Wiley & Sons (1946), pp. 633–66.

21. Dickinson, R. L., and Beam, Lura. *A Thousand Marriages.* Baltimore: Williams & Wilkins Company (1931). 482 pages.

22. *Dictionary of Occupational Titles, Part I.* Prepared by Job Analysis and Information Section, Division of Standards and Research, United States Department of Labor. Washington: United States Government Printing Office (1939). 1,287 pages.

23. Dublin, L. I., and Lotka, A. J. *Length of Life.* New York: Ronald Press Company (1936). 400 pages.

24. Ellis, Havelock. *A Study of British Genius.* London: Hurst & Blackett, Ltd., (1904). 300 pages.

25. Folsom, J. K. *The Family.* New York: John Wiley & Sons (1934). 604 pages.

26. Galton, Francis. *Hereditary Genius* (2d edition). London: Macmillan & Company, Ltd., (1892). 379 pages.

27. Goodenough, Florence L., and Anderson, J. E. *Experimental Child Study.* New York: Century Company (1931). 546 pages.

28. Greenleaf, W. J. *Economic Status of College Alumni.* United States Office of Education Bulletin (1937), No. 10. 207 pages.

29. Hamilton, G. V. *A Research in Marriage.* New York: Albert & Charles Boni, Inc. (1929). 570 pages.

30. Heilman, J. D. "The Relative Influence Upon Educational Achievement of Some Hereditary and Environmental Factors." *Yearbook of the National Society for the Study of Education* (1928), **27 (II)**, 35–65.

31. Hooton, Earnest. *Young Man, You Are Normal.* New York: G. P. Putnam's Sons (1945). 210 pages.

32. Hrdlička, Aleš. *The Old Americans.* Baltimore: Williams & Wilkins Company (1925). 438 pages.

33. Jackson, C. M. "The Physique of Male Students at the University of Minnesota: A Study in Constitutional Anatomy and Physiology." *American Journal of Anatomy* (1927), **11**, 59–126.

34. Jackson, C. M. "Physical Measurements of the Female Students at the University of Minnesota, with Special Reference to Body Build and Vital Capacity." *American Journal of Physical Anthropology* (1929), **40**, 363–413.

35. Keys, Noel. "The Underage Student in High School and College."

University of California Publications in Education (1938), **7**, 145–272.

36. KINSEY, A. C. "Homosexuality; Criteria for a Hormonal Explanation of the Homosexual." *Journal of Clinical Endocrinology* (1941), **1**, 424–28.
37. LANDIS, CARNEY, and PAGE, J. D. *Modern Society and Mental Disease.* New York: Farrar & Rinehart (1938). 190 pages.
38. LANGE-EICHBAUM, WILHELM. *The Problem of Genius.* New York: The Macmillan Company (1932). 187 pages.
39. LASSWELL, H. D. *Psychopathology and Politics.* Chicago: University of Chicago Press (1930). 285 pages.
40. LEARNED, W. S., and WOOD, B. D. *The Student and His Knowledge.* Carnegie Foundation for the Advancement of Teaching Bulletin (1938), No. 29. 406 pages.
41. LEHMAN, H. C. "Man's Most Creative Years. Quality versus Quantity of Output." *The Scientific Monthly,* New York (1944), **59**, 384–93.
42. LEHMAN, H. C. "The Age of Eminent Leaders Then and Now." *American Journal of Sociology* (1947), **52**, 342–56.
43. MACMEEKEN, AGNES M. *The Intelligence of a Representative Group of Scottish Children.* London: University of London Press (1939). 143 pages.
44. MCNEMAR, QUINN. "Sampling in Psychological Research." *Psychological Bulletin* (1940), **37**, 331–65.
45. MCNEMAR, QUINN, and TERMAN, L. M. "Sex Differences in Variational Tendency." *Genetic Psychology Monographs* (1936), **18**, 1–66.
46. OLSON, W. C. *The Measurement of Nervous Habits in Normal Children.* University of Minnesota Institute of Child Welfare Monograph Series (1929), No. 3. 97 pages.
47. POLLOCK, H. M. *Mental Disease and Social Welfare.* Utica, N.Y.: State Hospitals Press (1941). 237 pages.
48. PRESSEY, S. L. "Age of College Graduation and Success in Adult Life." *Journal of Applied Psychology* (1946), **30**, 226–33.
49. RAUBENHEIMER, A. S. "An Experimental Study of Some Behavior Traits of the Potentially Delinquent Boy." *Psychological Monographs* (1925), **34**, No. 159. 107 pages.
50. RECKLESS, W. C., and SMITH, MAPHEUS. *Juvenile Delinquency.* New York: McGraw-Hill Book Company (1932). 412 pages.
51. ROWNTREE, L. G. "The Health of Registrants and the President's Plan of Rehabilitation." *Science* (1941), **94**, 552–53.
52. RUBINOW, I. M. *Some Statistical Aspects of Marriage and Divorce.* American Academy of Political and Social Science Pamphlet Series (1936), No. 3. 36 pages.
53. SCOTTISH COUNCIL FOR RESEARCH IN EDUCATION. *The Intelligence of Scottish Children.* London: University of London Press (1933). 160 pages.

54. SHELDON, W. H. *The Varieties of Human Physique.* New York: Harper & Brothers (1940). 347 pages.
55. SHELDON, W. H. *The Varieties of Temperament.* New York: Harper & Brothers (1942). 520 pages.
56. *Sixteenth Census of the United States, 1940.* Washington: United States Government Printing Office (1942).
57. STEGGERDA, M., CRANE, JOCELYN, and STEELE, MARY D. "One Hundred Measurements and Observations on One Hundred Smith College Students." *American Journal of Physical Anthropology* (1929), **13**, 189–254.
58. STOUFFER, S. A., and SPENCER, L. M. "Marriage and Divorce in Recent Years." *Annals of the American Academy of Political and Social Science* (1936), **188**, 1–68.
59. STRONG, E. K. *Vocational Interests of Men and Women.* Stanford University: Stanford University Press (1943). 746 pages.
60. SWARD, KEITH. "Age and Mental Ability in Superior Men." *American Journal of Psychology* (1945), **58**, 443–79.
61. TERMAN, L. M. "A Study in Precocity and Prematuration." *American Journal of Psychology* (1905), **16**, 145–83.
62. TERMAN, L. M. "Genius and Stupidity; a Study of Some of the Intellectual Processes of Seven 'Bright' and Seven 'Stupid' Boys." *Pedagogical Seminary* (1906), **13**, 307–73.
63. TERMAN, L. M. *Psychological Factors in Marital Happiness.* New York: McGraw-Hill Book Company (1938). 474 pages.
64. TERMAN, L. M., and HOCKING, ADELINE. "The Sleep of School Children." *Journal of Educational Psychology* (1913), **4**, 138–47; 199–208; 269–82.
65. TERMAN, L. M., and MERRILL, MAUD A. *Measuring Intelligence.* Boston: Houghton Mifflin Company (1937). 461 pages.
66. TERMAN, L. M., and MILES, CATHARINE C. *Sex and Personality.* New York: McGraw-Hill Book Company (1936). 600 pages.
67. TERMAN, L. M., and ODEN, MELITA. "Correlates of Achievement in the California Gifted Group." *Yearbook of the National Society for the Study of Education* (1940), **39 (I)**, 67–89.
68. TERMAN, L. M., *et al. Genetic Studies of Genius, I. Mental and Physical Traits of a Thousand Gifted Children.* Stanford University: Stanford University Press (1925). 648 pages.
69. THORNDIKE, E. L. *The Measurement of Intelligence.* New York: Bureau of Publications, Teachers College, Columbia University (1927). 616 pages.
70. THORNDIKE, E. L. "The Causation of Fraternal Resemblance." *Journal of Genetic Psychology* (1944), **64**, 249–64.
71. WELLS, F. L., and WOODS, W. L. "Outstanding Traits: in a Selected College Group, With Some Reference to Career Interests and War Records." *Genetic Psychology Monographs* (1946), **33**, 129–255.
72. WHITE HOUSE CONFERENCE ON CHILD HEALTH AND PROTECTION.

Special Education: The Handicapped and the Gifted. New York: Century Company (1931). 604 pages.

73. *Who's Who in America* (24th edition). Chicago: A. N. Marquis Company (1946). 2,033 pages.
74. Woodbury, R. M. "The Relation Between Breast Feeding and Artificial Feeding and Infant Mortality." *American Journal of Hygiene* (1922), 668–87.
75. Woods, F. A. *Mental and Moral Heredity in Royalty.* New York: Henry Holt and Company (1906). 312 pages.

ADDITIONAL SELECTED READINGS

BENTLEY, J. E. *Superior Children.* New York: W. W. Norton and Company (1937). 331 pages.

BURKS, BARBARA S. "A Scale of Promise, and Its Application to Seventy-one Nine-year-old Gifted Children." *Pedagogical Seminary* (1925), 32, 389–413.

CARROLL, H. A. *Genius in the Making.* New York: McGraw-Hill Book Company (1940). 307 pages.

COHEN, HELEN L., AND CORYELL, NANCY G. *Educating Superior Students.* New York: American Book Company (1935). 340 pages.

CONKLIN, AGNES M. *Failures of Highly Intelligent Pupils. A Study of Their Behavior by Means of the Control Group.* Teachers College Contributions to Education (1940), No. 792. 250 pages.

GODDARD, H. H. *School Training of Gifted Children.* Yonkers-on-Hudson: World Book Company (1928). 226 pages.

HENRY, T. S. "Classroom Problems in the Education of Gifted Children." *Yearbook of the National Society for the Study of Education* (1920), 19 (II). 125 pages.

HOLLINGWORTH, LETA S. *Gifted Children: Their Nature and Nurture.* New York: The Macmillan Company (1926). 374 pages.

———. "The Development of Personality in Highly Intelligent Children." *Yearbook of the National Elementary Principal* (1936), 15, 272–81.

———. "An Enrichment Curriculum for Rapid Learners at Public School 500: Speyer School." *Teachers College Record* (1938), 39, 296–306.

———. "What We Know About the Early Selection and Training of Leaders." *Teachers College Record* (1939), 40, 575–92.

———. "Intelligence as an Element in Personality." *Yearbook of the National Society for the Study of Education* (1940), 39 (I), 271–75.

———. *Children Above 180 IQ, Stanford Binet.* Yonkers-on-Hudson: World Book Company (1942). 332 pages.

HOLLINGWORTH, LETA S., AND COBB, MARGARET V. "Children Clustering at 165 I.Q. and Children Clustering at 146 I.Q. Compared for Three Years in Achievement." *Yearbook of the National Society for the Study of Education* (1928), 27 (II), 3–33.

HOLLINGWORTH, LETA S., AND KAUNITZ, RUTH M. "The Centile Status of Gifted Children at Maturity." *Journal of Genetic Psychology* (1934), 45, 106–20.

KRETSCHMER, ERNST. *The Psychology of Men of Genius.* (Trans. by R. B. Cattell.) New York: Harcourt, Brace and Company (1931). 256 pages.

LAMSON, EDNA E. *A Study of Young Gifted Children in High School.* Teachers College Contributions to Education (1930), No. 424. 117 pages.

LANGE-EICHBAUM, WILHELM. *Genie, Irrsinn, und Ruhm* (2d ed.). Munich: E. Reinhardt (1935). 540 pages.

LEHMAN, H. C. "The Creative Years in Science and Literature." *The Scientific Monthly,* New York (1936), **43**, 151–62.

———. "The Creative Years: 'Best Books'." *The Scientific Monthly,* New York (1937), **45**, 65–75.

———. "Optimum Ages for Eminent Leadership." *The Scientific Monthly,* New York (1942), **54**, 162–75.

———. "Man's Most Creative Years: Then and Now." *Science* (1943), **98**, 393–99.

———. "Age of Starting to Contribute versus Total Creative Output." *Journal of Applied Psychology* (1946), **30**, 460–80.

LORGE, IRVING, AND HOLLINGWORTH, LETA S. "Adult Status of Highly Intelligent Children." *Journal of Genetic Psychology* (1936), **49**, 215–26.

MILES, CATHARINE C. "Gifted Children." In L. Carmichael (editor) *Manual of Child Psychology.* New York: John Wiley & Sons (1946), pp. 886–953.

ROOT, W. T. "A Socio-psychological Study of Fifty-three Supernormal Children." *Psychological Monographs* (1921), **29**, No. 4. 134 pages.

STEDMAN, LULU M. *Education of Gifted Children.* Yonkers-on-Hudson: World Book Company (1924). 192 pages.

SUMPTION, M. R. *Three Hundred Gifted Children.* Yonkers-on-Hudson: World Book Company (1941). 235 pages.

TERMAN, L. M. "The Intelligence Quotient of Francis Galton in Childhood." *American Journal of Psychology* (1917), **28**, 209–15.

———. "Psychological Approaches to the Biography of Genius." *Science* (1940), **92**, 293–301.

TERMAN, L. M., AND FENTON, JESSIE C. "Preliminary Report on a Gifted Juvenile Author." *Journal of Applied Psychology* (1921), **5**, 163–78.

THORNDIKE, E. L. "How May We Improve the Selection, Training, and Life-work of Leaders?" *Teachers College Record* (1939), **40**, 593–605.

THORNDIKE, R. L. "Problems in Identification, Description, and Development of the Gifted." *Teachers College Record* (1941), **42**, 402–6.

WHIPPLE, G. M. (ed.) "The Education of Gifted Children." *Yearbook of the National Society for the Study of Education* (1924), **23 (I)**. 444 pages.

WHITE, R. K. "The Versatility of Genius." *Journal of Social Psychology* (1931), **2**, 460–89.

WITTY, P. A. "A Study of One Hundred Gifted Children." *University of Kansas Bulletin of Education* (1930), **2**, No. 7. 44 pages.

WITTY, P. A. "A Genetic Study of Fifty Gifted Children." *Yearbook of the National Society for the Study of Education* (1940), **39 (II)**, 401–9.

WITTY, P. A., AND LEHMAN, H. C. "A Study of the Reading and Reading Interests of Gifted Children." *Journal of Genetic Psychology* (1932), **40**, 473–85.

———. "The Reading and the Reading Interests of Gifted Children." *Journal of Genetic Psychology* (1934), **45**, 466–81.

YATES, DOROTHY H. "A Study of Some High School Seniors of Superior Intelligence." *Journal of Educational Research Monographs* (1922), No. 2. 75 pages.

APPENDIX

APPENDIX

INFORMATION SCHEDULES OF 1936, 1940, AND 1945

The information blanks of 1936, 1940, and 1945 were 8½ by 11 inches in size. They are reproduced here in small type. The list that follows includes all the blanks used between 1936 and 1945 except two: (1) a 4-page blank on which gifted mothers supplied information on the development of their children who had been given a Stanford-Binet test; and (2) the Concept Mastery test.

Blanks reproduced:

Information Blank (1936), for subjects
Home Information Blank (1936), for parents
General Information (1940), for subjects
Supplementary Information (1940), for parents
Report of Field Worker (1940), on individual subject
Personality and Temperament (1940), for subjects
Marriage Blank (1940), for married subjects
Information Blank (1945), for subjects

Gifted Children Follow-Up
Stanford University, 1936

Date of filling out this blank..............................

INFORMATION BLANK (1936)

(To be filled out by the subjects)

Full name.. Age.....................

Address ....

1. Date of completing: (*a*) Eighth Grade............ (*b*) High School..........
   Years required to complete High School..
   Number of recommended units on graduation..
   High School honors (scholastic honors, offices, societies, etc.).................
   ....
   Special activities and hobbies during High School..................................
   ....
2. Other schools or institutes attended (not college or university) such as business, technical, art, dramatic, etc...
   ....
   For how long (give dates)........................... Diplomas.......................
3. If no longer in school, give date of leaving......................... Last grade or college year of attendance.............................. Reason for leaving..........
   ....
4. College Record:

Colleges Attended	For How Long	Average Grade	Degrees (give month and year)	Your Age at Time
a) Undergraduate..................				
b) Graduate..........................				

c) Undergraduate major.............................. Minor..............................
Graduate major .... Minor..............................

d) Graduation honors (such as with great distinction, *cum laude*, etc.)
....

e) Scholastic honor societies (such as Phi Beta Kappa, Sigma Xi, professional fraternities)..

f) Undergraduate scholarships or fellowships (with dates and stipend)
....

g) Graduate scholarships or fellowships (with dates and stipend)..........
....

h) Assistantships (with dates and stipend. Specify nature of work)......
....

i) Activities participated in while in college (such as dramatics, journalism, sports, music, etc.) ....

....

Activity honors (societies, athletic letters, etc.) ....

....

Other hobbies during college years ....

....

j) Have you belonged to a social fraternity, sorority, or house club? .... Which one? ....

k) To what extent did you put yourself through college?

i. Undergraduate years: (Underline) All, ¾, ½, ¼, Less than ¼

ii. Graduate years: (Underline) All, ¾, ½, ¼, Less than ¼

Under what circumstances: (Underline) Working while in college; Working during vacation; Remaining out of college to work.

List the kinds of work done for self-support in *undergraduate* years

....

....

Approximate total earnings as an undergraduate ....

Kinds of work in *graduate* years ....

....

Kinds of work done to earn college expenses while remaining out of college. (Indicate amount of time given to each, and rate of compensation) ....

....

Did you borrow money for your college expenses? ....

If so, how much? ....

5. Any long absences from school before completing education? ....
How long? .... Reason ....

6. Are you making plans for any further education? ....
Of what nature? ....

7. Occupations since leaving school. Indicate amount of time if less than full time.

Occupation	Indicate Exact Nature of Work	Compensation per Month	DATES From Mo. Yr.	DATES To Mo. Yr.

8. Have you definitely chosen your life work? .... Describe your ultimate goals as fully as you can at this time ....

....

What factors have influenced your choice? ....

Page 2]

9. Professional or business organizations to which you belong...................

....

Other special accomplishments, honors, or promotions.............................

....

....

10. Avocational interests and hobbies since leaving school (such as music, art, writing, sports, aviation, photography, etc.)...

....

Special instruction in any of the above interests (amount and kind).....

....

11. Your general health since 1928 has been: (Underline) Very good; Good; Fair; Poor; Very poor.

Illnesses, accidents, or surgical operations since 1928...............................

....

Aftereffects ....

Any tendency toward nervousness, worry, or special anxieties in recent years? ....

Over what? ....

12. Have any disappointments, failures, bereavements, uncongenial relationships with others, etc., exerted a prolonged influence upon you? Describe ....

....

Has any good fortune, accomplishment, or change of status had a profound effect upon you?..

Describe ....

Do you consider that any person, book, philosophy, or religion has had a profound influence on your life?..

If so, describe it..

....

13. Members of family (parents, grandparents, brothers or sisters) who have died since 1928. Give relationship, age at death, year of death, and cause ....

....

14. Have you contributed to the support of any relatives (not including your spouse or children)?..

Which ones and to what extent?...

15. Are you married?.............................. If so, give date...............................

Name of spouse (maiden name of wife)...

His or her present age..

Highest grade or college year of spouse's schooling...................................

Diplomas or degrees received...

What school or college?.................. Special scholastic honors.......................

Exact nature of his or her present work..

....

What are his or her plans for a life career?...

....

What are his or her chief avocational interests or hobbies?.................................

....

Occupation of his or her father.............................. mother..................................

Your husband's or wife's general health is: (Underline) Very good; Good; Fair; Poor; Very poor.

Other information regarding husband or wife that you think would be of interest..

....

Marital data: death of spouse, separation, divorce, annulment, remarriage .... Cause?..

Have you any children?............................ How many?..............................

Give for each the sex, name, and date of birth...

....

16. List your publications, if any. For each, give the title, date, publisher, and type of material (e.g., poem, short story, scientific article, etc.)

....

....

....

....

(Please send me copies of as many of your publications as possible)

17. How old were you when you first learned that you were a subject in an investigation of gifted children?...

What effects (favorable, unfavorable, or both) has this knowledge had upon you?...

....

18. Other significant information regarding yourself or your family. (If space is inadequate, answer on additional sheet.)

[*16 blank lines followed here*]

Page 4|

Gifted Children Follow-Up
Stanford University, 1936

HOME INFORMATION BLANK (1936)

Name of subject.. Present age..................

Parent ....

This report made out by...

1. General health since 1928 has been: Very good; Good; Fair; Poor; Very poor. (Underline)
2. Illnesses, accidents, or surgical operations since 1928..
   ....
   ....
   Aftereffects ....
3. Has subject any tendency toward nervousness, worry, or special anxiety in recent years?..
   Describe and give cause, if known..
   ....
   ....
4. Underline to indicate how well the subject is maintaining his or her early mental superiority *as compared to the average*: superiority is now much more marked, somewhat more marked, unchanged, less marked, much less marked.
   Remarks: ....
   ....
   ....
5. Has special ability in any field become either more or less marked in recent years (as in science, literature, music, art, mechanics, etc.)? If so, give details..
   ....
   ....
   ....
   ....
6. To what extent has the subject developed qualities of leadership or managerial ability? ....
   ....
   ....
   ....

[*Page 1*

7. In general does the subject prefer to be with large groups, small groups, one or two persons, or alone? (Underline)

   Remarks: ....

   ....

8. How popular is the subject with others of his or her age? ....

   ....

9. What do you regard as the subject's most serious faults of personality or character?

   Explain ....

   ....

   ....

   ....

10. The most outstanding favorable qualities of personality or character

    ....

    ....

    ....

    ....

11. Does subject show the normal amount of interest in members of the opposite sex? (Underline) More than average amount, average amount, less than average, very little, none.

    Remarks: ....

12. Significant events in the subject's life since 1928, such as travel, good or bad fortune, emotional experiences, etc. ....

    ....

    ....

    ....

13. For what occupation or occupations do you think the subject is best suited? ....

    ....

14. To what extent is subject characterized by ambition, drive, and willingness to work in order to attain success? ....

    ....

    ....

    ....

Page 2]

15. If subject is married, do you regard the marriage in all respects as a fortunate one?.. If not, explain.......................

....

....

16. Subject's father: present occupation if living..

Special accomplishments, activities, honors, or misfortunes of father since 1928..

....

17. Subject's mother: present occupation if living..

Special accomplishments, activities, honors, or misfortunes of mother since 1928..

....

18. Have parents separated or been divorced since 1928?..............................

If so, when? ....

Has either parent remarried since 1928?..

19. Subject's brothers and sisters: mark with a cross (X) any half brothers or sisters:

NAME	Age	Amount of Education	Occupation	Married?	Number of Children

Special accomplishments, activities, honors, or misfortunes of brothers or sisters since 1928..

....

....

....

[*Page 3*

20. Other significant information regarding subject's near relatives, especially brothers, sisters, parents, and grandparents. (Physical and mental health, economic changes, vocational success or failure, etc.)

....

....

....

....

21. At what age did subject learn that he or she was included in this study of gifted children? ....
What effects (favorable, unfavorable, or both) has this knowledge had on the subject? ....

....

....

22. Add any other information that you think would contribute to a more complete understanding of this subject.

[*19 blank lines followed*]

Page 4]

Gifted Children Follow-Up
Stanford University, 1940

Date of filling out this blank..

GENERAL INFORMATION (1940)

Full name.. Birth date.............................. Age..........
(Married women include maiden name)

Address ....

1. Date of completing: (*a*) Eighth Grade.............. (*b*) High School..............
2. Other schools or institutes attended (not college or university) such as business, nursing, technical, art, dramatic, etc..
   ....
   For how long (give dates)..
   Type of course ....
   Diplomas or certificates...
3. College Record:

Colleges Attended	For How Long	Average Grade	Degrees (give month and year)	Your Age at Time
a) Undergraduate				
....	....	....	....	....
....	....	....	....	....
....	....	....	....	....
b) Graduate				
....	....	....	....	....
....	....	....	....	....

4. Subjects in which you received best grades..
   Subjects which you found difficult..
5. Undergraduate major .... Minor..............................
   Graduate major .... Minor..............................
6. If no longer in school, give date of leaving...
   Last grade or college year of attendance...
   Reason for leaving..
7. Were you ever "flunked out" of college?.................. When?..........................
   Causes that led to this difficulty..
   ....
8. Graduation honors (such as with great distinction, *cum laude*, etc.)........
   ....
9. Scholastic honor societies (such as Phi Beta Kappa, Sigma Xi, professional fraternities)..
   ....
10. Undergraduate scholarships or fellowships (with dates and stipend)......
    ....
    Graduate scholarships or fellowships (with dates and stipend)................
    ....

[*Page 1*

Assistantships (with dates and stipend. Specify nature of work)........

....

....

11. Activities participated in while in college (dramatics, journalism, sports, etc., indicate degree of participation and level of success)..........

....

....

Activity honors (athletic letters, societies, etc.)..........

....

12. Other hobbies or extracurricular activities during college years..........

....

....

13. Have you belonged to a social fraternity, sorority, house club, etc.?........ Which one?..........

14. To what extent did you support yourself during college (excluding scholarships and fellowships)?

a) Undergraduate years: (Underline) All, ¾, ½, ¼, Less than ¼, None

b) Graduate years: (Underline) All, ¾, ½, ¼, Less than ¼, None

Under what circumstances: (Underline) Working while in college; Working during vacation; Remaining out of college to work.

List the kinds of work done for self-support in *undergraduate* years

....

....

Approximate total earnings as an undergraduate..........

Kinds of work in *graduate* years..........

....

Kinds of work done to earn college expenses while remaining out of college. (Indicate amount of time given to each, and rate of compensation) ....

....

....

....

Did you borrow money for your college expenses?..........

If so, how much?..........

15. Any long absences from school before completing education?..........

How long?.......... Reason..........

....

16. Are you making plans for any further education?..........

Of what nature and when?..........

....

....

....

....

Page 2]

17. Occupations since leaving school. Indicate amount of time if less than full time.

Occupation, Job or Position	Indicate Exact Nature of Work	Compensation per Month	DATES From Mo. Yr.	DATES To Mo. Yr.

(In front of each occupation place an L, I, or D for like, indifferent, or dislike, depending on your attitude toward the work.)

18. Did you definitely choose your present work or drift into it?..................
Would you prefer some other kind of work?..................
If so, specify..................

19. Have you definitely chosen your life work?.................. Describe your ultimate goals as fully as you can at this time..................

What factors have influenced your choice?..................

What have you done to prepare yourself for the accomplishment of your goals?..................

20. To what professional or business organizations do you belong?..................

Offices you have held..................

21. Special accomplishments, honors, or promotions since leaving school

22. List your publications, if any. For each give title, date, publisher, and type of material (e.g., poem, short story, musical composition, plays, scientific or critical articles, etc.). If you find too little space, attach further sheets listing such publications.

(Please send me copies of as many of your publications as possible.)

23. List other creative work accomplished (e.g., architectural, engineering, inventive, scientific, artistic, dramatic). (Note any special recognition.)

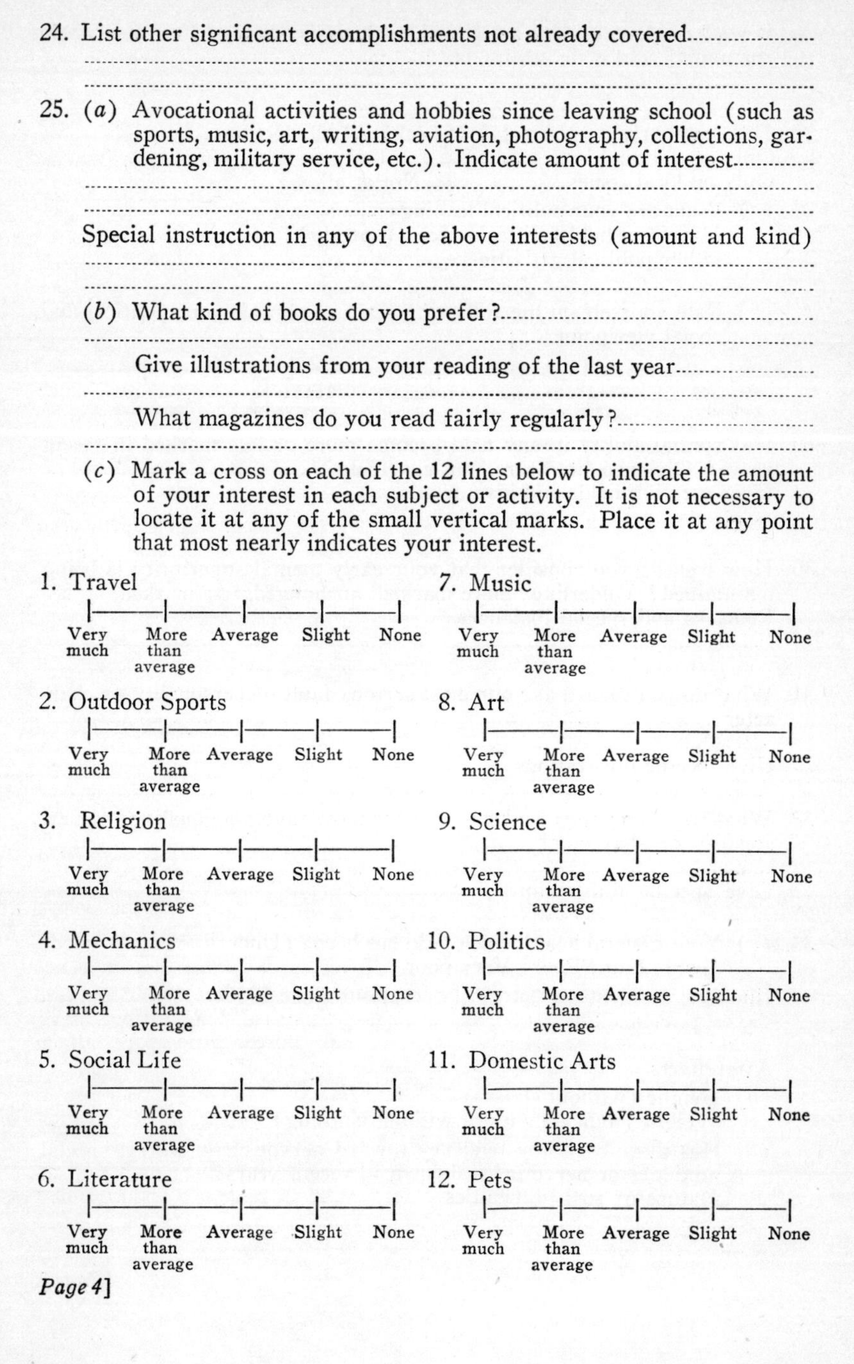

24. List other significant accomplishments not already covered..........

25. (*a*) Avocational activities and hobbies since leaving school (such as sports, music, art, writing, aviation, photography, collections, gardening, military service, etc.). Indicate amount of interest..........

Special instruction in any of the above interests (amount and kind)..........

(*b*) What kind of books do you prefer?..........

Give illustrations from your reading of the last year..........

What magazines do you read fairly regularly?..........

(*c*) Mark a cross on each of the 12 lines below to indicate the amount of your interest in each subject or activity. It is not necessary to locate it at any of the small vertical marks. Place it at any point that most nearly indicates your interest.

1. Travel — Very much | More than average | Average | Slight | None
2. Outdoor Sports — Very much | More than average | Average | Slight | None
3. Religion — Very much | More than average | Average | Slight | None
4. Mechanics — Very much | More than average | Average | Slight | None
5. Social Life — Very much | More than average | Average | Slight | None
6. Literature — Very much | More than average | Average | Slight | None
7. Music — Very much | More than average | Average | Slight | None
8. Art — Very much | More than average | Average | Slight | None
9. Science — Very much | More than average | Average | Slight | None
10. Politics — Very much | More than average | Average | Slight | None
11. Domestic Arts — Very much | More than average | Average | Slight | None
12. Pets — Very much | More than average | Average | Slight | None

Page 4]

26. Record of your service activities (such as Scout work, welfare work, community and civic affairs, etc.)..........

27. How regularly do you vote? (Check) At all elections..........
Only on national issues.......... Only on state issues..........
Only on local issues.......... Not at all..........

28. (*a*) What are your political leanings?..........
Have you held political office? (specify)..........
Other political activities..........

(*b*) Rate yourself on the following scale as regards your political and social viewpoint.

Extremely radical	Tend to be radical	Average	Tend to be conservative	Very conservative

29. Has special ability in any field become more or less marked in recent years? (Science, literature, music, art, etc.)..........
If so, mention fields and give details..........

30. How well do you consider that your early mental superiority is being maintained? Underline: more marked, unchanged, less marked.
Remarks and special instances..........

31. What do you regard as your most serious fault of personality or character..........
Give specific illustrations..........

32. What traits do you consider to be your most favorable qualities of personality or character?..........
Give specific illustrations..........

33. (*a*) Your general health since 1936 has been: (Underline) Very good; Good; Fair; Poor; Very poor.
Illnesses, accidents, or surgical operations since 1936..........
Aftereffects..........
(*b*) Height (without shoes)..........
Weight (indicate with or without clothing)..........
(*c*) Has there been any tendency toward nervousness, worry, special anxieties or nervous breakdown in recent years?..........
Nature of such difficulties..........

How did you handle such difficulties?..

....

....

Present condition (free from such difficulties, improved, no change, worse, etc.)..

....

....

(*d*) Check:

...... I have never used liquor

...... I take a drink occasionally for social reasons

...... I am an occasional drinker; I have not been drunk more than a few times

...... I am a moderate drinker, have been drunk occasionally, but have never felt it necessary to stop

...... Alcohol is a problem; I drink periodically or steadily, am drunk fairly often, and attempts to stop have been unsuccessful

34. Have you ever been arrested? (do not include *minor* traffic violations)

....

If so, give facts regarding each instance, including disposition of case

....

....

35. Were you greatly accelerated in school?.................. If so, to what extent do you consider this was an advantage or disadvantage..............................

....

36. Has any good fortune, accomplishment, or change of status had a profound effect upon you?......................... Describe...................................

....

....

37. Do you consider that any person, book, philosophy, or religion has had a profound influence on your life?.................... If so, describe it..............

....

....

38. What factors do you think have contributed most to your happiness in recent years?..

....

....

39. Have any disappointments, failures, bereavements, uncongenial relationships with others, etc., exerted a profound influence upon you? Describe..

....

....

40. List any members of your family (parents, grandparents, brothers or sisters) who have died since 1936. Give relationship, age at death, year of death, and cause..

....

....

Page 6]

41. (*a*) List members of the household in which you are now living, giving their relation to you (e.g., mother, father, grandmother, wife, sister, brother, son, daughter, friend, boarder, etc.). Check those who are in some degree financially dependent on you.

Name	Relationship to you	Check those dependent on you financially

(*b*) If living alone, give circumstances..

(*c*) Are there others than those mentioned above financially dependent on you?.................. If so, how many?..................
Give relationship ....

42. (*a*) Occupation of father, if living..
Special accomplishments, activities, honors, or misfortunes of father in last few years..
....
....

(*b*) Occupation of mother, if living..
Special accomplishments, activities, honors, or misfortunes of mother in last few years..
....
....

43. Subject's brothers and sisters; mark with a cross (X) any half brothers or sisters.

Name	Age	Amount of Education	Occupation	Married Yes or No	No. of Children

Special accomplishments, activities, honors, or misfortunes of brothers or sisters in the last few years..
....
....

44. Are you married?.............. If so, give date.............. Age at marriage: Yrs..................... Mos..................... Name of spouse (maiden name of wife).. Age of spouse at marriage: Yrs............... Mos............... Highest grade or college year of spouse's schooling...................... Diplomas or degrees received.............................. What school or college?... Special scholastic honors...................................... Present Occupation....................................
What are his or her plans for a life career?..
....
What are his or her chief avocational interests or hobbies?....................
....
Occupation of his or her father......................... mother.........................
Other information regarding husband or wife that you think would be of interest...
....
....
Changes in your marital status: (Underline) death of spouse, separation, divorce, annulment, remarriage
Cause of separation or divorce...
....
Have you any children?....................... How many?...............................
Give for each the name, sex, and date of birth.

Name	Sex	Date of Birth	If Not Living, Age at Death

45. Give any other significant information regarding yourself or your family which has not been covered in the questionnaire. (If space is inadequate, answer on additional sheet.)

[*13 blank lines followed here*]

Gifted Children Follow-Up
Stanford University, 1940

Date of filling out this blank..............................

SUPPLEMENTARY INFORMATION BLANK (1940)

(To be filled out by parent or close relative of subject)

Name of gifted subject..............................
This report made out by..............................
Relationship to subject..............................
Address of person filling out blank..............................

1. General health since 1936 has been: Very good; Good; Fair; Poor; Very poor. (Underline)
2. Illnesses, accidents, or surgical operations since 1936..............................
....
Aftereffects ....
3. Has subject shown any tendency toward nervousness, worry, special anxiety, or mental breakdown in recent years?..............................
Describe and give cause, if known..............................
....
Subject's present condition in this respect..............................
....
4. Underline to indicate how well the subject is maintaining his or her early mental superiority *as compared to the average*: superiority is now much more marked, somewhat more marked, unchanged, less marked, much less marked.
Remarks: ....
....
5. To what extent has the subject developed qualities of leadership or executive ability? ....
6. What do you regard as the subject's most serious faults of personality or character? (Explain)..............................
7. The most outstanding favorable qualities of personality or character........
....
8. To what extent is subject characterized by ambition, drive, and willingness to work in order to attain success?..............................
....
9. Do you think the occupation of the subject is the one best suited to his ability and interests?..............................
....
If not, for what occupation do you think the subject is best suited?..........
....
10. Other significant information regarding subject's near relatives, especially parents, brothers, sisters, and grandparents. (Physical or mental health, economic changes, vocational success or failure, special accomplishments, honors, misfortunes, etc.)

[*9 blank lines followed here*]

11. Add any other information that you think would contribute to a more complete understanding of this subject.

[*19 blank lines followed here*]

PERSONALITY RATINGS

Directions: In each of the following traits or characteristics, compare this subject with the *average* person. Then make a small cross somewhere on the line to show how much of the trait the subject possesses.

Locate your cross *any place on the line* where you think it belongs. It is *not* necessary to locate it on any of the small vertical marks.

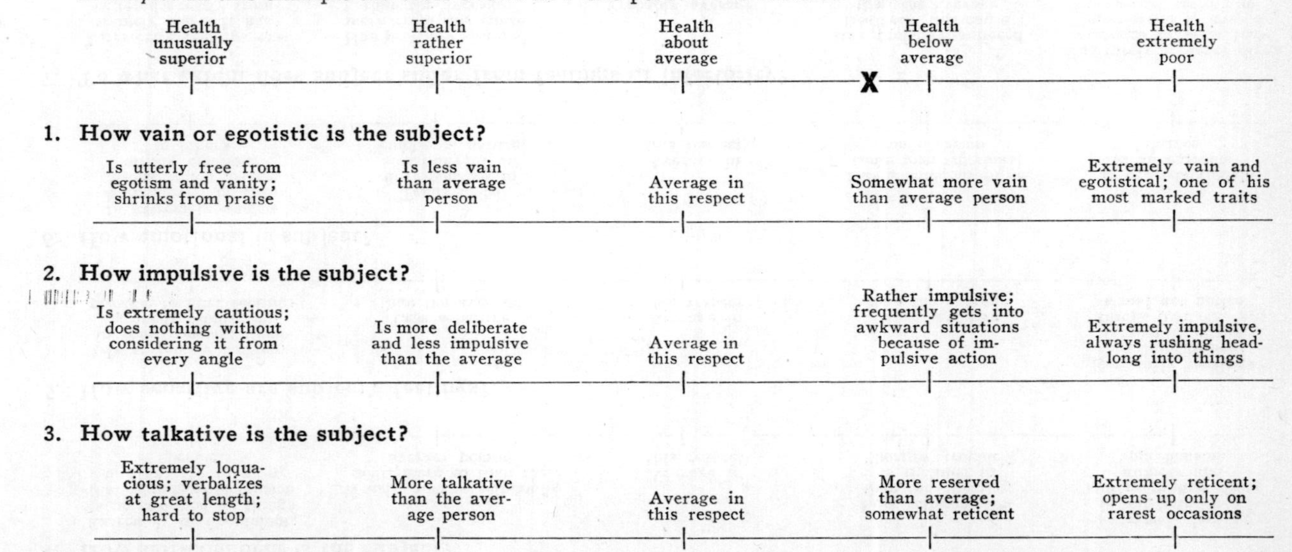

Example. In this example the cross shows how one person was rated for health.

Health unusually superior	Health rather superior	Health about average	Health below average	Health extremely poor

(The cross X is placed on the line just before "Health below average".)

1. How vain or egotistic is the subject?

Is utterly free from egotism and vanity; shrinks from praise	Is less vain than average person	Average in this respect	Somewhat more vain than average person	Extremely vain and egotistical; one of his most marked traits

2. How impulsive is the subject?

Is extremely cautious; does nothing without considering it from every angle	Is more deliberate and less impulsive than the average	Average in this respect	Rather impulsive; frequently gets into awkward situations because of impulsive action	Extremely impulsive, always rushing headlong into things

3. How talkative is the subject?

Extremely loquacious; verbalizes at great length; hard to stop	More talkative than the average person	Average in this respect	More reserved than average; somewhat reticent	Extremely reticent; opens up only on rarest occasions

4. How self-confident is the subject?

Extremely self-confident; is not worried by things that would cause tension and anxiety in most people	Nearly always self-confident, more so than the average person	Average in this respect	Less self-confident than the average; is inclined to "borrow trouble"	Extremely lacking in self-confidence; suffers greatly from anxiety and apprehension

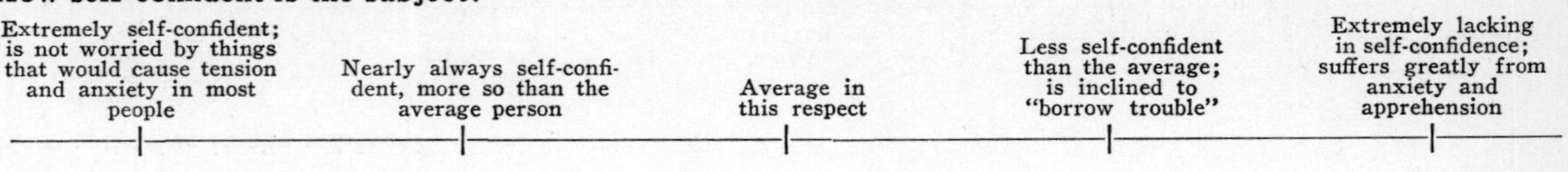

5. How sensitive are subject's feelings?

Is extremely lacking in sensitiveness; thick-skinned; almost impossible to hurt feelings	Less sensitive than the average	Average in this respect	More sensitive than the average	Extremely sensitive and thin-skinned; is hurt by many things that others would not notice

6. How emotional is subject?

Is extremely *un*emotional, even in situations which arouse strong emotions in others	Tends to be unresponsive to situations of an emotional nature	Average in this respect	Has a tendency to become over-emotional on occasion	Is over-emotional to an extreme degree

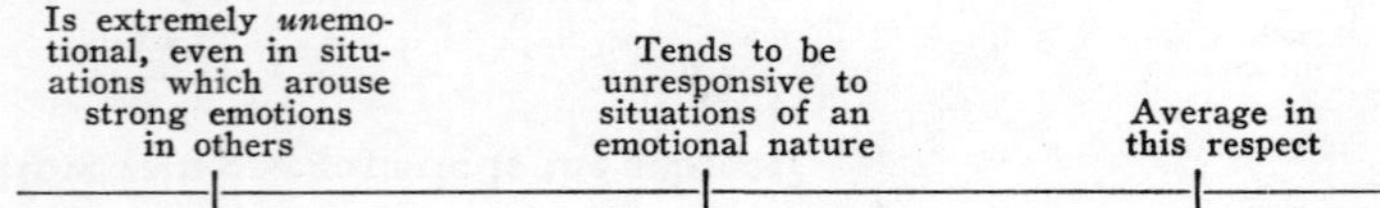

7. To what extent does subject suffer from feelings of inferiority?

Inferiority feelings extremely marked; has suffered greatly from them and still does	Has probably suffered more from this cause than the average person	Probably average in this respect	Has probably suffered less from this cause than the average person	Has rarely or never given evidence of such feelings; seems to have a perpetual feeling of complete adequacy

8. To what extent does subject conform to authority and the conventions?

No tendency whatever to resent or criticize authority, either personal or in the form of conventions	Less resentful than the average	Average in this respect	Is more rebellious than the average	Is inclined to be extremely antagonistic toward authority and conventions

9. Is subject recognized as having good judgment and common sense?

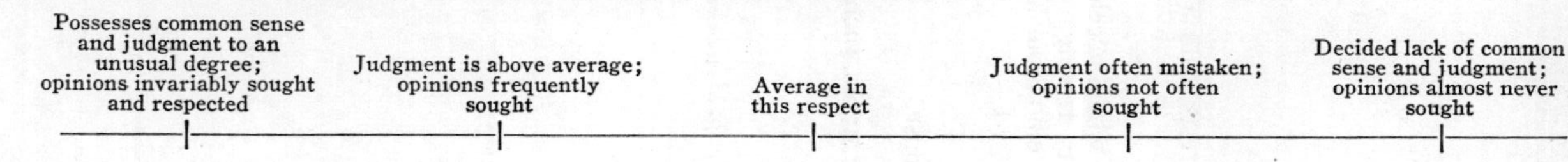

10. How much does subject enjoy social contacts?

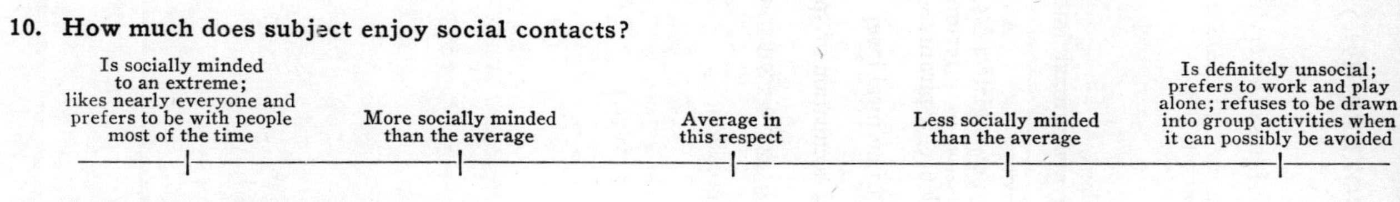

11. How popular is the subject?

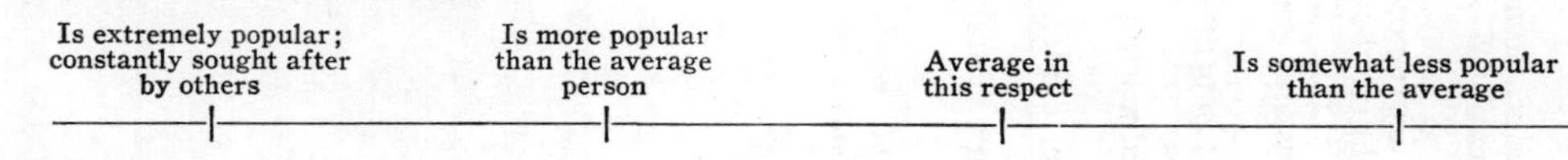

12. How persistent is subject in the accomplishment of ends?

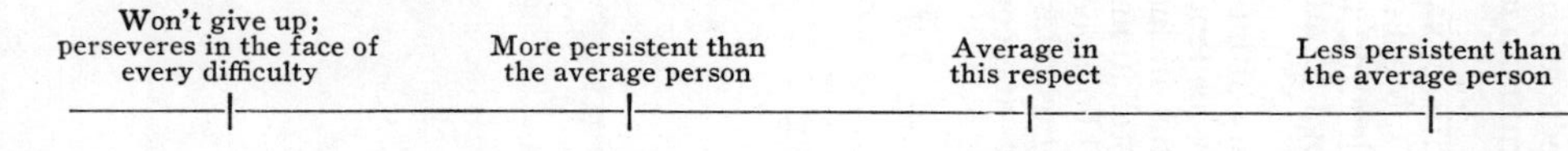

13. Does subject have a program with definite purposes in terms of which time and energy are strictly apportioned?

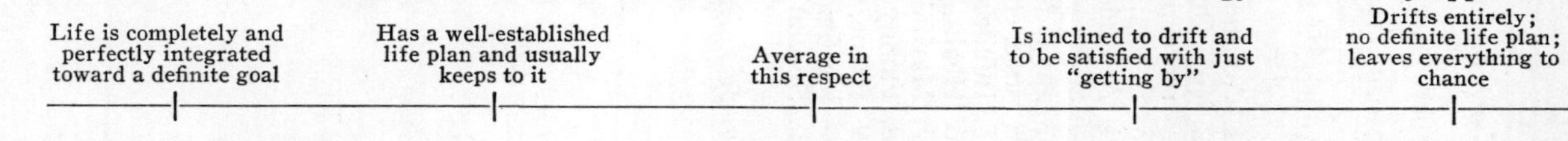

Gifted Children Follow-Up
Stanford University, 1940

Date..

REPORT OF FIELD WORKER (1940)

Name of subject..

Name of field worker.................................... Date of interview.......................

Informants ....
(If not subject, give relationship to subject)

Address ....

1. Additional education and educational plans.
2. (*a*) Occupation, (*b*) vocational and avocational interests, and (*c*) recreation.
3. Special abilities: Nature, degree of success.
4. Attitude of subject toward gifted study, own giftedness, school acceleration, etc., leading possibly into discussion of inferiority feelings (if any), feelings of adequacy and confidence, aspirations, emotional balance, etc.
5. Intellectuality of interests; impression of cultural level.
6. Health, nervous tendencies.
7. Marital status, including education and occupation of spouse.
8. Family constellation.
9. Home, neighborhood, other evidences of socio-economic status, including financial worries.
10. Special notes and comments. Total impression.

[*Here followed two and one-half pages of ruled space for the field worker's report on the ten items above.*]

RATINGS OF SUBJECT BY FIELD WORKER

Subject						Spouse				
1	2	3	4	5	**1. Appearance**	1	2	3	4	5
1	2	3	4	5	**2. Attractiveness**	1	2	3	4	5
1	2	3	4	5	**3. Poise**	1	2	3	4	5
1	2	3	4	5	**4. Speech**	1	2	3	4	5
1	2	3	4	5	**5. Vanity**	1	2	3	4	5
1	2	3	4	5	**6. Alertness**	1	2	3	4	5
1	2	3	4	5	**7. Friendliness**	1	2	3	4	5
1	2	3	4	5	**8. Loquacity**	1	2	3	4	5
1	2	3	4	5	**9. Frankness**	1	2	3	4	5
1	2	3	4	5	**10. Attention**	1	2	3	4	5
1	2	3	4	5	**11. Curiosity**	1	2	3	4	5
1	2	3	4	5	**12. Originality**	1	2	3	4	5

Stanford University, 1940

PERSONALITY AND TEMPERAMENT (1940)

Note. The questions in this blank, if carefully and truthfully answered, will give valuable information regarding your personality and temperament. They have been selected as the most useful for this purpose from more than a thousand that have been tried out with large groups of adults. Your answers will afford, among other things, a basis for estimating your aptitude for social adjustment, personal happiness, and happiness in marriage.

To be of any value your answers must be as **true to fact** as you can make them. Carefully avoid the natural temptation to picture yourself more favorably than the facts warrant.

Fill out the blank **entirely alone.** Do not consult with anyone regarding any of your answers. I am interested only in your own report uninfluenced by the opinion of any other person.

LEWIS M. TERMAN

Begin here:

1. Your name..

2. Date of filling out this blank: year..........; month..........; day of month........

3. Date of birth: year..........; month..........;. Your age at last birthday..........

4. Your present occupation. If not employed now, give the main occupation or occupations you have followed in recent years:..

....

5. Draw a circle around the highest school grade which you completed:

   Grade 1, 2, 3, 4, 5, 6, 7, 8, 9, 10, 11, 12;

   College 1, 2, 3, 4,;

   Postgraduate 1, 2, 3, 4.

   If you have also had special schooling *in addition to that specified above,* indicate how many years by circling the appropriate number below:

   Business School 1, 2, 3, 4;

   Music or Art School 1, 2, 3, 4;

   School for Nurses 1, 2, 3, 4;

   Other Kind of Special School 1, 2, 3, 4.

PART I—ATTITUDES

The questions in this list are intended to indicate your usual reactions and attitudes. Answer them so as to give as true a picture of yourself as you possibly can. Work fairly rapidly. Do not study long over a question.

In front of each question you will find: "Yes No ?"

If your answer is "Yes," draw a circle around the "Yes." If your answer is "No," draw a circle around the "No." If you are entirely unable to answer either "Yes" or "No" to the question, then draw a circle around the question mark.

1. Yes No ? Do you day dream frequently?
2. Yes No ? Are you much affected by the praise or blame of many people?
3. Yes No ? Do people often come to you for advice?
4. Yes No ? Do you want someone to be with you when you receive bad news?
5. Yes No ? Do you often feel just miserable?
6. Yes No ? Are you touchy on various subjects?
7. Yes No ? Do you often experience periods of loneliness?
8. Yes No ? Do you usually try to avoid arguments?
9. Yes No ? Do you often feel lonesome when you are with other people?
10. Yes No ? Do you try to get your own way even if you have to fight for it?
11. Yes No ? Do you frequently feel grouchy?
12. Yes No ? Are you thrifty and careful about making loans?
13. Yes No ? Does some particularly useless thought keep coming into your mind to bother you?
14. Yes No ? Are you frequently burdened by a sense of remorse or regret?
15. Yes No ? Do you ever upbraid a workman who fails to have your work done on time?
16. Yes No ? Can you play your best in a game against a greatly superior opponent?
17. Yes No ? Do you lack self-confidence?
18. Yes No ? Do you usually avoid asking for advice?
19. Yes No ? Do you worry too long over humiliating experiences?
20. Yes No ? If you came late to a meeting would you rather stand than take a front seat?
21. Yes No ? Do you ever take the lead to enliven a dull party?
22. Yes No ? Do you prefer a play to a dance?
23. Yes No ? Do you prefer to be alone at times of emotional stress?
24. Yes No ? Do your feelings alternate between happiness and sadness without apparent reason?
25. Yes No ? Do you prefer making hurried decisions alone?
26. Yes No ? Are you often in a state of excitement?
27. Yes No ? Are you considered to be critical of other people?

28. Yes No ? Can you be optimistic when others about you are greatly depressed?
29. Yes No ? Does discipline make you discontented?
30. Yes No ? Are your feelings easily hurt?
31. Yes No ? Are you always careful to avoid saying anything that might hurt anyone's feelings?
32. Yes No ? Would you rather economize on most other things than on clothing?
33. Yes No ? Do you have an extreme dislike for dictatorial or bossy people?
34. Yes No ? Do you often ignore the feelings of others when doing something that is important to you?
35. Yes No ? Do many people think you have an extra good opinion of yourself?
36. Yes No ? Do you lose your temper easily?
37. Yes No ? Are you the carefree sort who never worries over possible misfortunes?
38. Yes No ? Do you strongly dislike men who are feminine in their tastes?
39. Yes No ? Do you think our present social order so unjust that revolution will be necessary?
40. Yes No ? Do you think most religions do about as much harm as good?
41. Yes No ? Is it harder for you to be serene and cheerful than it is for most people?
42. Yes No ? Do you ever make wagers?
43. Yes No ? Do you make excuses more often than the average person?
44. Yes No ? Do you usually feel that you are well-dressed and make a good appearance?
45. Yes No ? Are you of the "stay-at-home" rather than "gad-about" type?
46. Yes No ? Do you enjoy planning your work in detail?
47. Yes No ? When working for someone are you often inclined to rebel inwardly at orders?
48. Yes No ? Would you rather change from place to place than work in one location?
49. Yes No ? In your work do you usually drive yourself steadily?
50. Yes No ? With the opposite sex do you tend to be dominant and to have your own way?
51. Yes No ? Would you rather have a quiet mate than a very vivacious one?
52. Yes No ? Do you prefer to have many women friends rather than just a few?
53. Yes No ? Should personal happiness be regarded as of paramount importance in marriage?

PART II—SOME LIKES AND DISLIKES

Below you are asked to express your likes and dislikes with reference to a selected list of occupations, activities, etc.

Indicate LIKE by drawing a circle around L
If you are INDIFFERENT, draw a circle around I
Indicate DISLIKE by drawing a circle around D

Work rapidly. Your first impressions are desired. Answer all items.
Selected occupations. After each occupation, indicate whether you would like that kind of work or not. Disregard considerations of salary, social standing, future advancement, etc. Consider only whether you would like to do what is involved in the occupation.

1. Clergyman ....L I D
2. Editor ....L I D
3. Hotel Keeper or Manager.L I D
4. Laboratory Technician ....L I D
5. Landscape Gardener ......L I D
6. Lawyer, Criminal ....L I D
7. Librarian ....L I D
8. Music Teacher ....L I D
9. Orchestra Conductor ....L I D
10. Poet ....L I D
11. Real Estate Salesman........L I D
12. Reporter ....L I D
13. Secret Service Man..........L I D
14. Stock Broker ....L I D

Activities. Indicate in the same way whether you like the following activities or not. If in doubt, consider your most frequent attitude. Work rapidly.

1. Picnics ....L I D
2. Attending smokers ....L I D
3. Reading comic strips.....L I D
4. Bible study ....L I D
5. Public speaking ....L I D
6. Teaching children ....L I D
7. Teaching adults ....L I D
8. Writing personal letters......L I D
9. Contributing to charities......L I D
10. Living in the city...........L I D

Types of people. Indicate in the same way whether you like the following types of people. Record your first impressions.

1. Conservative people ......L I D
2. Emotional people ....L I D
3. Negroes ....L I D
4. Cautious people ....L I D
5. Very old people...........L I D
6. People with hooked noses.....L I D
7. Methodical people ....L I D
8. Teetotalers ....L I D
9. Women cleverer than you are.L I D
10. Fortune tellers ....L I D

PART III—CHILDHOOD AND FAMILY BACKGROUND

1. Enter the following information for each of your brothers and sisters in order from oldest to youngest. *Place circle around the number which indicates your place in order of birth.* Be sure to give year of birth of *all* including yourself.

Order of Birth	1st Child	2nd Child	3rd Child	4th Child	5th Child	6th Child	7th Child	8th Child	9th Child	10th Child
Year of birth										
Sex M or F										
If not living, age at Death										

2. Which brother or sister in the above table were you *most attached to*? (indicate 1st, 2nd, 3rd, etc.)................. If you were not more strongly attached to one than to others, check here.................
3. Where was the larger part of your childhood spent? (check) city..........; small town..........; country..........
4. My childhood, on the whole, was: (check) extremely happy................; more happy than average................; about average................; rather unhappy................; extremely unhappy................
5. Type of training in my home: (check) exceedingly strict..........; firm but not harsh..........; usually allowed to have my own way..........; had my own way about everything..........; irregular (sometimes strict, sometimes lax)..........
6. Amount of punishment: (check) was punished severely for every little thing..............; was punished frequently..............; was occasionally punished..............; rarely..............; never..............
7. Religious training received: (check) very strict............; strict............; considerable............; little............; none............
8. Sunday School attendance *before marriage*: (check) never went..........; stopped before age 10..........; stopped between 10 and 15..........; stopped between 15 and 20..........; stopped between 20 and 25..........; still going at marriage..........
9. Were you a church member at the time of marriage? (check) yes........; no........
10. Check each of the following church activities that you engaged in *before marriage*: held office..........; sang in choir..........; attended prayer meetings..............; member of young people's society in church..............; other activity (specify)..
11. Your present religious affiliation: (check) Protestant..............; Catholic..........; Jewish..........; other (specify)..; no church affiliation..........
12. The sex instruction which I received from *responsible adults* before I was eighteen years old was: (check) entirely adequate..........; reasonably adequate............; rather inadequate............; very inadequate............; none whatever............
13. My sex information before I was eighteen years old was received chiefly from: (check one or more) parents..............; physician..............; teachers..............; other adults..............; other children..............
14. When did you first learn that babies are born of their mother's bodies?

(check) Before 6........; 6 to 11........; 12 to 16........; over 16........; can't remember........

15. Parents' attitude to your early curiosities about birth and sex? (check) Frank and encouraging........; answered briefly........; evaded or lied to me........; rebuffed or punished me........; I did not disclose my curiosity to them........

15a. Women check here age at first menstruation: 10........; 11........; 12........; 13........; 14........; 15........; 16........; 17 or later........

16. Before the age of 15, did you encounter any incident connected with sex, which shocked or greatly disgusted you at the time? (check) Yes........; no........ If so, at what age, or ages? Before 6........; 6 to 10........; 10 to 15........

17. At the High School age what was your general attitude toward sex? (check) Disgust and aversion........; indifference........; interest and pleasant anticipation........; eager and passionate longing........

18. Have you sometimes wished that you were of the opposite sex? (check) Yes........; no........

19. During the High School period did you indulge in petting, spooning, kissing, etc.? (check) Very frequently........; frequently........; sometimes........; rarely........; never........

20. During the High School period, how bashful and shy were you in the presence of the opposite sex? (check) Painfully so........; considerably........; slightly........; not at all........

21. Amount of *conflict* (before marriage) between you and your *father*: (check) none........; very little........; moderate........; a good deal........; almost continuous conflict........

22. Amount of *attachment* (before marriage) between you and your *father*: (check) none........; very little........; moderate........; a good deal........; very close........

23. Amount of *conflict* (before marriage) between you and your *mother*: (check) none........; very little........; moderate........; a good deal........; almost continuous conflict........

24. Amount of *attachment* (before marriage) between you and your *mother*: (check) none........; very little........; moderate........; a good deal........; very close........

25. Everything considered, which was your favorite parent? (check) Father........; mother........; had no favorite........

26. Which of your parents had the greater influence in determining family policies and decisions? (check) Father........; mother........; it was about 50-50........

27. In general appearance and looks, my father was: (check) exceptionally attractive........, above average........, just average........, below average........, distinctly unattractive........

28. In general appearance and looks, my mother was: (check) exceptionally attractive........, above average........, just average........, below average........, distinctly unattractive........

29. Have your parents been divorced? (check) Yes........; no........ If not divorced, have they been separated? (check) Yes........; no........ If they were divorced or separated, did you thereafter live with your father........, mother........, neither........, or both alternately........? How old were you when your parents separated?........

30. Have you had a step-parent? (check which) Step-father........; step-

mother.................. How well did you like step-parent? (check) Very much..........; rather well..........; not very well..........; disliked..........

31. What was the attitude of your parents toward each other after separation? Very antagonistic............; unfriendly............; indifferent............; friendly............

32. To the best of your knowledge how happy was the marriage of your parents? Answer by drawing a circle below around 1, 2, 3, 4, 5, 6, or 7. Avoid giving a higher rating than the facts warrant.

    1 = Extraordinarily happy
    2 = Decidedly more happy than the average
    3 = Somewhat more happy than the average
    4 = About average
    5 = Perhaps a little less happy then the average
    6 = Definitely less happy than the average
    7 = Extremely unhappy

PART IV—YOUR VIEWS ABOUT THE IDEAL MARRIAGE

Directions: Of the things mentioned below some are probably essential to a happy marriage, some not desirable, and some not important one way or the other.

Before each statement draw a circle around a number, 1, 2, 3, 4, or 5, to indicate your opinion of the thing mentioned. What we want is *your own personal opinion,* whether it agrees with the opinions of other people or not.

1 = Very essential
2 = Usually desirable
3 = Makes little or no difference
4 = Usually *not* desirable
5 = Decidedly *not* desirable

How important for the ideal marriage is it:

1 2 3 4 5 That the husband should be some years older than the wife? 1
1 2 3 4 5 That the husband should "wear the pants"? 2
1 2 3 4 5 That husband and wife, if congenial, should take their vacations together? 3
1 2 3 4 5 That marriage be postponed until income permits a comfortable living without serious skimping? 4
1 2 3 4 5 That the wife should have money of her own, or should earn her own living by paid employment, and not be financially dependent upon her husband? 5
1 2 3 4 5 That the wife be allowed a definite budget for the household and for her personal expenditures? 6
1 2 3 4 5 That the wife should be kept fully informed of the family finances and of her husband's business? 7
1 2 3 4 5 That the father should take an active interest in the discipline and training of the children? 8
1 2 3 4 5 That children should be given religious instruction? 9
1 2 3 4 5 That husband and wife should frequently express their love for each other in words? 10
1 2 3 4 5 That the same standard of sexual morality should apply both to husband and wife? 11
1 2 3 4 5 That the wife should not have had sexual intercourse with any *other* man before marriage? 12
1 2 3 4 5 That the husband should not have had sexual intercourse with any *other* woman before marriage? 13
1 2 3 4 5 That after marriage the wife should be 100 percent faithful to her husband in regard to sex? 14
1 2 3 4 5 That after marriage the husband should be 100 percent faithful to his wife in regard to sex? 15
1 2 3 4 5 That husband and wife should be well-mated sexually? 16

PART V—SELF-RATINGS ON PERSONALITY TRAITS

Instructions. On the next two pages you will be asked to rate yourself on twelve personality traits. Each trait is represented by a straight line, the two ends of the line representing the extremes in the trait. Place a cross (X) on the line at the place you think it should go to describe you correctly. The cross does *not* have to be placed at the small vertical bars; put it wherever on the line you think it should go.

Try to view yourself objectively. Don't hesitate to rate yourself at or near the extreme if that is where you belong. The extremes do not usually represent clear-cut faults or virtues. Try not to think of the traits in terms of "good" and "bad."

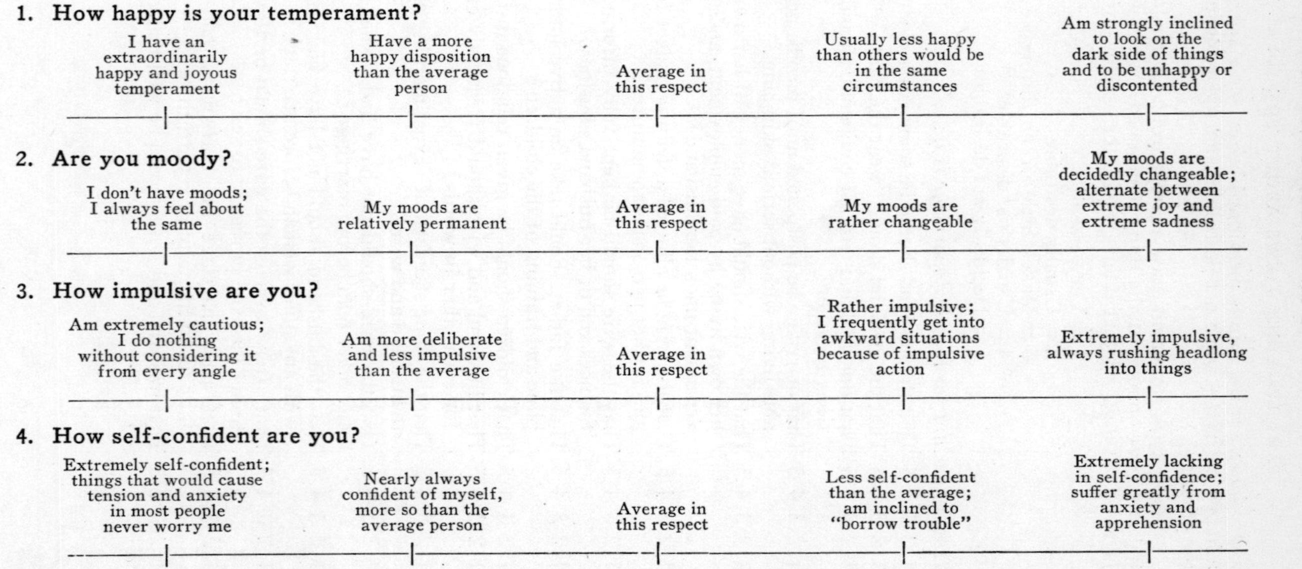

5. How emotional are you?

Am extremely *un*emotional, even in situations which arouse strong emotions in others	I tend to be unresponsive to situations of an emotional nature	Average in this respect	Have a tendency to become over-emotional on occasion	Am over-emotional to an extreme degree

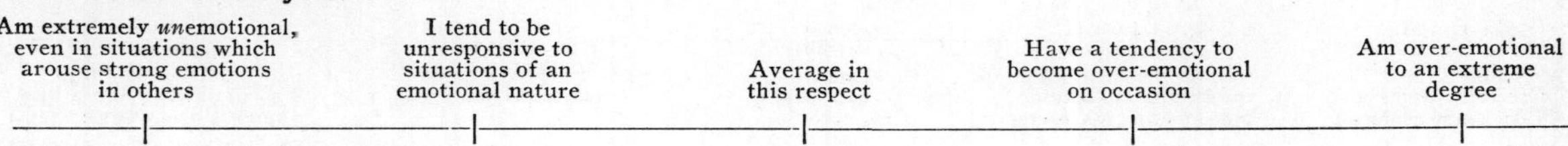

6. To what extent do you conform to authority and the conventions?

No tendency whatever to resent or criticize authority, either personal or in the form of conventions	Less resentful than the average	Average in this respect	Am more rebellious than the average	Am inclined to be extremely antagonistic toward authority and conventions

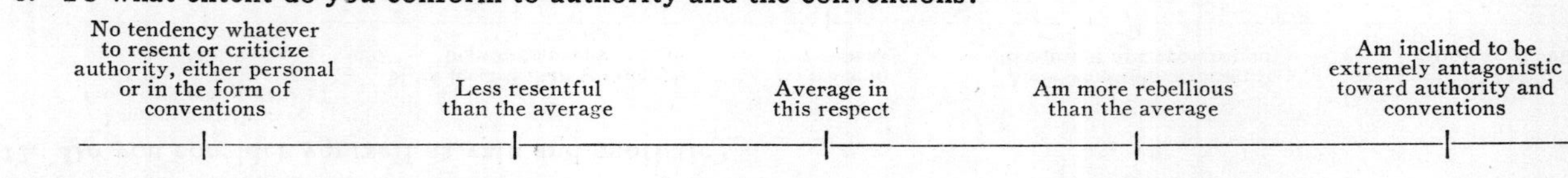

7. In general, how easy are you to get on with?

Extremely good natured, never irritable, always avoid every kind of quarrel or altercation	Am easier to get on with than the average person	Average in this respect	Am harder to get on with than the average person	Am rather inclined to be irritable, quarrelsome, or resentful at slight provocations

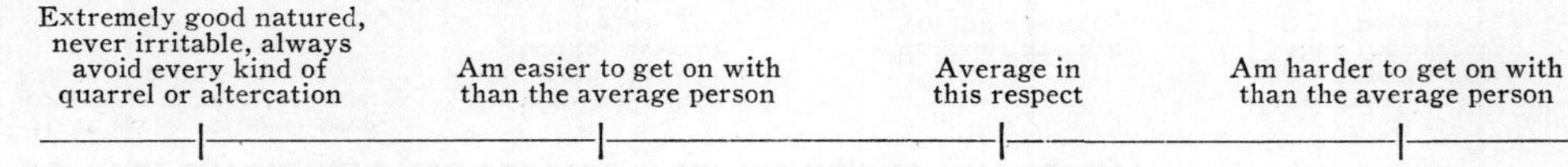

8. How much do you enjoy social contacts?

Am socially minded to an extreme; I like nearly everyone and prefer to be with people most of the time	More social minded than the average	Average in this respect	Less social minded than the average	Am definitely unsocial; prefer to work and play alone; refuse to be drawn into group activities when I can possibly avoid them

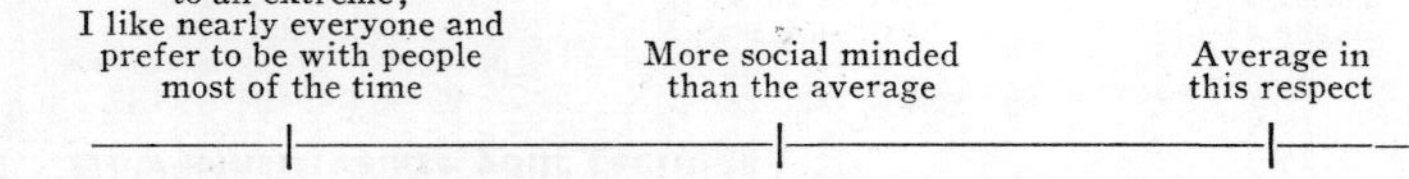

9. How persistent are you in the accomplishment of your ends?

I won't give up; I persevere in the face of every difficulty	Am more persistent than the average person	Average in this respect	Less persistent than the average person	Very easily deterred by obstacles; give up in the face of even trivial difficulties

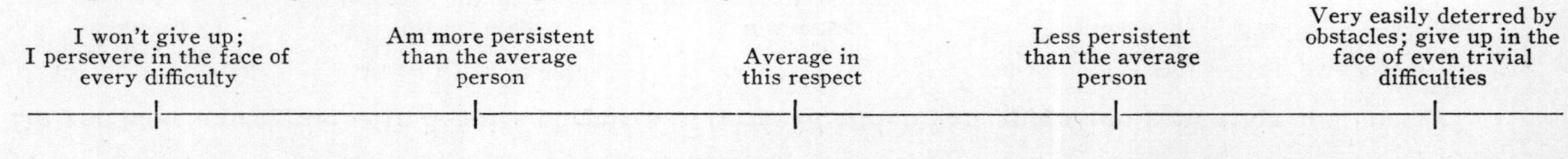

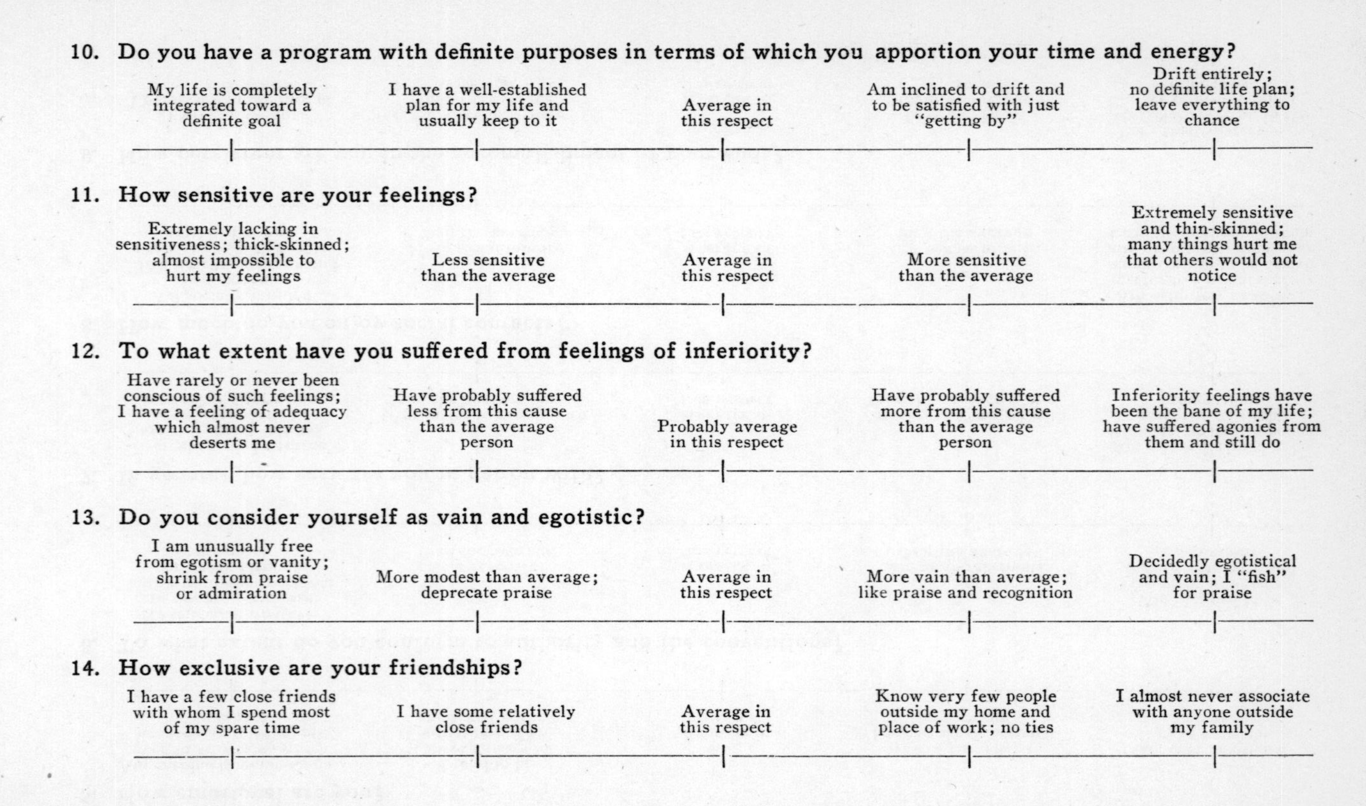

10. Do you have a program with definite purposes in terms of which you apportion your time and energy?

My life is completely integrated toward a definite goal	I have a well-established plan for my life and usually keep to it	Average in this respect	Am inclined to drift and to be satisfied with just "getting by"	Drift entirely; no definite life plan; leave everything to chance

11. How sensitive are your feelings?

Extremely lacking in sensitiveness; thick-skinned; almost impossible to hurt my feelings	Less sensitive than the average	Average in this respect	More sensitive than the average	Extremely sensitive and thin-skinned; many things hurt me that others would not notice

12. To what extent have you suffered from feelings of inferiority?

Have rarely or never been conscious of such feelings; I have a feeling of adequacy which almost never deserts me	Have probably suffered less from this cause than the average person	Probably average in this respect	Have probably suffered more from this cause than the average person	Inferiority feelings have been the bane of my life; have suffered agonies from them and still do

13. Do you consider yourself as vain and egotistic?

I am unusually free from egotism or vanity; shrink from praise or admiration	More modest than average; deprecate praise	Average in this respect	More vain than average; like praise and recognition	Decidedly egotistical and vain; I "fish" for praise

14. How exclusive are your friendships?

I have a few close friends with whom I spend most of my spare time	I have some relatively close friends	Average in this respect	Know very few people outside my home and place of work; no ties	I almost never associate with anyone outside my family

Name..

Blank number..............................

Stanford University, 1940

YOUR PRESENT MARRIAGE

HUSBAND'S BLANK

Please answer *all* the questions. Do not hesitate to be *completely frank.* Three measures have been adopted to safeguard the anonymity of your responses:

(1) Husband and wife will fill out the blanks separately and will seal them in the accompanying envelopes. This insures that neither husband nor wife will see the other's answer to any question.

(2) As soon as the blank is returned to me I will scissor off your name from the upper right-hand corner of this page and will assign to the blank a number which will identify the blank for me (but for no one else). This insures that your identity will not be known to any assistant who tabulates data from the blank.

3. This blank will *not* be kept in the regular files which contain the rest of the data on the gifted group, but in my *private confidential file* to which I alone have access.

LEWIS M. TERMAN

[NOTE TO READER: Wife's blank was the same as husband's except for (1) minor differences in wording and (2) the inclusion of three questions in Part III that were to be answered by the wife only.]

PART I—GENERAL INFORMATION

Begin here:

1. Date of marriage to your present wife: year............; month........................ How old were you then? Years..........................; months..........................
2. Where were you married? (check) At home............; at church............; elsewhere (specify)..
3. Who performed the marriage ceremony? Minister..............................; other person (specify)..
4. How many months or years before marriage had you known your wife? Months........................; years........................
5. How long before marriage did you keep company with her? (insert figure ....months, ...years.
6. How long before marriage were you engaged? (insert figure) ....months, ...years.
7. What was your father's attitude toward your present marriage? (check) Favored it............; mildly disapproved...........; strongly disapproved............; no indication given............
8. What was your mother's attitude? (check) Favored............; mildly disapproved..........; strongly disapproved..........; no indication given..........
9. Number of your women friends before marriage: (check) almost none............; a few............; several............; many............
10. How many women besides your wife had you kept company with before marriage? (check) None..........; 1 or 2..........; 3 to 5..........; 5 to 10..........; more than 10..........

11. To what extent, if at all, does your wife resemble your mother in *general physical type?* (check) Marked resemblance............; some resemblance..........; no particular resemblance..........; opposite types..........
12. My general mental ability, compared to my wife's, is (check) very superior to hers............, somewhat greater............, about equal............, somewhat less than hers............, considerably less............
13. Your occupation at the time you were married..
14. Proportion of the time you have been *unemployed* since your marriage, not counting school attendance or vacation periods: (check) none........; about 5%..........; 10%.......... 15%..........; 20%..........; 30 to 50%..........; more than 50%..........
15. How often have you changed your position voluntarily without bettering yourself? (check) Never........; rarely........; several times........; many times..........
16. Your monthly income at time of marriage.......................... Amount saved before marriage $..........................
17. Estimate the average monthly income of your family (yourself *and* wife) for the past 12 months. Count income from all sources. $.................. per month.
18. Do you own your home? (check) Yes................; no................ If not, do you plan to buy one later? Yes............; no............
19. Size of community where you live: (check) over 100,000..........; 25,000 to 100,000..........; 5,000 to 25,000..........; 1,000 to 5,000..........; live in the country............
20. Record here your height (without shoes): ....feet, ...inches.
21. Your present weight: ....pounds. Your weight at the time you were married: ....pounds.
22. On the whole, how good has your health been since your marriage? (check) Perfect..........; superior..........; good..........; fair..........; rather poor..........; very poor..........
23. How good has your wife's health been since marriage? (check) Perfect..........; superior..........; good..........; fair..........; rather poor..........; very poor..........
24. Check all of the following organizations you have ever belonged to: none at all........; church club........; athletic club........; social club........; Kiwanis........; Rotary........; luncheon club........; fraternal order........; labor union..........; others (specify)...
....
25. What marriage is your present one? (check) First........; second........; third..........; fourth..........
26. Did any previous marriage end in divorce? Yes..........; no.......... If so, how many?............
27. Number of children born to this marriage........ Did you want children? (check) Yes............; no............ If no children, do you want children? Yes............; no............
28. Give age and sex of each child of this marriage..
....
29. Have you one or more children by a previous marriage? Yes............; no............ If answer is yes, state number............

PART II—THE HAPPINESS OF YOUR PRESENT MARRIAGE

1. Do you and your wife engage in outside interests together? (check) All of them..........; most of them..........; some of them..........; very few of them..........; none of them..........
2. State approximate extent of agreement or disagreement on following items: (Please place a check opposite every item.)

Check one column for each item below		Always agree	Almost always agree	Occasionally disagree	Frequently disagree	Almost always disagree	Always disagree
Handling family finances	(*a*)						
Matters of recreation	(*b*)						
Religious matters	(*c*)						
Demonstrations of affection	(*d*)						
Friends	(*e*)						
Caring for the children	(*f*)						
Table manners	(*g*)						
Matters of conventionality	(*h*)						
Philosophy of life	(*i*)						
Ways of dealing with in-laws	(*j*)						

3. When disagreements arise, they usually result in: (check) you giving in............; your wife giving in............; agreement by mutual give and take............
4. Make ONE check (√) on the line before each activity you enjoy doing with average frequency when you have opportunity. Make TWO checks (√√) BEFORE EACH THING YOU ENJOY DOING WITH YOUR WIFE.

... 1. Exchange visits with old friends.
... 2. Attending a particular church.
... 3. Playing with children.
... 4. Talking about yourself.
... 5. Discussing social problems.
... 6. Meeting new acquaintances.
... 7. Engaging in outdoor sports.
... 8. Arranging and preparing meals.
... 9. Planning Christmas gifts.
...10. Making plans for children.
...11. Planning family budgets.
...12. Inspecting newly purchased clothes.
...13. Planning for the future.
...14. Listening to the radio.
...15. Discussing intimate personal experiences.
...16. Confiding worries.
...17. Exchanging visits with relatives and "in-laws."
...18. Discussing work done outside the home.
...19. Explaining your moods.
...20. Discussing literature.
...21. Listening to music.
...22. Discussing politics.
...23. Drinking.
...24. Planning home decorations.
...25. Theater going.
...26. Exchanging jokes.
...27. Discussing scientific topics.
...28. Dancing.
...29. Discussing friends.
...30. Observing outdoor sports.
...31. Singing or playing.
...32. Card playing.
...33. Planning investments.
...34. Reading the newspaper.
...35. Motoring.
...36. Going away for long trips.
...37. Gardening.
...38. Going shopping.
...39. Attending lectures.
...40. Visiting art exhibits.

5. Do you ever regret your marriage? (check) Frequently..........; occasionally..........; rarely..........; never..........
6. If you had your life to live over do you think you would: (check) marry the same person............; marry a different person............; not marry at all............?
7. Have you ever seriously contemplated separation? (check) Yes.........., no..........
   Have you ever seriously contemplated divorce? (check) Yes.........., no..........
8. If your marriage is now unhappy, how long has that been true? (Put down number of years. ....years.)
9. Consider each of the following statements one by one and indicate how true it is for you.
   a) Whenever I have any unexpected leisure I always prefer to spend it with my wife. (check) Completely true..........; almost completely true..........; questionable..........; untrue..........
   b) When I get money unexpectedly my first thought is how I can use it for my wife's pleasure. (check) Completely true..........; almost completely true..........; questionable..........; untrue..........
   c) When my wife and I are alone together we are almost continuously gay and delighted with each other. (check) Completely true..........; almost completely true..........; questionable..........; untrue..........
   d) My wife never does or says anything that either irritates or bores me in the slightest. (check) Completely true..........; almost completely true..........; questionable..........; untrue..........
   e) My wife's personality is so completely satisfactory that I would not want to change it in the slightest degree. (check) Completely true........; almost completely true........; questionable........; untrue........
   f) I feel certain that there is no one else in the world with whom I could be as happy as I am with my wife. (check) Completely true........; almost completely true........; questionable........; untrue........
   g) If my wife were to die, I would prefer to die with her, provided I were not prevented by family responsibilities or religion. (check) Completely true...............; almost completely true...............; questionable...............; untrue...............
10. Everything considered, how happy has your marriage been? (Draw a circle around 1, 2, 3, 4, 5, 6, or 7.)

    1 = Extraordinarily happy
    2 = Decidedly more happy than the average
    3 = Somewhat more happy than the average
    4 = About average
    5 = Perhaps a little less happy than the average
    6 = Definitely less happy than the average
    7 = Extremely unhappy

Page 4]

11. Below is a list of faults often charged by husbands against their wives. Make ONE check (√) on the dotted line before each fault YOUR WIFE HAS.
Make TWO checks (√√) before each fault that HAS AFFECTED THE HAPPINESS OF YOUR MARRIAGE.

... 1. is argumentative
... 2. is not affectionate
... 3. is narrow-minded
... 4. complains too much
... 5. is lazy
... 6. is quick-tempered
... 7. criticizes me
... 8. spoils the children
... 9. is untruthful
...10. is conceited
...11. is easily influenced by others
...12. is jealous
...13. is selfish and inconsiderate
...14. is too talkative
...15. drinks too much
...16. pays attention to other men
...17. is nervous or emotional
...18. neglects the children
...19. is extravagant
...20. lets her feelings be hurt too easily
...21. has annoying habits and mannerisms
...22. has been unfaithful to me
...23. interferes if I discipline children
...24. tries to improve me
...25. lacks ambition
...26. is insincere
...27. has had much poor health
...28. is slovenly in appearance
...29. snores badly
...30. often has offensive breath
...31. is bored if I talk about my business
...32. is too interested in social affairs
...33. nags me
...34. interferes with my hobbies
...35. interferes with my business
...36. is a poor housekeeper
...37. is too interested in clothes
...38. gossips indiscreetly

PART III—SEXUAL COMPATIBILITY

1. On the average, about how many times *per month* do you and your wife have sexual intercourse? (Put down the number that tells the average *per month*.)..............................
2. About how many times *per month* would you *prefer* to have sexual intercourse?..............................
3. Do you think your wife is *more* or *less* sexually passionate than you are? (check) Wife much more............, somewhat more............, same............, somewhat less............, much less............
4. How long does a single intercourse usually last? (Do not count preliminary "petting.") Average time: ....minutes.
5. Everything considered, how well mated are you and your wife from the strictly sexual point of view? (check) No two could possibly be more perfectly mated sexually..........; extremely well mated..........; reasonably well..........; not well..........; very badly..........

PART IV—PERSONALITY RATINGS OF YOUR SPOUSE

Instructions. Please rate your spouse on the following personality traits. Each trait is represented by a straight line, the two ends representing the extremes of the trait. Place a cross (X) on the line at the place you think it should go to describe your spouse correctly. The cross does *not* have to be placed at the small vertical bars; put it wherever on the line you think it should go.

Try to view your spouse objectively. Don't hesitate to give an extreme rating when that would express your best judgment. The extremes do not represent clear-cut faults or virtues. Try not to think of the traits in terms of "good" or "bad."

1. How happy is your spouse's temperament?

Has an extraordinarily happy and joyous temperament	Has a more happy disposition than the average person	Average in this respect	Usually less happy than others would be in the same circumstances	Is strongly inclined to look on the dark side of things and to be unhappy or discontented

2. Is your spouse moody?

Does not have moods; always seems to feel about the same	Moods less changeable than those of average person	Average in this respect	Moods are rather changeable	Moods are decidedly changeable; alternates between extreme joy and extreme sadness

3. How impulsive is your spouse?

Is extremely cautious; does nothing without considering it from every angle	Is more deliberate and less impulsive than the average	Average in this respect	Rather impulsive; frequently gets into awkward situations because of impulsive action	Extremely impulsive, always rushing headlong into things

4. How self-confident is your spouse?

Extremely self-confident; is not worried by things that would cause tension and anxiety in most people	Nearly always self-confident, more so than the average person	Average in this respect	Less self-confident than the average; is inclined to "borrow trouble"	Extremely lacking in self-confidence; suffers greatly from anxiety and apprehension

5. **How emotional is your spouse?**

Is extremely *un*emotional, even in situations which arouse strong emotions in others	Tends to be unresponsive to situations of an emotional nature	Average in this respect	Has a tendency to become over-emotional on occasion	Is over-emotional to an extreme degree

6. **To what extent does your spouse conform to authority and the conventions?**

No tendency whatever to resent or criticize authority, either personal or in the form of conventions	Less resentful than the average	Average in this respect	Is more rebellious than the average	Is inclined to be extremely antagonistic toward authority and conventions

7. **In general, how easy is your spouse for people to get on with?**

Extremely good natured, never irritable, always avoids every kind of quarrel or altercation	Is easier to get on with than the average person	Average in this respect	Is harder to get on with than the average person	Is rather inclined to be irritable, quarrelsome, or resentful at slight provocations

8. **How much does your spouse enjoy social contacts?**

Is socially minded to an extreme; likes nearly everyone and prefers to be with people most of the time	More socially minded than the average	Average in this respect	Less socially minded than the average	Is definitely unsocial; prefers to work and play alone; refuses to be drawn into group activities when it can possibly be avoided

9. **How persistent is your spouse in the accomplishment of ends?**

Won't give up; perseveres in the face of every difficulty	More persistent than the average person	Average in this respect	Less persistent than the average person	Very easily deterred by obstacles; gives up in the face of even trivial difficulties

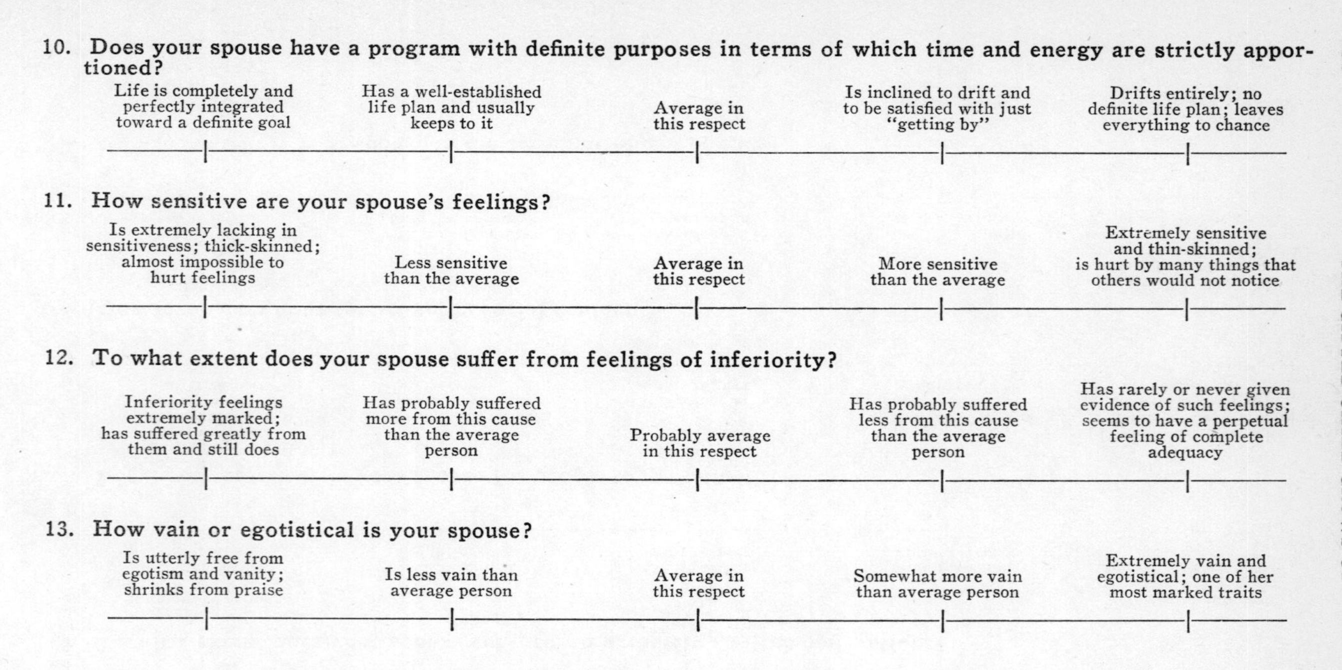

10. Does your spouse have a program with definite purposes in terms of which time and energy are strictly apportioned?

Life is completely and perfectly integrated toward a definite goal	Has a well-established life plan and usually keeps to it	Average in this respect	Is inclined to drift and to be satisfied with just "getting by"	Drifts entirely; no definite life plan; leaves everything to chance

11. How sensitive are your spouse's feelings?

Is extremely lacking in sensitiveness; thick-skinned; almost impossible to hurt feelings	Less sensitive than the average	Average in this respect	More sensitive than the average	Extremely sensitive and thin-skinned; is hurt by many things that others would not notice

12. To what extent does your spouse suffer from feelings of inferiority?

Inferiority feelings extremely marked; has suffered greatly from them and still does	Has probably suffered more from this cause than the average person	Probably average in this respect	Has probably suffered less from this cause than the average person	Has rarely or never given evidence of such feelings; seems to have a perpetual feeling of complete adequacy

13. How vain or egotistical is your spouse?

Is utterly free from egotism and vanity; shrinks from praise	Is less vain than average person	Average in this respect	Somewhat more vain than average person	Extremely vain and egotistical; one of her most marked traits

[*One blank page followed*]

Gifted Children Follow-Up, 1945 Date of filling out this form..............................

INFORMATION BLANK (1945)

Full name.. Birth date........................ Age........
(Married women include maiden name)

Address ....

Name and address of relative or friend through whom you could be reached

if your address should change...

....

1. Education. Circle highest grade completed. High school 1 2 3 4 College 1 2 3 4 Postgraduate 1 2 3 4
If now a student, give college year............ College record (enter below):

Name of college	Degree received	Date received	Scholastic honors

Other courses taken, technical, business, or professional..............................

....

2. Occupation and earned income. (Under income report annual salary before income tax deductions are made. If self-employed [doctor, lawyer, business owner, etc.] give equivalent of salary, i.e., earned income less operating expenses.)

Year	Profession, job, or position	Exact nature of work	Earned income per year
1941			
1942			
1943			
1944			

3. Military service, if any: Date entered.............. Branch of service..............
Grade or rank on entry.......................... Present grade or rank......................
Special citations, decorations, etc...
If no longer in service, give date of leaving........................ Reason..........

....

4. Volunteer war work. List all kinds you have done, including such activities as Red Cross, Civilian Defense, Nurse's Aide, A.W.V.S., U.S.O., Ration Board, Blood Bank, etc...

....

....

5. List your publications, if any. For each give title, date, publisher, and type of material (e.g., poem, short story, musical composition, plays, scientific or critical articles, etc.). If you find too little space, attach further sheets listing such publications...

....

....

....

(Please send me copies of as many of your publications as possible)

over

6. General health since 1940:
   a) Physical condition has been: (underline) very good; good; fair; poor; very poor.
   Illnesses, accidents, or surgical operations since 1940:........................
   ....
   Aftereffects ....
   b) Has there been any tendency toward emotional disturbances, nervousness, worry, special anxiety, or nervous breakdown in recent years?.................... Nature of such difficulties..............................
   ....
   How handled? ....
   Present condition..
7. Are you married?............ If so, give date............ Age at marriage............
   Name of spouse (maiden name of wife)..
   Spouse's age at marriage........................ Highest grade or college year of spouse's schooling................................ Degrees received................................
   What school or college........................ Scholastic honors........................
   Present occupation of spouse (if in military service give branch and grade or rank) ....
   ....
   Spouse's prevailing peacetime occupation if different from above............
   ....
   Changes in your marital status: (underline) death of spouse, separation, divorce, remarriage. Date and cause of separation or divorce.......
   ....
8. Offspring:

Name	Sex	Birth date	If in school, give grade	If not living, age at death
....	....	....	....	....
....	....	....	....	....
....	....	....	....	....
....	....	....	....	....
....	....	....	....	....

9. Illnesses, nervous breakdowns, deaths, etc., among near relatives (parents, grandparents, brothers, or sisters) since 1940:..................................
   ....
10. Give any other significant information regarding yourself or your family which has not been covered in the questionnaire, e.g. (a) changes in your plans due to wartime conditions, (b) any special accomplishments, recognition, or honors of your own or of members of your family, (c) any misfortunes or disappointments that have seriously affected your life, etc. (If space is inadequate, answer on additional sheet.)
    ....
    ....
    ....
    ....
11. Check here if you would like the summary mentioned in enclosed letter
    ....

INDEX